EARLY AMERICAN JEWRY

VOLUME TWO

The publication of this book was made possible by a gift to The Jewish Publication Society of America from the estate of Jacob R. Schiff.

Early American Jewry

THE JEWS OF PENNSYLVANIA
AND THE SOUTH

1655–1790

Jacob Rader Marcus

*Director, American Jewish Archives;
Adolph S. Ochs Professor of Jewish History, Hebrew Union
College—Jewish Institute of Religion, Cincinnati*

VOLUME TWO

PHILADELPHIA
The Jewish Publication Society of America
1953-5713

Printed in the United States of America
American Book–Stratford Press, Inc., New York

*Many years ago a graduate student at the
University of Berlin dedicated his thesis
To
Pretty Nettie Brody
Today, after twenty-five years of married
life, he dedicates this book to the same woman,
His Wife*

Preface

THE reader of this volume is referred to the Preface of Volume One for the approach and the methodology employed by the writer. Through the use of personal letters and documents, the effort was made to recapture the spirit of American Jewry in the late seventeenth and eighteenth centuries. The author hopes that he has succeeded. At the end of this work there is a very extensive systematic survey of the history of the American Jews from 1654 to about 1790. This is the first attempt of this sort. The summary is based, of course, on the contents of the two volumes of *Early American Jewry*. In addition, much that is new has been added: facts that did not lend themselves to incorporation in the preceding chapters, and material that has come to light since Volume One was published.

A word of explanation is due to the *cognoscenti* in this field. This relates to the proportionate space and emphasis devoted to the different Jewish settlements. Pennsylvania, as the colony and state of the largest Jewish community during the days of the Revolution, merits the detailed treatment which it has received. But South Carolina was important, too; it was the metropolis of the South. Yet it has been afforded less notice, less space, than either Virginia or Georgia—and the latter two Jewish communities were not particularly significant. The reason for my action is obvious, I hope. The South Carolina Jewry of the period has already received adequate treatment. Barnett A. Elzas, in *The Jews of South Carolina* (1905), collected almost every historical fact to be found in his day; Charles Reznikoff and Uriah Z. Engelman, in *The Jews of Charleston* (1950), added what new material turned up in the last two generations. In writing this chapter on that colony and state, the author of this book has no desire or intention to regurgitate the findings of his predecessors in the field.

There remains once more the pleasant task of thanking many of those who have been helpful in the preparation of this work. We say "many," for it is impossible to thank all. A researcher today writes to dozens of people, to many libraries and learned societies, for information; he consults hundreds of books, and gleans ideas from his colleagues in letters and in conversation. It is almost impossible to keep a detailed record of all those to whom we are indebted. Nevertheless, it is our desire, if only in this far too impersonal fashion, to thank the dozens of people and institutions who have generously and patiently answered our queries and proffered their aid.

The writer is very thankful to the following persons and institutions for permission to print or republish manuscripts or printed letters and documents: the late Dr. A. S. W. Rosenbach; the American Jewish Historical Society Library—and particularly its Librarian-Editor, Rabbi Isidore S. Meyer; the Historical Society of Pennsylvania; the Library of Congress; the Library Company of Philadelphia; the New York Public Library; the William L. Clements Library, Ann Arbor, Michigan; the Newport Historical Society Library; the State Library of Virginia; the Massachusetts Historical Society Library; the State Department of Archives and History, Raleigh, N. C.; Mr. and Mrs. B. H. Levy, of Savannah, Georgia; the Georgia Department of Archives and History; the Brown University Library, Providence, R. I.; Mikveh Israel Congregation, Philadelphia; and the American Jewish Archives.

The staffs of the University of Cincinnati Library, of the Historical and Philosophical Library of Ohio, of the Hebrew Union College Library, and of the American Jewish Archives have always been most helpful. Dr. Selma Stern-Taeubler, the archivist of the last-named institution, has read through this manuscript more than once and has given the writer the benefit of her wide experience as a historian. Charles Reznikoff has offered some excellent suggestions on the chapter dealing with South Carolina; and Dr. Sidney Fish has generously given me the benefit of his unparalleled knowledge of early Pennsylvania Jewry. Prof. Alexander Guttmann, of the Hebrew Union College-Jewish Institute of Religion, Cincinnati, has always been available for advice in matters touching on rabbinic law. M. Myer ("Max") Singer—a friend since high school days—has always been at my service in all matters touching on typography and printing style. His competence is proverbial. My secretary, Mrs. Etheljane Callner, worked enthusiastically to prepare the typescript, and an old secretary of many years ago, now Rabbi Eugene J. Lipman, of the Union of American Hebrew Congregations, will no doubt take pride in the completion of a work which he helped to initiate. To all these good helpers and good friends, many thanks.

As in Volume One, I received help from Rabbi Abraham I. Shinedling, Edwin Wolf 2nd, and Dr. Samuel Sandmel. Rabbi Shinedling saw this volume through the press and made the Index. Let it be noted that the Index includes also the material in Volume One. For all your labors, dear Abe, my heartiest thanks. Edwin Wolf 2nd, of Philadelphia, took time out of a busy professional life and the many demands of community service to revise the manuscript most carefully. Dr. Sandmel, now my colleague here in Cincinnati, again scrutinized this work and made many worth-while suggestions. To Edwin Wolf 2nd and Samuel Sandmel my deepest thanks and gratitude for their labors and this evidence of their friendship.

Jacob R. Marcus

Cincinnati, Ohio
September 1, 1952

Contents

Contents

Contents

–his daughter Rebecca, a partisan of the British—Myer Hart of Easton, an agent of Franks—Joseph Simon also an agent to supply the prisoners

Rebecca Franks and the *Meschianza*—General Charles Lee and Rebecca—David Franks arrested for Toryism—Franks banished—Rebecca retails the latest New York gossip—the last days of David Franks

Rachel Gratz in Lancaster—Benjamin Seixas does business in Philadelphia for Aaron Lopez—the Philadelphia synagogue again reorganized by *émigrés*—trouble with the intolerant German Reformed church—why the Jews sold their lot and moved away from the neighborhood of the church—a new synagogue is built and dedicated

The controversy about the merit of building a monument to Haym Salomon—the legendary story of Salomon—the facts about Salomon—his career as underground agent in British-occupied New York—Salomon is discovered and flees to Philadelphia—he becomes a broker for the French army—Salomon is employed by Robert Morris to sell bills of exchange—toward the end of the

Contents

war Salomon turns to commerce and trading
—he lends money to James Madison—Eleazar
Levy, Salomon's friend, loses money at
West Point—Salomon sends money to his
family in Poland—he plays an active part in
the Philadelphia Jewish community—Salomon initiates a protest against an illiberal
clause in the Pennsylvania constitution of
1776—the achievements of Salomon, symbol
of the Jew in the Revolution

Contents

Contents

Sheftall petitions Congress for reimbursement—Sheftall Sheftall as Flag Master—privateering—gossip in the Jewish community—
the dawn of freedom

SURVEY AND RETROSPECT

Contents

List of Illustrations

xix

List of Illustrations

List of Illustrations

THE JEWS OF PENNSYLVANIA
AND THE SOUTH
1655–1790

Chapter 1

Pennsylvania — 1734

URING the Revolution, Philadelphia was the second largest city in the English-speaking world. It sheltered the most important Jewish community in the United States, though by no means the oldest. New York, Newport, and probably even Savannah had synagogue organizations that antedated the one in the City of Brotherly Love.

Most of the Jews in this Pennsylvania capital—where they were first reported as being numerous enough to note by a traveler in 1734—were of Central European origin. Probably some of them were attracted to the city because of the large number of German Christians who had settled in eastern Pennsylvania. Individual Israelites had traveled to Pennsylvania much earlier, coming down from New Amsterdam no later than 1655 to trade with Indians on the Delaware. William Penn had theorized that the Indians were descendants of the Ten [Lost] Tribes—they looked just like the Jews in the London ghetto! We must look, however, for less aboriginal specimens, if we wish a persuasive authenticity for the first Jew who settled perma-

3

nently in Pennsylvania. He may have been a certain Jonas Aaron, who was already settled in the colony in 1703. But his Jewishness is indicated only by his biblical name, at best an uncertain identification.

It is more likely that the first Pennsylvania Jew, of whom we can be sure and whom we know by name, was Isaac Miranda. He was probably a Tuscanian; at least this is known, that his brother Joseph was steward to the Duke of Tuscany.

Though we have identified Isaac as a Jew, he may already have been a convert to Christianity when he appeared on the Pennsylvania frontier.

On occasion the pioneer Jew in a new area becomes a convert. Alone, cut off from any close Jewish community, eager to establish himself, he marries out of the faith and ultimately leaves it. The change of faith makes him somehow a little more acceptable to his neighbors; nevertheless, they continue to think, and frequently speak, of him as "the Jew." Their criteria of Jewishness are "racial" and ethnic. After the first Jew, the convert, has settled in a village or hamlet, succeeding Jews, unconverted, who wander in are more readily accepted. The ice has been broken, and the community has been prepared to receive these others.

Miranda had settled on Conoy Creek, in what was later Lancaster County, by about the year 1715. Although he was primarily an Indian trader, he also dabbled in politics. Sometime in 1727 he was appointed a deputy vice-admiralty judge, and later the same year he was dismissed when he refused to do the bidding of his superior, the vice-admiralty judge Joseph Browne, in a case smelling of corruption.

4

This "apostate Jew or fashionable Christian proselyte," as he was called by an unsympathetic Christian contemporary, died in 1732. Apparently a man of some wealth, he left his heirs two houses in Philadelphia, silver plate, furniture, books, a farm in Lancaster County, and several thousand acres of land. One of his two sons, George, carried on the family business of trading with the Indians, and in the 1730's was well-known in the Allegheny area as a trader among the Shawnees.

The elder Miranda was very eager for his daughter Mary to wed the aristocratic James Hamilton, the son of Andrew Hamilton, the famous lawyer who had defended John Peter Zenger in the well-known suit involving freedom of the press. In order to stimulate his interest, Miranda made liberal provision in his will for the young scion if he espoused the daughter, but the future lieutenant-governor of the colony did not marry Miss Miranda. Fate, however, had evidently ordained that there should be a "Jewess" in the Hamilton family. In the next generation, Andrew Hamilton III did marry Abigail Franks.

Jews, that is, unconverted Jews, did immigrate in increasing numbers to Pennsylvania in the first half of the eighteenth century. By 1730 the London De Pazes were building boats in Philadelphia shipyards, and by the 1750's there were isolated families, or groups, or even communities in Philadelphia, Easton, Reading, Heidelberg, and in other villages and townships as far west as the foothills of the Blue Ridge Mountains.

Lancaster, in the middle of the eighteenth century, had a little community and a cemetery. It was the most important frontier post for the western fur trade. There were ten families or male adults there in the 1740's, and the leading Jew, Lancaster's most prominent merchant, was Joseph Simon.

As for Philadelphia, there was a modest little congregation of Jews worshiping in a rented room on Sterling Alley as early as the 1750's. They had been holding services at least since 1747. Their first cemetery—originally the private burial plot of Nathan Levy—had been purchased in 1738; Levy sought a second plot from the Penns several years later.

This Levy, the founding father of the Jewish community, was a son of the well-known New York merchant-shipper, Moses Levy. Through the marriage of his sister Abigail, Nathan became a brother-in-law of Jacob Franks, the enterprising New York businessman. By 1731 young Nathan, then twenty-seven years of age, was an officer of the New York congregation, and by 1747 he was the third largest taxpayer in the synagogue, ranking just below Mordecai Gomez and Jacob Franks. The records of the 1740's and of the year 1750 disclose the fact that he continued to pay liberally for the upkeep of the New York congregation in spite of the fact that he had been living and doing business in Philadelphia since the late 1730's. No doubt it was filial loyalty and piety that prompted him to remain a member of Shearith Israel while doing what he could to establish a new Jewish community in Philadelphia.

Being a cemetery owner was not without its problems, and a Jewish cemetery was nearly always subject to desecration. In 1751 Levy was forced to insert the following advertisement in a September issue of Franklin's *Pennsylvania Gazette:*

Whereas many unthinking people have set up marks, and fir'd several shots against the fence of the Jewish burying-ground, which not only destroyed the said fence, but also a tomb-stone inclosed in it; there being a brick-wall now erected, I must desire those sportsmen to forbear (for the future) firing against the said wall. If they do, whoever will inform, so that the offender be convicted thereof before a magistrate, shall have twenty shillings reward, paid by Nathan Levy.

For at least nine years before his death Levy was a partner of David Franks in the firm of Levy and Franks, merchant-shippers who owned a number of good-sized schooners, sloops, and ships registered in Philadelphia. The firm had a store on Second Street and dealt in all sorts of merchandise, and from a letter which Nathan wrote in 1742 to James Dinnen (Dunning), the Indian trader and guide, we see that he also handled furs, bartering bundles of skins for goods and cash:

Mr. James Dinnen,
S'r:
I received your favour with six bundles summer skins for which have credited your account, and have according to your desire sent you all the goods you wrote for, excepting 1 p's match coating [coarse woolen cloth] and brass kettles, being I had them not.
The rum I bought for cash and so I did the vermillion, and therefore could not send you so much cash as I would. I alsoe paid John Smith, the waggoner, £4.17 for bringing the skins and carrying the goods out. I hope they may please you, and

7

wish you good success in trade is the needfull at p[re]'sent from, s'r,

Your most humble servant,
Nathan Levy.

Philad'a, Octo'r 15, 1742.
I have sent you £6.10 cash by Walker.[1]

The Levys of Philadelphia were very definitely "society." When Dr. Alexander Hamilton, a Maryland physician, made his "Gentleman's Progress" through the colonies in the summer of 1744, he went to a session of the Music Club in Philadelphia, where he "heard a tollerable concerto performed by a harpsicord and three violins." The leader of this club was the Attorney General Tench Francis, who "play'd a very indifferent finger upon an excellent violin that once belonged to the late Ch. Calvert, Govr. of Maryland." Apparently the only good fiddler of the three was "One Levy there [who] played a very good violine."

This violinist was almost certainly our Nathan Levy. Music was cultivated in his family, as we know from a letter written by his sister, Abigail Levy Franks, to her son Naphtali Franks in London in 1735. She recounted how her youngest son, Moses, was attracted to the instrument played by a daughter: "Richa does pretty well with her musick, Moses would fain learn if he could, he has stole some parts of tunes by seeing her taught." David Franks, still another son, then in Boston, continued Abigail, had studied the "fidle." From the mention of the "fidle" Abigail automatically went on in the very next sentence to say a word about her brother, Nathan Levy. The inference

8

seems unmistakable that her train of thought led from the fiddler son to another probable fiddler, her brother.

The Levys, people of culture and wealth, were city-folk, as were most Jews in the colonies, but many individuals seeking a larger opportunity—with little capital and less competition—moved out into the wilderness. By 1744 some Jews, probably Alsatians, were settled in the little village of Conestoga at the edge of Lancaster County. Our source for this information is the same *Itinerarium, Gentleman's Progress*, of Hamilton, which tells us that he met a French Jew, Abraham Dubois, who had just returned from a visit to his relatives in this little Pennsylvania town on the frontier. Although Dubois spoke an execrable English, he was evidently something of a student of the Hebrew Bible, for he carried on a religious discussion with a skeptical Scotsman on the subjects of creation and the authority of the Old Testament writings.

Dubois had no hesitancy in engaging in a religious dispute in public in an American colony. In spite of the laws against blasphemy found in most colonies—and in Pennsylvania, too—there was freedom of expression here. Back home in France, he might have been sent to the galleys for an inadvertent remark. Almost up to the French Revolution a generation later, Jews (and Christians, too) were being sentenced to death for religious "violations" which were not even misdemeanors after the fall of the Bastille in 1789.

As in many other English colonies, Jews had been able to secure naturalization in Pennsylvania after 1740, and a few did take advantage of this opportunity. Judging, however, from the small number that had themselves natural-

of the fact that he was an assimilationist, he was not, as others became, a Jew-hater. He always maintained close contact with his Jewish friends, particularly with the Simon and Gratz families of Lancaster and Philadelphia, and in his own letters to them occasionally added a Hebrew word or two. On October 12, 1765, on one of his numerous visits back home, to New York, he did attend services at the synagogue. It was the Saturday when the cycle of Pentateuchal readings started all over again, and to commemorate this happy event the congregational trustees all got gloriously "high." David gleefully reported all this—with a Hebrew word thrown in—to his good friend Barnard Gratz.

Who was this good friend Gratz? In the 1750's David Franks took into his employ this young emigrant from the German-Polish border, from Langendorf in Upper Silesia. There was no reason for Gratz to remain in his native province. It had fallen to Frederick II of Prussia. In 1750 that monarch had issued his *Reglement,* a charter detailing the rights and disabilities of Prussian Jews. A generation later this charter of the enlightened (!) king was termed by Mirabeau "a law worthy of a cannibal."

As for Silesian Jewry, Frederick made an effort to limit the number of Jews who were to be allowed to remain, even if born in the land. It was difficult, even for a successful businessman, to secure residential rights for more than one son. "Surplus" sons were often compelled to leave the parental home and to wander off. Indeed, Jews were ruthlessly driven out of the countryside where they had leased and worked the distilleries, bakeries, mills, and dairies of the feudal gentry. Though individual entrepreneurs were successful in some of the towns, the cities, in general, were not discouraged from exercising their medieval prerogative of excluding Jews as residents. Accordingly, German Jewish boys of spirit refused to remain in eighteenth-century Silesia and Germany.

Barnard Gratz was born about 1738. He had clerked for a while in London for his cousin, Solomon Henry; then, in January, 1754, he had come to Pennsylvania to work for Franks. Barnard could not have been more than in his early teens when he left Silesia. It was such resolute and courageous youngsters who did so much to build this country.

Working for David Franks did not mean that young Barnard could not engage in business "adventures" for himself. Undoubtedly his employer encouraged him to do it, and was his partner in shipments. They often bought and sold on "joint account." People were glad to help a young beginner.

One of the "concerns" of Gratz was a partnership with Benjamin Moses Clava, which began in 1755 and lasted until 1769. Clava had married out of the faith—a Christian minister officiated—but did not withdraw from the Jewish community. The business which the two men carried on was an exceedingly modest one. They had very little capital. One of their customers was Mrs. Hannah Moses, obviously one of those traditional mothers in Israel, a type common among the Jews of Europe, where the wife girded up her loins and supported the family. Evidently she took seriously the dictum of the Jewish sage who had said: "In a place where there are no men, strive to be a man." Hannah sold cheap jewelry, knives, snuff-boxes, brass and enamel fountain pens, children's rings, and the like.

Barnard lived at Hannah's house for a while and credited his board bill against what she owed the firm of Clava and Gratz. A scrutiny of the firm's accounts shows that the members found some time to relax—or were the following entries in the line of business: "Rum, sug'rs, and limes"—and, immediately following, "ditto" and "entertainm't given gentlemen from N. Y."

In 1758, after Barnard had been in the country for almost five years, he heard that his younger brother Michael had left the East Indies and was in London. (The source of his information was his cousin Jacob Henry, now Franks's agent in Lancaster. Jacob was a younger brother of Cousin Solomon Henry, the London merchant.)

Barnard was upset at the news. Michael was something of a problem; he was always getting into trouble and failing to make good. He had done poorly in Berlin and Amsterdam. Obviously he was now coming from the fabulous Indies without the expected sackful of diamonds or rupees.

Barnard, on the other hand, was a sober person; he was working laboriously to get ahead. His account books disclosed his studious practice in the English script. Not that Barnard was without sentiment. On the last page of one of his account books he wrote:

> Now by love [Jove?] the gratees oath that is,
> None loves you half so well as I.
> I due not ask your love for dis,
> For Heavens sake belive me or I die.

Underneath is sprawled his signature: Barnad Grates. Off
to a corner he wrote, "Mary Samuel . . . in London." But
it was not Mary Samuel whom he ultimately married.

As an older brother seriously beginning to find his stride,
Barnard had little patience with a rolling stone. On Novem-
ber 20, 1758, Barnard wrote to Solomon Henry, for whom
Michael also had worked before going to the Indies:

Philadelphia, November 20, 1758.

Dear Cousin Solomon:

I have not had the pleasure of a line from you this great
while. Only had the satisfaction to hear from your brother,
Jacob Henry, of y'r being in good health, which I wish may
continue.

I likewise heard my brother Michael is coming back from
the East Indies, which am very sorry for, and I should be glad
to know his reason for returning. I don't know what advice to
give him that would be for the best of his interest, as I do not
know his disposition. If he could content himself with living
in the [American back] country, or else with living here [in
Philadelphia] at Mr. David Franks's in my place, [he might
do well,] as I intend to leave him next spring, as I've wrote for
a cargo to Mr. Moses Franks by direction of Mr. D. Franks.
With their assistance, I believe I could soon get him my place,
where he could learn the business of this country by staying
with him two or three years, and might do a little business
for himself as he has some money of his own.

This place requires honesty, industry, and good nature, and
no pride, for he must do every thing pertaining to the business. So if you and he think he is capable of the last—I have no
doubt of his honesty—and he has a *mind* not to be stubborn
but to take advice after his arrival, I would advise him to come
by the first vessel in the spring. I would assist him as far as in
my power as a brother. That is not a great deal, as I am poor

15

my self. But if he thinks himself wise enough and refuses to take advice of Cousin Jacob [Henry] and myself, then let him do what he pleases; I would not advise him to come here, as it would give me much pain and uneasiness.

I regret I cannot remit you y'r money before next spring.

Your kindness shall always be acknowledged by, dear sir,

Your aff'te cousin and most humble servant,

Barnard Gratz.

Respects to Miss Hart. Will remit her money p'r next vessel.[2]

It is evident what brother Barnard was after. Let Michael —his synagogue name was Yehiel—come to America, take Barnard's place with David Franks, live at Franks's house, work for him, and put his money into "ventures" now and then. But no "monkey business"!

That same day, in the same mail, he sent a Judaeo-German letter to Michael himself. Though the florid salutation in Hebrew need not be taken literally, for it was an old epistolary formula, Barnard did love Michael—there is no record that they ever quarreled:

Greetings to my dearly beloved brother who is as dear to me as my own life, the young man, Yehiel—long may he live— that princely, scholarly, and incomparable person:

I report that I am in good health, and I hope you are too.

I learn, dear brother, from the letter of our relative Solomon [Henry] to our relative Koppel [Jacob Henry] that you have returned from India. I am very much surprised, but I cannot say much because I do not know the reason [for your return].

Only if you are satisfied to live in the country and keep a shop—if you are at all able to do that—or to live with my employer, Mr. David Franks, would I advise you to come here in the spring by the first boat. But you must agree to follow our advice while you are here. In that case I hope everything

16

will turn out satisfactorily to you. My plan would be that you come here and stay with my employer two or three years until you learn the business. Meanwhile you will get the same wages that I got.

[In that case] You might turn your money over to Mr. Moses Franks and take an order on Mr. David Franks, to be paid here when you arrive. I think this would be better than keeping a shop in the country. Mr. David Franks is a very good man, and you will be able to make some money with your capital here. Otherwise, "do as is good in thine own eyes," do what you want, but do let me know through someone what you have in mind. And don't be too proud. From me,

Your brother,

Issachar Ber[Barnard].

Remember me to everybody in our family.

P.S. Dear brother, if you intend to come here and live with Mr. Franks, you should not bring with you any merchandise whatsoever. You will be able to earn more with your money here. Will you please, therefore, do me the favor of paying our relative Solomon [Henry] nineteen pounds, i.e., £19 ster. on my account. When you arrive, I shall return the sum at once. The rest you ought to give to Moses Franks, and have him issue an order on Mr. David Franks here. Come over by the first boat, as I have already spoken to my employer about you, and he will wait for you until the month of Nisan or Iyyar [April-May]. However, you may do as you please.

I have just reconsidered the matter with our relative Jacob. If you have some money, you might bring with you about eighteen or twenty silver watches, worth from forty-five to fifty-five dinars [shillings?] a piece, some new-fashioned watchchains, about twenty dozen of women's shoes made of calamanco and worsted damask of all colors, a few dozen of women's mittens of black worsted, and a few other articles. In this case you can invest your money [in these articles] and not turn it over to Moses Franks. You might ask him what he

thinks you ought to bring here, if you have more money than
you need for the articles mentioned above. Let them be in-
sured.[3]

Michael left England in April, 1759, and about twelve
weeks later, by the second week of July, he was already in
this country at work selling his "cargo" of goods.

Back in London Cousin Solomon learned that the new
immigrant had purchased a pair of expensive buckles—
knee buckles?—not for resale but for his own use. "Time
enough for you to wear such things when you are worth
a hundred thousand," admonished Cousin Solomon.
Michael was apparently getting off to his usual bad start!
How he must have chuckled in later years at Cousin Solomon's strictures, as he sat for his portrait to Thomas Sully!

MAIN PART OF PHILADELPHIA, 1754

DAVID FRANKS AND PHILA, HIS SISTER

Chapter 2

Pennsylvania — 1771

L ESS than ten years after Michael Gratz landed in the colonies he was well on the road to a successful business career. In fact, within three years of his arrival he was already sending money out of his profits to his sisters in Silesia. He adjusted himself with natural facility to the needs of this pioneer land. The spirit of initiative that had prompted him as a young man to make the long trip to India stood him in good stead when he crossed the Alleghenies, relying more on his common sense and nerve than on his pistols to get along with the Indians.

Both brothers, Barnard and Michael, were engaged in foreign commerce, initially in "concerns," but ultimately on their own. Commerce was the royal road to wealth. The merchants of Philadelphia sent furs, grain, lumber, and cattle abroad in exchange for hard cash and consumers' goods. Barnard engaged in the coasting trade from New Orleans to Quebec; Michael, the more enterprising, sent cargoes to Canada, Georgia, and to the Dutch and British West Indies. Theirs was the typical career of colonial merchants, as exemplified in the activities of an Aaron Lopez.

But they were more malleable, more open to change and to new opportunities than the dignified Newport shipper.

Sometime after the French and Indian War (1763) the Gratzes realized that the turn in political and economic conditions would profoundly affect their mode of doing business. Following the defeat of the French, the English, it will be recalled, had acquired Canada and practically all of North America east of the Mississippi. To help finance the cost of the long war with the French and to raise money for administration and future defense, the colonists were called upon to pay additional taxes and duties. The old colonial system of winking at smuggling and at illicit trade and of conniving at disregard for the Navigation Acts was scrapped. The attempt was now made really to enforce the laws. Paper currency was prohibited. A Stamp Act was imposed, and new duties were levied in spite of the outcries of the colonists, who took refuge in the slogan: "No taxation without representation." England was now definitely embarked on a mercantilistic policy which the colonists felt was unjust and which they believed was intended primarily to further the interests of the English at home.

The American merchants determined to bring the home government to terms by a boycott expressed in nonimportation agreements and resolutions. Along with many others Barnard and Michael Gratz signed the nonimportation resolutions in Philadelphia in 1765.

One of the obvious effects of this more rigid control of colonial commerce and the resultant American boycott was the decline of foreign commerce, or at least of its profits. Many merchants were bankrupted; others realized that they would have to find additional sources of trade and income or go under. The Gratzes, to survive, began to put more time and effort into the fur and Indian trade.

The English policy toward the Indians supported this economic shift of the Gratzes. The authorities in London proposed to set aside the huge trans-Allegheny area as a vast reservation for the Indians, who would be encouraged to supply furs for the English market. The colonists were forbidden to establish settlements on the other side of the mountains—that would carry them farther and farther away from English traditions and from control by English cannon. As long as they lived along the tidal rivers they would be oriented toward Europe and would remain English in their loyalties.

But all such commercially slanted legislation was more easily planned than carried out. Colonists were beginning to cross the mountain barriers. Land companies in the Ohio basin had been in the making now for almost a generation. By punitive exactions and by purchase the Indians were brought to cede large areas to the white man. Thereupon the government reluctantly changed its mind with regard to the colonization in the Indian country.

Enterprising merchants were intent upon exploiting the wilderness country, and that meant, first of all, bringing out the furs; they established depots at important river junctions and at portage points. There the fur traders and hunters were "staked" to an outfit, stocked up with "Indian goods," and were paid for the furs in food, drink, ammunition, and other necessities.

It was but a short step from supplying trappers and buying their peltries to the much bigger game of securing huge land grants, getting colonial and royal confirmation, and then throwing the vast areas open to land-hungry colonists.

One of the leading figures in this phase of American tramontane expansion was David Franks. Like most successful merchants of his day, Franks ran a general store, operated a commission business, owned and freighted his own ships, underwrote maritime insurance, and bought and sold commercial paper. His specialty was army supply, especially of the interior posts; this heightened his interest in the fur trade and led him ultimately into land speculation. His mercantile and shipping pursuits served as underpinning for these activities, which he furthered through his influence in high places both here and in London. Though he was not in politics himself, his "connections" were of the best. His father-in-law, Peter Evans, was in politics; and his daughter, Abigail, had married Andrew Hamilton III. The Hamiltons were a powerful clan, related to the Penns, the Allens, and the like.

For decades prior to the Revolution, Franks was an active, perhaps the dominating figure among a group of businessmen who sought to control the western fur trade all the way to the Mississippi River. They were particularly eager to pre-empt the Ohio River and the Illinois River traffic. (The assumption that Frankstown, a portage point on the Kittanning Path, was named after him or his family is wrong. This village, and another Frankstown below Wheeling, owe their name to Frank Stevens, an Indian trader of the 1730's.)

Throughout the 1760's Franks appears as a partner in a variety of enterprises, all of which were directed toward the West. In the 1760's and 1770's, David Franks operated under the firm name of (Isaac) Levy and Franks. This concern is not to be confused with the older firm of (Nathan) Levy and Franks, which was dissolved about 1754, although the Levys were all related through David Franks's mother. The frequent change in name is to be accounted for by the fact that any time an important "venture" was made a loose, temporary, and new partnership might be formed, and when the transaction was finished the partners frequently entered into other ventures separately. A man might be "concerned" in two or three firms at the same time. In 1760 Franks was in a firm which included William Trent, Joseph Simon, and Levy Andrew Levy. A few years later he was concerned with almost the same partners in a new company. For a number of years he was closely associated with George Croghan, deputy superintendent for Indian affairs under Sir William Johnson.

Croghan and his partner, William Trent, had been pushing into the Upper Ohio River Valley, trading with the Indians, as far back as the 1740's. They were in the van of that westward movement which was just beginning to reach out across the mountains as far as the Ohio. In the year 1754 the struggle between the English and the French for control of the Ohio Valley broke out. The English, pushing up from Virginia, and the French, coming down from Canada, met head-on in the Ohio valley; this was the "wilderness beginning" of the French and Indian War, a war in which the English traders, in the first years, were beaten back and suffered severe losses.

After the conflict was over, in 1763, the Indians (Pontiac!) again attacked the traders who had pushed in with large supplies of goods. Throughout the whole western country, as far north as Detroit and Mackinac, merchants were robbed and harassed and killed. Croghan and Trent again suffered losses at the hands of the Indian marauders, as did Simon and Levy of Lancaster, their associate Franks, and the rival Baynton-Wharton group of Philadelphia, all of whom lost valuable stocks. Preliminary to a demand for satisfaction from the Indians, the traders and merchants submitted their bill to Sir William Johnson, the superintendent for Indian affairs. The total loss, so the claimants said, was about £81,000, sterling. Almost a third of the amount represented losses by Franks, Trent, Simon, & Co.

As compensation for their losses in 1763, the traders, and the merchants who had financed them, sought a grant of land from the Six Nations (the Iroquois), whom they held responsible for the attacks of their tributaries, the Shawnees, the Delawares, and the Hurons. Influenced more through the presents offered them by Sir William Johnson than through any consciousness of their moral or legal responsibility, the Six Nations finally signed a treaty at Fort Stanwix in New York in November, 1768. Under the terms of this instrument, the Iroquois made large cessions of land east and south of the Ohio River, which included a large tract in what is today West Virginia, as compensation for the "suff'ring traders." In the expectation of receiving this land and exploiting it for purposes of colonization and speculation, the Indiana Company had been created in 1763–65 by these traders and their supporters.

It was but a step to the next move: compensation also for the losses suffered in 1754. The sufferers of 1754—in some instances identical with the traders who were despoiled in 1763—had been clamoring for relief for almost a decade. Later they combined their claims with those who had been despoiled in 1763; they turned to the British government for special financial reimbursement for their group alone, but they accomplished nothing. They were very dissatisfied. Finally, a representative group of six, which included David Franks and Benjamin Levy, sought relief from the Anglophile Iroquois for the damage done by the French and their Indians. When this farfetched claim was rejected by Sir William Johnson, the six conceived the idea of asking the king for a special compensatory grant in the new lands ceded by the Indians in 1768 at Fort Stanwix.

Again, in anticipation, a company was organized, with its shares divided into two equal parts. Out of one half, the traders, under William Trent, agreed to pay their creditors, the merchants; the merchants got the other half as compensation for the efforts and the money they were supposed to expend in securing the expected grant for the 1754 traders. But the merchants, apparently, were not willing to put out any cash if they could help it; instead, they offered David Franks's brother, Moses, one-ninth of their half of their stock if he would further their claim at the English court.

We have spoken above of David's brothers Moses and Naphtali. It was Moses, in all probability, who represented the family interests in London. His type of representation was most desirable. The colonies were on the frontier; the manufactories, the money markets, and the sources of political influence (contracts!) were in England. It was important, therefore, that every large firm have a London agent. This was one of Moses' jobs, and his career had equipped him for it. He had moved to England in the 1740's, before he was thirty. Thereafter he had become a prominent businessman, moving in high financial and political circles in spite of the fact that his own political rights as a Jew were limited. He had kept in constant touch with his family and his old synagogue, and was the agent of Shearith Israel in 1757–58 in its search for a new minister. Conscious of Moses Franks's success, the president and governors of the College of the Province of New York—later Columbia—appealed to him in 1762 to help raise funds in England for the school, which had been so hard hit by the "ravages of a destructive war."

Moses had already been appointed the London representative for the merchants and sufferers of 1763. Now he was offered the job of squeezing a grant out of the king for those traders and their backers who had experienced losses in the *opening* days of the French and Indian War. Here is the letter which David Franks, his cousin, Benjamin Levy, and their four associates sent to Moses:

Philad'a, 4th Jan'ry, 1769.
Sir:

We embrace the oppertunity of this packet to acquaint you that we have associated together in order, if possible, to obtain a compensation for the losses of the Indian traders whose

26

properties were violently and unjustly taken from them by the French on the River Ohio, on or about the year 1754.

At a late congress [1768] with the Six Nations Indians at Fort Stanwix, a large tract of country was ceded to his Majesty, and a boundary settled between the English colonies and the Indians. At the same time a tract of land lying on the Ohio, within the bounds of the ceded country ["Indiana," now largely part of northern West Virginia], was granted by the Six Nations to the Indian traders and others who suffer'd by the depredations committed by their dependant tribes in the year 1763. During the course of this treaty an application was made to Sir William Johnson by several merchants of this city, who had been sufferers in the year 1754, to request of the Indians a compensation for their losses likewise. This Sir Will'm refus'd to comply with, under a perswasion that it was extreemly improper to demand a satisfaction from the Six Nations for hostilities committed by the *French* and their *Indians only*, in which neither they, the Six Nations, nor their tributaries had born any part.

These merchants have since thought proper to prefer a petition to his Majesty to be included in the *grant* made by the Indians to the sufferers of 1763. Some of us were subscribers to that petition, but having since had an oppertunity of inspecting several letters, petitions, and other papers relating to that subject, which we were before unacquainted with, are sattisfyed there has been no unfairness in the proceedings of the sufferers of 1763, and that therefore it would be more proper and just to make an application to the Crown for a tract of land distinct from *theirs*, than to attempt to interfere with their grant.

We, the signers of this letter, are the legal representatives of the Indian traders who were the real sufferers in the year 1754, having a deed executed by Capt. William Trent who has been impowered for that purpose by regular letters of attorney under the hands and seals of those traders, vesting in us one moiety [half] of all such lands as shall be granted by the Crown as a compensation for their losses (we being at the expence and trouble soliciting such compensation), the other moiety to be divided among the traders themselves, out of which moiety all the merchants to whom any of them owe money may receive a payment of their several demands.

We, therefore, do request of you to make an application to the Crown in behalf of the sufferers of 1754 for a grant of land distinct from that granted by the Indians to the sufferers of 1763, as there is now an immence quantity of excellent unapropriated land within the boundary, exclusive of that. And we confide in the justice of his Majesty and his ministers that they will in this way reimburse those sufferers on account of whose losses reprisals were made on the French merchants' effects before the declaration of war, those reprisals not having been applied to the indemnification of the sufferers.

Capt. Trent and Mr. Sam Wharton will shortly embark for England. To these gentlemen we refer you for particulars. They will on their arrival wait on you and show you all the traders' powers [of attorney] and other papers, and inform you fully of every thing relating to this subject. And they will be able to point out to you a valuable tract of land, within the late cession [by the Indians] to the Crown, which it may be proper to apply for, and will in all respects afford you their best assistance.

As there will be no method of requiting you for your trouble in negociating our application (which you are to be the *sole agent* for), except out of a part of the grant, care has been taken to make over to your brother, Mr. David Franks, two-ninths of the whole moiety conveyed by Mr. Trent, in order that you may have one-ninth for your services.

We are, with great respect, sir,

Your most obed't hum. servants,
Edw'd Shippen, Jun'r, Jos. Morris, Benjamin Levy, David Franks, Thos. Laurence, Sam'l Wharton.[4]

28

Moses accepted the offer of this consortium to act as their lobbyist at the Court and soon presented a memorial on behalf of his clients setting forth their claim to compensation. We shall see the outcome of this and similar claims.

Reverting to the Gratzes, it was, very probably, David Franks and Joseph Simon who interested them in the peltry trade and in the prospect of land speculation. Simon and Barnard Gratz had married girls who were first cousins; Michael had cemented the relation by marrying Miriam, Simon's daughter.

Simon's headquarters were in Lancaster, a fast-growing village on the Pennsylvania frontier, destined within a few years to become the largest inland city in British North America. Simon's fur trading outpost was at Fort Pitt (Pittsburgh), where his associate Milligan looked after his interests. The Lancaster merchant had been a member of the old firm of Levy and Franks, probably since the late 1740's. Numerous partnerships were characteristic of this enterprising Lancastrian; we know of at least eleven different supply and mercantile companies in which he was active during the course of a generation. Practically all of them had been established by him.

Most of these partnerships were very informal. We have a contemporary description of how Simon and Lowrey dissolved their forty-year-old firm. Some time after the Revolutionary War, Colonel Alexander Lowrey and Simon, now elderly men, called in arbitrators and proceeded to wind up the business. No books, papers, or contracts were offered—and none were needed. Simon reminded Lowrey of a certain sum paid him at a certain spring while out West; Lowrey asked Simon to recall what he had paid him while sitting on a log out in the Indian country, and thus the discussion continued until a final settlement was reached, peacefully and amicably.

One of Simon's partners was William Henry, the inventor. The young mechanic had joined forces with Joseph Simon as far back as 1750, after he had finished his apprenticeship as a gunmaker. The business was known as Simon and Henry. Henry was famed as a master craftsman, and the Henry rifle was a prized possession in colonial days. The company manufactured and sold arms, ran a hardware store in Lancaster, and exported bar iron. Henry had built the first stern-wheel steamboat in America (1763), but this experimental boat sank in Conestoga Creek. Sometime about the beginning of the Revolution the partnership of Simon and Henry was dissolved, because the latter went to work for the new American government as a commissary officer and as an arms manufacturer.

In addition to his other ventures Simon had been interested in the development of the Illinois country since the middle '60's. Together with a number of other entrepreneurs, he formed what might be called the "Lancaster syndicate" (although some of those concerned, like the Gratzes, lived in Philadelphia). A rival firm—much larger, and known for its sharp practices—had settled on the Scioto among the Shawnees, attempting by this maneuver to throttle the Fort Pitt fur trade. This was the "Philadelphia syndicate" of Baynton, Wharton, and Morgan.

By 1768 Barnard and Michael Gratz were actively engaged in an Illinois venture, employing one William Murray as their agent in the Mississippi River country. Murray also served as an agent for David Franks and for the London army supply syndicate in which the Frankses were very active. The records show that the Gratz brothers sent Murray gloves, shoes, caps, handkerchiefs, cloth, knives and buckles, coffee, tea and sugar, mustard and pepper, gin, wine, spirits, and rum.

Not infrequently men like Colonel Croghan worked with both the Philadelphia and the Lancaster group; indeed, the rivals found it advisable, on occasion, to join forces in the attempt to secure confirmation of their far-reaching plans from the reluctant, slow-moving British ministry in London.

In the late summer of 1769 Barnard Gratz had made the long and arduous trip to England. No doubt he wanted to see his cousin Solomon Henry. More important was the need to renew old business connections and to establish new ones. In addition, he was certainly eager to note what progress was being made in securing the approval by the English government of the land companies in which he was interested, for these syndicates were now in the process of merger and reorganization. We may be sure that in London he kept a watchful eye on the new Grand Ohio Company which proposed to create the large colony of Vandalia in what is today the state of West Virginia. (The proposed charter of this settlement disenfranchised Jews—in spite of the fact that a number of the proprietors were Jewish. But no American colony at that time envisaged such political equality.)

During Barnard's absence Miriam Simon Gratz, who had married brother Michael about two months previously, sent him the following note:

Philadelphia, August 26, 1769.

My dear Brother:

As I have just now heard of this opportunity, I do myself the pleasure of dedicating a few lines to you, and I hope to be excused for not doing my duty before, but I can assure you that it was not neglected for want of regard for my dear brother. Therefore, as I know your goodness, I need not make any further apologies.

I have the happiness of acquainting you that our family enjoys perfect health. Dear little Rachel [your daughter] has escaped the small pox and is hearty. She often talks of her "dear little Daddy" and wishes to see him, as, indeed, we all do. But how could it be otherwise when a person whom we all love and esteem is at so great a distance from us.

Would it was spring. Then should we be in expectation of a new happiness [Miriam gave birth to a son in April, 1770]. But, alas, a long winter is before us, though I can assure you there is nothing wanting but your presence to make us completely happy. I have a dear, good, and kind husband and a dear little prattling niece, which is a great comfort. I pray that the Almighty may prosper you in all your undertakings and conduct you safe over the wide ocean to your dear friends here.

I hope you'll make yourself entirely easy about Rachel and be assured she'll be as well taken care of by us as she possibly can be. Becky is the same kind body she always was. She desired me to remember her kindly to you and to let you know that she is much pleased in living as she does. I can assure you that I do everything in my power to render everything agreeable to her.

Rachel gives her love to you and hopes *that* you won't forget her London doll. I hope after the receipt of this I shall be favored with a few lines from you. I could not expect it before as it was my place to write first. My dear Michael joins me in love for you. I must conclude, wishing you every felicity this world can afford. From

Your ever loving and affectionate sister,
Miriam Gratz.

P.S. I should be much obliged to you if you would make my kind love acceptable to my Aunt and to my new cousin, Mr. Solomon Henry.

"You must make haste home." Rachel Gratz. (This is Rachel writing. As she begged me to let her write, I was obliged to guide her hand to please her.) [5]

A week later Michael wrote Barnard a more important letter. He reported—and this was good news—that the first cargo of goods sent out West to William Murray had been profitably disposed of; but—and this was not so good—he also reported that one of their customers, Mr. Robert Callender, had lost a considerable sum of money through the "Black Boys."

The Black Boys were a sort of vigilante group of Pennsylvania frontiersmen who had united under Captain James Smith to protect the frontier against marauding Indians. In order the more effectively to accomplish their purpose, they were accustomed to stop the pack horse trains coming across the mountains and to search them for guns, munitions, and liquor going to the Indians. They frequently disguised themselves as redskins, hence "Black Boys." Sometimes they did not burn the "contraband" which they seized but appropriated it for themselves. In 1765 they had destroyed a valuable pack horse train consigned to George Croghan, who was awaiting its arrival at Fort Pitt. This occurred at Sideling Hill, west of Fort London, on what is today the Lincoln Highway, U. S. Route 30. Here is part of Michael's letter:

Philad'a, 31 August, 1769.

Dear Brother:

. . . . A few days ago receiv'd a letter from Mr. Wm. Murray of the Illinois who refers us to letters by . . . Mr. Morgan [of Baynton, Wharton, and Morgan], but none of them arrived as yet here. He [Murray] relates in regard of the goods he had with him turning out to great advantage, and hopes we have sent the like goods by first battows on our joint acco't with him, as else we will be only the poorer for it.

However, as there is a little [some] fear of an Indian war by what letters I saw from Mr. Milligan [Joseph Simon's partner at Fort Pitt], [inasmuch as] the Senecas Indians [are] much discontented on acco't of the purchase money that was given at the last treaty to the nether Indians, and their share not received of them, which makes them very insolent and daring, tho' is thought they want nothing but presents, and robb, if they can, mean time. So am no ways sorry that we did not send any more [goods], as [I am] much afraid of what we have there already if an Indian war should happen, though nothing [is] thought of [one] at present by the generality of people.

Mr. Callender has sustained a loss of about £300 by the Black Boys (as they call them) stopping twenty-four horse loads of Indian goods on the road to Fort Pitt, a little this side Bradford [Bedford], where they pretended to burn the goods, but the chief [the major part was] carried off by them, for which he will receive but little satisfaction tho' [he] is after them.

Mr. Croghan has wrote a letter to you wherin he promises to be here in September or October when perhaps he will want some goods. However, shall be glad to see him here whether he does or not. . . .

However, hope you will be able to settle [on] a good correspondent for a small cargo [of] Indian goods and the other articles of E[as]'t India goods, which am in hopes we will be able to make quick and good returns of, with the assistance of the great run [smuggling] and our friends. Especially when the goods are laid in on good terms, [I] think [we] cannot fail. And no doubt the difficult [Townshend] Acts [imposing duties on lead, paper, tea, etc.,] will be on the repeal before or upon your leaving England; so that [I] would not omitt bringing some goods if they even was to be stored here for a little time, till we have acco't of the repealing of those Acts. . . . However, [I] would do nothing if in case there is no prospect of the Acts being repeal'd, which you are to judge, as [you are] on the spot.

Should be glad [if] you could get in with the Levy's family and try if they would ship those East India nankeens, etc., as there we might do something profitable for them and ourselves too.

Find there is a lottery this year; so must desire you to concern me in a ticket: one-half, or a quarter in two tickets. . . .

[Michael Gratz.]

[To Barnard Gratz, London.] [6]

In the welter of a succession of proposed colonization schemes, with their interlocking directors, with their confluent and opposing interests, the names of Joseph Simon, the Gratzes, Levy Andrew Levy, and the Frankses frequently recur. The land settlement schemes of Franks and his associates were part of a persistent westward movement marked, however, by a sharp ebb and flow.

Many famous names are associated with these western settlements. Back in 1763 George Washington was among the almost forty enterprisers who had formed the Mississippi Company to establish a colony at the mouth of the Ohio. At this strategic point they would have been able to control much of the Mississippi and Ohio River fur trade with the Indians. Three years later, in 1766, Baynton, Wharton, and Morgan, working with Croghan, actively undertook the economic exploitation of the Illinois country. Just about the same time the Lancaster firm of Simon, Trent, Levy, and Company, which we have already mentioned, began to penetrate the same Lower Ohio and Mississippi area.

By 1768 Joseph Simon, the Frankses, the Gratzes, and their friends had begun to merge their interests in the Indiana-Grand Ohio-Walpole-Vandalia colony on the Upper Ohio. This latter company, encouraged and represented at London by Benjamin Franklin who wanted to unite the conflicting interests in the western lands, blithely talked of a colony of 30,000,000 acres. By 1773, the David Franks Company had supplanted Baynton, Wharton, and Morgan on the Mississippi as traders, and was ready to start colonizing in that area.

Thus we see that from Pittsburgh to the Mississippi large sections of the Ohio River Valley were ripe for mass settlement. The Pennsylvanians were making plans for their new Vandalia colony. Adjoining them, west of the Scioto River, there was to be a little colony which George Washington proposed to establish. Farther down at the Falls of the Ohio (Louisville), Simon and Campbell, with offices at Lancaster and Pittsburgh, proposed to lay out a city and, incidentally, to dominate the Ohio River fur trade.

Still farther down the stream, in present-day Illinois, David Franks and Company was determined to establish large-scale settlements in conjunction with its trade with the natives. (This "Illinois Land Company" had twenty-two shareholders; eight were Jews; two, the Hamiltons, were Franks's "in-laws.") To carry out this purpose the company's western agent and chief negotiator, William Murray, assembled a huge load of supplies and Indian small goods at Pittsburgh in May, 1773. It was anything but an easy task. Ten boatmen had been hired at Philadelphia, but only three showed up. The butchers, a sailor, and a tailor for the new colony had deserted, taking their guns with them.

But discouraged as Murray was and disgusted as he was with the town—"this wretched place"—he still took time out to tease his correspondent, Michael Gratz. Murray had delivered some horses, ordered from Michael, to a Mr. Mahon, a Scotch-Irishman. Mahon sold them within a few minutes at a profit of £11. "You see, Michael," Murray wrote, "that a Scotch-Irish man can get the better in a bargain of a Jew. I cannot have it in my power to transgress the Mosaic law by eating swine's fflesh," he continued facetiously, "not an ounce of it can be had in this beggarly place, nor indeed of anything else."

By July 5th, Murray had reached the Mississippi with his goods and had already negotiated the purchase of two huge tracts of land from the Indians.

This enterprise was big business. In later years the company claimed that the grant alone had cost them over $37,000. All of this was in barter goods, of course: cloth, blankets, shirts, stockings, gunpowder, lead, guns, brass kettles, tobacco, looking glasses, grain, horses, and cattle. And it was no mean achievement to send these "sundries" and Indian goods over the Alleghenies on pack horses to Fort Pitt, through Indian country and hostile "Black Boys," and then down the Ohio River on flatboats to Kaskaskia and Fort de Chartres on the Mississippi.

What the company received in exchange for the goods was even more imposing: the lower triangle of land between the Mississippi and the mouth of the Ohio—approximately the same area in which Washington and his friends had been interested in 1763—and a huge wedge of land between the Mississippi and the Illinois Rivers extending to the Checagou (Chicago) or Garlick Creek. This latter area provided one of the most important river highways between the Mississippi River and the Great Lakes and Canada; the former area dominated traffic on the Lower Ohio and Mississippi Valley—and the Ohio, it must not be forgotten, was the chief highway running east and west. It was a brilliant undertaking.

But it was one thing to buy an empire from the Indians; it was something else to have the title confirmed and to secure permanent settlers. Franks and his associates were conscious of the importance of securing proper sponsorship for the new colony. They turned to Virginia, which had always claimed that territory. From their offices in Philadelphia they petitioned Governor John Dunmore of Virginia in April, 1774, to take the Illinois company under his protection:

To His Excellency, the Right Honorable John, Earl of Dunmore, governor and commander in chief, in and over the colony and dominion of Virginia and Vice Admiral of the same:

The petition of the several grantees named in the deed (herein after mentioned), as well on behalf of themselves as in the names and on behalf of all the several persons settled upon the lands granted by the said deed to the petitioners, humbly sheweth:

That your petitioners having seen the opinions of Lords Chancellors Cambden and York relative to titles derived by his Majesty's subjects from the Indians or natives (an exact copy whereof is hereunto annexed), and being farther induced by motives of extending the British trade into the Indian country, and by equitable, fair, and open dealing to bring over the natives to a due sense of a peaceable and well regulated commerce, as well as to avert the evil consiquences that might ensue to his Majesty's good subjects from the great numbers of irregular and lawless emigrants that are about seating themselves upon the lands of the natives, without having obtained the consent of those native and natural proprietors to the making of such settlements, which irregular and unlicenced incroachments might very probably be productive of Indian insurections and depredations, the fatal consiquences of which have been experienced by many thousands of his Majesty's subjects;

Your petitioners have therefore at an expence of many thousand pounds, as well as with very great fatigue to some of your petitioners, in the most fair, open, and public manner, purchased in fee simple from the native proprietors two several tracts or parcels of lands as by the Indian deed of conveyance (duely executed in full and public council held with all the chiefs or sachems of the different tribes of the Illinois nations

39

of Indians, and recorded in the Secretary's Office at Williams-
burgh in the colony and dominion of Virginia) may more
fully appear. That no part of the lands in your petitioners'
purchase were heretofore ceded to, or purchas'd by, or for
either their Christian [French] or Britannic Majesty's or either
of their subjects;

That the purchase was fair, open, public, and satisfactory
to the Indians, appears from the affedavits of Richard Winston,
French interpreter, Michael Danné, and Piero Bloit, Indian interpreters (the latter of whom being Indian interpreter for
the Crown in that country), taken by the officer commanding his Majesty's troops in the Illinois country, which may
be farther proven, if necessary, by the testimony of many
other credible witnesses who were present at the several con-
ferances publicly held with the Indian chiefs, &cta., relative
to the petitioners' purchase, as well as subscribing witnesses to
the executing the deed of conveyance, and present at the delivery of the considerations expressed in the deed;

That your petitioners are at a very considerable expence
making settlements upon their purchase: as well by themselves
as by many orderly, industrious, and usefull British subjects
whom your petitioners are transporting to that country, which
'tis hoped and expected may soon become usefull and beneficial to their parent country, as well as to his Majesty's colonies in America. And also tend greatly to faciliate and expe-
dite the civilization of those Indians who have heretofore
been troublesom to the frontier inhabitants of the several
colonies. The settlers, upon your petitioners' purchase, becoming also a good barrier to cover the frontiers of the several
contiguous colonies, and particularly the present frontier inhabitants of Virginia;

That your petitioners shall be always willing to comply
with such rules and regulations with respect to quit rents as
the inhabitants of his Majesty's colony and dominion of Virginia are subject to, as well as ardently wishing to enjoy the

40

benifit of the laws, and as they aprehend their purchase to be within the limits of the colony of Virginia, tho' its jurisdiction has not hitherto been so far extended;

Your petitioners theirfor pray that your Lordship be pleased to take the petitioners and their settlements into the protection of your Lordship's government of Virginia and extend to them the laws and jurisdiction of your colony accordingly.

And your petitioners shall ever pray.

By order of the committee duely authorised by all the grantees.

David Franks,
J. Murray,
John Campbell.

Philadelphia, 19th April, 1774.[7]

It all sounded very promising. Yet less than a month after this, while in the Mohawk Valley conferring with Sir William Johnson, Barnard Gratz received an ominous letter from William Murray. The Illinois agent was impatiently waiting in Philadelphia for Michael Gratz to finish celebrating the Jewish festival of Pentecost—"as the Devil will have it . . . Moses was upon the top of a mountain in the month of May." Reports had just come in, Murray continued, that the Indians were being killed by the whites on the Ohio. "If this intelligence be true, it would be much against us and greatly endanger my scalp."

The intelligence was, unfortunately, true; the family of the Indian chief Logan had been murdered. Cresap's and Lord Dunmore's War was on, the frontier was ablaze, the settlers fled to the forts, and all hopes for a peaceful penetration of the West had to be given up for the time being. And in the following year, 1775, the outbreak of the Revolution was a further blow; extensive colonization was out of the question, certainly for the duration of the war.

The Illinois Land Company enterprisers were never able to salvage their investments. None of the proposed pre-Revolutionary colonies in the West were able to come into existence after the states ceded their western lands to the federal government. The dreams of landed empire faded away.

Chapter 3

Pennsylvania — 1771

IN the early 1770's, Michael Gratz was beginning to count his profits from his traffic in the Illinois country and to justify the wearing of that expensive pair of buckles to which his cousin Solomon Henry had voiced such pointed objection. Although concentrating on the western trade, Michael did not fail to keep in touch with various businessmen in other parts of the country. There were no adequate newspaper services, and no efficient credit bureaus to inform, to advise, or to warn. Throughout the American colonies, in the West Indies and on the mainland, merchants helped their friends with advice, price quotations, and other important bits of news.

In July, 1771, Michael received a short note from Manuel Josephson, a respected New York merchant whose harrowing experiences as a sutler during the French and Indian War were slowly receding into the mist of the past. In 1762 he had been elected president of the congregation; strangely enough, he had trouble with the synagogal leaders a number of years later. He was accused, in 1769, of opposing the "good rules and orders instituted by our community" and was threatened with expulsion.

But this letter which Manuel Josephson now sent to Michael had nothing to do with congregational discipline. It concerned itself with an entirely different problem:

New York, 17th July, 1771.

Mr. Mich'l Gratz,
D'r Sir:

On Friday last I wrote you, but the mail being closed I followed the post boy to the ferry and deliv'd him the letter, and as I have not heard from you p[er]. this day's post, fear it did not come to hand.

I therefore shall repeat the subject w'ch is: that a young rogue named Levy Marks, who came to your place [Philadelphia] with the Widow Jacobs from St. Eustatia [in the West Indies], this day a week, took from me severall goods to the amo't of £40 to sell on commission, or rather to take all the proffite to himself, as I charged him only prime cost in order to encourage him, and [he] went away w'th them.

Having from that day to this not had any intelligence from him, and as it is probable he may have gone to your place, if so shall take it as a particular fav'r if you could secure me, if not in the whole at least some part, and otherwise act with him as such a villain deserves.

This being what at pres't offers, remain w'th salutations to Mrs. Gratz, d'r sir,

Your most humb'e serv't,
Manuel Josephson.[8]

As early as 1760 we find a Levy Marks, a tailor, in business in Lancaster and Philadelphia, living intermittently in these two towns. When, in 1765, Michael Gratz set out for St. Eustatia and Curaçao, he made out his will, in which he

provided a legacy for a cousin, Levy Marks of Philadelphia.
In the spring of 1776 a Levy Marks, presumably the cousin,
advertised in *The Pennsylvania Packet* that he had an inn,
some houses, and some land for rent. He informed his
debtors and creditors that he was leaving town and asked
them to come in and settle their accounts. But while still
in Philadelphia, in 1777, he sent a petition to the Continental Congress asking for the job of superintending the manufacture of army uniforms. And that same year, back again
in Lancaster, he subscribed a sum of money to hire one or
more persons to keep a steady courier service between Lancaster and General Washington's army. Two years later
he was among those who took the oath of allegiance to the
free, sovereign, and independent state of Pennsylvania.

Obviously the "young rogue" Levy Marks is not to be
identified with that solid citizen, Levy Marks, the erstwhile
tailor. Indeed, there is sufficient evidence to indicate that
during this period there was even a third man by the name
of Levy Marks. As far back as 1750, Levy Marks, a member
of Shearith Israel in New York, was assessed the minimum
amount for a seat; and in 1770, he was still in New York,
although now dependent on congregational charity. This
is definitely not our *young* rogue of 1771.

There were thus three men of this name: one, an old
New Yorker; another, Michael's cousin; and the third, our
genial young scoundrel who made off with Josephson's
goods, and, probably, with the widow from St. Eustatia.

Exactly four months later, Joseph Simon of Lancaster
sent his "in-laws" Michael and Barnard Gratz a letter in

Yiddish, to which an English postscript was added, complaining of another rogue:

Here, Lancaster, Sunday, 10th of the month of Kislew, 532, according to the shorter reckoning [November 17, 1771].
Peace to my beloved son [in-law] and his brother, the distinguished princes and the honorable congregational leaders, the respected and scholarly Yehiel [Michael] and Barnard Gratz—May their Rock and Redeemer guard these distinguished and God-fearing gentlemen and may they and theirs enjoy the blessings of peace:
I cannot refrain from giving you an account of what happened here last Thursday.
At about six o'clock in the evening a man came here with the enclosed letter [of recommendation from a Philadelphia engraver] and described himself as a cousin of Levy's [my son-in-law, Levy Andrew Levy]. He was dressed like a gentleman, with boots and spurs, and he was mounted on a horse. He was accompanied by another man, very neatly dressed, whom he referred to as Master Bailey—he said that he was a lawyer—so Levy told him to put up his horse at Slough's [the innkeeper].
When he returned to Levy's, we examined him closely in the light and found that he had been here two weeks ago. At that time he was dressed in a Ferginny [Virginia] shirt with leggings and moccasins, and Lyon and Master Myers had given him something. We were therefore surprised to see him in such fine array. He then gave Levy the enclosed letter. We thereupon questioned him as to how he had come by the fine clothes and the horse. He told us that Master Abrams [Alexander Abrahams, a clerk of the Gratzes] in Philadelphia had given him the coat and the camisole, and that Master Abraham Franks [a Philadelphia Mason] had lent him the cape, coat, boots, and spurs, and that a certain man in Philadelphia called Lazah (the butcher's son) had given him his hat, wig, shirt,

and stockings. The last time he was here he wore his own hair. He said he was a barber by trade.

I have forgotten [to say that] Abraham Franks is surety for the horse he was riding. He had hired it for two shillings a day. A certain man in Philadelphia, the son of Wolf the beadle, had given him money for his expenses. He [the rogue] told us that he had been brought up with Levy in the same street in Oxford [England], that his uncle was married to Levy's mother, that he was the son of Hayyim Gast, and that he had a wife and two children in England. When we found out that he had been a convict, I told him to clear out the same evening, and I had nothing more to say to him. Then I went home.

Meanwhile, after I had left, he began to weep before Levy and Lyon, and so they gave him something. (But I did not give him a penny, and I was very glad that I had not given him anything.) Afterwards I let Slough know what birds these two were, and I advised him to beware of them and not keep them over night. But Slough did not take my advice; he let them stay over. Whereupon they certainly did repay him for his kindness; they paid him with counterfeit coin, of the same kind as you will find enclosed in this letter. Therefore, you people ought to be on your guard and treat such birds as they deserve when they turn up in Philadelphia. I believe that the other fellow who was with him, whom he addressed as Master Bailey, is also a Jew.

I am very angry at that old fool of an engraver for giving such birds a letter. He [the crook] had friends enough in Philadelphia who helped him with clothes, money, and a horse. Why did they not keep him with them? Why? Because like begets like! Therefore, if they ever get such guests again, let them keep them there. Let them enjoy themselves with such birds. He told us that they would go to Philadelphia by way of Reading.

With which we close and wish you both health. From me, your friend, Joseph ben Simeon.

Please try to get Slough's money for him from these birds. If you can get it, I shall be happy. Slough took the counterfeit money in exchange for a quarter of a moidore [gold coin]. They left Friday morning at five o'clock.

[The following postscript in English was addressed by **Levy Andrew Levy** to his "in-laws," the Gratzes.]

I am very angry with the ingraver for recommending a transport [a convict] to me, and a good for nothing rascall. I never shall countenance such sort, was it even a brother, tho' I believe it all false his being a cousin. I knew him not; very few of those sort reforms, a proof, the behaveour to Slough. He had neither bread nor watter from me, yet his deceetfull lammentations flung me of 10/6. I have taken a resolution that I will hereafter take no more notice of straglers, unless they can perduce a letter of recommendation.

I am gentlem'n,

Y'r h[umble]. s[ervant].

L. And'ew Levy.[9]

When the rogues, who had cozened Colonel Matthias Slough, owner of the tavern the "Swan," out of a gold coin, examined it at their leisure, they may not have been very gleeful, for if Lancaster gossip was well-founded, the worthy Boniface was not unaccustomed to clip the gold coins that came into his possession—close! But then even a clipped coin is better than a counterfeit coin.

Defaulters and crooks were resented bitterly; they were cheats depriving honest men of hard-earned savings which they had scraped together only through toil and drudgery —and they gave the Jew a bad name.

Jews even in a secure position are nearly always fearful. They have their reasons. They are afraid that their own hard-won status will be threatened by the actions of coreligionists of lesser culture and of seemingly baser character. Jews are under the impression that the world holds the Jews, as a group, responsible for the derelictions of the individual.

In that same year (1771) the former American merchant Naphtali Hart Myers, as head of The Great Synagogue in London, took the lead in driving Jewish criminals out of England. He successfully urged the Postmaster General to stop providing free transportation for emigrants from the Continent; he and his cohorts induced the Lord Mayor to offer the poor Jews already in England a passport to return whence they had come.

This action of Myers in policing his own people was patterned after the action taken by him and his coworker Naphtali Franks, five years before, in 1766. At that time the two men had offered their assistance to the magistrate, Sir John Fielding of Bow Street, in dealing with Jewish criminal elements. The aroused Jewish leaders excommunicated the evil-doers, expelled some of them from the synagogue, and did everything they could as heads of Ashkenazic Jewry in England to rid the country of "wretches who are a pest to every community." (The Protestants did not, as far as we know, so denounce their own criminal elements. They sat back and let the state ship them to the colonies.)

Scamps and rascals were regarded as real threats by men like Levy, Simon, and Josephson. Less troublesome, although still a sizeable expense, were the impoverished and broken men who were dumped into their midst. These they just as promptly forwarded to the next community. There was no attempt, as far as we can see, at social rehabilitation. A case in point was Jacob Musqueto.

He arrived in New York from the Island of St. Eustatia, a distance of about 2,000 miles, and, after throwing himself upon the mercy of the local Jewish community, asked to be sent to the Island of Barbados, only about 200 miles from the spot whence he had just come. With resignation— one might almost say with Christian resignation—and without any reproach as far as the records indicate, the Shearith Israel leaders provided for him for a while. Then they sent this "object of charity" on to Philadelphia, requesting Michael Gratz to collect sufficient funds to dispatch him back to the West Indies.

Whether the unfortunate Mr. Musqueto was a voluntary migrant, it is difficult to say. Jewry in the West Indies may have shipped him to New York just to get rid of him—the Americans no less expeditiously rose to the emergency by giving him a long and peaceful free ride back. (Maybe that was what he really sought!)

But let us not be unjust. It is by no means improbable that the quickest way that our impoverished itinerant could go from St. Eustatia to Barbados—both in the West Indies— was via the long trip to New York. Such was not an unusual route for a merchant going from Jamaica to Surinam, Dutch Guiana. The longest way round was the quickest— though not the shortest—way home!

But there was another type of itinerant who was treated with more consideration than the ubiquitous "objects of charity": the collector for Palestine. Emerging from the very ends of the earth, as rabbi, scholar, and pious man, such a person had to be shown every courtesy and all generosity before he, too, was respectfully but cheerfully forwarded by the relieved community to a sister congregation.

Both paupers and Palestinian emissaries were part of the tradition of Jewish communal life and were accepted with equanimity. But businessmen who defrauded their creditors were beyond the fraternal pale. When, in 1760, red-faced, black-bearded Myers Levy of Spotswood in East Jersey departed with his wife and five children—and £2,300 worth of unpaid supplies—the Gratzes and the Frankses and their Gentile fellow-victims offered $800 for his return with the goods, but only $50 if he were brought back sans property.

There was no question of what they thought of this Levy; it is difficult to know what they thought of another Levy who, in the same decade, gathered to his bosom the absconding wife of an irate citizen from the same colony of New Jersey. *The Pennsylvania Journal* of November 5, 1769, carried the dour announcement that John Farnsworth was no longer responsible for the debts of Deborah his wife: "She likes the said Levy better than me . . . intends to live with him as he will maintain her as a gentlewoman. I have waited on Mr. Levy respecting the affair from whom I have received no other satisfaction than insolent language. . . ."

The Mr. Levy who received Mr. Farnsworth's wife was no "criminal" measured by the standards of his day; he may have been in love, and love, we are told, covers a multitude of sins. But the sputtering letter of Joseph Simon, which we have just read, clearly indicates that the Jewry of his day was not devoid of unvarnished criminals. Among the thousands of redemptioners and indentured servants who were shipped to this country, among the military and political criminals transported here, were many scoundrels and petty villains condemned to slave in the colonies as bonded servants until their terms were up. Evidently Levy Andrew Levy's "cousin" and Mr. Bailey, "the lawyer," were two transported convicts who had either served their terms here as indentured workers or had escaped from their lawful masters and were on a tour of petty thievery. (The name "Bailey" may well have been an unwitting reminiscence of Old Bailey, the Central Criminal Court, in London!) There may have been little excuse for past criminality by bondsmen of this type; but there was justification, only too frequently, for flight from their present servitude.

It has been estimated that at least one-half of the immigrants who came to these shores in colonial days, Irish, Scotch, Germans, and others, came as indentured servants. Some of them found good homes, others were subject to brutal mistreatment. Two days after the battle of Lexington, on April 21, 1775, while the country was ringing with the cry of "Liberty or Death," Mr. Purdie's *Virginia Gazette* announced a substantial reward for the capture and return of seven English servants who had escaped from their masters in Harford County, Maryland. Among these fugitives was the Jew, Abraham Peters, about twenty-eight years of age, about five feet nine inches high, black hair and beard, of a swarthy complexion, lame, his left hand somewhat perished—and talks very good Dutch.

Peters and his friends and dozens of others who were hid-

ing in the fields and skulking in the forests in April, 1775,
may well have been no criminals, but poverty-stricken men
who had sold themselves to gain passage to a land where
they hoped to achieve the liberty and the opportunity that
were denied them at home.

Certainly, one of the reasons why Joseph Simon was so
irritated by the impostor Levy Marks was the fact that
Matthias Slough was the victim. Simon and Slough knew
each other very well; they did business together during the
French and Indian War.

Simon was the outstanding Jew in Lancaster, proud—we
may be sure—of the fact that his Christian acquaintances
referred to him as a "principal merchant," an "eminent
trader," "a man fair in his dealings and honest from principle." He was one of the two men who laid out the Jewish
cemetery, and he it was who established the synagogue—no
doubt only a modest room in his own home, graced by a
portable ark standing against the east wall.

Occasional services were held in Lancaster. On a holyday, when the heads of the different families were in town,
when Simon and his Jewish sons-in-law foregathered with
their Jewish clerks, and an extra Jew or two had come in
from Conestoga, Reading, or York, they must have had a
good-sized congregation—but those occasions cannot have
been too frequent.

It is doubtful if they held services every Sabbath. This is
not to imply that some of these Lancastrians were not Sabbath observers. Simon, for instance, kept kosher and would
do no business on his day of rest, as the Rev. David Mc-

53

Clure discovered when he passed through town on his way
to the Muskingum Valley to bring the gospel to the be-
nighted Indians. When Mr. McClure presented an order
for money on the Sabbath to Simon, the latter said to the
clergyman and his companion: "Gentlemen, to-day is my
Sabbath, and I do not do business in it; if you will please
to call tomorrow, I will wait on you." To this McClure re-
sponded that he as a Christian could not do any business on
his Sabbath, on Sunday. Simon realized the difficulty and,
in spite of the fact that in so doing he violated the Jewish
law, called in his neighbor Dr. Boyd and asked him to handle the financial transaction for him. McClure's "gratitude"
for this kindness is recorded in his diary: "The Jews in
general are said to be very strict and punctual in the observance of some of the traditionary ceremonies of their
law, but hesitate not to defraud, when opportunity presents. Like their predecessors, the Pharisees, they tythe
mint, annis, and cummin, and neglect the weightier matters
of the law, as judgement, mercy, and faith. They strain at
a gnat and swallow a camel."

Whenever Simon chanced to be in Philadelphia of a Saturday, he could always join the local congregants at their
devotions. Although tradition has it that prayers were heard
in a Philadelphia synagogue in the 1740's, one may well
doubt that regular services were held during that decade.
There is a Philadelphia tradition—for what it is worth—that
no permanent congregation could be established because
the original settlers, followers of the German or Polish rite,
could not agree on a common liturgy.

Pastor Henry Melchior Mühlenberg, father of the Lutheran Church in America, tells us that there were only a handful of Jews in town, and they were "practicing atheists." As a true Pietist in the Francke tradition, Mühlenberg was also an evangelist. He was interested in converting the children of Israel, and his colleague Callenberg, back at the University of Halle, kept him supplied with Yiddish missionary tracts. (As a student of the Bible in the original tongue, he was quite familiar with the Hebrew script.) Something had to be done about the Jews. It is true, so he preached to one of his religious classes, they are the cousins of our Lord, but only after the flesh, not in the spirit. Unless these Jews believed in Jesus, there was no salvation for them; they were eternally damned. No man to delay when precious souls were at stake, Mühlenberg asked a friend of his, a good Christian, to approach the outstanding Jew in town and to offer him some tracts on the true Messiah. The Jew who was solicited—either Nathan Levy or David Franks—sent the pastor the following message: "The most representative men in the city, with whom I associate, admit that their Messiah . . . was an impostor. Give your writings to these gentlemen. I have no intention or time to read them."

It was not until the late winter of 1760 that the Philadelphia congregation bestirred itself and took on a new lease of life, probably under the prodding of the Gratz clan. In January of the following year Jacob Henry wrote from New York to Barnard Gratz that he had heard that a synagogue was to be built. Henry was frankly incredulous and was convinced that "Eternity is nigh at hand." Ironically he speculated whether the ritual would follow the London

Ashkenazic, Prague, or Polish pattern; he implied, indeed, that the Philadelphia ritual would be a Quaker one—that is, none at all. There would be no organized synagogal community. Desiring, however, to end his letter on a serious note, he expressed the hope that they would really accomplish something: "I wish you may go through your good works; and *I wish* myself the pleasure to see it built."

Jacob Henry's skepticism was justified only in part. While no building was erected at that time, the congregation did perk up. A messenger was sent to New York that fall (1761) to bring back a Scroll of the Law as a permanent loan. Ten years later, then at least a dozen families strong, the congregation determined to open a synagogue. Through the agency of a Mr. Myers, it secured another Scroll from Jonas Phillips, a New York merchant.

A silver pointer—the *yad*—was needed for the Reader, and also, of course, prayer books, *tefillot*. All these were secured that same year, as we discover in letters which Barnard Gratz sent to two of his London agents, Jacob Barnett and Michael Samson. Barnett, an unsuccessful printer, supplied the prayer books, in response to a letter dated October 15, 1771. In the same letter, Gratz complained that the dark purple and deep red ribbons which he had ordered had arrived, but were light blue and half pink. Barnett, it would seem, had failed to check the color of the goods before they were packed for shipment. Gratz went on to warn Barnett that he did not think that there was a market in the colonies for such items as rose water and "hungry" [Hungary] water, but that ready-made shoes might possibly sell in small lots. Let us hope that the juniper berries [for gin?] which Barnett sent Gratz were of good quality. (One gathers the impression—it may be an unjustified one—that Barnett was just a little bit of a *shlemiel*—a "nebb." Michael Samson, however, was certainly no *shlemiel;* he was one of the leaders of Ashkenazic London Jewry and was soon to become a warden of The Great Synagogue).

On the same day that Gratz wrote to Barnett he sent a letter also to Samson, his banking correspondent for the nonce, asking him to settle for purchases made for the Philadelphia synagogue. Gratz's note is interesting because it is his own entry into his letter book, and had not been whipped into shape by a clerk. It reveals his knowledge of the vernacular. Evidently, in spite of his having lived for two decades under the British flag, his English still left something to be desired.

Philad'a, Oct. 15th, 1771.

Mr. Michael Samson,
D'r Sir:

Your fav'r of the 6th June I duly rece'd and was glad to hear of your and y'r familly's good health, which gave me a great deal satisfaction and pleasur.

In regard the *sefer torah* ["Scroll of the Law"] have only to say and to lett you know that we have the one you mentioned to me, that did belang to Mr. Jonas Philips from New York, from Mr. Myers, as Mr. Philips order'd, for which you will be kind anough to pay Mr. Philips for it. I suppose he will not charge too much for it, as he asked me but seven guenes, I think, for it. But shuld he ask somthing more now, you must pay him. Mr. Myers of New York, I heard, told sombody he thinks it will be nine guenes, but hope Mr. Philips will

57

lett it goe for the price he asked me for it, as above. However, I live [leave] this to you to agree with him.

You need not to send the silver *yad* ["pointer"] I mentioned to you before, as we had one made a pressent for the *shool* from New York. And shuld be glad if you would be kind anough, after paying Mr. Philips for the *sefer torah,* and if mony anough in your hands, you would pay Mr. Jacob Barnett seventy-five shillings sterling for some *tefillot* he sent me hear. And pleas to lett me know neeta [the net balance] that I might know how our acc'ts stand, as should not like to trouble you without proffit and to advance money [for me].

I am very much obliged to you for the trouble you have taken in forwd'g the letters to Amsterdam, and wish sinceerly it was in my power to serve you or any of yo'r familly, which would give me great pleasure. And should you or any of y'r familly incline to venture something this way in trade, shall allways be glad to serve them and adviceing them what would best answer this way.

I have now only to wish you and Mrs. Samson a great deal of joy on y'r familly increase with a son. Hope Mrs. Samson and y'r d'r children are well, which is the senceer wishes from, d'r sir,

Yo'r most hum'le servent,
B. G[ratz].[10]

Thus the congregation gradually acquired the inventory of cult utensils which it needed to carry on a proper and attractive service.

Among the Jewish settlers at this time in Philadelphia was a transplanted New Yorker, Jonas Phillips. Jonas was an American patriot, as we shall see; he had every reason to be one. He had emigrated from Germany when he was not yet twenty years of age, coming from one of the twin-villages Alten or Gross Buseck in Upper Hesse, not far from Giessen. With a chance to leave, it would have been foolish for him to remain in Hesse. In all the Hessian states of that time Jews paid exorbitant discriminatory taxes; in one of them they were excluded from most crafts and forms of commerce. Jonas went to London—where, no doubt, he Anglicized his name Feibush or Phoebus to Phillips—and then sailed, in 1756, for Charlestown, South Carolina, on the "Charming Nancy" with Moses Lindo, an expert in the indigo trade, who was taking him along as a clerk or as a servant.

He remained but a short time in Charlestown and then struck north. By 1759 we find him up the Hudson at Albany, a freeman of the city, bartering groceries, liquor, and drygoods for furs, and catering also to the military headed toward Canada; by 1761 he was back in New York, opposite the Fort, doing business with the soldiers again, we may be sure. The following year, 1762, in Philadelphia for the occasion, this twenty-six-year-old German immigrant married sixteen-year-old Rebecca Mendez Machado, a Sephardic Jewess, the daughter of a former *hazzan* of Shearith Israel.

The next fall, the first of their twenty-one children was born. The children came quite regularly, most of them survived, and they needed food. In 1765, after having become an insolvent debtor, Phillips accepted the position of *shohet* for Shearith Israel and kept the post till 1769. He was paid £35 a year, and although he complained that he received no perquisites, the *shohet* of that day usually did receive the tongues of the animals he killed. He almost lost this job in 1767 when he carelessly left his pinchers lying around. That instrument was used to stamp the lead kosher mark on the meat of the animals he had slaughtered. Anyone could have used it to put a kosher seal on an unfit piece of meat! He was given another chance, and the following year he even dared to ask for an increase in salary. He got it: the officers gave him a grant of £10 for firewood—and then they immediately revoked it.

Things seem to have picked up for him in 1769, for he was then given the freedom of the city of New York. He had business relations with Moses M. Hays in Newport, to whom he described himself as of a "poor but honest family." In those years he probably still had more downs than ups. Now that he was a recognized denizen of the city, he felt that he could strike out completely for himself. He resigned his position as *shohet* in the winter of 1769–70.

But, in order to help keep the pot boiling, he took a sick man in as a paying guest at the request of the community, which boarded out its impoverished and sick who had no homes of their own. For this he received fourteen shillings a week. The deal was made with Isaac Moses, who was then an important officer of the congregation. Jonas was glad, no doubt, of the extra income now that he was about to surrender his job as *shohet*, and, perhaps due to the boarder, he managed that same year to save enough to send some money home to his mother. It was his wife, we may rest assured, who took care of the sick man. After all, a young healthy woman of twenty-four, who had only three or four children of her own, could easily assume the care of another person, even if he was sick. Hard work certainly did not hurt her; we know that she lived to be eighty-five years of age.

Three years later, in 1773, Phillips experienced some obscure misfortune which severely threatened his status and touched upon his integrity, for we find him soliciting, successfully, a certificate of good character from his former employer, Moses Lindo. By 1775 he was settled in Philadelphia, doing business as a retailer and auctioneer, moving around from location to location, and striving to attract custom by extensive advertising. He sold everything from broadcloth to bacon. He dealt in pork—but one may rest assured that he never ate it himself, for he was an observant Jew and had a good knowledge of rabbinic law.

In July, 1776, he sent a letter to his relative and business correspondent in Holland, Gumpel Samson. Along with the letter went a copy of the Declaration of Independence. Because of the British blockade, Phillips sent his letter by way of the Dutch island of St. Eustatia. In it he enclosed a draft for his mother and hinted, rather broadly, as one might to a relative, that money was to be made by running the blockade. He thought he could fool the British by writing in Yiddish. He fooled only himself: they intercepted the mail, and it lies today in the British Public Record Office with the sage notation of an archivist that it was written in some shorthand! Jonas had been away from home for many years and flattered himself that he wrote a better English than Yiddish. Maybe he did—but there is nothing wrong with the original Yiddish of his letter:

61

Philadelphia, Sunday, 12 Menahem Ab, 536, according to the shorter reckoning [July 28, 1776].

Peace to my beloved master, my kinsman, the eminent and wealthy, wise and discerning God-fearing man, whose honored, glorious name is Mr. Gumpel—May his Rock and Redeemer protect him and all his family! Peace!

As it is not always possible to send a letter to England on account of the war in America, I must therefore write by way of St. Eustatia.

I have not yet had any answer to a letter of May, 1775, when I sent my master a bill of exchange for ten pounds sterling for my mother. Should that letter not have arrived, then the enclosed third bill of exchange will obtain the money, and please send it to my mother, long life to her. Should it, however, have already been obtained, you need not return the bill of exchange again, and a hint to the wise will suffice [Use it to buy goods for me to run the blockade!].

As no English goods can come over at all, and much money can be earned with Holland goods if one is willing to take a chance, should you have a friend who will this winter acquaint himself with the goods mentioned below, I can assure you that four hundred per cent is to be earned thereby. I could write my meaning better in English than Yiddish.

The war will make all England bankrupt. The Americans have an army of 100,000 soldiers [literally: "tough guys"], and the English only 25,000 and some ships. The Americans have already made themselves [free] like the States of Holland. The enclosed is a declaration [of independence] of the whole country. How it will end, the blessed God knows. The war does me no damage, thank God!

I would like to send you a bill of exchange, but it is not possible for me to get it. If my master, long life to him, will disburse for me 100 gulden to my mother, I can assure you that just as soon as a bill of exchange on St. Eustatia can be had, I will, with thanks, honestly pay you. I have it, thank

God, in my power, and I know that my mother, long life to her, needs it very much; and I beg of my master, long life to him, to write me at once an answer, addressed as herein written.

There is no further news. My wife and children, long life to her and them, together send you many greetings and wish you good health up to one hundred years.

Your friend, to serve. From me, Jonah, son of Mr. Feibush [Phoebus]—the memory of the righteous is a blessing—of Buseck,

Jonas Phillips.

[Address all goods sent:]
To
Mr. Jonas Phillips in Philadelphia to the care of Mr. Samuel Curson, merchant in St. Eustatia.

Goods that will sell to advantage in this place. All sorts of coarce and fine white linen, Russia sheetings, coarce white thread, ravens duck, Russia sail duck, oznabrigs [coarse linen made of flax and tow], drillings, check linens, Harlem stripes, thomoise [shomoise? = chamois type cloth], ivory combs, needles, pinns, drugs and medicines, sewing silks, worsted stockings, large, striped woollen blankets, different sorts of woollen goods for the winter season.
To
Mr. Gumpel Samson, merchant in Amsterdam, by way of St. Eustatia.

St. Eustatia, 24 Sep'r, 1776, Rece'd and forwarded by

Your hum'e serv't,
Sam. Curson.[11]

Less than two years later, Phillips and sundry other Philadelphia merchants did succeed in bringing a cargo of goods through the British blockade. It was an expensive load, for the insurance alone ran to fifty per cent of the cost, and they paid for everything in sterling. But, apparently, they were to derive no profit from this bold venture, for the goods were taken by the Clothier and Quartermaster Generals for the use of the army. In the meantime, the same goods had advanced forty per cent at the European source. Phillips and his friends now petitioned Congress to bear all these facts in mind when they set a price for these valuable wares. When and if they were paid, rest assured it was in Continental currency!

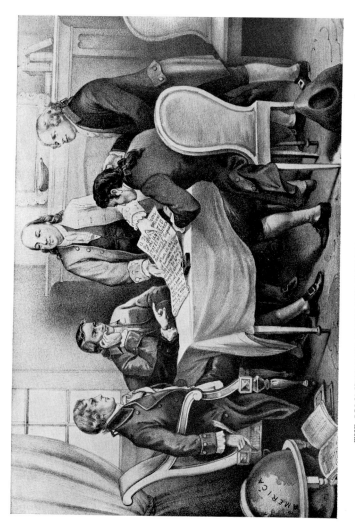

THE COMMITTEE TO DRAFT THE DECLARATION OF INDEPENDENCE, 1776

BALTIMORE IN 1752

Chapter 4

Pennsylvania — 1776

I N his July, 1776, letter to Amsterdam, Jonas Phillips had said of the war: "How it will end, the blessed God knows." He certainly could not have been very optimistic that winter as he received the news of the defeat at Long Island, the withdrawal of Washington's troops from the city of New York, the mishaps of Benedict Arnold at Lake Champlain, the surrender of Fort Washington and Fort Lee, and the steady retreat across New Jersey toward the Pennsylvania border. It looked as if Philadelphia itself was doomed, and no doubt Jonas wondered what he himself would do if the British entered the city.

At that time another Jew, a member of a prominent Philadelphia family, who had been living in Baltimore since the early '70's, sent a hasty note to his well-known friend Robert Morris offering him sanctuary in Maryland. This hospitable businessman was Benjamin Levy. (One of his sons was named Robert Morris Levy.)

The Pennsylvania Levys, whom we have already met through David Franks's partner, Nathan, included also

Samson and Benjamin Levy. Benjamin married Nathan's daughter, Rachel.

Like Nathan Levy, Samson and Benjamin moved in the best social circles. Samson was one of the subscribers of the first Philadelphia dancing "Assembly" in 1748. Both Samson and Benjamin, together with eight other Jews, were among the approximately 400 merchants who signed the 1765 agreement not to import goods from England until the Stamp Act was repealed. Robert Morris, whose firm was Willing, Morris, & Co., was also among the signers.

Much more than today, social relationships in old Pennsylvania followed closely in the wake of business deals, certainly as far as Jews were concerned. The Frankses and the Levys traded with the Hamiltons, the Shippens, and the Plumsteds, took their men as partners, danced with their women-folk—and intermarried.

When Benjamin Levy lost his money in 1768, in part no doubt due to the looting by the Indians during the early days of the French and Indian War, he was compelled to make an assignment of his assets to a group of Philadelphia merchants, some of whom were his social intimates, fellow-members of the aristocratic "Assembly." Business was, even then, always business.

Shortly thereafter Benjamin moved to Baltimore, hoping, doubtlessly, to take advantage of the growing West India trade and to improve his financial condition in that thriving city of 5,000.

There had been a "Jewes store" in Maryland in the seventeenth century. Benjamin, however, was one of the first permanent Jewish settlers in Baltimore, although individuals of his persuasion had been naturalized in the colony as early as 1757. At the most, however, there could not have been more than a dozen Jewish families in Baltimore during the 1770's. True, a cemetery was purchased in 1786, but no real Jewish community came into being until the second quarter of the nineteenth century.

There was little to attract a Jew to Maryland beyond its commercial opportunities. Even the so-called Toleration Act of 1649 extended its benefits only to those who believed in Jesus Christ. In 1659 an early Jewish settler in Maryland, Jacob Lumbrozo, was arrested under this Act and charged with "blesphemy ag'st Our Blessed Saviour Jesus Christ."

Lumbrozo, "the Jew doctor," did not start this trouble, or at least so he said. He became involved in a religious argument when questioned how he could deny that Jesus Christ was the savior in view of his resurrection from the dead and the miracles he had performed. Lumbrozo coolly answered that miracles had been performed by magic, as Moses and the Egyptians could well testify. As for the resurrection, well, the disciples had stolen and hidden his body. He told one disputant, who insisted that Jesus was the Messiah, that he was only a man, a human being, and when asked by another disputant if he thought that Christ was a necromancer, he said nothing but only laughed.

It was Lumbrozo's good fortune that he never had to stand trial, but was released under a general amnesty proclaimed a few days after he was arrested. Otherwise he might have lost both life and property, for blasphemy was no joking matter then, or even a half century later. In 1697, an eighteen-year-old student of the University of Edinburgh, Thomas Aikenhead, was executed on this charge in Scotland. A year later a law was almost passed in the English Parliament subjecting Jews to the older act "for the more effective suppressing of blasphemy and prophaneness." Had this law been passed and implemented, Jews would have been compelled to leave England.

In Maryland the Church of England was "established" in 1692–1702, and Jews were effectively barred from political life. The disability was preserved in a series of laws, promulgated in the years 1715–16, which opened offices of trust only to those who could take the oath "upon the true faith of a Christian." The constitution of 1776 continued these disabilities, thus offering full civil and political equality to those only who declared their belief in the Christian religion and thereby denying Jews their complete religious liberty. Indeed, it was not until 1826 that Maryland was ready to enfranchise its Jews.

Benjamin Levy, in all likelihood, was little concerned, in the 1770's, about these civil and religious disabilities. He was not greatly interested in matters Jewish. He was certainly not so orthodox as some of his fellow Baltimoreans. In 1782, Ezekiel Levy of Mikveh Israel in Philadelphia came to Baltimore on a business trip. He was discovered in the act of shaving on the Sabbath by Isaac Abrahams, one of the Jews in town. Isaac relayed the news to Mordecai M. Mordecai, then in Baltimore. The latter—a distiller of Lithuanian birth who maintained membership in the Philadelphia congregation—reported this offense to the head of the synagogue, Jonas Phillips, and Jonas brought the matter be-

fore his congregational board. But, after carefully considering the charges, the board finally dismissed them for lack
of corroborating testimony.

Benjamin Levy would certainly not have been interested
in informing on an errant Philadelphia Jew; there is no record that he was a contributor to any Jewish congregation,
and it is to be doubted that he was. In fact, the members of
the Levy family still left in Philadelphia were not active
any longer in synagogal affairs; some, indeed, had accepted
Christianity. When Rachel and Benjamin Levy died in Baltimore, they were both buried in an Episcopalian cemetery.
But such burial is no final proof that they were no longer
Jews; as late as 1786 Benjamin took oath on the Five Books
of Moses.

It was no doubt in his Philadelphia days that Benjamin
Levy had first become acquainted with Robert Morris, who
was then already a successful businessman. Later, during
the war, the Baltimore merchant stood ready to co-operate
with Congressman Morris in raising funds which the Continental Congress so desperately needed. In December,
1776, Levy was authorized to sign bills of credit emitted by
the Congress.

This is the note which Robert Morris received from Levy
in the trying days when Washington was retreating into
Pennsylvania, and it seemed that the fall of Philadelphia was
imminent:

My dear Morris:
It is said that if the Congress are oblig'd to leave Philadelphia, they intend coming to this town. We have two very
good rooms on our first floor upstairs, which we purpose for

you and Mrs. Morris. We have one spare bed, our house is good and large, and think if you can be supply'd with bedding from Mr. Aquilla Hall, who is but about 25 miles from hence, we could accommodate all your children and three or four servants, having other apartments that will do exceeding well. But sincerely pray that you may not be under the necessity of leaving your home and that we shall soon hear of the enemy' retireing. As these are not times for compliments and ceremony, I need not give you assurances of making you welcome as I ever profess'd myself,

Your truly affectionate humb. serv[an]'t,
Benjamin Levy.

Rachel [my wife] joins me in compliments to Mrs. Morris. Baltimore, Friday, 13 Decb'r, 1776.[12]

Another Philadelphia merchant who signed the 1765 nonimportation agreement, along with Benjamin Levy, was Mathias Bush. He was a brother-in-law of Barnard Gratz—he and Barnard had married two sisters named Myers. This marriage also brought Bush into the Joseph Simon family; Simon had married a cousin of the two sisters. It was not the Gratz-Simon connection that brought Bush into close touch with the wealthy and prominent Levy-Franks clan. The families had known each other back in London.

As early as 1748 Mathias Bush was a contributor to the New York synagogue, but by the next year he was in Philadelphia, engaged in trade and commerce, as a naturalized British subject. When the French and Indian War broke out, he was kept busy supplying the Pennsylvania military forces with firearms, munitions, and similar sundries. He was an observant Jew and participated in 1761 in the borrowing of the Pentateuchal scroll from Shearith

Israel of New York. (At least two of those who signed for
the *Torah* ["the Scroll of the Law"] were not actually living in Philadelphia. Therefore some historians have suggested that the *Torah* was for use either in Lancaster or in
Reading. Reading is quite improbable, since it had only one
or two Jewish families; Lancaster is less improbable. We
are inclined to regard Philadelphia, the largest of these
cities, as the place most likely to have housed the *Torah*,
since we saw above that the congregation at this time was
developing some vigor.)

Evidently the small Jewish group in Philadelphia was
being augmented in the 1750's and 1760's by a steady flow
of eager immigrants. By 1769—the year in which Bush became a partner of David Franks in the candle business—
there were enough "new Jews" to create trouble.

With rare exception, Jews have always resented Jewish
newcomers. The older element, even when it shared the
same ritual, stemmed from the same ethnic stock, and hailed
from the same distant province as the more recent immigrants, nearly always looked askance at them. The newcomers, for their part, were resentful of the snobbery and
prosperity of the older group.

All the frustrations which Jews experienced in the world
outside them they vented internally in bitter personal quarrels and mutual recriminations. Before the Dutch Jew, Leon
Norden, died in Savannah in the 1790's, he specified that
"None of the Sheftalls need be present" at the funeral.

Family and business jealousies and private feuds were
behind much of the synagogal dissension. Religious "differences" played only a minor part in the clashes of colonial

days. The Polish or Germanic rite differed somewhat from the Spanish rite, but such differences should not be over-emphasized. Moreover, wealth had a way of wiping out such religious disparities. Indeed, it is not unusual for the examination of a squabble in the "Spanish-Portuguese" synagogue to disclose that it was German Jews bickering with *Landsleute*. Wrangling, quarreling, petty sniping, were common in all Jewish pious associations in all lands, and certainly the Philadelphia Jewish congregation was no exception. (It was no different in the little Christian conventicles throughout the colonies!)

We do not know the substance of a struggle between two groups in Philadelphia at this time when their total number did not exceed twenty or thirty families. It is from Mathias Bush that we learn that there was trouble between the older and the new migration, and that one year the obstreperous newcomers even held separate services during the High Holydays. Mathias, of course, sided with the "old-timers"; he had been in this country now for a whole generation, at least since 1742, and he, too, looked down upon the more recent immigrants.

Curiously, the leader of the revolt of the "new Jews" chanced to be one of the older settlers, the Hebrew teacher. The newcomers documented their resentment against the older group in typically ghetto style by circulating a pasquil in which our old friend Joseph Simon was lampooned. When Barnard Gratz was in London, in 1769, he received some word of the affair in a letter from Bush. The "new Jews" were a "plague." "Pray prevent what is in your power to hinder any more of that sort to come!"

72

Such intramural Jewish squabbles and jealousies were nothing new in Jewish life. Six years before immigrant Bush wrote to immigrant Gratz to keep the other immigrant Jews out of this country, the Portuguese Jews in Bordeaux succeeded in inducing the king of France to sign a measure expelling German and Avignonese Jews from Bordeaux. Though this decree was not implemented, it is a grim reminder of the type of brotherly love that only too often obtained in some Jewish communities.

Because Mathias had a son named Solomon, one might with confidence hazard the guess that the surname "Bush" (*B'SH, Ben Shelomoh*) derives from an ancestor named after the wise king of Jerusalem. The guess is wrong. Mathias' Hebrew cryptogram, signed to the 1765 Philadelphia nonimportation agreement, reads, "From B. City (*MB'SH*, from *B. Stadt*)," obviously some town or hamlet in Germany or Bohemia.

Solomon Bush, a son of Mathias, was appointed a Deputy Adjutant General of the Pennsylvania State Militia on July 5, 1777, by the Supreme Executive Council of Pennsylvania. A few months later, in September, his thigh was shattered by a bullet in a skirmish—no doubt near the Brandywine— and he was carried, badly wounded, to Mathias' house in Chestnut Hill, near Philadelphia. In October, the month after General Sir William Howe took Philadelphia, Bush was discovered and made prisoner. The unfortunate officer described his plight in the following letter to his friend, Henry Lazarus, a merchant in Fredrick Towne (Winchester), Virginia:

73

Chesnut Hill,
15th Nov'r, 1777.

D'r Sir:

As Mr. [Joseph] Simons tells me that he is going to your town, cannot omit leting my good freind know how we all are, being sensible it will give him satisfaction to hear from his freinds.

I suppose you heard of my being wounded the 18th of Sept'r [a week after the Battle of the Brandywine] when with dificulty was bro't home in a most deplorable condition with my thigh broke, and the surgeons pronounced my wound mortal. Seven days after, the enemy came, who treated our family with the utmost respect. They did not take the least trifle from us, though our neighbours, the poor Tories, lost every thing. Howe's march this way has made many Wigs.

I was conceal'd after the British Army came here twenty-two days and shou'd have got clear, but a vilain gave information of me, when [whereupon] I was waited on by an officer who took my parole. When [whereupon] I wrote a line to the [British] commanding officer leting him know of my being a prisoner and requesting a surgeon which he imedeately comply'd with, and was attended every day during their stay at this place.

I am, thank God, geting beter and have the satisfaction to have my limb perfectly strait. My wishes are to be able to get satisfaction and revenge the rongs of my injured country. I wish you joy of the success of our troops to the northward [Burgoyne surrendered to the colonials at Saratoga, on October 17th] and hope to tell you New York is ours before long. The [English] shiping is not got up to Philad'a though this is the 9th time of their attacking the Fort [the English took Fort Mifflin the next day]. There is a cannonade whilst I am writeing; shou'd they not be able to carry the Fort their stay in Philad'a will be but short.

As it grows late and am seting in bed writeing, remain, with

74

my best wishes to Mr. and Mrs. Lazarus, Uncle Levy, and the
worthy Miss Brandla [your daughter],

> Your most affection'e friend and hbl'e serv't,
> Sol'n Bush.

My parents' best wishes to you all. Pray pres't my comp's to
Col. Johnson, Mrs. Charlton, and family.[18]

As an officer on parole it was necessary for Bush to report to the British. On one such occasion—apparently while
receiving medical attention at enemy headquarters—he was
an unobserved witness to a civilian's bringing a letter to
General Howe. Learning that this civilian was an agent
carrying messages to the British from a spy at Washington's
headquarters, he forwarded that important bit of news
to General Washington through General John Armstrong.

Bush's wound in his thigh never healed thoroughly; he
was ill for years. In April, 1779, he appealed for financial
aid to the federal Board of War. When help was not forthcoming from that source, he wrote in September to
Timothy Matlack, the fighting—and spending—Quaker,
who was secretary to the Supreme Executive Council of
Pennsylvania:

> Chesnut Hill, 27 Septem'r, 1779.
>
> Dear Sir:
> Pardon the liberty I take in troubling you with these few
> lines the purport of which as I well know you to be a friend
> to the Sons of Freedom, especially those who have been un-
> fortunate in the service of their country. I have, my d[ea]'r
> sir, lain in a most deplorable condition ever since I had the
> pleasure of seeing you in Lancaster, and still continue in a
> helpless state. This, with the expensive times, compels me to
> petition the Honb'le [Supreme Executive] Coun'ill to direct

me where I shall apply to have my acco't [for m]y pay and rations setled, as I have through [my] great indisposition been unable to apply for [the] same since my appointment. As I am still a prisoner on parole and in the service of the State [of Pennsylvania], have petition'd the Councill that I may draw my pay and rations (untill exchanged) monthly. I therefore beg your assistance in forwarding the same which will ever be gratefully acknewlidg'd by, d'r sir,

Y'r mo. obd. hbl. ser't,
Sol'n Bush.

The Hon'ble Timothy Matlack, Esqr.[14]

Finally, on October 20, 1779, the Supreme Executive Council of the state declared, after studying his case, that he had distinguished himself by his brilliant military career, especially in the winter of 1776 "when the service was critical and hazardous," and therefore recommended to the Board of War, in charge of army matters, that he obtain pay and rations equal to his rank. He was now a major; a week later he was made a lieutenant-colonel, thus becoming the highest ranking Jewish officer in a combat unit of the Continental army.

Although Bush was able to contribute a tidy little sum to the synagogue building fund in 1782, he may have been in need of assistance, for in 1785 the Pennsylvania Council, now under the presidency of Benjamin Franklin, awarded him a pension.

Like so many other veterans, Solomon Bush found it hard in postwar days to adjust himself to the humdrum routine of the prosaic world of peace. He was eager for a government appointment. And he was convinced that the sacrifices he had made and the sufferings he had undergone entitled him to consideration at the hands of his old comrades in Pennsylvania and of his old commanding officer, President Washington.

Modesty ill becomes a man conscious of his own worth. Solomon made several efforts to obtain an appointment to public office. In 1780 he appealed in vain to Congress for the post of secretary to the Board of Treasury; in 1784 he turned to the Supreme Executive Council of his state, applying for the position of health officer of the Port of Philadelphia, and in 1793 to George Washington for the post of naval officer for the same port. Letters of recommendation for this latter post stressed his acquaintance with the merchants of Philadelphia; his appointment, they said, would give general satisfaction. Shortly before his death— which was the result of his wound, as it was commonly believed—Bush had no hesitation in writing to the President (1795), petitioning him for the position of postmaster general to succeed Colonel Timothy Pickering, who had entered upon his new post as secretary of war.

When Colonel Bush was asking his friends to support his candidacy for the federal berth of naval officer for the port of Philadelphia, he had just returned to his home town after an intermittent stay of several years in London, from the late 1780's to 1793. He had been summoned to straighten out the affairs of his father, who had died a few years earlier. It was his duty, as the oldest son, to look after the family.

In Philadelphia, conditions were bad, both generally and for Solomon in particular. The yellow fever was taking its toll. Mathias Bush had left three orphan daughters, all young, whose support devolved upon Solomon. In addition, he had to support a brother who had been imprisoned by the British, had fought in the campaign under General Nathanael Greene in the South, and had finally lost his reason. Added to all this he had a wife and family of his own. The task of earning a livelihood, the new responsibilities, and the distress occasioned by the reopening of his old wound made it necessary for him to secure some sort of suitable, pleasant, but light work—a government position. Hence his several efforts.

Still another effort, an earlier one, is worth pausing over. While in London, Colonel Bush had been Dr. Bush, a practitioner of medicine. Just when he acquired his training is not known, but if we may accept his word, he had built up a good clientele in the English capital. But his heart was not in medicine; he was always the Revolutionary soldier and staunch American, proud of the fact that he was one who had "fought and bled in the service of his country."

Bush was one of the leaders of the "patriots" in London, a group of Americans and Englishmen who were devoted republicans and watched with fascinated anticipation and sympathy the unfolding drama of the French Revolution. When Bush heard, in July, 1789, that Captain Watson, commander of a New York ship, had been seized together with part of his crew, on the charge that the men were natives of Great Britain, he at once stepped into the breach. On behalf of the American government, which then, seemingly, had no diplomatic or consular representative in the country, he approached the English authorities and made a vigorous protest. (This case of Captain Watson was one of the early instances of visit and search of American boats in port and of the impressment of their sailors. By the spring of the following year this abuse had become so patent that Washington sent Gouverneur Morris from France to ask the English, among other things, to stop boarding American vessels. Morris warned them that the consequences in the United States might be serious. The War of 1812 is eloquent testimony that he was not exaggerating.)

The Watson ship and crew were released, largely through the exertions of Bush. The Colonel was so elated that he sat down, in August, 1789, and reported the good news to the President. In the back of his mind was the conviction that he had demonstrated his capacity to serve as a representative of his country: "From my acquaintance and connection w'th personages of the first consequence in this country," he had written the President in an earlier letter, "I dout not of rendering my country many services. Believe I have nothing in view but the prosperity of America." Here is the letter in which Bush suggests rather pointedly his availability for appointment:

London, 5th August, 1789.

I did myself the honour to address your Excellency a few days since, congratulating you on the happy event of your appointment to the Chief Magestracy of the United States, a country to establish whose liberties I have bled in her cause, and now feel happy in her prospects in having one to preside over her liberties for whose welfare and felicity I daily offer up my most fervent prayers.

I took the liberty to mention to your Excellency the seizure of the ship commanded by Capt. Watson belonging to New York, and am happy to say by a spirited exertion and due representation the ship is again liberated. From this event and a number of American seamen daily comeing to this metropolis, it points out the necessity of a minister or consuls being appointed for the United States.

From my connection in this kingdom, I think it wou'd be in my power to serve my country shou'd they think proper to confer a deplomatic appointment on me. Believe I do not speak from interested or picuniary principles, as I will undertake to serve my country from the same principles I step'd forward to the field.

I am happy to find the warm affection between the people of this country and their former bretheren, the Americans, residing here, which is a pleasing presage of the happy union which every good man wishes to take place between the two countries.

With every mark of sincere respect and true affection, I beg leave to subscribe,

Your Excellency's most obd't faithfull hbl. ser't,
S. Bush.

His Excellency
Gen'l Washington.[15]

It was November before Washington's secretary found time to answer the Colonel's two letters and to express the President's appreciation of his proper and spirited conduct. "As a citizen of the United States of America I offer you my thanks for the assistance which you afforded towards saving the property of our countrymen." Discreetly, the President said nothing about a diplomatic or consular appointment. In the postscript the President acknowledged the receipt of a book, *City Petitions* (London, 1778), which an English admirer had asked Bush to forward to the General. John Trumbull, the painter, had personally carried the book to the States. (This very volume of petitions, addresses, and remonstrances of Londoners on behalf of the colonists appeared in the book market in 1949 with Washington's autograph, bookplate, and a presentation inscription of the "left wing" English donor: *Manus haec inimica tyrannis* ["This hand is the enemy of tyrants"]. The price asked was $2,000.)

Bush never became a distinguished diplomat; he was never offered a post in the cabinet of a Washington. Nevertheless, this fervent republican was crowned with titles far more resounding and exalted than any republic could vaunt —he became a Mason of high degree. The last years of his life were devoted to intense activity in the Sublime Lodge of Perfection. He had been made Deputy Inspector General of Masonry for Pennsylvania in 1781 by virtue of an appointment by Moses M. Hays, and was finally elected Grand Master of the lodge for the years 1787–88; he had gone to Britain on a mission to further relations with English Masonry.

One of the pleasant duties of his Masonic career was to indite a letter to Frederick the Great, head of the Grand Council at Berlin and Paris. In this letter, written in 1785, Bush described himself as follows: "I, Solomon Bush, Grand Elect, Perfect and Sublime Knight of the East and Prince of Jerusalem, Sovereign Knight of the Sun and of the Black and White Eagle, Prince of the Royal Secret, and Deputy Inspector General, and Grand Master over all Lodges, Chapters, and Grand Councils of the Superior Degrees of Masonry in North America within the State of Pennsylvania, etc." He signed this grandiloquent effusion: "Your very humble and most affectionate brother."

It is interesting to speculate what thoughts ran through the mind of the cynical Frederick as he read this letter—if he ever did—from the offspring of a Germanic Jewish immigrant to the Prussian autocrat who denied his German Jews the most elementary of civil, political, and social rights. Frederick probably laughed—out loud.

BARNARD GRATZ, PHILADELPHIA MERCHANT

MICHAEL GRATZ, PHILADELPHIA MERCHANT

Chapter 5

Pennsylvania – 1777

IF Frederick the Great had been in a laughing mood during the last few years of his life, he might have smiled very broadly also at a letter addressed to him and to one of his bureaus by a famous magician and fellow-townsman of Solomon Bush. Or, perhaps, he might not have smiled.

Sometime in the first half of the eighteenth century there was a Jewish family in Pennsylvania that had a son named Jacob. The young man later called himself Jacob Philadelphia. Evidently he grew up in that city. Inasmuch as it is known that he traveled in Portugal years later, it has been surmised that his family was of Portuguese origin. But Jacob journeyed to many lands and he was, it would seem, a fine linguist. The last half of his life was spent largely in Germany.

One student of American Jewish life ventured the opinion that he was the son of Barnard Jacobs, a Lancaster County merchant. Jacobs was living in Heidelberg and in Lancaster in the early 1740's. For a while he and a partner, a man named Levi, ran a country store near Conrad

Weiser's inn, bartering notions for furs, hides, grain, and fruits. In one of their advertisements in a German-language newspaper they warned their clientele: "They further announce that they do not trade on Saturday and Sunday because they are Jews." Jacobs' distinction lies in the fact that he was in all probability the first *shohet* ("slaughterer") and *mohel* ("circumciser") in the colony. Responding to the religious needs of his neighbors, he circumcised children in most of the towns of Eastern Pennsylvania. It seems hardly likely, however, that Jacob Philadelphia was a son of this Lancaster merchant, for the latter fathered a child as late as 1777.

Somehow or other, young Jacob managed to secure training in the natural sciences, possibly through an apprenticeship to the pietistic mystic, Dr. Christopher Witt, a member of the older queer communistic Society of the Woman of the Wilderness. Early in the 1750's Jacob went to England and worked in the experimental laboratories of the Duke of Cumberland. In the next few years, by dint of work and wit, he transformed himself into the prodigious combination of physicist, chemist, astrologer, expert mechanician, submarine pioneer, and prestidigitator. With this background he was soon hailed as one of the most famous magicians in Europe, traveling, lecturing, and experimenting in public before learned and unlearned audiences—for a good fee. Apparently he was part magician, part scientist, part charlatan—but certainly no one's fool, and the ultimate product of his varied genius was an attempt to promote a German-American trading company.

The European trading companies were organized to bar-

84

ter colonial raw materials for domestic finished wares. The pattern was old, and was followed by the medieval trading companies and by the later Dutch, English, and French corporations which penetrated the East and the West Indies. In December, 1745, during a period of imperialistic aspiration, Sweden licensed the Christian bankers, Abraham and Jacob Arfwedson, to establish an overseas trading company to exploit African and American lands, especially the isles of the West Indies. To secure the necessary capital the Swedes went out of their way to invite all groups, of all nationalities and religions, to send in their subscriptions, and despite the fact that Jews were not tolerated in Sweden at this time, the "Hebrews" were specifically encouraged to purchase shares. Evidently the Swedes believed that the merit of supporting their commercial enterprises had the sacramental power of transmuting Jews into Hebrews.

As early as 1747 Frederick the Great had thought of exchanging American tobacco for Prussian textiles. After the War of Independence had begun, American commissioners sent out by Congress tried persistently to negotiate with the Prussians a treaty of amity and commerce which would involve recognition of the new American state. This recognition Frederick refused to grant.

Yet, he was eager to trade with the colonies; he needed their products; he wanted them to buy his manufactured goods. But he had no navy and no desire to run afoul of the powerful English, whom he hated. They had left him in the lurch in 1761 during the French and Indian War, and he would gladly have turned against them now, but he dared not. Nonetheless, the Prussian king did not prevent his merchants from making formal arrangements with the Commonwealth of Pennsylvania to carry on trade and shipping. This was in 1781. However, it was not until June, 1783, that Frederick empowered Baron von Goltz to prepare the way for a commercial treaty. By then it was evident that the British themselves would recognize the independence of the United States.

In May, 1783, our Jacob Philadelphia wrote a letter designed for Frederick, outlining his scheme for a German-American trading company which would further economic relations between the two lands. This letter was transmitted through an intermediary, one Stilcke, to Frederick William von der Schulenburg, who was now in charge of the state's maritime affairs:

Most Humble Memorial to the Honorable Royal General Directorium in Berlin:

I was in America from my youth and was reared there. Consequently, I have traversed that part of the world by land and sea and am acquainted with all its commercial harbors and markets. I know, therefore, the trade which is carried on there and which can be carried on even more profitably in view of the present changes in North America. I know this better than anyone else, for I have carried on a legitimate and smuggling trade by land and by sea with the English, the inhabitants, and also the savages, and I have been as far as eighty German miles beyond Quebec. I have spent considerable time there, have associated with the savages, and I am so well-informed that I not only know the American language which is spoken with the savages, but also the English and the African-Guinea which are spoken with the Negroes. I speak all these languages better than I speak German, and certainly nobody in Germany can make a similar boast. Therefore, in view of the prevailing modes of free trade, any nation that would want to carry on commerce there would have to spend many years and expend much money to acquire the necessary experience before it would be able to gauge the true advantage of the American trade.

To be sure, there will be no lack of a market for the goods to be transported to America. There will also be plenty of goods that are to be transported to Europe. The question is whether there will be the same profit which one might derive therefrom if one has a proper experience with and understanding of the American trade. That is the principal thing. For just as one can sell his linen better by ten to twelve per cent in Cadiz and Lisbon than in Hamburg, Luebeck, or Bremen— all three places in Europe, too—similarly the same circumstances and conditions are true of America and its commerce. Here one can lose ten or more per cent on every account at the wrong places and markets, if one has no further knowledge of them, and if one unloads and sells his wares in the first available harbor.

Inasmuch as I possess a knowledge of all the advantages of American commerce and am in a position to prove this, I therefore take the liberty of presenting my most humble proposal, first and foremost of all, to the Royal Honorable General Directorium, and I offer my most submissive services to establish commercial relations with America. I am able to indicate those harbors, commercial emporia, and markets where all goods sent to America can be sold most advantageously, and where, on the other hand, one can buy most profitably the goods which can be transported to Europe. I have in mind particularly the prime staples, articles such as linen, ordinary cloths, woolen socks, caps, etc. Just as I can point out the best harbors and markets for selling, even so I can indicate the best places for buying tobacco, wild animal- and raw hides and furs, the very articles from which England has drawn such great advantage up to this time.

There are still a number of various products and wares which are manufactured and can be obtained in your Royal Highness' Prussian states and which can also be sold to an advantage in America, as for example, porcelain, velvet, iron, blue dyes, gold and silver laces, hats, mirrors, glassware, etc., and other similar articles. I know one article in particular—concerning which I reserve making a statement at the present time—on which one can make a pure profit at any time of twenty per cent.

I offer not only to sail with the ships and goods three to four times, but personally to take charge of the buying and selling of the goods and to get the project started.

For this service, for initiating and regulating this American commerce, I most humbly ask for an annual pension for life. If this pension be granted me, together with my traveling expenses—first of all to Berlin—then I am prepared immediately to disclose and to explain the secrets and the details of this trade. I will indicate, in addition, the best seasons for ships to sail, and I will direct the ships at sea myself. For I am experienced at sea, and I have not only visited America but also Asia and Africa; I have full knowledge of navigation, can steer ships, and know how to sail to America. I am known by the people in America and England inasmuch as I have made sea trips with the greatest sea heroes of the present generation in England, with men such as the well-known and famous sea-captain, Locks. The latter and the unfortunate technician who locked themselves in their boat and let themselves down to the bottom of the ocean to rise to the surface again with their boat were my very intimate friends, and I worked on this last project with them for many years. If they had followed my plans they would not have met with an accident.

If such an American commercial trade were to be established on His Royal Highness' own personal account, a very handsome profit could be derived. The cost of outfitting the ships would be paid through one cargo of American tobacco alone. Or, if a joint-stock or a trading company should be organized, then the various subscribers would not only get their interest at six per cent, in the course of five to six years, but would also get back their capital and could carry on this business in the future out of their own profits. The responsible authorities will understand, even better than I could explain, what great profits and advantages would also accrue to the factories and to the royal states in general through the establishment of such a commercial company.

Your most humble servant,
Jacob Philadelphia.

Euthen, May 27, 1783.[16]

This letter is of value, not only because it reflects the cockiness, conceit, and confidence of Jacob, but because it offers an insight into the economic and commercial opportunities which intelligent observers glimpsed in the new American state.

Schulenburg decided not to forward the letter to the monarch, even though it was just the sort of proposal that should have appealed to the mercantilistic ruler. In a short note of reply to the intermediary Stilcke, he wrote, rather vaguely, that he had certain objections to the proposal and deemed it inexpedient. It would not be shooting too wide of the mark to assume that this Prussian bureaucrat had little respect for our magician, whom he looked upon as something of a faker; and he may have objected to the financial demands which the petitioner made for himself. The basic idea was certainly not farfetched, for the very next year the state of Saxony attempted to establish such a company, with an office in Philadelphia, and the year after that, in 1785, Prussia signed its first treaty of trade and amity with the young republic.

During the early years of the Revolution, Colonel Solomon Bush, as we saw, was cooling his heels as an officer on parole, but he was more fortunate than many others, for while on parole he lived with his father, Mathias Bush, and had a good many comforts. Other American prisoners in the hands of the British did not fare nearly so well, especially those who were not officers. Thus, hundreds who were unfortunate enough to be confined in the prison ships at Wallabout Bay, Brooklyn, died of brutal mistreatment.

On the other hand, there were many British captured by the Americans, and their lives were by no means lives of ease and luxury. As early as 1775 there was a pressing need to provide the minimum necessities of food and clothing for them in some systematic fashion, and the man eventually selected by Congress and the British to feed and outfit most of the Tories and English prisoners was our old acquaintance David Franks of Philadelphia.

There was no question but that David was ideally fitted for this particular job, as a brief glance at his career reveals. Through his brothers Naphtali and Moses in London he had good connections with the British government, which was expected to foot the bill for the men in the hands of the Americans. His father, Jacob, as the king's agent for the Northern Colonies, had been actively engaged in army victualling, and Jacob in New York, David in Philadelphia, and his two other brothers in London worked closely together, probably as partners, serving as purveyors to the

British army and navy in the American colonies for almost two generations.

David had been very active as an army supplyman during the French and Indian War. After Braddock's defeat by the Indians, he was one of those who contributed to a defense fund, and in 1758, when Colonel George Washington led the Virginia expedition that participated in the reconquest of Fort Duquesne, it was in part equipped by Franks. He then acted as the agent for a powerful business group in England, James and George Colebrook, Arnold Nesbitt, and Moses Franks, which had the contract, beginning in the late 1750's, of feeding and equipping the British armies in the American colonies. (Some of these men were also his partners in later land and colonizing schemes.)

The English syndicate with which David Franks was associated was more than a supply agency. It was in itself a quartermaster corps, or even more. It made a courier service available, forwarded the latest news dispatches, carried government baggage, and acted in a general advisory capacity. Its prime job, on the western frontier, was to provide the troops with flour and cattle, bread and meat. These staples were assembled at the various depots along the main highway and the Forbes Road, at Lancaster, Carlyle, Fort Loudon, Bedford, Ligonier, and Fort Pitt. (George Croghan once suggested that David Franks might well lease grazing lands in the neighborhood of Fort Pitt and raise his own beef. It is probable that his good advice was acted upon; we know that Croghan did sell some of his improved lands to one of the Franks companies.)

The difficulties under which the purveyors labored were

almost insurmountable. At times the colonies themselves refused to co-operate with the Crown and the contractors; the sub-contractors were often unreliable or dishonest; the roads, after November, were impassable. In the dead of winter supplies had to be carried in by pack train, and it was no light task to take a train of 100 horses, loaded down with flour, across the mountains.

In June, 1763, one of the supply companies, of which Franks was a partner, submitted the following grim account to the British. It is also eloquent evidence of the manner in which the government handled the Indian problem.

D[ebto]'r, The Crown to Levy, Trent & Comp'y, for sundries had by order of Capt. Simon Ecuyer, Command't.
. . . To sundries got to replace in kind those which were taken from people in the hospital to convey the smallpox to the Indians, viz.,

2 blankets at 20 shilling	£2.0. 0
1 silk handkerchief, 10 s.	.10
1 linnen do. 3 s.6	. 3.6
	2.13.6

Fort Pitt, Aug't 15th, 1763.
I do hereby certify that the above articles . . . were had for the uses above mentioned.

S. Ecuyer, Capt. Command't.

Sir Jeffrey Amherst's troops finally drove the French out and won the trans-Allegheny region for England. It was the Franks family and their partners who had helped in the arduous job of feeding and supplying the victorious armies of conquest.

But opportunities continued to knock at David's door

even after the French and Indian War. He and his partner for the time being, the politically well-connected William Plumsted, served as the American agents for the British. After 1765, Plumsted dropped out; the agency name changed four times in the years 1764 to 1768, but David remained. In England the names of the companies changed at least three times between 1761 and 1766, but David's brother, Moses, was always included. For at least twenty years, Moses Franks and his varying associates, Nesbitt, the Colebrooks, Drummond, and Fludger, carried out contracts amounting to over £764,000, extending their operations as far north as Canada, as far west as the Illinois country, and as far south as the West Indies.

The money that David Franks made came from merchandising and from army contracting. He made precious little, if anything, in the land colony business.

With this background we can see why, after the Revolution broke out and British prisoners began to be a governmental problem, David Franks was appointed to provide for them. It was a continuation of his work, army purveying. He undertook this special task at the request of Congress in the late winter of 1775. In the following February, General Washington suggested to the President of Congress that Franks expand his activity by appointing a deputy to help him take care of the men and the officers in the Massachusetts area: "It will save me much time and much trouble."

The General also asked Congress to appoint a supreme commissioner to be responsible for all the prisoners, both British and American. This appointment was finally made in June, 1777, when Elias Boudinot became commissary general of prisoners and succeeded the committee that had functioned up to this time. Boudinot, to whom Franks was then subordinate, accepted the job not only that he might "be of some service to the prisoners," but also in order "to watch the military and to preserve the civil rights of my fellow citizens."

Franks found himself in a very difficult position. He, an appointee of the United States, was presumably a patriot—or at least a neutral. But at the same time he was the agent whom the English contractors, Nesbitt, Drummond, and (Moses) Franks, had appointed to victual imprisoned British troops. Moreover, he was also a commissary officer appointed by General Sir William Howe to provide for any special needs of the captured English. Accordingly, he had to keep in constant touch with the British army in America and with his brother's firm in London. And, finally, a number of his business associates, relatives, and society friends were loyalists. (One may realize how thin was the line between patriot, neutral, and loyalist by remembering that Commissary Elias Boudinot, who was later to become president of the Continental Congress, refused, as late as April, 1776, to be stampeded into favoring a declaration of secession from the mother country, and that Robert Morris, in July, 1776, refused to vote for the Declaration of Independence.) Franks's connections could easily make his American loyalties suspect.

In 1776 Franks experienced difficulty in collecting from the British authorities the monies which he had expended on behalf of prisoners. In October he asked Congress for permission to go to New York with his clerk Patrick Rice to submit his claims to the British general for certification. He and Patrick were allowed to go on the conditions that they "give their parole not to give any intelligence to the enemy, and that they will return to this city." Patrick Rice, in spite of his Hibernian name, was a Jew—unless he was an Irishman who could write the Hebrew script. His original name, we may surmise, was probably Feibush (Phoebus) or Phinehas Reis.

On June 28, 1777, just a few weeks after Boudinot had taken up his new duties as commissary general of prisoners, he wrote from Washington's camp at Middlebrook, New Jersey, to Franks that he was sending some "necessaries" for British prisoners located in Lancaster, probably the largest such depot in the country. The letter mentioned a bag sealed with an impression of a cupid and two hearts, and a hogshead of clothes. Boudinot also had in his possession, he wrote, thirty-one guineas for the prisoners but deferred sending the money until he could "get an opportunity I can trust." In a postscript he asked for a roster of all the prisoners. Within a week Franks answered him from Philadelphia:

Philadelphia, July 4th, 1777.

Sir:

Yesterday I had the pleasure to receive your favor of the 28th ultimo with a h[ogs]h[ea]'d and bag containing sundry necessaries for the British prisoners. The contents of the hogshead I know not, as I shall send it up to Lancaster unopened, but the bag, tho' sealed up as you describe, does not contain what is specified in the letter wrote by Adjutant Ward of the 33d Regiment, as some articles are wanting. Whenever the

95

guineas comes to hand they shall be properly paid, some [of the prisoners] being here, and some at Lancaster and Reading; for which reason it will be best to send whatever may come to your hands for them, here, to prevent your sending up and down.

There's about *sixteen hundred* prisoners who draw provisions in this State: men, women, and children, as p[er]. return herewith. I have sent to Virginia, Maryland, etc. for a return of the prisoners in those states, which when comes to hand shall transmit you. There are likewise many captains and mates of transports and merchant men to whom I also issue provisions, being prisoners here.

I am very respectfully, sir,

Your most humble serv't,
David Franks.[17]

Elias Boudinot, Esqr.

The suspicion that Franks was a Tory sympathizer and not to be trusted induced the Congress, in the winter of 1777–78, to keep a watchful eye on him and to circumscribe his privileges as a contractor.

His uncertain position was certainly not made easier for him by the fact that his daughter Rebecca was notoriously a partisan of the British.

When the British took Philadelphia the Franks home, like many of the best homes in the city, was open to the British officers. Rebecca was a charming, brilliant girl, one of the wits of her generation, and a great favorite of the English, who were very much drawn to the attractive young lady.

There is no record of her baptism, but it is safe to assume that she was reared by her mother as a Christian. Unlike her father, there is no evidence that she had any interest whatsoever in Jews and Judaism. Yet she was constantly referred to as the "Jewess"; in the mind of the average Gentile, a person is a "Jew"—until the fact of Jewish origin is no longer known.

One of Rebecca's good friends was Anne Harrison of Wye Island, Maryland, who had married the patriot William Paca, a signer of the Declaration of Independence. Paca was considerably older than Anne, who was his second wife. Loyalist Rebecca kept up a correspondence with Nancy, as she called her, even though Nancy was the wife of a delegate to the Congress. Rebecca even asked General Sir William Howe, then in command at Philadelphia, for permission to send Nancy a little gift through the lines, and prepared to make arrangements to have her come to visit her. Evidently her political prejudices did not extend to her patriot friends—nor theirs to her. One of her letters to Nancy gives us an excellent picture of social life in the occupied city:

[Philadelphia.]

Dear Nancy:

. . . . You can have no idea of the life of continued amusement I live in. I can scarce have a moment to myself. I have stole this while everybody is retired to dress for dinner. I am but just come from under Mr. J. Black's hands, and most elegantly am I dressed for a ball this evening at Smith's where we have one every Thursday. You would not know the room 'tis so much improv'd.

I wish to Heaven you were going with us this evening to judge for yourself. I spent Tuesday evening at Sir Wm. Howes where we had a concert and dance. I asked his leave to send you a handkerchief to show the fashions. He very politely gave me permission to send anything you wanted, tho'

I told him you were a delegate's lady. I want to get a pair of buckles for your brother, Joe. If I can't, tell him, to be in the fashion, he must get a pair of harness ones.

The dress [I am wearing] is more ridiculous and pretty than anything that ever I saw: great quantity of different coloured feathers on the head at a time, besides a thousand other things; the hair dress'd very high in the shape [the Wilmington beauty] Miss Vining's was the night we returned from Smiths. The hat we found in your mother's closet wou'd be of a proper size. I have an afternoon cap with one wing, tho' I assure you I go less in the fashion than most of the ladies, no[t] being dress'd without a hoop. B[ecky]. Bond makes her first appearance tonight at the rooms.

No loss for partners, even I am engaged to [dance with] seven different gentlemen, for you must know 'tis a fix'd rule never to dance but two dances at a time with the same person. Oh, how I wish Mr. P[aca]. wou'd let you come in for a week or two. Tell him I'll answer for your being let to return. I know you are as fond of a gay life as myself. You'd have an opportunity of rakeing [having a good time] as much as you choose, either at plays, balls, concerts, or assemblys. I've been but three evenings alone since we mov'd to town. I begin now to be almost tired.

Tell Mrs. Harrison [your mother] she has got a gentleman in her house who promises me not to let a single thing in it be hurt, and I'm sure he'll keep his word. The family she left in it still remain. I had a long conversation about you the other evening with John Saunders. He is just the same as when you knew him. Two or three more of your old acquaintances are in town such as Prideaux and Jock DeLancy [my cousin]. They often ask after you.

Is Mrs. White with you? I long to hear all that concerns you. Do pray try to get an opportunity [to send a letter]. The clock is now striking four, and Moses [my brother] is just going out to dinner, quite the Congress hours. Moses wrote to

98

your mother about her house six weeks ago. Did she get the
letter? All your Philadelphia friends well, and desire their
loves; mine to all in Maryland.

When you see the Miss Tilghmans, tell them I never hear a
new song or piece of music that I don't wish them to have it.
I must go finish dressing as I'm engaged out to tea.

God bless you,
B[ecky]. F[ranks].

Thursday,
Feb'y 26, '78.

I send some of the most fashionable ribbon and gauze; have
tried to get Joe's buckles in all the best shops, but in vain.
B[ecky]. Redman is here and sends her love.[18]

While Rebecca was living this "life of continued amusement," her father was having his headaches with his prisoners. They were scattered in various towns of Pennsylvania, Maryland, and Virginia, and there they were provided for by sub-contractors who were often friends and
old business associates.

David's agent in Easton was the pioneer Jewish settler
Myer Hart, who was sometimes referred to as Myer Hart
de Shira (Texeira), and was reputed to be of Spanish descent.

When Easton was established by the Penns in 1752, Hart
was one of the founding fathers and soon its most substantial citizen. Though he was involved in many lawsuits, he
was not ungenerous. He contributed twenty pounds of
nails to the building of the local school, a worth-while gift
in the days of hand-wrought nails.

Hart was landowner, innkeeper, and general merchant.
He did business occasionally with the Gratz brothers and

their associates, and it was probably to them that he consigned the wheat which he shipped down the Delaware on flat-bottomed barges.

When the Congress quartered some of the prisoners in Easton, it was logical that Franks should give Hart the job of feeding them. Since David's sub-contractors furnished their own capital, periodic settlement with him was both desirable and necessary. In December, 1777, Congress insisted that British payment for the prisoners had to be made in specie. Franks could secure no specie for this purpose. Hart, at this juncture, felt that it was opportune to balance his accounts with his employer. Also, we may be sure, he sensed that Franks was under suspicion for his Tory leanings. In January, 1778, Hart asked Boudinot to have him passed into Philadelphia, within the British lines, on a flag of truce, in order to see Franks and straighten out their finances. Evidently this was not feasible, for about four weeks later he again approached Boudinot. We do not know the outcome of Hart's efforts to settle the accounts; we only know that he wanted to. In March, in answer to rumors that the British prisoners in Easton were being mistreated, Hart submitted the following statement:

March 19, 1778.

I, the subscriber, do hereby declare, that I have had the care of the prisoners in the British service at Easton in Pennsylvania from last September, as agent to Mr. David Franks of the city of Philadelphia. That during the whole time I have seen nothing like cruelty exercised towards them nor heard of any insult offered to them. On the contrary, I have observed a care and attention have been paid to their wants, and that the commissary and goal keeper have behaved to them civilly and with humanity.

That the greatest part of them have had the liberty of several miles limits, and do know that they have faithfully rec[eiv]'d one pound of meat and one pound of bread p[er]. man p[er]. day till within about two months past, when they were restricted to twelve ounces of each. That they have frequently been allowed to work out for the inhabitants and rec[eiv]'d a dollar p[er]. day wages. That surgeons are appointed to attend the sick who have necessaries provided for their comfort. That all the officers are and have been on their parole, and none have ever been confined to my knowledge. That such prisoners who have wanted necessaries, as shoes, shirts, etc., have had liberty to purchase them in the town when they had money.

Myer Hart.[19]

Myer Hart's operations were probably petty compared with those of Joseph Simon. That same month of January, 1778, when it appeared that Franks was not going to be able to pay his agents in specie, Franks was already in debt to Simon for thousands of pounds. The latter was afraid he might never receive his money. Accordingly, he asked Elijah Etting of York to consult with Congress, then meeting there, and determine if it would permit him to pay for the upkeep of the prisoners in Continental paper currency. In the meantime he continued to pay in bundles of paper money, which he had received from Franks, in spite of the Congressional insistence on specie. Inevitably Simon was summoned to York by Boudinot and by General Horatio Gates, President of the Board of War, and was instructed to comply with the order of Congress.

Simon thereupon informed Franks—in April—that if the

latter could not supply him with hard cash, "I shall be obliged to decline acting as commissary for the prisoners." Again the following month Simon wrote a letter, a "tough" letter, to his principal:

Lancaster, May 12, 1778.

Sir:

The 9th instant I received a letter from George Murdoch, Esq'r, [a well-known patriot leader of] Frederick Town, who supplys the prisoners of warr in the state of Maryland on my acco't. He received a letter from Colo[nel]. Daniel Hughes, a copy of which as follows:

"Hagers Town, April 16th, 1778.

Sir:—I am desired by the Board of Warr to inform you that you are to furnish provisions [in specie] for the prisoners of warr, agreeable to the late resolves of Congress. I purpose to collect all the prisoners in this state to Fort Frederick by the fifth of May. Till then, you are to furnish them as usual. I am, sir,

Your humb'e s[ervan]'t,

Daniel Hughes.

George Murdoch, Esq'r."

In consequence of said letter, I waited on the Board of Warr and acquainted them [with] the inconvenianceys I labour under. I have often troubled them and prolong'd time, still expecting to here from you, that you would have answer'd my letters before this time, respecting my department, how I shall act. I am blamed greatly [for] not adhereing to the resolves of Congress, *which I sent you before*, and the Hh'ble Board of Warr have still indulg'd me till the first of June by their letter, a true copy of which I now inclose you for perusal, that I may have early instructions from you how I shall act.

I shall prepair my acco't of imbursements for the prisoners in this and the state of Maryland by the first of June for a settlement, as I must then positiv'ly give up my departments respecting the victualling and furnishing the prisoners with necessarys, if not furnished with specia to pay for the same, agreeable to the late resolves of Congress. And I should be very sorry, as I fear the prisoners will be neglected and not supply'd with the usual necessarys they receiv'd from me. I do assure you, the gentlem'n of the Hh'ble The Board of Warr have not alone given me great indulgence, but have acted in regard of the prisoners with a tenderness and feeling greatly to their honour. They have also told me that if provisions should be sent out [by the British] for the prisoners, they will not make it inconveniant or expensive to transport the provisions to the different places, but will receive them at any of the ports of the Army of the United States and order their commissary to replace the same quantity at the places where the prisoners resides, so that [so long as] the provisions sent out be good. Should they be otherwise, they will not be rec'd.

I supose about 1200 prisoners will be remoov'd to Fort Frederick in the state of Maryland. The prisoners are intirely distitute of cloathing, shirts and shoes in perticular. Colo. Boudinot order'd the commissary I imploy at Reading to rece've no other money from me then specia which I have not.

I intended this letter to the care of Colo. Boudinot, but as I am inform'd he is now at New York I have taken the liberty to trouble his Excellencey, Gen'l Washington, to forward it to you, if his Excellencey should thing proper. I am in advance upwards of £15,000 and been oblidge to borrow money. I have accepted to pay a draft from Mr. Philip Bush. The fourth past, I sent you to the care of Colo. Boudinot receipts to the amount of 44,926 rations. Please to advise me if you have reciv'd them. I dayly expect the receipts from Maryl'd and have a number by me to send but would not trouble his Excellencey with them. I am, sir,

> Your very humb'e s[ervan]'t,
> Joseph Simon.

David Franks, Esq'r.[20]

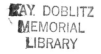

Chapter 6

Pennsylvania — 1779

IT is by no means improbable that David Franks received this last letter from Simon on the very day that he was out on the river witnessing the most brilliant social event in the history of Philadelphia, an event in which daughter Rebecca played a leading part. In order to honor the British general, Sir William Howe, who was returning home, his officers determined to hold a tournament-festival, somewhat on the order of the medieval fete at the Field of the Cloth of Gold. Two of its "directors" were good friends of Rebecca: Major John André and Captain Oliver DeLancey, Jr. André, after being captured at Saint John's in 1775, had been paroled to Philadelphia, and spent many a pleasant hour in the Franks household painting a miniature of Miss Rebecca—she was then all of fifteen or seventeen years of age—and inditing poetry to her. Oliver DeLancey, Jr., was Rebecca's first cousin, for Oliver's mother was Phila Franks, David's sister. Rebecca's very prominent role in the festivities, however, rested not only on her social background, but also on her personal charm.

The fete, called the *Meschianza*, began at 4 o'clock in the afternoon of the 18th of May and continued for twelve hours, until the dawn of the next day. There were a regatta on the river, processions under triumphal arches, and a climactic grand ball with fireworks and a royal repast.

In the tournament two parties were represented: the Knights of the Blended Rose and the Knights of the Burning Mountain. The former chose a Miss Auchmuty as their Queen of Beauty; the latter, Miss Rebecca. We have a description of her costume on that great occasion. She was dressed in a "white silk gown, trimmed with black and white sashes, edged with black. It was a polonaise dress which formed a flowing robe and was open in front to the waist. The sash, six inches wide, was filled with spangles, as was the veil, which was edged with silver lace. The head-dress was towering, in the fashion of the time, and was filled with a profusion of pearls and jewels."

This grand "medley" of extravagant entertainment, "the notorious *Meschianza*," took place at the Wharton estate, "Walnut Grove," not many miles from Valley Forge where the harried Continental troops, still encamped, had spent a bitter winter. Hundreds of invitations were issued, and it is reported that £12,000 worth of expensive silks and laces were sold by one London firm.

A month later the English left Philadelphia, to be repulsed at Monmouth as they marched across New Jersey.

Two months later the memory of the *Meschianza* still rankled in the heart of General Anthony Wayne as he caustically wrote: "Tell those Philadelphia ladies, who attended Howe's assemblies and *levees*, that the heavenly, sweet, pretty red-coats, the accomplished gentlemen of the guards and grenadiers have been humbled on the plains of Monmouth. The Knights of the *Blended Roses* and the *Burning Mount* have resigned their laurels to rebel officers, who will lay them at the feet of *those* virtuous daughters of America who cheerfully gave up ease and affluence in a city, for liberty and peace of mind in a cottage."

But the Revolutionary General Charles Lee, whose inglorious conduct at Monmouth led to his suspension for a period of twelve months, nursed no such grudge against the female Tories of Philadelphia. While in temporary retirement in the Pennsylvania capital during the winter of 1778, he carried on a spirited correspondence with Rebecca Franks, whom he greatly admired. In a mock-heroic letter, studded with *double-entendre*, he reproached her for attacking him. He could have borne the accusations of treasonable correspondence with the enemy (an unconscious slip?), of getting drunk, of theft, of never parting with his shirt until his shirt parted with him—all these calumnies he could endure, but she had diabolically slandered him by reporting that he wore green breeches *patched* with leather, rather than genuine riding breeches *reinforced* with leather!

"You have already injured me in the tenderest part," he cried out grandiloquently, "and I demand satisfaction. And as you cannot be ignorant of the laws of duelling . . . I insist on the privilege of the injured party, which is, to name his hour and weapons; and as I intend it to be a very serious affair, I will not admit of any seconds. And you may depend upon it, Miss Franks, that whatever may be your spirit on the occasion, the world shall never accuse General Lee with having turned his back upon you."

This sort of thing was just a little too crude for Rebecca, and when the General later realized that his *jeu d'esprit* had deeply offended her, he apologized most abjectly and most charmingly.

But while she was skirmishing flirtatiously with British officers, while she was enjoying her day of triumph at the *Meschianza*, certainly she had no thought, even for a second, that she was doing her father a great disservice. The British had left Philadelphia. Public opinion associated Franks with his Tory daughter—and his other loyalist associates. In September, 1778, Franks was unable to supply the British prisoners for lack of specie, and hence he could be dispensed with. In October or early November he was thrown into jail by the federal authorities. Possibly some ambitious patriot had his eye on Franks's lands which might be confiscated and sold cheaply after his conviction for treason.

The actual charge against Franks was that he had written to his brother Moses in England and had expressed "intentions inimical to the safety and liberty of the United States." This letter, which he had attempted to forward through his brother-in-law, the British general, the senior Oliver DeLancey, was intercepted and sent to the Congress. In November, Franks was formally deprived of his position as commissary to the British prisoners in the United States. But when he stood trial no convicting evidence could be produced, and he was soon released. The letter to his brother is no longer extant.

In the meantime, a dispatch reached Moses Franks in England with the news that David had been arrested. The anxious brother, not knowing that David had long since been released, sent a hasty note to Sir Grey Cooper, one of the secretaries of the Treasury, asking him to arrange immediately with General Sir Henry Clinton for the exchange of his brother, "tho' God knows whether he will be alive when such an act of benevolence and mercy shall reach him." Moses Franks had gone to school with Henry Clinton in America and hoped that the General would be mindful of the common tie.

David Franks made further efforts to get in personal touch with the English army authorities, but the suspicious Congress refused him permission. There was, however, a plain and simple reason for these repeated requests: it was imperative that he be reimbursed for the large sums he and his agents had put out for the British prisoners. Franks kept appealing to his principals, Nesbitt, Drummond, and Franks, to pay his drafts; they in turn appealed to the Lords of the Treasury, and these august gentlemen referred them back to Sir Henry Clinton, maintaining that Clinton had repeatedly been instructed to pay for the victuals for the prisoners out of the army contingency fund.

Neither Congress nor the Pennsylvania Supreme Executive Council would let Franks go to New York under a flag of truce to induce Clinton to pay the bills or to certify to the food delivered, but they did permit his clerk, Patrick Rice, to go in his stead. In December, 1778, Franks owed his creditors and agents for 500,000 rations supplied the British prisoners in American hands. In March, 1779, Nesbitt, Drummond, and Franks not only refused to honor his drafts, but, washing their hands of the whole affair, left him "holding the bag." He needed money badly, and in December of that year he smuggled through the following letter to his friend Major John André, Adjutant General of the British Army:

Sir:

I had the pleasure of addressing you in the month of February last, by Mr. Rice, my clerk and agent, praying for your friendly advice and assistance in the settlement of some interesting accounts at Head Quarters. I call them interesting because they really are so, both to my constituents in England and to myself and friends in this country, owing to the very long delay of payment of the large sums advanced so cheerfully, not only for our attachment to Government, but from inclination on my part to render essential service to the Crown, and also to distressed suffering prisoners. And my being able to render those unfortunate prisoners such necessary comforts during my agency always gave me the greatest pleasure and satisfaction, and indeed I sincerely wish that those troops were since that period as well supply'd, but that is not the case.

As for my own late sufferings, on acco[un]'t of my loyalty, I have cheerfully submitted to it, notwithstanding my imprisonment, trial for life, the unhappy situation my large family were necessarily thrown into, and the heavy expence to lawyers, etc., of *two hundred guineas.* Yet find myself involved in great difficulties by the contractors [in London] suffering my drafts on them to the amo[un]'t of £4,370, st[erlin]'g, to be return'd protested for want of proper certificates being sent them for the said provisions as usual, or on acco[un]'t of the Lords of the Treasury directing the Commander in Chief [Sir Henry Clinton] to settle the price of said provisions with me here and pay the amo[un]'t thereof as by the contractors' letter will fully appear. And the hardships that attend us, on acco[un]'t of the delay is great, as some of the holders of said return'd bills [of exchange], on this side, threaten imprisonment and seizure of effects.

Upwards of three months have I been applying for liberty to pass into New York to endeavor to do something towards a final settlement, but cannot yet obtain it, and it is deemed a great indulgence my being permitted to come thus far [to Elizabeth Town, New Jersey].

I therefore beg of Major André to give Mr. Rice his assistance in this settlement, or even for the present to procure a partial payment, in order to take up those bills as that would be a temporary relief to the concern'd, which, depend, we shall always retain a gratefull sense of.

I am, sir,

Your most obedient h'ble servant,
David Franks.

Elizabeth Town, December 2d, 1779.

P.S. Mrs. Hamilton [Abigail Franks], Miss Franks, and all the ladies of your acquaintance in Philadelphia present their best compliments to Major André and all their military friends, at or in the vicinity of New York, and, indeed, to make use of Miss F[rank]'s own expression, they would be very happy in taking a view of the Mall, or having a ramble under the *holy old trees* in the Broad-way.[21]

Less than a year later, in October, 1780, Franks was again arrested, this time by the Pennsylvania state authorities, on the charge of corresponding with the enemy at New York. If they meant that he was writing letters to the British, they were quite right; how else was he to secure payment for the large sums he had expended on their behalf? A second time, apparently, no evidence was brought against him, although it was suggested that he had depreciated the currency by buying specie. Continental paper was falling so rapidly that ultimately it was not even to be "worth a Continental." Quite properly, Franks indignantly denied any direct responsibility for this inflation. But what was true, as Washington intimated in an earlier letter, was that the very use of American paper money in large sums, by the British and by men like Franks, to feed prisoners in the hands of the Americans, coupled with the British refusal to accept this same currency to feed prisoners in their hands, tended to undermine the value of the Continental dollar.

There was a Pennsylvania statute (1779) which permitted the Supreme Executive Council to arrest, place under bond, or to imprison any suspected British sympathizer. This statute was invoked, and though there was no specific provision permitting expulsion into the enemy's lines, David and his daughter Rebecca were sent to New York before the year was out. (This Franks incident is somewhat reminiscent of the banishment by Lincoln of former Congressman Vallandigham into the Confederate lines in 1863.) Rebecca got her wish; she had her ramble under the holy old trees in the Broad-way.

She kept constantly in touch with both patriot and Tory friends back home through letters. Her father's tribulations did not lessen her frivolous chatter, and her letters retailed the choicest Gotham gossip.

During the hot summer days there were parties with the British officers. A captain's barge, she wrote, was ready down at the wharf to carry guests to General Robertson's summer home. They were always chaperoned, for in New York no unmarried girl went out without an older woman to accompany her. In Philadelphia, of course, all this was unnecessary: "We Philadelphians, knowing no harm, fear'd none." There was an ample supply of attractive officers eager to dance attendance, the handsome Captain Montague, for instance—"Such eyes!" In her more quiet moments Rebecca went to church or yearned for her sister and the familiar scenes at home, or at "Woodlands," the Hamilton estate. But she could never quite keep the men out of her thoughts, and the choicest blessing she could conjure up for sister Abigail's girls back home was their choice of the wealthy titled suitors who were floating about: three Honorables, one with £26,000 a year!

Her father, David, was not lonely, either, in New York; he had many friends there. His sister Phila, Oliver De-Lancey's wife, was in town. She could match his "escape" with a story of her own, for she was almost burnt alive in a kennel when the Whigs destroyed her home at Bloomingdale. Franks also wrote home frequently, but there is little, very little, in his letters to betray the fact that he had just gone through a harrowing experience which might have cost him his life. He showed no rancor, no resentment; he maintained an almost studied calm, preferring understatement to exaggeration. He kept busy, for there were prisoners' commissary accounts to be straightened out at British headquarters, deeds and bills of exchange and loose ends to be taken care of. He wrote to his daughter Abigail Hamilton in Philadelphia, asking her to attend to matters at home that required attention. Apparently financial jargon made sense to her; one gets the impression that she was her father's daughter—solid, sensible.

But business details by no means monopolized the pages of his correspondence. He was interested in the family and said "how doo & loves de" to his son-in-law and children. Tell the young ones to take care of their teeth—I just sent Peg a toothbrush. When "By"—short for Becky?—went out to the General's on a hot summer day, David went swimming in the river. He felt lazy after his plunge—boasted that he could still swim like a boy: Wish I had your children with me "to dipp and learn." And after he had sent them all his prayers and good wishes and love he added: Tell Bernard Jacobs, the Lancaster merchant, that there's a Nathan Levy in a British prison ship and he wants Jacobs to send him some money.

One of Rebecca's long chatty letters was sent to Abigail from the Flatbush country estate of the Van Horn's. It gives us an excellent opportunity to study social life in aristocratic, Tory New York during the Revolution:

Flat Bush, Saturday, 10 o'c[lock]., August 10th, [17]'81. My dear Abby:

The night before last I receiv'd y'r letter by *Comfort* [the messenger]. I wish I had been in town to have answer'd it and sent the things out, but I fancy eer [ere] I cou'd have receiv'd y'rs, he must have left E[lizabeth]. Town. And a few days ago I got y'rs and the chicks [my nieces], all of which I thank you and them for. If I have time this morning I'll answer them and the girls' letters.

You will think I have taken up my abode for the summer at Mrs. V[an]. Horn's, but this day I return to the disagreeable hot town much against my will and the inclination's of this family, but I cannot bear papa's being so much alone; nor will he be persuaded to quit it, tho' I am sure he can have no business to keep him. Two nights he staid with us, which is all I've seen of him since I left home. I am quite angry with him.

I have wrote you several times with in these two weeks; you can have no cause to complain, with out it is of being too often troubled with my nonsense. Those [letters] you mention'd sending by P[olly]. R[edman]. have not yet come to hand. The ham is safe; the cracker's haven't as yet made their appearance. I fear they never will tho' I heard they were safe on S[taten]. Island. I fancy the person to whose care they were sent thought them too good to part with. The *person* who sent them and the ham, I beg you'll *give* my sincere thanks to.

You ask a description of the Miss V[an].Horn that was with me, Cornelia. She is in disposition as fine a girl as ever you saw, a great deal of good humour and good sense. Her person is too large for a beauty, in my opinion (and yet I am not partial to a *little* woman). Her complection, eyes, and teeth are very good, and a great quantity of light brown hair (*Entre nous*, the girls of New York excell us Phil[adelphi]'ans in that particular and in their form), a sweet countinance and agreeable smile. Her feet, as you desire, I'll say nothing about; they are V[an]. Horn's and what you'd call Willings. [The Willings, who evidently had big feet, were partners of Robert Morris.] But her sister Kitty is the belle of the family, I think, tho' some give the preference to Betsy. You'll ask how many thousand there are, only *five*. Kitty's form is much in the stile of our admir'd Mrs. Gallwey [Galloway], but rather taller and larger, her complection very fine, and the finest hair I ever saw. Her teeth are begining to decay, which is the case of most N[ew].Y[ork]. girls after eighteen—and a great deal of elegance of manners.

By the by, few N.York ladies know how to entertain company in their own houses unless they introduce the card tables, except this family (who are remarkable for their good sense and ease). I don't know a woman or girl that can chat above

114

half an hour, and that's on the form of a cap, the colour of a ribbon, or the set of a hoop stay or *jupon* [petticoat]. I will do our ladies, that is Phila'ans, the justice to say they have more cleverness in the turn of an eye than the N.Y. girls have in their whole composition. With what ease, have I seen a Chew, a Penn, Oswald, Allen, and a thousand others entertain a large circle of both sexes, and the conversation without the aid of cards not flag or seem the least strain'd of [or] stupid.

Here, or more properly speaking in N.Y., you enter the room with a formal set curtesy and after the how do's, 'tis a fine or a bad day, and those triffling nothings are finish'd, [then] all's a dead calm 'till the cards are introduc'd when you see pleasure dancing in the eyes of all the matrons, and they seem to gain new life. The misses, if they have a fav'rite swain, frequently decline playing for the pleasure of making love, for to all appearances 'tis the ladies and not the gentlemen that shew a preference now adays. 'Tis here, I fancy, allways leap year. For my part that am us'd to quite an other mode of behaviour, cannot help shewing my surprize, perhaps they call it ignorance, when I see a lady single out her *pet to* lean all most in his arms at an assembly or play house (which I give my honor I have too often seen both in married and single), and to hear a lady confess a partiality for a man who perhaps she has not seen three times. [These women say] "Well, I declare, such a gentleman is a delightfull creature, and I could love him for my husband," or "I could marry such or such a person." And scandle sais [with respect to] most who have been married, the advances have first come from the ladies side. Or she has got a male friend to introduce him and puff her off. 'Tis really the case, and with me they loose half their charms; and I fancy there wou'd be more marriage was an other mode adopted. But they've made the men so saucy that I sincerely believe the lowest ensign thinks 'tis but ask and have; a red coat and smart epaulet is sufficient to secure a female heart. . . .

And now, my d'r Abby, I am going to tell you a piece of news that you'll dislike as much as I do. What do you think of Moses [our brother in London] coming out with a cockcade [an officer's insignia]! He writes to papa and me 'tis his serious resolve, and we must not be surpriz'd if we see him this summer. The idea of ent'ring an ensign at his time of life [he was probably close to thirty] distresses [me] more then any thing I've met with since I left you. All the comfort I have is that his Uncle M[oses]. will not allow him. I have not had an oppor[tuni]'ty of asking papa's opinion of it, as I receiv'd the letter's since I've been here, but I am certain he must disapprove of it as much as I do. Was he ten or twelve years younger, I should not have the smallest objection, but 'tis too late for him to enter into such a life, and after the indulgence he's ever been us'd to he'll never brook being commanded from post to pillow by ev'ry brat of [or] boy who may chance to be longer in the service. Tomorrow I shall write to him and make use of ev'ry argument I am misstress of to disuade him from so mad a project, which I hope will arrive in time to prevent it, for if he once enter's I wou'd be the first to oppose his quiting it, as I ever lov'd a steady character. The danger of the war I have in a measure reconcil'd myself to. 'Tis only his age I object to and the disagreeable idea of his being sent the L[or]'d knows where. If he does enter (which I hope to God he may not), I wish he may join the 17th, or els get into the dragoons; the latter I think he'll prefer on account of his lameness. He has not, I believe, wrote to you by this oppor-[tuni]'ty; Aunt [Moses?] Franks and Aunt Richa [father's sister], I believe, have. . . .

Nanny VaHorn and self employ'd yesterday morn'g in trying to dress a rag baby [doll] in the fashion, but cou'd not succeed. It shall however go, as 'twill in some degree give you an idea of the fashion as to the jacket and pinning on of the handkerchief. . . .

Yesterday the granadiers had a race at the Flatlands [Long

Island], and in the afternoon this house swarm'd with beaus and some very smart ones. How the girls wou'd have envy'd me cou'd they have peep'd and seen how I was surrounded, and yet I shou'd have [felt] as happy if not much more to have spent the afternoon with the Thursday Party at the W[oo]'dlands. I am happy to hear you'r out there as the town must be dreadfull this hot summer. N.Y. is bad enough tho' I do not think 'tis as warm as Phil'a. . . .

Well, this is sufficiently long; love to everybody. . . .

Y[ou]'rs,

[R. F.] [22]

The "17th" which Rebecca mentions as her choice for brother Moses was no doubt the 17th Foot Regiment, whose lieutenant-colonel, Henry Johnson, was a beau of hers. Six months later, in January, 1782, she married Henry at her father's house on Broad-way. After the war the Johnsons went to England, and there it was, about the year 1816, that Winfield Scott saw Rebecca, a prematurely aged but still charming woman. In the course of the conversation with the young hero of the War of 1812—he was a general at twenty-eight—she said emphatically: "I have gloried in my rebel countrymen! . . . Would to God I, too, had been a patriot!"

David went to England after Rebecca's marriage, remained there with his son Jacob for a while, and then returned to the States. In 1786, a David Franks issued the first New York city directory, and some historians have credited this to Rebecca's father, but in error, for the David Franks of the directory was a Gentile, the son of a Dublin attorney.

It is difficult to determine whether our David Franks

upon his return was in reduced circumstances, or not. In England, about 1782, he had told the Commission for the Relief of American Loyalists that he once possessed personal property worth £20,000 sterling, all this exclusive of his extensive land holdings, and that he had had to sell some of his furniture to pay his debts—yet he asked for only £1,125 as compensation. The Commission awarded him £125 and recommended an annual pension of £100 in view of his "loyalty and zeal." In 1791, in Philadelphia, he was in the habit of borrowing small sums from Michael Gratz, now a well-to-do and respected merchant. When Franks died of yellow fever two years later his administrators supplied a bond of only £500, a relatively small sum. His estates apparently were never confiscated by the American authorities, although there is no question that his loyalty lay with the mother country. He was a Tory.

HOME OF DAVID FRANKS IN PHILADELPHIA, 1771

WOODLANDS, HOME OF THE FAMILY OF ABIGAIL FRANKS HAMILTON

Chapter 7

Pennsylvania — 1781

WHEN Congress removed David Franks as British commissary of prisoners in the winter of 1778, his chief associate in this work, Joseph Simon, asked the Board of War for authority to continue supplying "necessaries" to the captured. But, as we know, purveying was by no means the only economic outlet of Joseph Simon; we recall his interest in land-settlements and his participation in the Lancaster consortium with the Frankses and the Gratzes.

During the summer and fall of 1779, the Lancaster group lobbied diligently to get the Virginia legislature to acknowledge their claims to the "Indiana (West Virginia)" lands across the mountains. Barnard Gratz· went to Williamsburg, the Virginia capital, in October for that purpose. He traveled about a great deal during the difficult war days, working hard to make a living, but he kept his family in Lancaster, where food was plentiful and where there was no danger of the enemy. There his "in-law," Joseph Simon, could be depended upon to look after the welfare of the womenfolk and children.

Barnard Gratz's only surviving child was his young daughter Rachel. (She grew up to marry the widower Solomon Etting of Baltimore, whose first wife had been a daughter of Joseph Simon. The Ettings of Baltimore were a very important family in the history of early nineteenth-century American Jewry.) When she was seven or eight years of age, "her honored farther" showed her how much he loved her. He and Uncle Michael wrote William Murray telling him that an agent was bringing out a shipment of goods to the Illinois country. And among the supplies was a small package of jewelry which Murray was to sell, the profits to go to Rachel and two other Gratz youngsters. This was Rachel's first "adventure" in business, and Murray was asked to watch the account and remit the profits separately.

As she grew up her father lavished all his love on her. She, too, was very fond of her "dear little daddy," and she missed him very much when he left on a long trip to England or crossed the mountains into the dark forests.

Although Rachel was in her teens in 1779, she was apparently getting her first formal instruction in arithmetic—rather late, to be sure—but then all sorts of things happen in wartime. But she had already learned to write, as the following letter testifies. Barnard received it from her while he was away from Lancaster. He was probably at his business, in Philadelphia, at the time.

Lancaster, August 3, 1779.

Hon[ore]'d Farther:

I cannot let slip this favorable opportunity after my long silence to let you know that I am in good health, thank God, as *I* hope this may find you in the same. You mention in your letter about my minding my schooling, which shall do my endeavors to learn as I know it is my dear daddy's desire. I have just begun to cipher and I am very much delighted at it. I am in averdepois weight and now can cast up anything. I should be very much obliged to my good daddy if you see a pretty fan to get it for me, as they are very dear in this place. Today I was at a French colonel's funeral who was buried with all the honors of war. The day before that he was buried but it was not regular; so they took him up again. Today was the finishing.

I must conclude, hon'd father, with wishing you every earthly felicity this world can afford.

Your ever-loving and obedient daughter,
Rachel Gratz.

Aunt [Miriam Gratz?] and all the children desire their love to you. Aunt Bush desires to be remembered to you. Becky's [Richea Bush's?] compliments to you. Please remember me to Moses.

My d[ea]'r daddy, I have one favor to beg of you, not to forget to get me a lining for my cloak and some lace. Becky begs of you the favor to get her three yards of linsey, please.[23]

We do not have the slightest idea where Barnard got the three yards of linsey-woolsey for Becky. If it could not be gotten in Lancaster, which was something of a textile center in those days, it must indeed have been a scarce item. Perhaps Barnard had some of it in stock in Philadelphia. If not, then he probably made the rounds of his fellow-merchants, and among his associates in the synagogue who might have been able to help was Hayman Levy.

Hayman's daughter Zipporah ("Birdie" in English) had married Benjamin Mendes Seixas, of the New York and

Newport family, in January, 1779, in Philadelphia. Levy had then taken his very capable son-in-law under his wing in matters economic, and they began to work together also in local congregational affairs. Seixas was already an up-and-coming Philadelphian; that very year, 1779, he protested with other solid citizens against the endless issue of worthless bills of credit by Congress.

Because of the Newport connections he was in frequent touch with Aaron Lopez, to whom he usually wrote through his brother Moses Seixas in Newport, or through Josiah Hewes, the Philadelphia agent of Lopez. Occasionally, as in the following letter, Ben wrote directly to Lopez:

Philad'a, Jan'y 16th, 1781.

Dear Sir:

We were yesterday week fav[ore]'d with yours of 22d Dec'r and note the contents. Mr. Hewes called on us and we have since rec'd £106.15. Cont[inenta]'l currency, and £37.10s. in specie, which closes our acct's for the present.

Accept of our thanks for your kind wishes of success in our business. We have for this some time past done but very little which made it necessary for each [Hayman Levy and myself] to seek singly, the profits being by no means sufficient to maintain two families.

Prices are very fluctuating with us, rise and fall 20 p'r cent in two or three days. Annexed you have the prices current, which will be some compensation for the postage. Nominal exch[an]'ge [of paper for specie] here is at seventy five for one, though in reality nothing less than one hundred [for one]. People governing themselves and asking in proportion to the latter.

Our city has been in a little confusion within these few days past oweing to the Pennsylvania Line having mutinied [at Morristown, January 1st], and on their march for this place. We dreaded the consequences of such a proceedure. Happily for us, our governor [Joseph Reed, President of the Supreme Executive Council of Pennsylvania], with a comittee of Congress, had influence enough to stop them at Trenton where matters were accomodated. They are most all discharged.

Gen[era]'l Clinton [the British general], watching every opportunity, sent two men with great offers to them. They [the rebellious troops] had virtue sufficient to refuse him and delivered his emissaries to our Light Horse, who [the two emissaries] were last week executed as spies. Arnold [Benedict, the traitor,] has landed at Richmond in Virginia where he has done a great deal of mischief.

Our families join in best wishes for your and Mrs. Lopez's with all the worthy families prosperity. Believe me to be with respect in behalf of Mr. Levy and self,

Your assured friend, etc., etc.,
B[enjamin]. S[eixas].

West India rum, 90 to 100 doll'rs
Muscovado sugar 1100 to 1200 [dollars a loaf?]
Havannah brown [sugar], 10 doll. p. lb.⎫
D[itt]o. white, 12 do. ⎬ falling
Bohea tea, 90 [$] p'r. lb.
Choco[la]'te 18 [$ per] lb. by the box
Coffee 16 & 17 [$] per lb.
Allum salt 240 doll. per busshel
Fine imported [salt] 240 [doll. per bushel]
D[itt]o. country [salt] 160 [doll. per bushel]
Port wine has been sold as low as £9 to £12 per gall., there being a great quantity brought in [by] the several prizes lately arrived here.[24]

The list of prices current which Seixas annexed to this letter gives a graphic picture of what deep inroads inflation had already made by the beginning of 1781. Pepper sold for $98 a pound in February, so Josiah Hewes wrote in a letter to Lopez; in April it rose to $130 a pound, and when Seixas left on a business trip that spring for Boston and Newport, he carried with him $32,000 in Continental currency in payment for two barrels of pepper!

The following year, in 1782, the Jews of Philadelphia wanted to improve their synagogue quarters. For a generation prior to the war, the Jewish families in Philadelphia had held services in rented rooms. Now the *émigrés* who had streamed into town wanted something better. Most of them were voluntary exiles who had fled from the British-occupied cities of Newport, New York, Charlestown, and Savannah. But Philadelphia was more to them than a city of refuge. It offered them opportunities. It was the country's most important financial center, and, as the capital city, it afforded them a chance to secure their share of government contracts.

Nearly all these *émigrés* were sincere Whigs. Early in the war, Dr. Benjamin Rush had remarked that "the Jews in all the States" were Whigs. The good doctor erred; all were not on the Continental side, although the majority were. The large influx to Philadelphia, however, illustrated the basic correctness of Rush's observation.

The newcomers soon assumed control of the local Jewish congregation which at the time was already called Mikveh Israel, "The Hope of Israel." This was not the first American Mikveh Israel; the name had been adopted about 125 years before this by the congregation in Curaçao, one of the oldest in the Western Hemisphere.

When the Philadelphia synagogue was reorganized in 1782, only one Pennsylvanian, Barnard Gratz, who had been its *parnas* or president, was put on the board of six; the rest were from out-of-town. Isaac Moses, a man of large affairs, was the new president; the others were Hayman Levy, Simon Nathan, Benjamin Seixas, and Jonas Phillips.

The new leaders moved with dispatch. A vigorous campaign to raise money was promptly started, and soon an old house and a lot were purchased on Sterling Alley. They thought that the house could be remodeled, but when they discovered that it was almost as cheap to build afresh, the house and lot were sold and a new location chosen. Such, at any rate, is the story as Hyman Polock Rosenbach gave it in *The Jews in Philadelphia*. But this was only half the story.

The facts are that the congregation liked the location and had decided to build its synagogue there. The contract had already been signed with the builders. Why, then, did it go somewhere else? Here is what really happened.

The lot on Sterling Alley, purchased from Robert Wall, was "contegious" to the "lott" of the Reformed German Congregation, a local Protestant group. As soon as the church found out that the Jews were going to build next door, its members objected, and vigorously.

As Germans, or children of Germans, they reflected faithfully traditions that had characterized their ancestral land for hundreds of years. Indeed, as far back as the sixth century, Pope Gregory the Great had declared that no synagogue should be so close to a church that the sound of the singers, the *hazzan* and the congregation would disturb the devotions of the Christian worshipers. Gregory's declaration prevailed throughout Christendom, and thereby set the pattern for Germany. The German Protestants of Philadelphia had probably never heard of Pope Gregory, and would have indignantly repudiated him as a Catholic had they known of him, but they had more recent and more acceptable authority. *Der alte Fritz* himself, Frederick the Great of Prussia—still living, too!—had been very specific on this matter in the charter which he granted his Jewish subjects in the 1750's. Prescribing for Jewish conventicles, he had ordered that: "The assembly is to be held at all times in a house back from the street, or in such a place where the neighbors and the public in general will not be inconvenienced by too much clamor."

But Philadelphia, in spite of its numerous Germans, was not Berlin; Pennsylvania was not Prussia. This was a free country, bringing to a successful conclusion a great war that was supposed to guarantee to every citizen certain unalienable rights, included among which was certainly the concept of freedom of conscience. As a matter of fact, the pastor of the German Reformed Church in Philadelphia was a patriot. And like his fellow-Philadelphian Haym Salomon, whom we shall soon encounter, he had urged the Hessian mercenaries to desert the British, and he had been imprisoned for his known Continental sympathies. Many of his flock were Whigs—but, apparently, they could see no connection between American patriotism and religious tolerance. They knew what tolerance was, for when they built their beautiful church many of the Christian denominations showered them with good wishes and, what was more important, with money. It was, therefore, with a glow of exaltation that they had reported to their spiritual leaders back in Europe: "The assistance rendered . . . by other denominations convinces us that that is done in America which has long and vainly been sighed for in Germany." Nonetheless, they objected to having a synagogue next door, but out of deference to this new American sentiment, the new spirit of the times which scorned bigotry, they resorted to vague generalities.

The officers of the synagogue believed that inasmuch as the church did not want them as neighbors, the least it could do was to take the lot off their hands at the price they had paid for it; that was only fair. Such a proposal was made to the German Reformed Church:

[Philadelphia, May 1, 1782.]

Gentlemen:

We find a misunderstanding has operated respecting the lot of ground and building thereon, lately purchas'd from Mr. Rob't Wall. In order therefore that we may understand each other, and to prevent any future disputes, we now again offer you the same.

Our intention was to build a synagogue and school house thereon for the use of our congregation, not conceiving that we should in the least disturb you. To our great surprize we are told it will.

We can now supply ourselves with another lot, not so convenient for our purpose, nor on such good terms, though it will cost more. But as we would wish to live in friendship with our neighbours, and to convince you it is our mean[in]'g, we are willing to take the same price we gave for the place, with

the charges, which is £540, specie, to be paid in the following manner, viz't, £350 immediately, and £190 in one year
with interest. These are the conditions we must bind ourselves
to if we purchase another, and these are the only terms we
have in our power to offer.

The season of the year advances, the tradesmen [mechanics]
are wait'g to begin their work agreable to contract, and we
are in want of our synagouge. We therefore request you
answer by Monday or Tuesday next.

Annexed is a copy of the conditions agreed to with Mr.
Wall, for your better information.

We are, gentlemen,

In behalf of the Hebrew Congre'n,
Your very h'bl serv'ts,
Isaac Moses, Pres't,

Barnard Gratz, Jonas Phillips, Benj'n Seixas, Simon Nathan,
Assistants.
To the President and Vestry of the Reform'd German Con-
gregation.

Fifty-eight and a half feet in front on Sterl'g Alley, and in
depth forty-seven feet, together with the privilege of a cellar
under, and building over a four and half foot alley, subject to
a ground rent of nine Spanish milled dollars per annum.[25]

The church did not accept the proposal. Thereupon the
leaders of Mikveh Israel called a meeting of the entire congregation and secured authority to buy another lot. Before
the month of May had passed they had purchased one on
Cherry Alley. Ben Seixas was appointed chairman of the
building committee, or, as they expressed it: he was to give
directions to the carpenter and to the mason. In June the
Jews finally decided to advertise the lot for sale and, if no
buyer could be found within a month, to dispose of it at
public auction.

One wonders what motivated the leadership of Mikveh Israel to urge the congregation to move elsewhere. Did they not have the courage, in a free country, to build a house of worship on a lawfully acquired piece of ground? Were their leaders afraid to insist on their rights?

Hayman Levy and Simon Nathan were skilled and aggressive merchants, men highly respected and admired by their associates. Levy had left a successful business behind him in New York to throw in his lot with the Whigs in Philadelphia. His certainly was not the action of a fear-ridden man.

Together with Barnard Gratz and others, Simon Nathan was to sign a strong appeal to the Council of Censors of the Commonwealth of Pennsylvania, asking them so to modify the constitution that Jews might take the oath with good conscience if elected to the Pennsylvania state legislature. These two men were ready to fight vigorously for the rights that were theirs.

Barnard Gratz was no coward. It took courage to engage in commercial ventures that carried him into almost every colony of North America, to ride the solitary trails over the mountains into Indian country, and to fight, as he did, even in old age, for equality before the law for the Jewish citizens of Maryland.

Benjamin Seixas, Simon Nathan, Isaac Moses, and Jonas Phillips had served in the militia during the Revolution.

Isaac Moses, the richest man of the lot, had excellent relations with powerful people. A patriot, who had pledged his credit for a substantial sum on behalf of the American government in one of its dark hours when supplies were sorely needed, who sent his privateers to scour the seas for British prizes, had no fear of those little men who called themselves Christians but were alien to the spirit that distinguished the founder of their own faith.

The belligerent Jonas Phillips was indubitably a man of moral courage. In later years he was to stand out for his insistence on his rights as an American citizen; he petitioned the Continental Congress in the mistaken notion that it had the authority to revoke the Christian test oath of the Pennsylvania Frame of Government. When summoned to court on a Sabbath, he refused to be sworn because of his religious convictions even though he was fined £10.

The president and *junta* ["board"] of this congregation were anything but servile men. What motivated them to move was simply their self-respect, their inner dignity. They refused to live with people who did not desire to live with them.

The dedication of the synagogue on Cherry Alley took place on September 13th, and the following invitation was sent to the President (the Governor) and the Supreme Executive Council of Pennsylvania:

Memorial of the Jewish Congregation of Philadelphia, 1782:
We, the president and representatives of the Jewish congregation in this city, humbly beg leave to approach his Excellency, the President, his Honour, the Vice President, and the Honourable, the Executive Council of the Commonwealth of Pennsylvania.

The Congregation of Mikve Israel (Israelites) in this city, having erected a place of publick worship which they intend to consecrate to the service of Almighty God, tomorrow afternoon, and as they have ever profess'd themselves liege subjects to the sovereignty of the United States of America, and have always acted agreeable thereto, they humbly crave the protection and countenance of the chief magistrates in this state to give sanction to their design, and will deem themselves highly honoured by their presence in the synagogue, whenever they judge proper to favour them.

The doors will be open'd at 3 o'clock and the service will continue 'till seven.

The uncertainty of the day of consecration was the sole cause of having delayed this matter 'till now, but earnestly hope it will not be thought too late.

With prayers to the God of Israel for the safety of the United States in general and this commonwealth in particular, we are, gentlemen, most respectfully and most devotedly, in behalf of the congregation,

Jonas Phillips, President,

Michael Gratz, Sol. Marache, etc., etc.

Philadelphia, 12th September, 1782.[26]

Chapter 8

Pennsylvania — 1782

AMONG those who were certainly present at the dedication of the synagogue was Haym Salomon. At this time Salomon, a prosperous Philadelphia merchant and broker, was in one respect the congregation's most important member. He was its most liberal contributor.

This man is one of the most fascinating figures in American Jewish history—and one of the most debated. The controversy about Salomon became quite acute in the early 1920's, when the Federation of Polish Jews in America formed a Monument Committee to erect a memorial to him as one of the great financiers of the American Revolution. Thereupon a number of publicists and scholars, believing that there was no justification for a monument to his memory, set out to prick the Haym Salomon "bubble."

The root of the controversy extends back as far as 1827. At that time Haym M. Salomon, a son, wrote to James Madison about his father's affairs, thereby taking the first steps to recover large sums which the son claimed the father had advanced to the government during the period of the Revolution.

Salomon, as this legend has it, was a Polish Jewish immigrant who had fled his native land after the partition of 1772. A friend of Pulaski and Kosciusko, he turned, like them, to these hospitable shores. He landed in New York, became a patriot forthwith, and along with others was commissioned by Washington to destroy the warehouses and the ships of the city after its occupation by the British in 1776. In this underground activity he worked closely with General Alexander McDougall, the New York political radical. He was finally caught, thrown into prison, sentenced to death by General Clinton, but managed to free himself by a bribe of a large sum of gold, and fled on August 11, 1778, to Philadelphia.

By this time France had recognized the United States; the Dutch were moving or were being driven by circumstances into the American orbit, and ultimately both began to lend the American government money. It was Haym Salomon—so this story goes—"who was charged with the negotiation of the entire amount of those munificent grants of pecuniary supplies from the governments of France and Holland."

As the French troops began to pour in, he handled all the funds for the support and maintenance of their sea and land forces, 150,000,000 livres, on which he received the regular mercantile commission. All the money he made through these transactions he invested in the Revolutionary cause.

But these large financial dealings—so the tale continues—

by no means exhausted his contribution to the struggle for American liberty and independence. Frequently he supplied funds to members of Congress, who without his aid could not have remained in office, for they were reduced to their last dollar. Among those whom he so helped were James Madison, Thomas Jefferson, Edmund Randolph, Joseph Reed, Arthur St. Clair, James Wilson, and a number of others.

He was reputed to be close to the French minister, Chevalier de la Luzerne, and to his subordinates, Marbois and La Forest. Even Don Francisco Rendon, the Spanish agent, was dependent on Salomon, for in a letter to Don Diego José de Navarre, Governor-General of Cuba, he is reported to have written: "I am entirely indebted to the practical kindness of Mr. Salomon to support my credit with any degree of reputation, and without it I certainly could not have been able to render that protection and assistance to the subjects of His Most Catholic Majesty which is enforced on me by his royal commands."

Haym Salomon, continues the legend, was the real financial hero of the Revolution: "the man that stood behind Morris and actually produced the actual sums with which the Revolution moved on." He advanced to the government —in one form or another—about $800,000 of his own money, but when he died, leaving a young widow and helpless children, nothing was left for them. Thus far the story is a curious hodgepodge of fact and fiction.

In spite of the claims made by his family a century ago, and despite the fact that at various times committees of Congress recognized a validity in their demands, members of the family have never received one cent. In 1893 the Salomons were willing to waive all rights to financial reimbursement, if only a medal were struck recognizing the services of their distinguished ancestor. Still nothing was done, even though a Congressional committee viewed the suggestion favorably.

When the Federation of Polish Jews of America sought, on the basis of the family tradition, to erect a monument to his memory in New York, it met with strenuous opposition and a denial of the truth of the Salomon story. Indignantly the proponents countered: "America failed to repay the money he advanced, and now men seek to rob him of his posthumous fame."

Max J. Kohler, of German Jewish descent and an able student of American history, was among those who opposed the monument. The project to honor Salomon, he maintained, was motivated not so much by the wish to enshrine the memory of the man, as by the desire of the Polish Jewish federation to emphasize the fact that Polish Jews had come to these shores long before the Russian pogroms of 1881. The sharp differences between Kohler and his cohorts on one side, and the "Polish" Salomonians on the other side, were to some degree a reflection of the rivalry between the old-line German Jewish settlers and the newer, aspiring East European element in American Jewish life. Haym Salomon was accordingly caught in between the disputants; it is our hope to rescue him—if we can—from this awkward position.

It is only fair to Kohler's memory to insist that he was certainly not consciously whipping Polish American Jewry with the Salomonic cudgel; he strove to be a conscientious, cautious, and accurate historian, and he nearly always succeeded.

Was the monument justified, or was Professor Worthington C. Ford, the eminent American historian, right when he said that the "story itself is incredible. . . . only as an estimable merchant has he claims to any recognition"? Let us look at the facts.

That Haym Salomon had met his compatriots Pulaski and Kosciusko is possible, yet is nowhere documented. Salomon was undoubtedly a Polish Jew, born in Lissa about the year 1740. At an early age, like all poor Jews of his day, he set out to make his fortune; he could not have been out of his teens. It is very doubtful if he was given even the most elementary and usual Hebrew training; he was certainly never a *yeshibah bahur*, a student of a rabbinical academy. It is true that he knew the Hebrew alphabet, but he wrote the most common Hebrew words phonetically, and the few Yiddish words he used are evidence of an incomplete knowledge of his own mother tongue. We know that he usually pressed his friends into service when he found it necessary to write a letter to his family back in Poland.

In his wanderings he acquired a working knowledge of German, French, Italian, Russian, Polish, English, and perhaps some other tongues. Far more to the point, he did acquire an unusual knowledge of finance and made friends among the bankers of the most important European commercial centers.

Haym Salomon was not a member of Shearith Israel in New York. He probably came to America about 1775 or even early in 1776, just about the time the patriotic members of the congregation were getting ready to flee before the British invaders. Salomon thus did not have time to affiliate himself with the Jewish Whig group. The new loyalist congregation which soon assembled in the old synagogue has left us no records.

In the summer of 1776, while suttling at Lake George for the American troops, he became known for his warm attachment to their cause, and it was not long, therefore, after the British took New York that Salomon incurred their suspicion. There is every reason to believe that he was an ardent patriot working zealously to undermine them. The facts are that he was arrested by General Robertson and thrown into the military prison, but soon released. There were large numbers of Hessians with the English, and a skilled businessman and interpreter like Salomon would have been invaluable to them. It is by no means improbable that his release was arranged without bribery, through the intervention of some of the Jewish commissary officers who came over from Germany with the Hessians. (There were a number of them, and some of them remained in this country after the war.)

For the next year or two Salomon enjoyed a considerable measure of prosperity in New York. He married, probably for the first time, on July 6, 1777, on a Sunday. We specify "for the first time," because he was already thirty-seven years of age. The bride was fifteen.

Haym's wife, Rachel, was the daughter of Moses B. Franks, a member of the widely-known Anglo-American family. Franks is usually referred to as a wealthy New York merchant, probably on the strength of his kinship with Jacob Franks. Actually, as late as 1774, the rolls of the congregation show that he received a load of wood. This may have been charity, or Franks could have received it as the perquisite due him as a synagogal employee, and, if he was working for the congregation, then he was indeed a poor man! On the other hand, Rachel Franks brought Salomon a dowry of 200 pounds New York currency; if this is to be accepted at its face value, it means that Moses B. Franks was no longer impoverished in 1777. It is by no means improbable, however, that the stipulated sum brought by the bride existed only in the contract, and nowhere else, and was inserted as a face-saving device. Such things were done.

The man who engrossed the marriage contract and also served as one of the witnesses was Abraham I. Abrahams. (We now know that the unexplained "I" stands for Isaac, and that he was by origin, though not by birth, a Lithuanian Jew, a "Litvak," one of the first of his tribe in the colonies!) No doubt Abrahams, who was not only scribe but *mohel* as well, also looked forward piously to the merit of another circumcision, and he was not disappointed, for on Tuesday, July 28th, the following year, he officiated for Haym's firstborn son, Ezekiel. (The lad grew up to become cashier of the New Orleans branch of the United States Bank.)

While working for the Hessians in New York, Salomon used the opportunity to help his adopted country by propagandizing the mercenaries, but he was finally betrayed, and on August 11, 1778, fled for his life. He barely managed to reach Philadelphia, and there, two weeks later, he penned the following appeal to the Continental Congress:

To the Honorable, the Continental Congress:
The memorial of Hyam Solomon, late of the city of New York, merchant, humbly sheweth:

That your memorialist was some time before the entry of the British troops at the said city of New York, and soon after taken up as a spy and by General Robertson committed to the Provost; that by the interposition of Lieut. General Heister—who wanted him on account of his knowledge in the French, Polish, Russian, Italian, etc., languages—he was given over to the Hessian commander who appointed him in the commissary way as purveyor chiefly for the officers; that being at New York he has been of great service to the French and American prisoners, and has assisted them with money and helped them off to make their escape; that this and his close connexions with such of the Hessian officers as were inclined to resign, and with Monsieur Samuel Demezes, has rend'red him at last so obnoxious to the British head quarters that he was already pursued by the guards, and on Tuesday, the 11th inst., he made his happy escape from thence.

This Monsieur Demezes is now most barbarously treated at the Provost's and is seemingly in danger of his life. And the memorialist begs leave to cause him to be rememb'red to Congress for an exchange.

Your memorialist has upon this event most irrecoverably lost all his effects and credits to the amount of five or six thousand pounds sterling, and left his distressed wife and a child of a month old at New York waiting that they may soon have an opportunity to come out from thence with empty hands.

In these circumstances he most humbly prayeth to grant him any employ in the way of his business whereby he may be enabled to support himself and family. And your memorialist as in duty bound, etc., etc.,

Haym Salomon.

Philad'a Aug't 25th, 1778.[27]

Salomon's petition was referred to the Board of War and was probably buried there under hundreds of similar requests.

At thirty-eight, with a wife and an infant child, he began life anew in Philadelphia. He had just lost a fortune, at his own appraisal; five or six thousand pounds sterling was a great deal of money in those days. He settled down to start all over again, as a commission merchant and bill broker, and for three years we hear nothing of him: it is obvious that he was struggling to get a toe hold.

By 1781 it seems that he was on the way up. Following the methods he had used in New York, he began to advertise extensively in the local newspapers, emphasizing his financial connections with France, Holland, and St. Eustatia. (Until its seizure that same year by the English this neutral Dutch island had been the most important depot for commerce between the blockaded United States and Europe.)

The French armed forces in America now employed the multilingual and skilled Salomon to sell their bills of exchange, and we may assume that this one client alone was sufficient to put Salomon back on easy street.

Commissions were liberal, and huge amounts, millions of livres, were involved. Salomon took his orders, probably, from John Holker, the French consul, and Holker, we know, worked hand in glove with Robert Morris.

The latter had, in May, 1781, just accepted the post of superintendent of finance, with the top salary of $6,000 a year. His was the almost impossible task of whipping the chaotic finances of the struggling country into some sort of shape. To accomplish this, he needed an able, honest broker to help sell the bills which were coming in from France, Holland, Spain, and other sources. Salomon was just the man for him and—at Holker's suggestion?—Morris chose him as his chief agent. This was in June, 1781.

Two months later the campaign to corner Cornwallis in Virginia was set under way; Robert Morris was called in and promised to raise the money to make it possible. Judging from the fact that Mr. Salomon the broker is mentioned more than one hundred times in the diary of the superintendent of finance, we may rest assured that Haym pitched in vigorously to help Morris.

Cornwallis surrendered at Yorktown in October. The end of the war was in sight, but the peace was not yet at hand. Salomon continued to serve Robert Morris as one of his chief aides, selling bills of exchange, negotiating drafts, and floating securities. He undoubtedly did a very satisfactory job, for the following summer, in July, 1782, Morris permitted Salomon to advertise himself as "Broker to the Office of Finance." "This broker has been usefull to the public interest," Morris wrote in his diary, "and requests leave to publish himself as broker to the office to which I have consented, as I do not see that any disadvantage can possibly arise to the public service but the reverse, and he expects individual benefits therefrom." (It has been suggested that one of the reasons which prompted Salomon to publicize himself in the newspapers as the Broker to the Office of Finance was the need to meet the growing competition of brokers like Isaac Franks, and, later, of Benjamin Nones, Lion Moses, and others.)

In an advertisement in *The Pennsylvania Packet* of Philadelphia, for July 20, 1782, Salomon informed the public that he was Broker not only to the Office of Finance but also to the consul general of France and to the treasurer of the French army. He stressed that he bought and sold on commission all kinds of commercial paper and bonds for all parts of Europe, the West Indies, and the United States. Bills of exchange excepted, he charged one-half of one per cent commission on all transactions. (Robert Morris, as per contract, paid him only one-half of one per cent on the bills as well.) He lent money, he discounted notes, and he stored and sold on commission tobacco, sugar, and tea. "He flatters himself," continued the advertisement, that "his assiduity, punctuality, and extensive connections in his business, as a broker, is well established in various parts of Europe, and in the United States in particular."

Banking did not exhaust his interests. In the summer of 1782 he engaged actively in the mercantile and import fields. That his entry into commerce was a relatively new venture for him is evidenced by the fact that his name does not occur in the Lopez or Gratz correspondence. With the war approaching its end, the long-blockaded United States was hungering for consumers' goods. In May, he tells a merchant in Virginia, he is ready to ship such goods.

Philadelphia, May 7th, 1782.

Mr. John Brownlow,
Frederickbourg.
Sir:

I have yours of 30th ulto. and am now preparing what you wrote for to be ready againts the waggons come. The hats are so much higher than what you judged that I shall defer sending them till I hear further from you. They cannot be got less than 10½ dollars. Silk stockengs are also high and scarce, and am afraid shall not be able to send the quantity you want. Goods are grown scarce, and from the number of vessels we have lost, and our capes being now swarming with enemy cruizers, we expect they [the goods will] rise conseiderably. Inclosed is Major [Robert] Forsyth's draft which I have thought best to send back as they will not accept it till they have all the acc'ts from that department [of the Virginia militia].

> I am, sir,
> Your hum[bl]'e ser[van]'t,
> Haym Salomon.

The forty dollars in fav'r of Rob't B. Chew I have paid.[28]

Four months later Haym Salomon was in communication with the firm of Watson and Cossoul of France. Elkanah Watson, apparently the senior member, was a remarkable person. Then only twenty-four years of age, he was the head of a large mercantile and banking house. When only seventeen this Massachusetts boy had been sent by the Providence merchant, John Brown—an old business associate of Aaron Lopez—to General Washington at Cambridge, with the welcome load of a ton and a half of gunpowder. In 1779 Watson carried dispatches to Franklin at Paris. After that Watson settled down in partnership with Cossoul in Nantes. It was during that period in his career that the famous writer, agriculturist, and far-visioned transportation economist corresponded with Salomon.

As early as January, 1782, Salomon had sufficiently recovered from his losses in New York to be able to think again of helping his family back in Poland. He sent them money through Gumpel Samson in Amsterdam. But when he heard nothing from Samson, he wrote to Nantes, to Watson and Cossoul, asking them to investigate. (Also he wished to remind this French firm of his letter of July, 1782, asking them to report on a Mr. John Cuming of L'Orient, France; Salomon had sent Cuming £1,000 for goods over a year earlier, but had gotten nothing in return.)

Philadelphia, 4th Sept., 1782.

Mess'rs Watson and Cossoul,
Gent'n:

Some few months ago I remitted a bill [of exchange] to Amsterdam to one Mr. Gumple Samson for the purpose of his forwarding the same to some particular persons as directed. I have certain acc'ts that the bill remitted was paid, and Mr. Samson rec'd the money, but have not been favou'd with a line from said Mr. Samson. I have no manner of doubt but said Mr. Samson has done the needfull as I directed, and attribute his not writing to neglect and the little intercourse this country has as yet with Holland. As the intercourse with your place is more frequent, this is to request that any lettre to my address, directed to you, that you forward the same to me, for which purpose have by this conveyance requested Mr. Samson to forward my lettres to you. Any charges thereon will be thankfully reimbursed by me.

Hope you have rec'd the papers sent you for the recovery of my money in the hands of Mr. Cumings. As by appeerence peace [between England and the United States] is near at hand when bussiness can be transacted on some solidity, hope our connections will be established for our mutual interest and proffit. I am with great regard, gent'n,

Your very obe't and very h'e serv't,
H[aym]. S[alomon].[29]

The £1,000 which was astray with Cuming could be put to much better use. Salomon was in the habit of lending money to some of the delegates of the Continental Congress who were in desperate need, among them, James Madison. In August of 1782 the future president had written to Edmund Randolph: "I cannot in any way make you more sensible of the importance of your kind attention to pecuniary remittances for me than by informing you that I have for some time past been a pensioner on the favor of Haym Salomon, a Jew broker." The next month Madison was still in as bad shape as ever and reported that other members of the Congress were also in sore need of ready cash. He then borrowed some more money from Jacob I. Cohen, a Richmond merchant.

But evidently even that was not sufficient, and so he directed his steps again to the office of Salomon. It is to be noted that this time Madison does not refer to him as a "Jew." "I am almost ashamed to reiterate my wants so incessantly to you," he wrote to Randolph again, "but they begin to be so urgent that it is impossible to suppress them. The kindness of our little friend in Front Street, near the coffee-house, is a fund which will preserve me from extremities, but I never resort to it without great mortification, as he obstinately rejects all recompense. The price of money is so usurious that he thinks it ought to be extorted from none but those who aim at profitable speculations. To a necessitous delegate he gratuitously spares a supply out of his private stock."

The month of September was a busy one for Salomon. It is true that he was worried because he had no news of the remittance which he had sent his family, but he had his satisfactions too. For a generous man the pride and pleasure of helping a man like Madison to remain in Congress must have been great. And Salomon had the additional pleasure the same month of attending the dedication of the first real synagogue building in Pennsylvania, a building which he more than any other man had made possible through his financial contribution.

He was not an official of the congregation at this particular time; he was undoubtedly too busy to accept office. Certainly the choice of honors would have been offered any honorable man who had contributed so large a percentage of the total cost of the new structure erected on Cherry Hill. The building cost £1,815; something less than £1,000 was actually collected by Jonas Phillips. Salomon's contribution was £304, a large sum for a man who had arrived in Philadelphia more dead than alive just four years before. Later he added to his benefactions and gave the synagogue a very fine Scroll of the Law which he had imported from Europe.

Among those who were present at the dedication of the synagogue with Haym Salomon was his good friend, Eleazar Levy, a former Canadian trader. Levy was one of the New York *émigrés* to Philadelphia, "from principles repugnant to British hostilities," as he phrased it.

He was a man with a grievance. Late in May, 1772, he had lent £1,000 on a large plot of ground on the Hudson River known as West Point. The army had moved in, taken over, used up much of the timber for fuel and fortifications, and had thus reduced the value of the land. The borrower had finally agreed to pay the mortgage in paper money at forty to one, but Levy had indignantly refused to accept this offer which practically wiped out his equity. In 1779 he petitioned John Jay, President of the Continental Congress, and in 1783 the honorable delegates of the United States and their president, Elias Boudinot, asking for relief. He received but cold comfort from them. In 1779 they told him his petition would be acted upon at the conclusion of the war; in May, 1783, they informed him "that in their opinion it is not expedient for Congress to take any order therein." That ended the matter.

It was to this man that Salomon turned in January, 1783, in the matter of the money sent to his family in Poland. Aware of Levy's many connections, he asked him to write to his friend "Samy" in Amsterdam. "Samy," Samuel Myers, was a member of the firm of Isaac Moses and Company and of the interlocking firm of Samuel and Moses Myers with offices at Amsterdam, Philadelphia, and New York.

. Philadelphia, 9 Jan'y, 1783.
Dear Samy:

At the request of my friend, Mr. Haym Salomon, [I] inclose you two lettres for Mr. Gumple Samson, a Jew merch't or trader, at Amsterdam, which request you will deliver into his own hands. The intent is to be asured that he has received the lettre, and you will be pleased to advise of the delivery.

Some considerable time since, Mr. Salomon, reflecting on the circumstances of his family in Poland, which, when he left many years ago, consisted of a father, a mother, brothers, and sisters, from whom he has not heard, thinking it his duty, now it is in his power to afford them assistance, he upwards of a year ago remitted a bill on Amsterdam for five hundred guilders to Mr. Gumple Samson with directions where his relations lived, and how Mr. Samson was to dispose of the money among them. Tho' many oppurtunities have offered and vessells arrived from Amsterdam, Mr. Samson has not answered Mr. Salomon's lettre or in any manner acknowledged his receipt of the money remitted, tho' the house on which the bill was drawn advise the bill was presented and the money paid by them to Mr. Samson.

Mr. Samson was further requested to forward his lettres to Nantz to Mess'rs Watson and Cossul who had Mr. Salomon's directions thereon. In this Mr. Samson has also been remiss.

Thus having related the circumstances, you will judge of Mr. Salomon's anxiety to hear of his parents and his ardent wish to relieve them, for could he once know Mr. Samson was not inclined to trouble himself with this charitable, tho' unproffitable commission, Mr. Salomon would immediately use his utmost endeavour with some other people and remit another bill.

I need not enlarge further on this matter. Your own feelings will direct you what's necessary in order to [bring] the accomplished relief to these poor relations of Mr. Salomon, whose blessing must follow every individual that in any shape is instrumental therein, I am,

> With true regard,
> Your affect. friend,
> Eleazer Levy.[30]

A few months later, in April, Salomon finally heard from his folks back home. The money which he sent them had finally come. All told, he received four Yiddish letters from them. These Salomon forwarded to New York, through the courtesy of Eleazar Levy, to Israel Myers, with the request that he answer them. Myers no doubt was proficient in Hebrew and Yiddish. Here is Salomon's note to him:

Philadelphia, 29 April, 1783.

Mr. Israel Myers,
New York.
Sir:

I take the liberty in sending you, by Mr. Eleazer Levy, sundry letters rec'd from my parents, which I have to beg of you to answer in the best manner you can and according to the directions that Mr. Levy will give you. I dare say you will partake with me of the joy that I feel on receiving those letters so long wished for, and in relieving them in their necescity. Beg you will answer the four letters, and also please to write duplicates of each which in so doing you will confer an obligation on

Your very obe't serv't,
H[aym]. S[alomon].

N. B. Please to mention to my father the difficulty that I have laboured under in not having any learning, and that I should not have known what to have done had it not been for the languages that I learned in my travels, such as French, English, etc. Therefore would advise him and all my relations to have their children well-educated, particularly in the Christian language[s], and should any of my brothers' children have a good head to learn Hebrew, would contribute towards his being instructed.[31]

Our Eleazar Levy—who was one day to be an administrator of the estate of his deceased friend Haym Salomon—is not to be confused with an Ezekiel Levy to whom Salomon wrote a sharp note the next month through one of his clerks, Samuel Hays. Indeed, there were apparently several Ezekiel Levys at this time: one in Pennsylvania, one in Charlestown, and another in Virginia.

149

The Pennsylvania Ezekiel Levy worked in Northumberland in 1777–78 for Aaron Levy, the land agent and founder of Aaronsburg. For part of this time Ezekiel was a soldier—probably a militiaman—and fought at the battle of Germantown. The Charlestown Ezekiel Levy served in Captain Lushington's "Jew Company," and fought at the battle of Beaufort in February, 1779. The Pennsylvania Levy reappeared in September, 1782, as the member of Mikveh Israel who, we recall, was haled before Jonas Phillips and the board and was charged with having shaved on the Sabbath. The third Ezekiel Levy, presumably a converted Jew, was a Virginian who, late in the 1780's, was a vestryman in the Protestant Episcopal church at Williamsburg. The latter was in all probability identical with the Richmond Levy to whom Salomon and Hays wrote in 1783.

It is also possible that the three were one and the same person.

The Pennsylvanian, leaving Northumberland after his enlistment had expired, may well have gone down to Charlestown where, perhaps, he was conscripted to serve with Lushington. After the British occupation of the South Carolina capital, he may have gone north to Philadelphia with the hundreds of other Charlestonians who fled the city. The Northumberland-Charlestown-Philadelphia wanderer could then have migrated to Virginia after the war was over, and there have become a convert. The acerbity of the note to Levy may have been due not only to Salomon's concern for his "hankerchiefs" but also to his distaste for a Jew whose religious fidelity was suspect.

Philadelphia, 29th May, 1783.

Mr. Ezekiel Levy,
Richmond, Virginia.

Sir:

My patience is almost exausted with your procceedings with regard my hankerchiefs. You having disposed of them nigh these eight months without sending me the acc't of sales, altho' you have been repeatedly solicited to do it. I therefore desire you will imediately send it, and if you have trusted them away [sold them on credit], it must be on your own acc't, as it was my expres orders not to sell one farthing's worth on credit, as will appear [in] my leters [to] you. I am, for H[aym]. S[alomon].,

Your obe't serv't,
S[amuel]. H[ays].[32]

Occasionally Salomon took time out to write a purely gossipy note. A fellow-member of Mikveh Israel, Bar't Moses Spitzer, was on a trip to Charlestown. (In the Philadelphia congregational records Bar't was listed as Barendt Barnett, Bernard.) Spitzer had been appointed a Deputy Grand Inspector of Masonry for Georgia by Moses M. Hays, but there is no evidence proving that he ever participated in the development of the fraternal order in that colony. It was a paper appointment.

Here is Salomon's note to Bar't:

Philadelphia, 20 June, 1783.

Mr. Bar't M. Spitzer,
Charlestown, South Carolina.

Sir:

I am surprised after the many assurances that you gave of writing to me that you have not yet done it. However will admit this as an excuse, that your whole time is devouted to

the lady's and can't spare time to inform a friend of your welfare, how ever desireous he may be of hearing.

I doubt if the lady's here have the same reason to coplain
of your neglect. Am certain you would not make it long
before your return, was you to know how disereous the lady's
are of your presence. And one in particular who wishes that
no pecuniary vews [views] may get the better of the partiality
you always entertained for her.

Time will not permit me to inlarge, but be asured that you
may command any thing that is in the power of

> Your obe't servant.
>
> [Haym Salomon.] [33]

The impression was abroad that *Reb Hayyim* ["Mr.
Haym"] was a *nadib meod*, a "great philanthropist" and a
man of wealth, and there is evidence of his generosity to
some European suppliants. Salomon, who was no bluffer,
admitted in a letter to John Strettel, a London merchant:
"My bussiness is a broker, and chiefly in bills of exchange,
and so very extensive that I am generally known to the
mercantile part of North America." As the chief broker
for Morris, as an agent for the French army and navy, for
the French diplomatic representative and consuls, for the
Dutch and the Spanish, he was in truth no small fry.

Salomon's earnest effort to help his family in the 1780's
was something of a strategic error. His relatives, discovering
his affluence, now descended upon him—at least through
letters. (Jewish relatives, particularly the learned among
them, do not ask for help; they demand it as a matter of
right. After all, haven't all American relatives always been
rich!)

The following letter, an answer to a wandering uncle in

England—Joseph Elis?—shows that the importunities of his relatives were beginning to get under his skin.

Philadelphia, 10 July, 1783.

[Dear Uncle:]

I rec'd your last letter inclosing a letter for Aaron Levy [the merchant and founder of Aaronsburg]. I will now answer your several letters fully. I have ordered fifty guilders to be paid you by Mr. Gumple Samson in Amsterdam, which letter giving that order you must already have rec'd, and I now send you an order for six guinies.

Your bias of my riches are too extensive. Rich I am not, but the little I have I think it my duty to share with my poor father and mother. They are the first that are to be provided for by me, and must and shall have the preference. Whatever little more I can squeeze out I will give my relations, but I tell you plainly and truly that it is not in my power to give you or any relations yearly allowances. Don't you nor any of them expect it. Don't fill your mind with vain and idol expectations and golden dreams that never will nor can be accomplished. Besides my father and mother, my wife and children must be provided for. I have three young children, and as my wife is very young may have more, and if you and the rest of my relations will consider things with reason, they will be sensible of this I now write. But notwithstanding this I mean to assist my relations as far as lays in my power.

I am much surprised at your intention of coming here. Your *yikes* [family and academic background] is worth very little here; nor can I emagion what you mean to do here. I think your duty calls for your going to your family, and besides these six guinies you will receive in Amsterdam fifty guinies of Mr. Gumple Samson.

You are pleased to say you have done a great deal for my family. Let my father and the *a"bd dk"k Lissa* ["rabbi of Lissa"] write me the particular services you have done to my

153

family, and I will consider in what manner to recompense them.

I desire no relation may be sent. Have I not children, are they not relations? When I shall be fully informed of all the young people of our family and their qualifications explained, I may then perhaps advise sending one or two to this country, and I will at my leisure explain to you the nature of this country: *vinig yidishkayt* ["little Jewishness"].

I am, with true respect, dear uncle,

Your affec'te nephew,

Your very hum'e serv't,[34]

[Haym Salomon.]

By the fall of 1783 Salomon found time for a more active interest in congregational life and became a member of the *junta* of Mikveh Israel. The trustees and their "rabbi" were men who knew the cost of freedom through bitter experience for, with the exception of one man, they were all refugees. These were the men who addressed themselves, in December, 1783, to an old problem: the limitation of their political and religious liberties.

When, in 1776, a new constitution was adopted by the Commonwealth of Pennsylvania, section ten of the Frame of Government had the following provision: "Each member [of the House of Representatives] before he takes his seat, shall make and subscribe the following declaration, viz.: 'I do believe in one God, the creator and governor of the universe, the rewarder of the good and the punisher of the wicked. And I do acknowledge the Scriptures of the Old and New Testament to be given by Divine Inspiration.'" Such a declaration could be made in good conscience only by a Christian. The provision—with its belief in the divinity of Jesus—was a serious obstacle to Jewish citizens; it barred them from serving as members of the state legislature.

Jews in this country had a tradition of fighting for their rights ever since the time of Asser Levy, who, in 1655, protested against the refusal to permit him to stand guard on the walls of New Amsterdam. After the adoption of the act of 1740, when Jews were allowed to become citizens, Aaron Lopez was compelled to fight for the privilege of naturalization. He had been denied that right in the colony of Rhode Island. Moses Michael Hays, in 1776, had been vigorous and forthright in refusing to take a special oath after some overzealous people had tried to "smear" him as a Tory.

Jews understood the meaning and the significance of the Declaration of Independence; the universality of its concept was imbedded deep in their religion. Jonas Phillips, we will recall, had sent a copy to Gumpel Samson in Amsterdam, in July, 1776, just a few weeks after it was issued.

Philadelphia Jewry was fully aware that there was a church minority who were eager to deprive all but Protestant Christians of the privileges of civil and religious equality, even in the millennial days of '76. This conservative group was convinced that the proposed new state constitution, even though it imposed a Christian test oath, was much too liberal. Their leader, Henry Melchior Mühlenberg, the outstanding Lutheran of his generation, believed that if the new constitution was adopted, Christian people would be "ruled by Jews, Turks, Spinozists, Deists, perverted naturalists." The American republic would become another "Sodom"!

A Mr. "R.," in *The Pennsylvania Evening Post* for September 24, 1776, wanted to impose constitutional safeguards that would expressly deny Jews and Turks the opportunity of becoming large landowners in the state and officers of the government. Such a situation would create "national slavery"; it would be "unsafe for Christians."

Two days later "A Follower of Christ" wrote even more frankly in the same newspaper: "An Episcopal church, a Presbyterian meeting-house, a Roman Catholic church, a mosque, a synagogue or heathen temple, have now in Pennsylvania all equal privileges! Will any Christian power call this state for the future a Christian state? Will it not be an asylum for all fugitive Jesuits, and outcasts of Europe? . . . If blasphemers of Christ and the holy blessed Trinity, despisers of revelation and the holy Bible, may be legislators, judges, counsellors, and presidents in Pennsylvania. Wo unto the city! Wo unto the land."

For Jews this was medieval bigotry, un-American and dangerous doctrine. But as long as the war was on, they did not feel it expedient to protest against "section ten." However, in 1783, when the conflict was over and the enemy had been routed, the issue of political freedom could be raised. The spirit of liberty was in the air: the wide estates of the Tories were broken up and distributed; the old English laws of primogeniture and entail that made for aristocratic control and tradition were abolished; the Anglican church was in the process of disestablishment; the

Catholics were given more opportunity; and even anti-slavery sentiment began to flourish.

The doughty trustees of Mikveh Israel addressed the following memorial to the Pennsylvania Council of Censors, an official committee of the state charged with safeguarding the rights of the people:

[December, 1783.]

To the honourable, the Council of Censors, assembled agreeable to the constitution of the State of Pennsylvania.

The memorial of Rabbi Ger. Seixas of the synagogue of the Jews at Philadelphia, Simon Nathan, their *parnass* or president, Asher Myers, Bernard Gratz, and Haym Salomon, the *mahamad*, or associates of their council, in behalf of themselves and their bretheren Jews, residing in Pennsylvania, most respectfully sheweth:

That by the tenth section of the Frame of Government of this commonwealth [adopted in 1776], it is ordered that each member of the general assembly of representatives of the freemen of Pennsylvania, before he takes his seat, shall make and subscribe a declaration which ends in these words, "I do acknowledge the Scriptures of the Old and New Testament to be given by divine inspiration," to which is added an assurance that "no further or other religious test shall ever hereafter be required of any civil officer or magistrate in this state."

Your memorialists beg leave to observe that this clause seems to limit the civil rights of your citizens to one very special article of the creed, whereas, by the second paragraph of the declaration of the rights of the inhabitants, it is asserted without any other limitation than the professing the existence of God, in plain words, "that no man who acknowledges the being of a God can be justly deprived or abridged of any civil rights as a citizen on account of his religious sentiments." But certainly this religious test deprives the Jews of the most emi-

157

nent rights of freemen, solemnly ascertained to all men who are not professed atheists.

May it please your Honors: Although the Jews in Pennsylvania are but few in number, yet liberty of the people in one country, and the declaration of the government thereof, that these liberties are the rights of the people, may prove a powerful attractive to men who live under restraints in another country. Holland and England have made valuable acquisitions of men, who, for their religious sentiments, were distressed in their own countries.

And if Jews in Europe or elsewhere should incline to transport themselves to America, and would, for reason of some certain advantage of the soil, climate, or the trade of Pennsylvania, rather become inhabitants thereof, than of any other state, yet the disability of Jews to take seat among the representatives of the people, as worded by the said religious test, might determine their free choice to go to New-York, or to any other of the United States of America, where there is no such like restraint laid upon the nation and religion of the Jews, as in Pennsylvania.

Your memorialists cannot say that the Jews are particularly fond of being representatives of the people in assembly or civil officers and magistrates in the state, but with great submission they apprehend that a clause in the constitution, which disables them to be elected by their fellow citizens to represent them in assembly, as [is] a stigma upon their nation and their religion, and it is inconsonant with the second paragraph of the said bill of rights. Otherwise, Jews are as fond of liberty as other religious societies can be, and it must create in them a displeasure when they perceive that for their professed dissent to a doctrine, which is inconsistent with their religious sentiments, they should be excluded from the most important and honourable part of the rights of a free citizen.

Your memorialists beg farther leave to represent that in the religious books of the Jews, which are or may be in every man's hands, there are no such doctrines or principles established as are inconsistent with the safety and happiness of the people of Pennsylvania, and that the conduct and behaviour of the Jews in this and the neighbouring states, has always tallied with the great design of the Revolution; [they beg farther leave to represent] that the Jews of Charlestown, New-York, New-Port, and other posts occupied by the British troops, have distinguishedly suffered for their attachment to the Revolution principles; and their brethren at St. Eustatius, for the same cause, experienced the most severe resentments of the British commanders.

The Jews of Pennsylvania, in proportion to the number of their members, can count with any religious society whatsoever the Whigs [the patriots] among either of them. They have served some of them in the Continental army; some went out in the militia to fight the common enemy; all of them have chearfully contributed to the support of the militia and of the government of this state.

They have no inconsiderable property in lands and tenements, but particularly in the way of trade, some more, some less, for which they pay taxes. They have, upon every plan formed for public utility, been forward to contribute as much as their circumstances would admit of, and as a nation or a religious society, they stand unimpeached of any matter whatsoever against the safety and happiness of the people.

And your memorialists humbly pray that if your honours, from any other consideration than the subject of this address, should think proper to call a convention for revising the constitution, you would be pleased to recommend this to the notice of that convention.[35]

The memorial reflects almost every nuance of apologetics which the modern Jew has employed in his search for a fuller life. In touching upon the philosophic bases of freedom, in stressing the political rights to which he was entitled, and in pointing to the economic advantages which the Jew brought to every country that had the wisdom to grant him the liberty he sought, the document is a classical example of similar memorials in other lands.

When this memorial was read by the Censors it was ordered to be laid on the table, and was forgotten—for the time. Yet there were some who recognized the reactionary nature of the disability. A correspondent who commented on this memorial in *The Freeman's Journal* of January 21, 1784, said "that he could wish, as a friend to the state of Pennsylvania, and as a friend to Christianity, that the religious test that should be required before the admission to any office whatever in the commonwealth, were, what the declaration of rights avows to be sufficient, simply this, 'I believe in one God, the creator and governor of the universe, the rewarder of the good and the punisher of the wicked.' " Continuing, the correspondent wrote that "he conceives that this abridgment of our religious test would be attended with the most beneficial consequences. It would benefit the state, by inviting hither a great number of Jews, who for their wealth, their information, and their attachment to the cause of liberty, might be of extensive and permanent service. It would tend to the propagation of Christianity by impressing the minds of the Jews, from this generous treatment, with sentiments in favour of the gospel, etc."

Protests of this type were not without influence. Although in general a much more conservative attitude was reflected in the new constitution of 1790, in one respect at least it was more liberal. The disability against Jews was removed, and it was now declared "that no person, who acknowledges the being of a God and a future state of rewards and punishments, shall, on account of his religious sentiments, be disqualified to hold any office or place of trust or profit under this commonwealth."

Salomon and his associates had made their appeal on behalf of the Jews of Pennsylvania, yet all these signers, with the exception of Barnard Gratz, the Philadelphian, eventually returned to their home, New York, or prepared to move there.

In the spring of 1784 Salomon bought a house at the corner of Wall and Pearl Streets, New York. He formed, with Jacob Mordecai, a partnership which advertised that they would open an auction house, receive merchandise and wares for sale on commission, and act as brokers to buy and sell commercial paper and bank stocks.

Salomon seemed at the peak of his powers, a relatively young man of forty-four, with a young wife and an increasing brood, but his health was poor. He made final provisions for his aged parents: he sent his mother a gold chain, and for his father back in Poland he purchased denization rights and a burial plot.

Several months later *The Pennsylvania Packet* of Philadelphia carried the following simple notice on January 11, 1785: "Thursday last, expired, after a lingering illness, Mr. Haym Salomons, an eminent broker of this city; he was a native of Poland, and of the Hebrew nation. He was remarkable for his skill and integrity in his profession, and for his generous and humane deportment. His remains were on Friday last deposited in the burial ground of the synagogue, in this city." Four children, all under seven, and a young widow remained behind to mourn him.

We can now revert to the original question. Several years after the death of Max Kohler a monument was finally erected to the memory of Salomon, not in New York, but in Chicago. Did Salomon merit the monument, as the Federation of Polish Jews contends? Or was Kohler right?

The *Dictionary of American Biography* informs us that Salomon either gave or lent to the government and to its servants sums aggregating almost $700,000 which were never repaid. Yet the facts are—Kohler demonstrated this in his *Haym Salomon, the Patriot Broker of the Revolution* —that he did not lend or give the government sums of such size. Indeed, he never had them to give away; he could not have had them, for by his own admission he landed in Philadelphia in 1778 without any money. It was not until 1782 that he was again back on his feet and able to send some money to his impoverished family in Eastern Europe. It would have been impossible for him to have made such fabulous sums in four years; had he done so, he would have been the richest man in America, and there is no real evidence to prove that he ever possessed substantial wealth.

Salomon himself, moreover, never made the claim that the government owed him huge sums. It was the son who did so, many decades after the father's death. While it is a fact that the extant records show that Salomon paid the government, through Morris, large sums of money, those sums were for drafts and bills which were sent by the French, Dutch, Spanish, and others to the United States and turned over to Morris for negotiation and sale. Salomon sold these bills, deposited the money initially to his own account in the bank, and then turned it over to Morris and the government. He was an agent; the money only passed through his hands. It was all government money, not his own. Later generations, either deliberately or unwittingly, chose to believe that his own money was handed over, because the records showed that it was originally deposited in his name.

Why, then, a monument to this man? If it is understood that Salomon is a symbol of the participation of the American Jew in the struggle for independence, then he merits the memorial. The American Revolution was a "Battle of the Nations" for freedom: English, Scots, Irish, Germans, Dutch, and a host of others . . . the "huddled masses yearning to breathe free, the wretched refuse . . . the homeless, tempest-tost." All these groups have helped build America, and monuments have been erected to representative leaders of the ethnic elements, to individuals like Kosciusko and Pulaski.

Salomon did a craftsman's job for Robert Morris. He was without doubt the most competent bill broker in America—and an honorable man. We have every reason to believe that his work met with the unreserved approval of the French, the Dutch, and the Spanish. Of course he received his commissions. But Robert Morris was paid, too; while Superintendent of Finance he carried on a thriving private business and emerged an even richer man than when he started.

When Salomon died—in the midst of a severe postwar depression—he left a modest estate, but his obligations swallowed it up. He died insolvent. Merchants who found it difficult to pay were indebted to him for considerable sums. He made himself personally liable, through his own signature, for many of the drafts and bills of exchange which he handled on behalf of the government. And when these bills were not honored, he accepted liability without protest. This may have ruined him. Practically all of his estate was assigned to his chief creditor: the Bank of North America, Morris' bank.

At the risk of his own life—in New York, from 1776 to 1778—he helped French and American prisoners to escape; he induced Hessians to desert; he went to prison for his patriotism when he could well have made his peace and fortune with the English in New York; he fled from his home and left behind him wife and infant; he floated securities to the amount of $200,000; he helped keep Madison and others in Congress by lending them money without charge; he fought for political and religious liberty in Pennsylvania; and he gave liberally, munificently, that his fellow-Jews might worship the God of their fathers in dignity and devotion in a synagogue of their own.

He was Colonial America at its best. As a symbol and as a man he merits not only the respect and the affection of this generation, but also the monument which his admirers built to do him honor.

ROBERT MORRIS · GEORGE WASHINGTON · HAYM SALOMON

★ ★ ★

THE GOVERNMENT OF THE UNITED STATES
WHICH GIVES TO BIGOTRY NO SANCTION TO PERSECUTION
NO ASSISTANCE REQUIRES ONLY THAT THEY WHO LIVE UNDER
ITS PROTECTION SHOULD DEMEAN THEMSELVES AS GOOD CITIZENS
IN GIVING IT ON ALL OCCASIONS THEIR EFFECTUAL SUPPORT
PRESIDENT GEORGE WASHINGTON 1790

★ ★ ★

Photo by Ewing Galloway, N.Y.

THE HAYM SALOMON MONUMENT IN CHICAGO

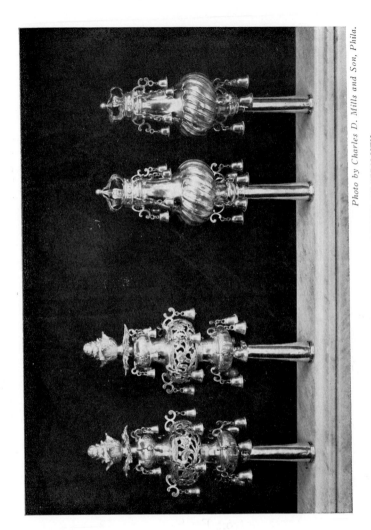

Photo by Charles D. Mills and Son, Phila.

RELIGIOUS ORNAMENTS BY MYER MYERS, SILVERSMITH
IN MIKVEH ISRAEL SYNAGOGUE, PHILADELPHIA

Chapter 9

Virginia, 1658 – 1786

AT first glance it seems very strange that Virginia, the oldest and most populous colony and state in the Union in the eighteenth century, was the last to witness the establishment of an organized Jewish community. Economic, political, and religious factors provide the answer.

Individual Jews, of course, were always moving in and out of the colony on business ventures. For example, David Ferera of New Amsterdam imported Virginia leaf tobacco as early as 1658, the very year that one Moses Nehemiah, Virginia's first known Jew, was engaged in litigation at the York County courthouse. (Nehemiah may have been from Barbados.)

There were a number of Spaniards or Portuguese who were resident in the colony in the seventeenth century, and, in all probability, some of these were Marranos or crypto-Jews who had fled there from Europe or South America to escape the forces of the Inquisition. Yet, as far as we know, they did not live as Jews. Many of the Marranos who must have come to America's shores in the seventeenth century had no Jewish sympathies. Only too often they had fled from the Iberian peninsula not because they wished to live as Jews, but to escape the prying of the Inquisition over-zealous in its searching out of heretical infractions. Christian descendants of Jews were only too frequently tortured by the Holy Office till they confessed, often falsely, to the practice of Jewish ceremonies. Flight to a foreign country gave them a fair chance to live unmolested as Christians.

But no permanent Jewish communal life could be established in Virginia in the early or middle eighteenth century, because there were no towns of any size, no vigorous independent urban middle class. The large plantation owners dominated the colony politically, socially, and economically. Much of what they needed in the way of goods they bought directly from factors and merchants in England, thereby eliminating the services of the small-capital middlemen who could not afford to extend them the long-term credits which they required and demanded.

In the seventeenth century, in Virginia, individuals were naturalized after rendering the usual oaths. Practicing Jews who would not profess faith in Jesus the son of God, or who would not take the sacrament, were thus ineligible for citizenship and office. A law of 1705 specifically excluded non-Christians, together with Negroes, Catholics, and convicts, from testifying as witnesses in court.

There were, seemingly, no specific laws which denied suffrage to Jews as such as long as they met the financial requirements for the franchise. In actual practice, however, it is doubtful that Jews voted or even applied for denization or naturalization in the pre-Revolutionary period.

The temper of the times is reflected in a petition of a group of men who wished to settle a colony of Swiss and German Protestants in the western part of Virginia in 1730. The new colony was to be called "Georgia." Like the later Georgia to the South, it was designed to serve as a barrier against the encroachment of the enemy, in this case the competing French of Canada. Representations were made that such a colony would supply raw materials for England: hemp, flax, silk, potash, wines, and, above all, furs. In return, the colonists would take large quantities of coarse English woolens to be used in trade with the Indians.

The petitioners asked for "unlimited liberty of conscience" for "the publick profession of all religions, excepting heathenism, Jews, and papists who are to be utterly disqualified and for ever excluded from holding any office of trust or profit in that province." At this time the petitioners themselves would have been denied religious liberty in some of the eastern counties of Virginia! The colony was never established.

Denial of the Trinity deprived "offenders" of their civil rights and could even subject them, ultimately, to imprisonment. In 1753, if not later, Virginia forbade Jews to employ Christian servants. Anti-Catholic Virginia did not hesitate to coincide, in this last prohibition, with medieval Catholic law.

If the Parliamentary Naturalization Act of 1740 had been followed in Virginia, Jews could have been naturalized there as they were in some of the other colonies, but there is no record that any Virginia Jew took advantage of the terms of this English statute. Nor is there any evidence that any professing Jew was naturalized or given letters patent of denization by the House of Burgesses or the governor.

Furthermore, if he had applied for those privileges, it is probable that his petition would have been rejected. The Church of England was securely entrenched and closely integrated with the civil authority. For the political leaders there was only one true church, the Church of England, and the Church-State autocrats could not tolerate, let alone encourage, the idea of political equality for Jewish infidels.

The colony was unsympathetic to non-Anglicans. Under the "establishment," Jews as well as Christians were taxed for the support of the Anglican Church. Attendance at Anglican religious services was compulsory. Whether individual Jews in the pre-Revolutionary period were mulcted for non-attendance is difficult to determine. Christian Dissenters were frequently persecuted. Non-Anglican Christian clergymen were, on occasion, not even allowed to speak or write on matters religious. Some two and a half years before the Declaration of Independence, Baptist ministers—unlicensed clergymen—were beaten and sent to jail for "disturbing the peace," that is, for preaching the word of God as they understood it.

It is therefore hardly likely, in a colony where almost every Protestant Dissenter had to fight for toleration, that Jews would be encouraged to come in and would receive religious and political privileges. The handful who did enter in the third quarter of the century were ignored because they were few and because of their "low visibility."

Liberal Virginians were quite conscious that the prevailing economic, religious, and political disabilities were injurious to the colony. As late as 1774, James Madison wrote to William Bradford, Jr., of Pennsylvania:

> You are happy in dwelling in a land where those inestimable privileges [of religious liberty] are fully enjoyed; and the public has long felt the good effects of this religious as well as civil liberty.
>
> Foreigners have been encouraged to settle among you. Industry and virtue have been promoted by mutual emulation and mutual inspection; commerce and the arts have flourished; and I cannot help attributing those continual exertions of genius which appear among you to the inspiration of liberty, and that love of fame and knowledge which always accompany it.
>
> Religious bondage shackles and debilitates the mind, and unfits it for every noble enterprise, every expanded prospect.

Nevertheless, after the middle of the eighteenth century more and more Jewish merchants, artisans, silversmiths, watchmakers, chandlers, and fur traders landed on the coast, sailed up the tidewater streams, or wandered south along the main highway from Baltimore, or down the Shenandoah from Lancaster. Ever alert to economic opportunity, they could not afford to ignore Virginia, the largest of all the colonies.

It was only natural that the far-ranging Aaron Lopez of Rhode Island should dispatch an agent to Virginia, in the days before the Revolution, to sell a load of goods for him. The man whom he employed was Enoch Lyon, who, like many other Jews, had come to the colonies during the days of the French and Indian War, or shortly thereafter. For

a time he had lived with Lopez and, no doubt, worked for
him too. Like many young men who were clerks, he engaged in ventures on his own account. His father-in-law
back in London made arrangements to send him about
£200 worth of goods on credit, and another London
merchant, without even consulting him, consigned another
£200 worth of merchandise to him.

Apparently he was doing well. At least he felt he was,
for he gave some beautiful brass lamps to the new synagogue in Newport. They are still there today, proudly
bearing his name in Hebrew, "the young man Hanok ben
Joseph," and in English, "Enoch Lyon." Though the adjective "young man" in Hebrew usually implies that he was
not married, we know he had a wife in London. What happened to her, and why he apparently remained for so many
years in the colonies without her are questions without answers. The sad lot of the wife of the itinerant merchant is
a theme that runs all through Jewish history.

By 1767 Lyon was being persistently dunned for the
goods which he had bought years before, and paid for only
with fair promises. But Lopez intervened on his behalf;
Lyon, he pointed out, had not solicited the last batch of
goods—a load of unmarketable expensive hardware—and
had barely managed to get rid of it on a long-term credit
sale, to be paid, when due, in West India goods. Lyon was
honest, a "young beginner. . . . Use him with all the tenderness you can in settling this matter." We do not know
whether those debts were ever settled. We do know that
the young merchant was still in the country doing business
in Newport and Philadelphia in the days of the Revolution.

While in the former city, in 1772, he called on the Reverend Ezra Stiles one Saturday night and spent four hours talking theology with the convert-hunting Congregationalist pastor. Jesus, said Stiles, was the suffering Messiah foretold in the fifty-third chapter of Isaiah. He had died for the sins of mankind. Yes, admitted Lyon, Jesus was a holy and good man and his teachings were also fine, but there was no need for him to die on the cross to expiate the sins of the world. God, he argued, was infinitely merciful and did not require any vicarious atonement for the sins of mankind. The good-natured disputation between the Jew and the Christian preacher took place in the month of February.

Three months later Lyon was carrying on a disputation of a different nature with his Jewish former patron. It was not on theology, and it was anything but friendly. Lopez had taken possession of a ship owned by Lyon—apparently for a debt—and the former clerk had threatened suit unless the matter were submitted to arbitration.

But squalls such as these blew over quickly in the small circle of Jewish businessmen. They were too few to stay angry for any great length of time. They could ill afford the luxury of unending feuds. About two and a half years later, Lyon was once more working for his old employer—this time in Virginia—as the following letter indicates:

Philadelphia, Octo. 18th, 1774.

Mr. Aaron Lopez,
Kind Sir:

When I arriv'd at Virginia the wheather was so extream hot that the people could not relish cordials so well as rum. Nevertheless I have sold about sixteen gallons of your clove at 4

shillings, 6 pence p. gallo. Now the cold wheather is coming on.
I expect on my return to Virg'a to dispose of the remainder
quickly, and when I have finish'd the sales I shall remitt you
the neat proceeds in cash by the first good opportunity. I am

> With the greatest respect, sir,
> Your very hb'l serv't,
> Enoch Lyon.

P.S. I hope Mrs. Lopez and your whole family enjoy a perfect
state of health, to whom please, sir, to give my best respects.

I shall be oblig'd to tarry here about three weeks before I
can return. If you should have any commands, please to direct
for me at [the tavern of] Mr. Israel Jacobs in Third Street.[36]

Apparently he settled down in Virginia permanently.
There was an Enoch Lyon in Gloucester County as late as
1790. If this is our man—and it may well be—he was unmarried, living isolated from all contacts with fellow-Jews.

The business done by Enoch Lyon in Virginia was inconsequential compared with that of the Simon-Bush-Gratz
clan. These men had interests in Virginia and visited the
colony often. At times they operated on their own account,
as individuals. At times two or more of them were partners.
Not infrequently the Gratz Brothers—like Joseph Simon—
worked through Gentile partners in Western Pennsylvania,
in Virginia, and in the West, as far as the Mississippi River.
The Gentiles carried on the business locally; the Jews, in
metropolitan Philadelphia, supplied the credits and the
goods. The Gratzes had correspondents in most of
the towns of Virginia: in Norfolk, on the coast, and, in
the interior, in Dumfries, Fredericksburg, Williamsburg,
Richmond, Petersburg, and Winchester.

Since 1760 Simon and his associates had brought furs up through the Shenandoah from the Old Southwest. Simon and Campbell—one of his concerns—acted as an agent for Virginia during Lord Dunmore's War (1774), and the firm advanced money and supplies for repairing Fort Pitt and for building Fort Fincastle, later to become Fort Henry, the site of present-day Wheeling.

Speculations in Virginia lands occupied the attention of the Philadelphia and Lancaster Jewish merchants down to their last day. Much of the land in which they were interested in the area south of the Ohio was claimed by Virginia. Like the Washington family and many others, Barnard Gratz sank money in the Dismal Swamp.

When the Revolution was over the Gratzes marketed Virginia land warrants in Pennsylvania and in the Northern states for their partners in the Old Dominion who had bought up the certificates. One deal alone with land-office warrants involved 81,000 acres. Virginia, watching the New Englanders settling in the North-of-the-Ohio region, was eager to encourage settlement on its own lands on the southern side of the river.

It was during the Revolution, however, that Simon and the Gratzes were most active in Virginia. Simon, as we have seen, was busy providing for the British imprisoned in the Virginia towns, working, as was his wont, through sub-agents. The Philadelphia merchants freighted goods, financed and shipped hemp and tobacco crops, and bought and sold all types of merchandise. Using small shallow draft vessels, the Gratzes sent goods down from Philadelphia and up the Virginia rivers, bringing out tobacco in payment.

Some of this tobacco they processed in a Philadelphia snuff mill in which they were interested. Michael Gratz speculated with Carter Braxton and other Virginians in privateering and, it would seem, lost money.

Virginia was a state without sufficient manufactories. It was badly in need of arms, clothing, shoes, and other supplies which could not easily be imported because of the British blockade. It was because of these circumstances that men like the Gratzes were employed by the state as purchasing agents, for occasionally they succeeded in running the blockade with a load of goods from the West Indies.

Operating through Gratz and Gibson, a Fort Pitt branch, the Philadelphians helped outfit an abortive Virginia expedition for George Rogers Clark in 1781. The latter had captured the towns of Kaskaskia, Cahokia, and Vincennes in 1778–79, thus securing the Northwest territory for the United States. To insure his victory, however, and to protect the Virginia frontier (Kentucky) from a threatened raid by the British and the Indians, it was necessary also to take Detroit and, if possible, Michilimackinac. Capture of these two towns would not only protect the new conquest but would also threaten Canada, lost to the Continental Congress in the unhappy campaign of Benedict Arnold and Richard Montgomery in 1775–76. But nothing came of Clark's proposed expedition against Detroit in that year, 1779.

The historic dash of George Rogers Clark which had resulted in the conquest of the Illinois territory had been financed in part by the issue of bills of exchange, some of which were put up for sale in the New Orleans market.

Unfortunately, since Virginia could not ship tobacco or other commodities to New Orleans to meet its obligations, the bills and drafts which George Rogers Clark and his associates issued were not honored, and the state's credit in that town was shattered. In the meantime the Havana merchant Simon Nathan—the ancestor of the well-known American Nathan clan—bought about $50,000 worth of these New Orleans bills. He purchased them very likely for speculative purposes. When they remained unhonored, Nathan went to court to recover his money, and for this reason—and because of other financial difficulties with the state—he was involved in litigation for over a decade.

In 1781, General Washington, Governor Thomas Jefferson of Virginia, and Clark were still interested in an expedition against Detroit. The motives were still the same as in 1779. In addition, there was the realization that success would add new domains to the "Empire of Liberty" and would divert the coveted western fur trade from Canada to the American states.

The expedition was to start in June. Clark, as we saw, turned to Gratz and Gibson at Fort Pitt for supplies. Though Virginia had not authorized any expenditures, the Fort Pitt firm supplied the necessary goods, taking the personal bond of the General and his adjutant, Colonel Dorsey Pentecost, as a guarantee of payment. But without money or credit, fearful of the British invaders in the tidewater and of the Tories on the border, the Virginia Assembly finally ordered Clark to move south of the Ohio. There was to be no march against Detroit.

Two years later the accounts of Gratz and Gibson were

still unpaid, and Michael Gratz sent the following petition
to the Virginia authorities:

The Honorable, the Speaker, and Gentlemen of the House of
Delegates:

The memorial of Michael Gratz of Philadelphia humbly
sheweth that your memorialist had been concerned for several
years past in trade with a certain John Gibson, and in the
course of their dealings, and particularly at Fort Pitt, your
memorialist, at the special instance of Brigadier General
George Rogers Clarke, did furnish, on account of the State of
Virginia, sundry merchandizes and other things to the amount
of £1,425.16.9 specie, for which said sum of £1,425.16.9 a
bond was obtained from General Clarke and Dorsay Penticost,
payable in three months after date.

At the same time, General Clarke wrote a letter to the executive of the state, in which he informed them that he had
made a purchase of goods from John Gibson at Fort Pitt, composed of such articles as were absolutely and indispensably
necessary to further his designs in the Western Country—
being then on an expedition—and requested that speedy pai-
ment might be made, as well for his bond granted to John
Gibson as aforesaid, as [for] the said Gibson's expenses in
negotiating this business.

Your memorialist is much concerned when he informs your
Honorable House that notwithstanding several years has
elapsed since the first transaction of this matter, and application having been made a considerable time past without receiving any kind of payment, he therefore most humbly prays
that your Honorable House will be pleased to direct that his
demand may be recognized, and provision made for the discharge thereof as will relieve your memorialist from the em-
barrassments which he is at present under for the want of this
money.

Your memorialist wishes only to share with other creditors

of the State of Virginia, but when he reflects on the principles which primarily governed him in this matter, and the attention he has at all times paid to the Virginia officers on public business, he is induced to hope his demand will meet with an immediate payment. And your memorialist, as in duty bound, will pray, etc.

Michael Gratz.

May 17, 1783.[37]

The Gratzes and their partner had no desire to be reimbursed by forcing Clark and Pentecost to pay. Fortunately, the firm's demands were deemed "reasonable," and in 1784 they were paid in full with interest at six per cent. The payment was in tobacco, and the partners probably lost money on the deal.

In that same decade the Gratz brothers were thinking seriously of opening stores in Richmond, Williamsburg, and Norfolk. Obviously, their prime motivation for the proposed extension of their business was to take advantage of the growing economic opportunities in Virginia. Less obvious, but probably not unimportant, was the realization that the rapidly expanding political, civil, and religious rights and liberties were broad enough to include even the Jews.

The first significant change in Virginia was made on June 12, 1776, when the colonial House of Burgesses adopted a bill of rights almost a month before the promulgation of the Declaration of Independence. The Virginia Bill of Rights declared (section one) "That all men are by nature equally free and independent, and have certain inherent rights . . .: namely, the enjoyment of life and liberty, with the means of acquiring and possessing property, and pursuing and obtaining happiness and safety." Section sixteen affirmed "That religion, or the duty which we owe to our Creator, and the manner of discharging it, can be directed only by reason and conviction, not by force or violence; and therefore all men are equally entitled to the free exercise of religion, according to the dictates of conscience; and that it is the mutual duty of all to practise Christian forbearance, love, and charity towards each other."

This bill of rights was incorporated into the state constitution on June 29, 1776. In effect, however, it was little more than a pious wish. It abolished no disabilities applicable to Christian Dissenters or to Jewish and Moslem infidels. Nor did the state constitution itself make provision for the abolition of current disabilities. That the House intended to continue withholding rights and citizenship from Catholics, certain Protestants, and Jews was grimly documented, in the fall of 1776, by the fate of a naturalization bill. This proposed law, as revised by Thomas Jefferson, encouraged the immigration and naturalization of the above religious groups. The great Virginian stressed the physical advantages which such settlers would bring to the state, spoke of their high moral qualities, and expressed his belief that Jews would make good citizens, but all to no avail. The bill never came up for a vote. The Anglican Church remained the only legalized religion in the state. Jews, and certain others, were not permitted to perform marriages until 1784.

Nevertheless, the vigorous efforts of the Dissenters and

the genius of George Mason, Jefferson, and Madison did much to transmute into law the spirit and intent of the Bill of Rights. Within a few years after the adoption of the constitution, Dissenters and Jews were exempted from paying taxes to the established church, and the penalties for divergence from the old state religion were abolished.

But there was still another obstacle to be hurdled. Many of the Dissenters, now that the Anglican Church had been disestablished, were eager to have Christianity adopted—and supported!—as the state religion. This produced the "general assessment plan" which, if accepted, would, as Beverley Randolph wrote to James Monroe (1784), "mean that Turks, Jews, and infidels were to contribute to the support of a religion whose truth they did not acknowledge."

For a time it seemed that this plan to levy an annual tax for the support of the Christian denominations would pass. Patrick Henry was its impassioned protagonist. Washington was not disturbed by it, but hoped that if it passed, Jews and other non-Christians would not be subject to it. Madison was the spearhead of the fight to defeat the assessment, and in his famous *Memorial and Remonstrance* (1784) wrote that "the proposed establishment is a departure from that generous policy which offering an asylum to the persecuted and oppressed of every nation and religion, promised a luster to our country, and an accession to the number of its citizens." The Baptists and many of the Presbyterians were bitterly opposed to the plan. At a general assembly in August, 1785, the Presbyterians evidently had the Jews in mind when they stated that the assessment bill "unjustly subjects men who may be good citizens, but who have not

179

embraced our common faith, to the hardship of supporting a system they have not as yet believed the truth of; and deprives them of their property for what they do not suppose to be of importance to them [by taxing them for the benefit of Christian religious institutions]." That year the plan was finally defeated.

In 1786, Jefferson's Bill for Establishing Religious Freedom was adopted as law. This statute went a step further than the 1776 bill of rights by stating categorically "that no man shall be compelled to frequent or support any religious worship, place, or ministry whatsoever, nor shall be enforced, restrained, molested, or burthened in his body or goods, nor shall otherwise suffer on account of his religious opinions or belief; but that all men shall be free to profess and by argument to maintain their opinion in matters of religion, and that the same shall in no wise diminish, enlarge, or affect their civil capacities."

The opponents of this legislation died hard. A final attempt was made—so Jefferson said years later—to amend the preamble of the 1786 bill so as to identify "Almighty God . . . the Holy author of our religion," with Jesus Christ, but this failed.

It was the bill of 1786 which gave the Jews, among others, complete religious and political freedom by divorcing church and state. Yet even this was not the last word. In 1798–99, legislation was enacted formally repealing all existing laws in seeming contradiction with the intent of the constitution and the bill of rights. In 1802 all churches were given equality of rights. It had taken a generation to bring this measure of equality to the people of Virginia.

It has been suggested that Jefferson and Madison may have been influenced in their liberal attitude by the consciousness of their duty to their Jewish fellow-citizens whose patriotic devotion and economic contribution to the state and country, particularly during the war, entitled them to the rights of political and religious equality. This is very much to be doubted, for although Jefferson, Madison, and others had Jewish friends, and although these men were quite conscious of the fact that the religious liberties of the Jews had to be safeguarded, they did not fight this battle with one specific group in mind. The issue for them was fought out on the basis of principle and ideology.

The two acts of 1776 and 1786 at once assumed importance, not because of the two dozen or so Jewish families in Virginia, but because of the influence of these laws on the Declaration of Independence, on the first amendments to the Federal constitution, on the other state constitutions, and, above all, on the growing liberal sentiment in Europe soon to culminate in the French Revolution. Jefferson arranged for the wide dissemination in Europe of his version of the 1786 Act for Establishing Religious Freedom; it was soon translated into French and Italian, and in 1790, when the French Jews petitioned the National Assembly for political and religious liberty, they referred specifically to American precedents.

It was not until after the War of Independence that a real Virginia Jewish community, most of whose members lived in Richmond, began to emerge. It was a small group, but constantly growing.

One of the earliest settlers, if not the first, was Isaiah Isaacs, who came, no doubt, by way of England. A silversmith by trade, he was in the colony as early as 1769, for he was then being dunned for a debt by a London creditor.

It was probably sometime toward the end of the war that he entered into partnership with Jacob I. Cohen, and the firm of Cohen and Isaacs soon became the largest Jewish business house in town. Their interests were varied; they were primarily merchants, but the firm also owned land, houses, and slaves. One of their buildings was the tavern Bird in Hand, one of the oldest in town. Years later, when the firm dissolved partnership (1792), the agreement in Yiddish, dividing the firm's holdings, assigned this tavern to Isaacs. In addition, both Cohen and Isaacs had property in their individual names. The latter possessed lands in a half-dozen counties and also speculated in Dismal Swamp tracts.

Isaacs went into politics sometime before the 1786 Bill for Establishing Religious Freedom passed; he sought election to the Common Hall (Council). Obviously, the civil disabilities that then still obtained against Jews were disregarded in practice. Though not elected to the office, he was appointed Clerk of the Market that year (1785); later he became a tax assessor and a councilman.

Apparently he was married at least twice. His first wife, it would seem, was a Gentile. Intermarriage was almost a rule for the individual settler in the back country. His second wife, Hetty Hays, was a Jewess, a member of the well-known New York family of that name, whom he must have met on a business trip to New York after his first wife died. He kept in touch with the eastern communities, and when the Philadelphia synagogue was built in 1782 he made a very substantial contribution. In his will he asked that his children—two of them may have been by his first wife—be given a good education that they might become useful citizens. In spite of the fact that he had lived for years as probably the only Jew in a Christian community, he retained a strong attachment to Judaism. This loyalty to his faith was reflected in his last testament, in his request that his orphaned children—his second wife had also predeceased him—be brought up in good Jewish homes.

Isaacs had little facility in the use of English, or else, for reasons best known to him, he preferred signing his name and writing important documents in the Hebrew script. But the extent of a man's Americanization cannot be gauged by his ability or inability to handle the Latin script or the English language. Witness the will of this Virginian who made provision for the emancipation of his slaves in the following phrases redolent of the spirit of the great Virginians of his generation:

Being of opinion that all men are by nature equally free, and being possessed of some of those beings who are unfortunate, doomed to slavery, as to them I must enjoin upon my executor a strict observance of the following clause in my will. My slaves hereafter named are to be and they are hereby manumeted and made free, so that after the different periods hereafter mentioned they shall enjoy all the privileges and immunities of freed people. . . . Each one of my slaves is to receive the value of twenty dollars in clothing on the days of their manumission.

183

When Isaacs died after the turn of the century, his former partner, Cohen, was appointed one of the executors of the estate.

It is somewhat confusing that in the 1780's, when there were probably not more than two dozen Jews in the whole state, there were three Jacob Cohens. One was a cavalry officer who had served through part of the war as captain of a troop of state militia. That Cohen came from Cumberland County. Jacob Cohen, number two, was a silversmith living in Alexandria, in Fairfax County. These two Cohens had married Christian women and reared their children as Gentiles. We are not even sure that the two were born Jews.

Jacob Cohen, number three, had come to the colonies from Germany about two years before the Revolution and settled in Lancaster. With this town as his home station, he set out to trade with the Indians. During the war he drifted south to Charlestown, probably after a brief stay in Richmond. In Charlestown he joined Captain Lushington's militia company into which many of the Jewish merchants of King Street were conscripted. He fought at Beaufort, South Carolina, in 1779, under General Moultrie and, it would seem, was back in Richmond no later than 1781.

Like other merchants from the North, he may have decided to settle in Virginia permanently because its chief commodity, tobacco, offered a stable medium of exchange during the inflation of the 1780's.

Cohen and Isaacs formed their partnership about the year 1781. The following May, 1782, Cohen applied formally for membership in the Philadelphia synagogue. The fact that he spent a considerable part of that year in the Pennsylvania capital leads us to believe that he was a resident buyer for the new firm. In June, the thirty-eight-year-old merchant turned to President Isaac Moses of that synagogue, asking that arrangements be made for his marriage to Esther (Hester) Mordecai.

The ostensibly simple request was the beginning of what was to become a *cause célèbre*. Mrs. Mordecai was the widow of Moses Mordecai who had died the preceding year leaving three sons—and, it would appear, little money. She was, probably, the same Mrs. Mordecai who had applied to the congregation in May for help to pay her rent, and had received a grant of £9. Her poverty, of course, was no bar to the marriage, but there was a problem. The bride had been Miss Elizabeth Whitlock, a Christian, before she became a convert and married Mordecai. Cohen, as his name plainly indicates, was a *kohen*, a "priest," and, according to rabbinic law, a priest was forbidden to marry a proselyte. Cohen's proposed marriage was thus obviously improper, but the congregation, after a preliminary squabble over the membership of the legal committee which was to consider the problem, asked Cohen to make a formal application in writing.

Even though the Jewish law in the matter was plain, the decision of the congregation was not easy. The legal battle, we suspect, was not fought on its merits alone, but also on personalities. There were only five board members involved, but they were probably split into cliques, with personal grudges to be satisfied; and certainly the crisscross of business rivalries complicated the issue. The Gratzes and Simon Nathan had interests in Virginia; Benjamin Seixas' brother, Abraham, had soldiered with Cohen in South Carolina; and there was the usual extremist in the congregation who stubbornly insisted on a literal interpretation of the law. A decision had to be made. Pressed by Cohen, "Rabbi" Gershom M. Seixas wrote to the *junta* for permission to officiate, for in a Sephardic congregation the marrying official was always expected to ask for authorization if there was the least question of ritual legality.

The board finally decided, on August 25th, after a busy meeting both in the morning and in the afternoon, to send the following letter to the *hazzan:*

Sir:

In answer to your letter of the 24th of August, we now inform you that you are not to marry Mr. Jacob Cohen to Mrs. Mordecai. Neither are you to be present at the wedding, and you are hereby strictly forbid to mention the said Cohen or his wife's name in any respect whatsoever in the synagogue.

We are,
Your very humble servants,
Isaac Moses, Barnard Gratz, Jonas Phillips,
Benjamin Seixas, Simon Nathan.[38]

In effect, this letter ordered the imposition of a mild form of the traditional ban, if the couple married. The board also took action to inform the congregation that it would punish anyone who performed the marriage or was present at the wedding ceremony.

Cohen's answer was to marry the Widow Mordecai—who officiated is not known to us—and from all indications their marriage was a very happy one. It was not blessed with children, for neither was young. Twenty-eight years later, Cohen, by then a wealthy citizen of Philadelphia, became the president of Mikveh Israel. Time and circumstance often play strange tricks on congregations!

But we are running ahead of our story. In September, 1782, Cohen received a call in Philadelphia from "a necessitous delegate" from Virginia who was "relapsing fast into distress," financially. The man, as we have seen once before, was James Madison, who now received a loan of £50 from Cohen. Madison, in payment, gave him an order for that amount in favor of Isaiah Isaacs in Richmond.

After the war, Cohen and Isaacs, like many others, did a brisk business in land warrants. In December, 1781, they hired Colonel Daniel Boone to locate some land for them, giving him £6 specie as advance payment. After Boone signed the receipt for the warrants and the cash, the document was filed among the firm's papers. As was customary in those days, a brief description of the contents was scrawled on the back. This endorsement was in Hebrew script, in excellent and typical American Yiddish: *Resit fun Kornel Bon far 10,000 agir lanit* ("Receipt of Colonel Boone for 10,000 acres land").

In 1783 or 1784 they again commissioned the Colonel to survey lands for them, this time on the Licking River in Kentucky, just a few miles south of present-day Cincinnati. Boone did the job and presented his bill for a little over £22. "Send the money by the first opertunety," he wrote. "Mr. Samuel Grant, my sister's sun, will lykly hand you this later. If so, he will be a good hand to send by, and I will bee acountable for any money put into his hands inless kild by the Indins."

One of the two witnesses to a Yiddish document dissolving the partnership of Cohen & Isaacs was Marcus Elcan. A man of twenty-five, in 1782 he was already well settled in Richmond.

Young Elcan had come from Central Europe, probably from Warburg, in Westphalia. Somehow or other he had managed to acquire a knowledge and appreciation of European languages and literatures. Had he remained in the Prussia of Frederick the Great he would, at best, have been a second-class citizen, resentful of his Gentile neighbors who in turn would have looked askance at him. In freer America, in Virginia, he became a highly respected, cooperative citizen. In his will, written in 1805, he gave $1,000 as an endowment for the Richmond Charity School, and left his library, as a token of his esteem, to one of his executors—Joseph Marx, a German Jewish compatriot. This was quite a gift, for it contained many fine works. It is strange, though, that among the almost two hundred volumes listed by name there was no Hebrew Bible. To be sure, the executors may have made their task easy for themselves by including all Hebrew books among the twenty-one "odd volumes."

It is worthy of comment that in the Richmond of early post-Revolutionary days—a town of about 2,000 people, half of whom were slaves—at least three of the ten Jewish householders were men of culture. These three, Marcus Elcan and his two friends, Jacob Mordecai and Joseph Marx, were all widely read in the theological and philosophical literature of the age, at home in the best of contemporary English and French writing. It is somewhat disturbing to our pat concept, that such culture as existed among early American Jews was to be found only in the larger Jewish communities on the coast, to discover men of genuine intellectual capacity in what was little more than a frontier shanty town in the early 1780's.

Chapter 10

Virginia, 1786 – 1789

ONE of the men mentioned before was Jacob Mordecai. He was the son of Moses Mordecai of Philadelphia and of Elizabeth Whitlock Mordecai. Jacob I. Cohen became his stepfather in 1782, and it may have been Cohen who sent the twenty-year-old businessman to Richmond that same year.

Jacob, a native of Philadelphia, had gone to Captain Stiles's school there and had received an excellent education from that severe disciplinarian, a former British naval officer who later threw in his lot with the colonials.

When the troubles with the British government became acute in 1774, young Jacob, an ardent patriot of twelve years of age, joined one of the many youthful military groups. He belonged to a company whose members wore fancy, colored hunting shirts, carried real arms, and made themselves useful and conspicuous by escorting the delegates to the First Continental Congress into the city that momentous September.

During the war young Mordecai worked as a clerk for David Franks, and it was at the latter's house that he saw

the thin and swarthy Major André, then a paroled prisoner.
Mordecai was not a successful businessman; the family jo-
cosely ascribed this to the fact that his mother had originally
been a Christian! He wandered about quite a bit—to New
York, for instance, where he formed a partnership with
Haym Salomon in 1784, and to three other places, including Richmond—before finally settling down, about the year
1792, in Warrenton, North Carolina, as a country merchant
and dealer in tobacco and grain. The Mordecais were one
of the few Jewish families, if not the only one, in that part
of the state.

The letters which Mordecai wrote reflect an acquaintance with literature, history, and theology certainly not
typical of the Jew of his generation. Influenced, in all
probability, by his very observant father, he was strongly
Jewish in his sympathies and in his religious practices. A
younger contemporary who knew him intimately said that
he was well-versed in Hebrew. This training, which he
must have received in the Jewish community of Philadelphia in the days before the Revolution, speaks well for
the congregational school or for the tutorial opportunities
available. Mordecai was very much interested in apologetics
and polemics. He was the author of an unpublished two-
volume work—the manuscript now in the American Jewish
Archives in Cincinnati—which demonstrated, to his satisfaction, the superiority of Judaism over Christianity.

Compensating, perhaps, for his own frequent failures as
a businessman, he devoted himself assiduously to the intellectual development of his children. He was determined

that they too should be well educated. His only real success in life, therefore, was the Female Academy in Warrenton, North Carolina, which he was one day to establish. He was always a student at heart.

At the age of twenty-two, Jacob married Judith Myers of New York, where he was living, engaged in the pursuit of commerce. By the winter of 1786 he was faced with financial difficulty and was compelled to make a settlement. Among those to whom he was indebted was Isaac Moses & Company, two members of which firm, Samuel and Moses Myers, were destined in a year to become Virginians.

Isaac Moses & Company, the American branch of the European house of Samuel & Moses Myers, was probably the largest Jewish mercantile business in the colonies during the days of the Revolution. It is questionable whether the operations even of David Franks during this period were as large.

There were three men in the firm: Isaac Moses, Samuel Myers, and Moses Myers. Isaac Moses, undoubtedly the chief, handled the American end in New York. Samuel and Moses Myers, with chief offices in Amsterdam, were in charge of European operations. All three were equally responsible for the debts incurred by the business as a whole. We have little positive evidence, but it seems fairly certain that the company was organized during the Revolution to run the British blockade via the West Indies, in order to supply the colonies with the foreign manufactures they so urgently needed. (Isaac Moses was a Whig; Samuel Myers may have been a tacit loyalist.) At first, during the war, the American office was in Philadelphia; the foreign offices were in Amsterdam, St. Eustatia, and, probably for a time, St. Thomas. The St. Eustatia office was closed, we may be sure, when this "rock" that "alone supported the infamous American rebellion" was captured by the British Admiral Rodney in February, 1781. (It was because of his knowledge of the West Indies that Samuel Myers was appointed that year Deputy Grand Inspector of Masonry for the Leeward Islands by his friend, Moses M. Hays.)

Moses Myers and Samuel Myers were native Americans, possibly of third or even fourth generation stock. They were not related. Samuel was the son of Myer Myers, the New York silversmith; Moses was the son of Hyam Myers, the New York and Canada trader. The two Myerses were close friends in spite of the formality that prevailed in their correspondence. Samuel was the older, and Moses deferred to him. The latter boarded with Samuel's married sister in New York, our Mrs. Jacob Mordecai.

The firm, like all others, was affected by post-war economic changes. The new American republic began to discover that independence from England was not an unmixed blessing. England treated the rival commercial state as a foreign power to which no favoritism was to be shown, and once the war was over, France and Spain, the former allies or friends of the United States, made few commercial concessions. All these states, and Portugal too, were in no hurry to sign treaties of commerce with a rival. The mercantilistic-minded countries of Europe wanted to sell to the Americans; they were not so eager to buy from them. As a matter of fact, they believed it necessary for their own welfare to impose restrictions on trade with the United States.

France and England both made it difficult for the Americans to do business, particularly in the West Indies. The British limited imports from America into the Islands, and even stipulated that those articles admitted had to be carried in British ships. Their merchants were forbidden to buy American-built vessels. Such restrictions were a severe blow to the country. The prosperity of New England and other sections of the country hinged on the traffic with the Islands.

Under the Articles of Confederation there was no effective union. "Each state," declared Article II, "retains its sovereignty, freedom, and independence." The power of Congress to impose commercial regulations was limited; it could not even levy taxes. Rivalry between some of the states was not uncommon. Each had its own system of customs and duties, and some even applied mutually discriminating tariffs. In the absence of close commercial integration, it was almost inevitable that economic, and ultimately political, anarchy should threaten the very existence of the new nation, affecting alike the farmers and the city folk, the merchants and the mechanics, the producers and the vendors.

Economic and financial distress was common in many parts of the country between 1783 and 1786. The decline of the West India and foreign trade limited the export market for American farm products. Their prices fell, yet taxes continued, and foreclosures increased. Families were dispossessed. A clamor arose for easy money, paper money.

The government, many believed, was responsible for the depression, and in Massachusetts aroused people, led by

Captain Daniel Shays, marched on the Springfield arsenal. There were similar agrarian uprisings in New Hampshire and in the back country of New York. The militia had to be called out to put down these revolts. The climax was reached in the winter and spring of 1786–87. "For my part," wrote Moses Myers to Samuel, "shou'd not be surpris'd at a civil war taking place on this continent. You will see by the papers the strides taken to overset [overthrow] gouvernment in eastern [New England] states which by and by will be a general case throughout."

The farmers, as we have said, were not the only ones affected. The merchant-shippers, as a class, suffered even more. Because of the trade regulations imposed by the unfriendly European powers, the American importers could not pay their obligations with exports to the West Indies. They were receiving little specie or good bills from that quarter to balance their accounts with their creditors in Europe. The local merchant was doing less and less business because the farmer, who could not sell, had no money to buy. Overstocked merchants, desperate for cash for current living expenses or to pay bills, began to sell their stocks below costs. Bankruptcy for farmers, merchants, and importers was inevitable. The protests against the bankruptcy laws became increasingly bitter: some said that the laws were too lenient; others said that they were too severe. It all depended on whose ox was being gored. Bankruptcies of great houses were ominously numerous. Only one man seemed secure beyond the ravages of even the most severe depression. Almost reverentially, Samuel Myers wrote the following paragraph to one of his creditors in Amsterdam (1785):

> Robert Morris is the richest man in America and the most enterprising. It is said, and with much truth, that during his officiating as Finincier [superintendent of finance] that he accumulated £100,000 cur'cy in cash. Indeed he has more at his command than most of the merchants colectively in the thirteen United States. He is much esteemed as a merchant and eaqually so as a man. His abilityes in trade are of the first rate, and he is much respected as a legislator.

Robert Morris survived the post-war depression to end up in a debtors' jail before the end of the century. One of the Winthrops of Boston, Samuel Wharton and James Wilson of Philadelphia, and hundreds of lesser lights were not so fortunate; their businesses were hard hit during the unsettled 1780's.

Isaac Moses and the Myerses were no different from anyone else. They ran into trouble right after the war, but made every effort to keep afloat. Through their New York office they continued to export tobacco, rice, lumber, grain, skins, furs, and naval stores. In exchange, operating out of Amsterdam—where they had devoted friends—they sent to America a large assortment of yard goods and textiles, gin, liquors, wines, glass and pottery, teas and spices.

The oriental products, such as tea, spices, and nankeen, they obtained from their Dutch friends, but after 1785, with the arrival of the first American ship direct from China, they realized that the day of Holland's advantage in that field was gone. Moses Myers, like a host of others, was thrilled by the arrival of the sloop "Experiment" from

China in 1787. This little eighty-ton boat, with only five men before the mast and a total of only eleven on board, had made the perilous trip from Canton with a valuable cargo in four months and twelve days. "This, I presume, was the boldest enterprize ever attempted from this country," he wrote.

But at least two years before American vessels began to tap the Chinese trade directly, S. & M. Myers in Amsterdam were already in money difficulties. They could not pay their Dutch and other creditors because their American debtors could not pay them. Consequently, when the Amsterdam people began to press for payment, the partners could not meet their obligations.

In July, 1783, Samuel Myers was in Paris and dined one evening with John Adams, but he was not in the French capital merely to pay homage to Adams or Franklin or Jay, the commissioners who were negotiating the peace with Great Britain. The American merchant was simply trying to save his firm by finding someone in Paris who would lend it £35,000 to £40,000. That sum was not available. The following year, in December, 1784, S. & M. Myers stopped payment; Isaac Moses & Company followed suit in April, 1785.

Assignees and trustees were set up in Amsterdam for S. & M. Myers; a similar body was constituted in New York for Isaac Moses & Company. The American trustees were Alexander Hamilton and two merchants. One was Daniel Ludlow, later destined to become the city's largest importer; the other was Nicholas Low, a merchant, and, later, a real-estate operator on a grand scale. Low had gotten his start, so a contemporary wrote, by clerking for Hayman Levy, and then started on his own, trading with the Indians with a hogshead of rum which Levy had supplied him.

The indebtedness of the firm amounted to somewhere between £150,000 and £160,000, New York currency, a sum which indicates that they were one of the great "houses" of American commerce. Some of their creditors were Jews; the majority by far were Gentiles. Among the former was the European firm of Mendes DaCosta, to which they owed £10,000. The partners expected to pay at least fifty per cent of their debts, and in order to help meet their obligations, they sold their surplus furniture and silver plate. Isaac Moses' plate alone totalled 445 ounces, a very sizeable amount.

In a misfortune of this type there are bound to be charges and countercharges, and, after the bankruptcy, there was indeed bad blood between the younger Myerses and the older Isaac Moses. The records as preserved—the letter books of Samuel and Moses Myers—tell only one side of the story.

According to these records Isaac Moses was a "damn'd villain." The Myerses claimed that he used the firm's money to buy some property for himself. It is now known that Isaac Moses purchased Tory estates as late as February, 1785, over two months after the Amsterdam house had stopped payment and less than two months before he himself was bankrupt! This item does not appear in the Myers' record of grievances. The real estate which Isaac Moses held in his own name was worth about £10,000. He surrendered it to the creditors on condition that all his debts, both personal and company, were to be thrown into the common pot with the others. His partners kicked like steers at this proposal, for evidently Isaac Moses' personal debts were huge. Yet they had no choice. Isaac had the property, and he could have secured relief for himself, as a bankrupt, through an act of the Assembly.

If we may accept the Myerses' estimate of themselves, as reflected in their correspondence, they did not lose their "good name" even after the trustees stepped in, and subsequent events support this contention. Their creditors continued to write to them and, what is far more convincing, to send them goods. "Our firm has been very unfortunate both here and there [Amsterdam]," wrote one of the Myerses, "but believe I may with safety assure you that our characters as men of honor remain unsullied, to preserve which ought to be the study of every man."

Only one firm sued them. But such was their standing in the New York community that the Sheriff, Marinus Willett, went out of his way to warn them. He passed by their store, and out of the corner of his mouth whispered that he had a writ which he would presently serve. This gesture gave them ample time to go out and get bail, and they never served a single day in a debtors' jail, certainly not for this failure.

Samuel Myers was in Europe during the greater part of 1785, trying to settle the firm's affairs. He returned in the fall to report on what he had done and to prod some of the customers into paying their debts. Here is one of the letters which he sent to Isaac de Jacob Mendes of Amsterdam, a creditor:

New York, December 5, 1785.

Dear Mendis:

I have done myself the pleasure of writing you by every convayance since my arrival, and should have been made happy by a few lines from my friend by the October packet, which arrived in a very short passage and did not bring me a line, my expectation being raised (for I confess there are many I truly love in your place, and you my friend among the first).

I felt the most poignant chagrin and cou'd only console myself for the disapointment in hoping and supposeing you were all well. For as bad news never wants convayance or wings, I was sure, if any disagreable occurences had taken place, I should have hered of it. And as I ever wish my friends well, I anticipate agreable tidings. It's that allone can reconcile absence which I sincearly feel. For although surrounded here by the tenderest and worthiest conexion [my parents, a brother, and a sister], I feel my heart incline towards your best of citys, Amsterdam.

I am serious, Mendas, and confess without blushing, that I find myself more attached to it than to my native (country) place. My mind seems to have been formed for it, and my heart is ever inclined to follow its dictates. But such I fear has fate ordain'd, that I must slave here to gain what I am deficent by misplacing confidence. That however will not take place before my return to Europe which will, I think, be next May, when I hope to have my buisness finally closed, it now being in a fair way. And altho' it will not turn out so well as I could wish, still am happy to see an end of it that dear Moses [Myers], who is now writing at my side, and my self may again git in buisness and be inabled in time to follow the dictates of our hearts in paying all our good Holland creditors twenty shilling in the pound. They merit it from us and shall have it, if we ever have it in our power. Had we been otherwise conected then we were [with Isaac Moses], we should have done well, but . . . we must now . . . make the best of it.

One thing alone I cannot forget, which is that the author of our ruin [Isaac Moses] has endeavour'd to asperse our character to clear his own, and reported that the cause of his failure was owing to us. Of this we leave the impartial world to judge, and being conscious of our own interest defy his malice. I have the pleasure to tell you that we are respected by the better sort of people here, and having every confidence placed in us, which greatly aleaveates our sufferings.

Tomorrow I set out for Phil'a, Baltimore, and Virginia to collect what is due us. Before my departure will endeavour to get a bill of exchange for the money I owe you and remit it in this letter, which I leave open for the purpose. I have the money by me, but so scarce are good bills that it's with the utmost difficulty they are to be had. Should I not succeed this time, I will in my next, and must crave your paitance.

Do, my friend, let me here from you. Deliver the inclosed to Beckey and make my respectfull compliments acceptible to all your familey and every friend of mine, and believe me truly, my dear Isaac,   Your affectinate friend,
Sam'l Myers.[39]

In the following January the partnership of the three men was formally dissolved. Samuel Myers, working for the trustees, went out on the road collecting debts. It was anything but pleasant to travel the boggy highways of Maryland and Virginia in winter through hail, rain, snow, and frost, but it was probably preferable to some of the summer trips which he and Moses Myers occasionally made. It was not unusual for one of the partners to cover 500 miles, see all the customers, and be back in New York in a period of nine days. On occasion they traveled 100 miles a day by stage through heat and dust and discomfort. On this January trip, Samuel conjured his debtors in Philadelphia, Baltimore, Fredericksburg, and Petersburg.

In the summer, June, 1786, Samuel returned to Europe to render an account, leaving Moses behind him to carry the burden. After his partner sailed for Europe on the eighth, Moses Myers was very much distressed. He was still a young man, but he had already gone through a lot. He was bankrupt; his best friends, men who trusted him, had lost thousands of pounds because of their confidence in him. His mother, whom he loved deeply, was mentally unbalanced. Isaac Moses, whom he distrusted, was a constant worry to him and, as he suspected, rightly or wrongly, always up to something. His future was uncertain. This is the mood of worry, of indecision, of loneliness, which is reflected in the following letter which he sent on to Samuel the day after the latter sailed for Europe.

New York, June 9th, 1786.

My dear Myers:

The packet not yet sail'd gives me an opportunity of informing you that I reach'd town at six last evening and found your dear sister [Judy Mordecai] compos'd and quite determin'd to bear your absence with fortitude.

She was very much surpriz'd to see me so soon back, and I assure you without disguise she is *entirely* compos'd and really merits applause for her deportment.

The dear boy [her infant son, Moses,] is well, as is every individual of the family.

Your letters are all deliver'd to the very great satisfaction of those to whom directed.

My mind, my dear Myers, is more at ease, but do assure you I slept but little last night. I walked the Battery alone till near one this morning, being lock'd out and not willing to disturb our dear Judy. I tried to awaken Solly [your brother] by breaking a window in our room. To no effect, he heard me not. I laid on the sopha at Mr. Gersham Seixas's most of the night reflecting on my situation, bereft of allmost every thing dear to me. You, my Myers, you are. But God is great and in him all my trust.

You have had a heavenly wind that has I hope wafted you along in the manner you wish. Your ship sail'd well, and as the wind favors I hope your passage will be short. Heaven grant that I may soon be bless'd with the agreable tidings. . . .

I have love in abundance to offer, and if the wishes of your friends (who are numerous) prevail, you will have a short passage. Depend, none wishes it more sincerely than, my ever dear Myers,

Your affectionate friend,
M. Myers.

I shall write fully p[er]. French packet.
Mention me to friends. [40]

Because they were going through bankruptcy, the partners were not legally permitted to do any business as individuals on their own account. Actually, however, this was a prohibition observed in the breach thereof. Obviously, they needed money to live; the bankruptcy—if we may judge again from the personal correspondence of the Myerses—had been an "honest" one. On occasion Moses Myers was almost down to his last £50. The Myerses—and we may assume that this was true of Isaac Moses, too—did try to secure a commission here and there. Once, Moses Myers sent a consignment of tea and kosher meat to James Murphy, to Europe. The roundabout expression by which Myers described the meat undoubtedly made its nature clear to Murphy, if he required any clarification: "It is beef put up on purpose for people of my profession."

Moses Myers could not have been uninformed on the

details of Jewish observance. His father, an observant Jew, had once been the *shohet* for the New York congregation. However, although he knew full well the meaning of kosher meat, it may well be doubted that he observed the dietary laws, particularly on his long sea and land trips.

Both he and Samuel were professing Jews. Samuel, however, was not a member of Mikveh Israel while in Philadelphia, and his contribution to its building fund in 1782 was but nominal. In later years he became a respected member of the Richmond synagogue.

Moses, however, seems to have been more active in the religious community. In 1786 he was chosen a minor officer of Shearith Israel. During the war he had been a member of the Philadelphia congregation and had made a very liberal gift to help build the new synagogue. Among a group of about sixty contributors, his gift was the seventh largest. It is eloquent testimony to the religious loyalties of the young merchant of twenty-nine or thirty, for just a year before the firm of S. & M. Myers had been dealt a crushing blow through the capture of their stocks when St. Eustatia was taken by the British.

Moses himself did not travel out of town during the High Holyday season. Some of the Jews with whom he did business would undoubtedly have resented a cavalier disregard of the most holy days in the religious calendar. It is quite likely that simple piety and loyalty motivated him. Every now and then, in his letters, Moses Myers used a Hebrew phrase which he wrote in English script. And when a collection was taken up for a poor Jew, his subscription was not wanting.

A case in point was the poor Mr. Shimelah (!) of
Montreal. As one who had grown up in that city and was
in constant touch with the Judahs of that town, Moses was
partial to Canadians. It would seem that he knew this Mr.
Shimelah, who was on his way to London via New York.
Moses helped raise £14 for him, put him on the fast
packet, the "Speedwell," on a Saturday night, bade him
goodbye and returned to his home convinced—if he believed in *mizwot*, "good deeds"—that he had performed a
mizwah. But, lo and behold, on Sunday morning Mr.
Shimelah was back on shore, still in New York. Aboard,
so he said, he could not use his phylacteries (*tefillin*) for
his prayers. And so Mr. Shimelah was sent back to
Montreal.

Throughout 1786, the two men traveled extensively as
agents for their bankrupt firm. They had made up their
minds to stick together as partners and ultimately to re-
establish their business here in the United States. In addition to pleading and arguing with "villains"—a synonym
for obstreperous creditors—they served as a sort of credit
bureau, rating all the big solid merchants in the larger
cities which they visited. These character and commercial
ratings they forwarded to their European creditors, the
Dutch merchants. Strangely, no Jews were listed, as far
as can be determined. (Some of the information was in
code.) Evidently at the time there were few or no Jewish
merchant-shippers of consequence in New England, in the
Middle Atlantic states, and in Virginia.

Toward the end of 1786 they began to note a change
for the better. They reported that goods were no longer

thrown on the market in large quantities, at auction. Inventories were depleted, and commodities commanded better prices. Almost reluctantly Moses Myers reported that the new paper money was holding its own. In one of his letters, in August, he wrote: "We find no ill consequences from a paper medium now in circulation. Tho' for my part I must confess I shall never have confidence in it untill a better fund is provided for its redemption, and a new system of gouvernment form'd to give more general consequence to the states at large."

The Myerses were in all probability nationalistic, that is, "federalistic," in their politics. They liked the idea of sound money and certainly approved of Alexander Hamilton's financial system. They watched with interest the calling of the Annapolis Convention in September, 1786, which was assembled to solve the complications of interstate commerce. Like Hamilton and the merchants, they wanted a uniform code for foreign and domestic trade. In their correspondence, one of the partners took pains to report that Colonel Hamilton had been selected as a commissioner from New York to attend the Convention.

In spite of their friends in Europe and of their appreciation of its life and culture, they were convinced, even during this critical period of civil unrest, of failures, and of bankruptcies, that America was destined for great things. "This country is so situated," wrote one of them, "that it must flourish, and time only is wanting to bring all again to rights."

Evidently the partners felt, in 1786, that the time was approaching when they could once again open their establishment. Wherever they traveled in the states they were on the lookout, constantly, for a place to settle. In the following letter to Samuel, Moses Myers weighed the different possibilities.

New York, June 13th, 1786.

Dear Myers:

. . . . Now my friend for our future establishment in life. It is time we think on it very seriously on this subject. Therefore I shall give you my opinion candidly.

It has ever been my opinion we might do considerable good business in this city [New York] with care and industry, but then it requires we shou'd be together. Except we shou'd form such a connexion as wou'd be an object worthy your stay in Europe. In that case only I shou'd think it adviseable. I see no prospect of making such a concern, or do I think it would be our interest so to do. I wou'd have you settle our affairs and fix such connexions as you can and find necessary. That done, wou'd have you embark in the spring for Maryland or Georgia where I will join you, or if you judge best, to this city.

Georgia is a young country and promises success. The exports will ever make it a place of consequence. And we know by experience that in all new country's most money is to be made. We shall doubtless meet many friends and support from every part of the continent. Our expences together wou'd be very little more than ea[ch]. apart, an object at the year's end, and business conducted with greater facility and peace of mind.

Wou'd you prefer Philad'a, I think money is to be made there with proper attention. Goods, I am convinc'd, cou'd be vended to a large amo't, and certain proffit and many advantages arise from commissions. In this case you may have it in your power to find such a man as James Duff [the merchant of Cadiz, Spain], who'd let you ship wheat, flour, etc., and give you credit in London, Amsterdam, etc. From circum-

stances and things in Europe you will best be able to form
your resolutions, weigh well all things, and deliberate on them
before you determine to not be precipitate. But when your
plan is once form'd, swerve not from it. Your experience and
thorough knowledge of the trade and people of this country
will enable you to form the most solid judgement of an establishment.

I wou'd in preference be alone [just the two of us], except
the advantage of a connexion is great indeed. You are too
well acquainted with the consequences of copartnerships to
need any coment thereon. Woefull experience has taught you
they are pernicious and if possible to be avoided. . . .

I am with sincere attachment, dear Myers,

Your f[rien]'d and ob't serv't,

M. Myers.[41]

Samuel had made a long trip southward for the creditors
during the first three months of 1786. For the same reason
Moses spent most of November traveling in Pennsylvania,
Maryland, and Virginia. His stay in Richmond was anything but productive. The two Mordecai brothers, Joseph
and Isaac, owed him a considerable sum which he needed
very much; if the money was not forthcoming, he wrote
Marcus Elcan in December, "I am ruin'd." He even quarreled with Jacob Mordecai over an unpaid bill, and the
usually reliable Elcan could do little for him.

Elcan was in debt to S. & M. Myers and he attempted
to balance his account by forwarding to them a note of
Barnard Gratz, who was in debt to him. But when S. & M.
Myers attempted to cash the note, Gratz said that he had
no money and asked the firm to wait. But what the Myerses
wanted was cash, not promises.

It may well be that the troubles Moses ran into in Rich-

mond soured him on that town when he again wrote Samuel
about opening their own business. Moses may also have
been mindful of the fact that Cohen and Isaacs were already
firmly entrenched there, and that Cohen was the stepfather
of the Mordecai boys.

In the June 13th letter Moses had thought in terms of
New York, Maryland, or Georgia. (Georgia was then the
second largest state in the Union!) Early in December,
after he had returned to New York and when he was
struggling again with the problem of deciding on a location, the choice was between Savannah, Charleston, and a
city in Virginia. By December 14th, as we see from the
following letter, Richmond was out of the running.

New York, Dec'r 14th, 1786.

Mr. Sam'l Myers,
Dear Myers:
  .... I have revolv'd over in my mind the circumstances re-
specting our future establishment and think that either Ch's
Ton, S. Carolina, or Norfolk in Virginia must be the place.

I always wou'd prefer a sea port town to any other. The
advantages are superior and need not be pointed out to you.

I presume that you will be able (at least) to establish a
credit in Amsterdam for such articles as either place wou'd
require, and from whence there can arise no difficulty to make
suitable returns.

Neither tobacco, rice, or indigo can possibly maintain these
present prices, and the state of Virginia having rejected paper
money altogether gives it a superiority over the other states
and establishes a confidence unknown heretofore.

I have observed that no or very little credit must be given
the planter, for thereby you frequently lay long out of your
money and lose their custom. The proffits are very great, and
goods suitable to the country can be vended in large quanti-

ties. Two thousand pieces of oz[nabrig]'s [coarse linen] cou'd have been dispos'd of for cash and to a considerable proffit. None was at market.

Money is certainly to be made in Ch's Ton. The trade you are no stranger to.

Georgia is a young state, and I think offers advantages to a trade with Holland. They have timber in abundance, rice, indigo, tobacco, corn for exportation, and being contiguous to the Spaniards I shou'd suppose wou'd give them great advantages.

Their emigration has been one-third of the inhabitants since the peace. This, says my informant, but really is not reasonable. Before the war they knew not what it was to raise tobacco, and the last year's exportation was three thousand h[ogs] h[ea]'ds.

It is impossible to enter minutely into the advantages or disadvantages of trade without being on the spot to collect the necessary informations. As we have both been lately in Virginia we can best judge for a certainty, and I think we can do well at Norfolk where, if you think proper, we will determine to set down in a snug business that will secure to us a sure income. We shall be enabled to get many comm[ission]'s from this [New York] and Philad'a.

As very much will depend on what can be done in Holland, I now leave you to finally determine. Let me know the place, and will repair there early in the spring and be ready to receive you.

Was it practicable to establish a credit such as I pointed out some time since, very great advantages wou'd arise from it, and money cou'd be made with care. This, however, you can best judge of being on the spot. I shall wait your reply, interim close our affairs with all speed. . . .

I am, with sincere attachment, dear Myers,

Y'r f[rien]'d and mo[st]. ob't serv't,

M. Myers.[42]

By the spring of 1787, Moses Myers was more determined than ever to open up somewhere. The depression was about over, and the national constitutional convention which had been called for May would certainly strengthen the Union. All he needed was capital—and he never had less money!

In this crisis he decided to get married. Ever since the previous April, if not earlier, he had had his eye on a likely young widow of twenty-four. Her name was Elizabeth Judd or Judah, and she was related to the Montreal clan of that name. Moses may even have known her in her youth.

While living in that city in 1771, still a child, she had woven a beautiful sampler which piously summarized the Ten Commandments. Though worn and ravaged by time, most of this versified Decalogue can still be read:

EXODUS   CHAP. XX
I
Thou shalt not have more gods than [me].
II
[Before] no image bow thy knee.
III
Take not the name of God in vain.
IV
Nor dare the Sabbath day profane.
V
Give both thy parents honour due.
VI
Take heed that thou no murder do.
VII
Abstain from words and deeds unclean.

VIII
Nor steal tho thou [art] poor and mean.
IX
Nor make a wit[ness fals?]e nor love it.
X
What is thy neighbours dare not covet.

— * —

With all thy soul love God above.
And as thy self thy neighbour love.

During her first marriage—to a man named Chapman—
Elizabeth had lived in England. With Chapman dead, the
widow, a woman of considerable wealth, had come to the
States accompanied by her brother. She and Moses Myers
were married in the month of March. In the traditional
Aramaic contract, the groom guaranteed his bride £150,
New York currency. Gershom Mendes Seixas, we may
suppose, performed the ceremony in New York; Benjamin
Nones, war veteran and flamboyant Republican of a later
decade, was one witness; Hayman Levy, president of
Shearith Israel, was the other. (Mrs. Hayman Levy was
Samuel Myers' aunt.)

The next month, at Moses' insistence, Norfolk was
selected as the new locale of the resurrected firm of
S. & M. Myers. Samuel had held out for New York, and
Moses had agreed that it was the best town—but our re-
spective families! That was the objection which changed
Samuel's mind.

Now that the die was cast, Samuel in Europe went to
work. Their credit was still excellent. A stock worth
15,000 florins was shipped to Norfolk: yard-goods, stock-

ings, textiles, steel, looking glasses, Swedish iron, window glass, and the inevitable cases of gin.

In June, Moses passed through Richmond—he got $1,200 on account from Elcan—and went on to Norfolk. Armed with letters of introduction from some of his Virginia clients, he was well received there on that exploratory trip. (He later sent a Mr. Bowdoin some essence of spruce because of the latter's hospitality. "You will find the necessary directions in the box." He was sorry that no canary seed could be gotten for Mrs. Bowdoin.) The more he saw of the town the better he liked it. On June 19th, he wrote to Marcus Elcan—who wanted some dry goods from the new firm—giving his impression of the place.

Mr. Marcus Elcan, Norfolk, June 19th, 1787.

Dear Elcan:

I have been busily employ'd ever since my arrival here which was not 'till the day after I left you.

I like the place and its inhabitants. They often brought to my recollection the friendly treatment I rec'd at all times under your roof. Time, or any other occurrence, will never erase it from my mind.

I have not had it in my power to open the articles you wish'd to have, for I have not fix'd on a place to put them. I have hired a store[room] by the month in which I have lodg'd the bales, etc.

I return this afternoon to Balt[imo]'re and expect to be here in three weeks. At any rate I shall have a person to take charge of our business. Then the goods will be open'd and such as you please at your command. Interim I have ship'd you one bale of oznaburgs and six pieces ravens duck on board the sloop "Nancy," Joshua Ventures [master], for which you've bill of lading inclos'd. . . .

I shall find no difficulty in geting a house and think from appearances we shall do well.

So soon as I return shall circulate our firm. Write me to New York and, believe me,

Truly yours, etc.,
M. Myers.[43]

After his return to New York, Moses Myers wrote and rented a house in Norfolk for a year, and arranged to have it properly altered and papered. On July 22nd, he and his wife set sail on the schooner "Sincerity" for their new home. In the hold were their furniture and a £1,000 cargo which he had secured on credit. The future looked good to him: "My prospects [in Norfolk] are better than they wou'd be here [in New York]," he informed one of the Canadian Judahs, "and I hope with prudence, industry, and frugality, in five or six years, to have it in my power to set myself at ease." And he continued, with possibly just a suspicion of regret: "The distance is not great. With a fair wind, 'tis but a run of thirty-six to forty hours [to New York]."

In August there was a formal announcement of his opening. Goods would be sold for cash only. He was ready to buy naval stores, grain, beeswax, deerskins, tobacco, and lumber. A few days later he filled his first order. A business house destined soon to make a name for itself had been established in Virginia.

After a few years Samuel left the firm to settle ultimately in Richmond. Moses remained in Norfolk to become one of Virginia's most distinguished and respected Jews. His features have been preserved for us in the fine portrait by Gilbert Stuart.

Four years after Moses moved there he built one of its most attractive Georgian homes. It is still standing, a beautiful and sturdy monument to the man himself.

For many years he was one of the city's best-known merchants, and in the heyday of his career, in the decade before and after the turn of the century, he served as the financial representative of the French and the Batavian republics, as a director of the local branch of the Bank of Richmond, and as an agent for Thomas Jefferson, Wilson Cary Nicholas, and other Virginia families. He was a major in the militia. After eight years in Norfolk, his fellow-townsmen elected him to the Common Council, and having received the highest number of votes, he became its president.

Just a few weeks after S. & M. Myers began to do business in Norfolk, Moses Myers offered the hospitality of his home to three guests on their way to Richmond. David Isaacs, a younger brother of Isaiah Isaacs, had arrived from Europe, and with him on the same boat were Israel I. Cohen and his bride. Cohen, a younger brother of Jacob I. Cohen, had been living in Richmond since 1784 but went abroad to bring back a bride, a girl from Bristol, England.

Richmond was growing. In 1782 there were only three male Jews listed on a tax return. In 1788, according to another list, there were at least twenty-five Jews. Out of a total of about 420 taxable free white adults in Richmond, there were ten Jewish householders. Six of the ten were in the lower middle bracket; three, Marcus Elcan, Cohen, and Isaacs, were fairly well-off; one, Isaac Mordecai, was in the lowest bracket. Mordecai was too poor to own a servant; the firm of Cohen & Isaacs owned three slaves; each of the other six householders had one Negro slave as a domestic servant.

These ten men were an interesting lot. We have noticed Elcan and his library. We have already described the two pioneer merchants, Jacob I. Cohen and Isaiah Isaacs. Israel I. Cohen's claim to fame came through his five sons, who moved to Baltimore with their widowed mother after the turn of the century. "Cohen of Baltimore" became a famous name. They were bankers, railroad promoters, engineers, physicians, and members of the town council.

As we have just read, Isaac Mordecai, one of Jacob I. Cohen's stepsons, had the unenviable distinction of being the least successful of the Jewish merchants in town at that time. Myer Cohen, a New York watchmaker, was one of the many Whigs who had sought refuge in Philadelphia during the war. He died unmarried, leaving a widowed mother up North, a small stock of sundries, and a number of bills collectable for watch and clock repairs.

Evidently Myer Derkheim, who came to town sometime during the middle 1780's, was not disturbed about the warning of the Psalmist: "He weakened my strength on the road." He was a wanderer. If his name means anything, he was a Rhenish Bavarian. England sheltered him for a while: London, York, Bristol, Plymouth. Then he came to these shores. We can trace him as far north as Pennsylvania and as far south as the Carolinas and, possibly, Georgia. In Virginia he also visited Petersburg and some other towns.

A Jew who travels to many places is either a peddler, a schnorrer (for himself), a collector (for others), or an itinerant circumciser. Derkheim was the last, and the records in his circumcision books are eloquent testimony that isolated Jewish families were to be found in even the most remote villages of this country, and that some of them attempted to remain Jewish.

What brought a man like Derkheim so far from home? Adventure? Hardly! Political and economic disabilities imposed on Jews in Europe, incapacity to meet the competition of abler men, the lack of any remunerative skills or techniques, the hope of making an easier and a better living on the periphery of civilization—only these could have induced such a man to uproot his wife and family and to brave the discomfort and danger of a voyage to the United States.

In Richmond, when he was not traveling on a ritual mission, Derkheim made and sold candles and turpentine soap in his "new" shop opposite the old Capitol. A little extra cash—always welcome to a man with a growing family—was supplied by the town fathers, who hired him as a lamplighter for the bridge which crossed the creek at Main Street. But even Richmond was not the last resting place for this wanderer. He and his wife Sara are buried in the old Spruce Street Cemetery in Philadelphia.

Isaac H. Judah was another of the early Richmondians. He was of Newport stock, for his maternal grandfather was Isaac M. Seixas and his father was Hillel Judah, the

Newport *shohet*. Like his father, Isaac was interested in religious affairs and was, in all probability, Richmond's first "rabbi." In later years he was active in Masonry.

There were two Cardozos in Richmond, but in the tax list of 1788 there is only one, Moses Nunez. A brother, Abraham N., came there later. They were two of the four sons of Aaron N. Cardozo. Aaron was already in New York, attending services at Shearith Israel by 1750. Later his wife joined him, bringing to these shores the two older girls and a young son born during his absence. This son, Isaac N., was for a time the fashionable tailor of Easton—for £1.8 he would make you a good suit, using your materials, of course; later he moved to New York where he died. (Benjamin N. Cardozo, the justice of the United States Supreme Court, was Isaac's great-grandson.)

The three other sons were born in the colonies. David N. became a Charlestonian and joined the South Carolina Grenadiers during the Revolution. As a "top sergeant" he led his company in a forlorn-hope assault on the British lines at Savannah in 1779; people recalled that act of heroism over fifty years later. Jacob N. Cardozo, one of the most distinguished economists of ante-bellum days, was David's son. (And if Carolina gossip was right, Francis L. Cardozo, the brilliant Negro politician of the Reconstruction period, was his grandson.)

Moses owned a farm near Richmond, and before he died asked that he be buried in his own lot close to his stables. But he warned his executors to fence the grave in securely. He did not want the cattle in the yard cropping the grass that grew over him.

The youngest brother, Abraham, was the first of the four to die. A bachelor, he left a sizeable farm, at the Bowling Green near Richmond, to his executor Joseph Darmstadt, and the balance of his possessions he ordered to be sold and divided among the Cardozo family. Moses N. protested the probate, indignant that the whole estate was not willed to the clan.

Joseph Darmstadt had originally come to these shores with the Hessian troops as a sutler, but, so we are told, he was captured by Continental troops and imprisoned in Virginia. And there it was that he remained after the Revolution, throwing in his lot with the new republic.

He came to Richmond no later than 1786. Like his neighbor, Isaiah Isaacs, the "Dutchman," as he was called, never acquired any skill in the use of the English language, but the German farmers of the Great Valley to the west, having faith in this Jew who spoke their tongue, drove into Richmond three or four times a year to do their trading with him. He fed, shod, and physicked a whole generation, till the panic of 1818 almost broke him. The townspeople, the judges and lawyers, the merchants and doctors, who did their own shopping in the wet and misty mornings, made it their custom to turn in at his store on the market square where a coffee pot bubbled hospitably on the fire and where the latest gossip was retailed.

An honest and able man, Darmstadt commanded the respect and the affection of the business and social leaders of the town, despite his accent. They accepted him as a member of the Amicable Society, an organization established to relieve helpless itinerants. When John Marshall assumed office as Grand Master of the Virginia Grand Lodge of Masons, Darmstadt became Grand Treasurer.

In the folklore of old Richmond the Hessian sutler is best remembered for his bucolic friendliness and humor. He was one of the participants in a practical joke that was played on the Irish mayor who had risen to his high office from the humble position of blacksmith. Some wag had solemnly informed the not overly bright official that a bottle could not be broken in an empty bag. His Honor was convinced that it could be done, and bet a bowl of punch for the entire Common Council that he could do it. Darmstadt supplied the bottle, blew into the bag, tied it up, and handed it over to the mayor, who swung it like a sledge hammer against a large block of stone on the sidewalk. The bottle was shattered, the whilom blacksmith bellowed, "Victory," but when the bag was opened it was *not empty*, and the mayor had to supply the punch.

A man like Darmstadt would not overlook the celebration of a joyous holiday such as Purim, which is the happiest and most boisterous of the festivals. Drinking and feasting are enjoined upon the Jews for this day to commemorate the rescue of their fathers in ancient Persia from the wicked Haman. In all Jewish lore there is no more popular heroine than good Queen Esther, the consort of the great King Ahasuerus.

When, therefore, Purim eve rolled around on March 12, 1789, Darmstadt would only too gladly have availed himself of an invitation to attend a party at Jacob I. Cohen's. He was fond of Cohen's wife, Esther, "Queen Esther," if you please. Unfortunately he could not come. He may have had a "roup," a cold, or an upset stomach. Not to be cheated out of his fun, however, he excused himself to the host in the following letter, written in doggerel. It is an excellent illustration of the spelling and the type of wit that characterized the erstwhile Hessian sutler. In addition, it may well be one of the oldest pieces of poetry (??) by an American Jew that we possess. Certainly it is the first American Purim skit. It speaks most eloquently for itself:

To Jacob I. Cohen, Esq.:   March 12th, 1789.

    My best respect & compliment
    To you all in this letter I sent.
    I hope this will find you all well and hardy,
    And excuse me also, as I can't [be] one
        of your party
    This evening with you to drink or soup;
    I mean to give you a hint by way of a roup.

    As I was in companie not very late,
    When we all joint in one debate,
    There was Cohnim, Levin ["priests and
        Levites"] and Quakers,
    Sadlers, leaf pikers [pickers], &
        candel makers.
    It was wen we was all in union,
    And we all joint in one opinion.

    Why is it sure a drohl afair,
    Out of 365 days in a year,
    Not to find one day which is feet [fit]
    To give a body a diner to eat?
    Or to have an inclination
    To give a body an invitation.
    Or to make us remember,
    As there was good porter in a hempr [hamper].

Or never should be handy,
As ther is spirits or brandy.
Or by good graces
As there is gin in cases.
. . . .
Then you find your only satisfaction.
Then you make us drink & sing,
Because you think like Ahasuerus the King
What—have not I Queen Esther's plasure
And, besides, silver, gold, and treasur.
Therefore at my ease
I can invite wen I please.

But remember, and not uncomon,
A man is born of woman,
Is cut down like a flower.
And why shall we drink porter wich is sour,
And like the dog in the manger,
Wen our stomags fear no danger.

But all these should not keep me away,
Was not another ca[u]se in the way,
Wich makes my [me] afrait,
If I should be the villan in the gate,
And by chance the spirit should my [me]
      mouve
And disagreable to the companie should
      prove.

All thes I say and no more.
May He who knows us all bless you as
      before.
And keep you many Purim marry [merry].
And I will drink your health in a glass
      of cherry.   I am, with respect,
                            Yours most humble serv.,
                                  J. Darmsdadt.[44]

When Darmstadt's will was probated in January, 1820, in the depths of the depression, the executors found that this old bachelor had left $500 to the Female Society and thousand-dollar legacies to several women friends, and had closed with this apologetic instruction: "I would have left more leagacis but on a/c property and evry thing else has deminest & our [are] worth less by half is the reason. The bond & book dep[osi]'ts you'il sue for et & the proceets given to such poor people as you'il thinck proper."

When the Purim party was held in Cohen's home, there were more than enough Jews in town—if all were united —to establish a congregation. The Jewish law merely requires that there be ten males over thirteen years of age. Individuals and families had been drifting into Richmond, gradually swelling the little community. On August 24, 1789, on a Sunday, a congregation was called into being in order to promote "the divine worship which by the blessing of God has been transmitted by our ancestors." At least two of the charter members of the Richmond synagogue had been members of Philadelphia's Mikveh Israel when it was reconstituted seven years earlier. The new organization was named The House of Peace, Beth Shalome, because it was dedicated not only to worship, but also to "peace and friendship."

Though most of the subscribers were of Germanic origin, the ritual adopted was the Spanish-Portuguese. The constitution or guiding rules of Beth Shalome, a copy of which is extant, indicates that it was one of the most democratic of the six synagogues in the country.

The group was small, and every individual was zealous

for his own prerogatives. One might even hazard the suggestion that the leveling influence of the frontier also made itself felt. It was easy to become a member. Any free man who had lived in town for three months could join. The emphasis on "any *free* man" would seem to be directed against Negro slaves who might be attracted to the synagogue of their masters; in the 1820 constitution of Beth Elohim, of Charleston, "people of colour" were excluded from membership. It is very probable, too, that the adjective "free" served to exclude indentured whites.

The *junta* was composed of three persons, a president and two "assistants." They could not serve together if related by ties of blood or of business. The *parnas* ran the congregation with the aid of his board which met monthly. Any decision they made was read to the membership at two successive weekly services. If there was any objection on the part of a member, it was his privilege to call a congregational meeting and to subject the ruling of the *junta* to the will of the majority. What could be fairer?

On Thanksgiving Day, Thursday, November 26th of that year, the newly formed group met for worship pursuant to a request of the federal authorities. Jacob I. Cohen wrote a prayer for the welfare of the government. In a part alluding to President George Washington he said:

O God of Hosts, thou has set peace and tranquility in our
    palaces,
And has set the President of the United States as our head.
And in prayer we humble ourselves before Thee, O our God.
Unto our supplications mayest Thou hearken and deliver
    us.

224

SAMUEL MYERS, VIRGINIA MERCHANT

MOSES MYERS, VIRGINIA MERCHANT

A mind of wisdom and understanding, set in the heart of the
    head of our country.
May he judge us with justice; may he cause our hearts to
    rejoice and be glad.
In the paths of the upright may he lead us.
Even unto old age may he administer and judge in our midst.
Pure and upright be the heart of the one who rules and
    governs us.
May God Almighty hearken to our voice and save us. . . .

These were the beginnings of the first synagogue in
Virginia, in the most western of the Jewish communities
of that day.

Chapter 11

South Carolina, 1690 – 1776

IN 1781 hundreds of Whigs had been ordered out of
Charlestown. Among them were a number of Jews.
One was a cocky young French immigrant known for
his radical political views, Benjamin Nones, who had
fought under General Pulaski in the South and had distinguished himself by his daring conduct.

Another who refused to "take protection" from the
enemy and was banished was Isaac DaCosta; he and his
wife and two children arrived in Philadelphia on December
31, 1781. Many of the Charlestown *émigrés* were so impoverished that they had to take advantage of the fund
which was set up for their relief by generous Philadelphians. (Haym Salomon and Jonas Phillips were among the
subscribers.) But DaCosta was not destitute, if we may
judge by the fact that he was able to make a contribution
to help build the Philadelphia synagogue, and when the
house of worship was dedicated on September 13, 1782,
that Charlestonian, we may be sure, was present. We can
imagine him sitting in his seat at three o'clock on a Friday
afternoon, on the eve of the Sabbath of Repentance. He

was in no hurry; the service was scheduled to last four hours.

What were his reflections as he looked about him? Surely he thought of his wanderings, his hopes, his struggles since the day he had left London almost forty years earlier. Now here he was in Philadelphia, the city of brotherly love—in a land of opportunity and liberty. Liberty—but would there be complete liberty for him as an American Jew? Six years after the Declaration of Independence, South Carolina—in whose defense he had suffered proscription—still frowned on Jews as officeholders.

As he looked about him he saw many of his neighbors from Charlestown who had fled even as he; he turned around and saw at least a dozen grim-faced men who had been driven out of Newport, New York, and Savannah by the coming of the British. Maybe that is our misfortune, he mused—always in the big cities, the storm centers, in the center of things. How will it all end?

What had brought DaCosta to South Carolina rather than elsewhere in the colonies? Economic opportunity was certainly one reason. Charlestown had a good port; it was a mercantile and commercial center, and it was strategically close to the rich islands of the West Indies. It was the fourth largest city in the colonies, the largest below Philadelphia, and the metropolis of the South.

But economic opportunity was only half the story; the other half was hope for civil liberty, religious freedom, and political equality. The Carolinas, both North and South, got off to a liberal start in 1663 when the original charter of Charles II encouraged the coming in of Protestant Dissenters. Two years later the tolerance accorded Dissenters was broadened to include all men without reference to their religious beliefs. The English, who were trying at this time to build in South America, in Surinam, and who were competing with the Dutch for settlers, realized that people had to be enticed into the wilderness by the promise of liberty. They offered the "Hebrew Nation" in Surinam religious, civil, and even political privileges; no price was too high to pay for men who would settle in their colonies.

It is not surprising, therefore, that when John Locke wrote an organic statute for the Carolinas, he went out of his way to encourage Jews. In the Fundamental Constitutions, which he wrote (1669) for the Lords Proprietors, the Jews were specifically granted religious toleration, and several provisions were included to protect them and non-Orthodox Christians from group libel:

> No person whatsoever shall disturb, molest, or persecute another for his speculative opinions in religion, or his way of worship.

> No man shall use any reproachful, reviling, or abusive language against any religion of any church or profession; that being the certain way of disturbing the peace, and of hindering the conversion of any to the truth, by engaging them in quarrels and animosities, to the hatred of the professors and that profession which otherwise they might be brought to assent to.

Though the Fundamental Constitutions were not officially adopted by the settlers, the spirit of that document may have created a climate of opinion favorable to the Carolinas—among Jews at least. In the first three decades of the settlement, the colonists were tolerant of each other through necessity. They wanted company, and they realized then, if not later, that so religiously diverse a group could not exist except harmoniously. Tolerance was the only solution in a new land which sheltered Anglicans, French Huguenots, Congregationalists, Presbyterians, Lutherans, and even Jews. Such tolerance did not remain unchallenged.

To be sure, there was only a handful of the last. As early as 1695 a governor had employed a Jew as a Spanish interpreter, and two years later four Jews were naturalized, all of whom were merchants. At least two of them were of Spanish-Portuguese stock.

One of the four was the brother-in-law of Asser Levy, Simon Valentine, who, probably in the late 1680's, had wandered south from New York to Jamaica. He did business on the island, at Port Royal it would seem, handling chiefly indigo, flour, sugar, and Negroes. One of the Jamaicans with whom he dealt was Jacob Mears, who sold him goods and occasionally lent him money to pay the merchant-shippers who sailed into port with their cargoes. In 1692 large parts of Port Royal sank into the sea during a terrible earthquake. Both Mears and Valentine escaped, but they lost their stocks and their account books. Valentine then migrated to Charlestown, where he again became a merchant, from all indications a successful one. For a while he was a police commissioner, a very responsible,

229

honorary position, and, as far as we know, he was the first Jew in the Carolinas to own land (1699).

Hearing that Valentine was making money, Mears, still in Jamaica, brought suit in the Court of Chancery at Charlestown to recover several hundred pounds which, he claimed, Valentine owed him. Mears admitted that he had no books to prove the case, but asked that Valentine be subpoenaed to appear in a Charlestown court and to testify under oath as to his indebtedness. The writ was issued and served (1701). Valentine was represented by one of the great colonial lawyers, Nicholas Trott, later chief justice of the colony.

Valentine not only denied the charges but admired the "assurance"—he meant the impudence—of a debtor who demanded money of his creditor! Jacob Mears owed him about £75! We do not know who paid whom, for the final decree in this suit has not been found.

By the early 1690's, the colony was so firmly established that the various Christian groups allowed themselves the luxury of bitter religious squabbles, and finally, in 1698, the Anglican Church was established, *de facto*, if not *de jure*.

In 1703, so an indignant remonstrant reported, Jews were voting in the elections for representatives to the Assembly. It is hardly to be doubted that they were entitled to vote, for an act passed the following year specifically permitted "aliens" to exercise the franchise. In any event, the Jews were not hesitant in exercising the privileges to which they believed they were entitled.

There was a common pattern in the action of colonial

and British Jews, in the eighteenth and nineteenth centuries, in their ceaseless struggle for enfranchisement. They did not ask for rights; they assumed them like others, unless or until they were contested—then, if possible, they re-assumed them after the protest had faded. This is what happened in New York in the first half of the eighteenth century in the elections for representatives to the Assembly, and this is what happened also in Georgia and in South Carolina.

In the latter colony a group of Dissenters, locked in a bitter political and religious struggle with Anglicans, pointed out that Negroes, Jews, sailors, and the like had presumed to vote for representatives. The hope of the Dissenters was to invalidate that legislation and to "smear" their Anglican opponents by linking them with "undesirable" elements.

In spite of the fact that settlers were badly needed in the early decades, there was a definite tendency to limit the franchise and other political rights. In 1704, aliens—this category included Jews—could still vote but could not aspire to office in the Commons House of Assembly. By 1716 the attempt was made to reserve the franchise and the right to sit in the Assembly to Christians only; under this act, which was repudiated by the Lords Proprietors in England, Jews were not to be allowed even to vote. Five years later active and passive voting privileges were again limited to Christians. By 1759 the colonists decided to restrict liberties still further: Protestants only were to hold office—but that provision too was disallowed by the royal authorities in London. As we shall see, a Jew served

in the First Provincial Congress in 1774, but that was
under exceptional circumstances.

Increasing political disabilities, however, did not deter
Jews from settling in South Carolina. Their rights to worship as they saw fit and to engage in any type of business
and commerce were unrestricted. (Throughout the Middle
Ages the Jews had discovered that they could survive,
comfortably, without political liberties, as long as they
had religious freedom and economic opportunity.) In the
eighteenth century, there was probably not a country or
colony where they enjoyed all rights.

And so Jews continued to come to South Carolina, but
the rise of a community was imperceptibly slow. The Jewish community in those days grew by slow accretion. By
the 1730's there were signs of an increase in the Carolina
port. Jewish shippers began to register their boats in town;
merchants from New York discovered that Charlestown
was an excellent depot for distributing goods throughout
the South; shopkeepers appeared and advertised their
wares. But there was still no quorum of ten males for a
religious service. There was no "community."

It was not until the following decade that a communal
organization could be created. More people had come in.
Discouraged settlers filtered in from Georgia. As a result,
during the High Holydays, in the fall of 1749, a congregation was formed which was to call itself The House of
God and Mansion of Peace ("Beth Elohim Unveh
Shallom").

One of the settlers, who had come in during the 1730's,

232

became the first president, another was nominated as "rabbi," and a third was appointed *hazzan* or cantor. The officiants were, of course, volunteers. We know very little about the "rabbi" except that his name was Moses Cohen, that he kept a shop, and that he once advertised for a runaway Dutch servant girl of about ten years of age.

We know much more about the *hazzan*, to whom we revert: Isaac DaCosta. He was the Carolina Whig *émigré* whom we have already met in Philadelphia. The English DaCosta family was one of the most famous among the Spanish-Portuguese Jews; it had branches everywhere; many of its sons achieved wealth and fame, as Jews and Christians, in Holland and in England. Isaac was from England, and was probably encouraged or even helped to leave his native London by some of his rich relatives in the Sephardic congregation of that city. By the late 1740's he was in Charlestown. We doubt very much that he was a man of wealth. Wealthy men were not in the habit of braving the rigors of the wilderness merely to increase their possessions.

Like most of his fellow-Jews in the South, he was a merchant. In that area of farms and plantations, where towns were few and small, the Jew found his opportunity as a purveyor to the planters. The service which the American commission-merchant performed for the large landowners was similar in many respects to that which the East European Jewish merchant rendered the Polish landed aristocracy.

By 1751 DaCosta was already a rising businessman—we can trace him through his "ads"—and by 1755 he was in partnership with Thomas Farr, Jr., under the firm name of DaCosta and Farr. As we have seen in our study of the Pennsylvania Jewish merchants, partnerships of Jews and Gentiles—often of short duration in a common venture— were very frequent in those days. This partnership lasted into the early 1760's. Later, as members of DaCosta's family grew up, they went into business with him.

Like many other Jewish merchants in the North American colonies, DaCosta did business with Aaron Lopez of Newport, and received the usual five per cent commission, exclusive of handling expenses, on the goods he sold. It was a mutually satisfactory arrangement. For example, on a consignment of spermaceti candles worth £520 DaCosta's commission amounted to a tidy little sum.

Here is a letter that DaCosta and Farr wrote in 1761 discussing the first consignment of rum sent them by the Newport merchant:

So. Carolina, C[harle]'s Town, June 1st, 1761.
Mr. Aaron Lopez,
Sir:
Your favour of the 14th April p[er]. Capt. [Thomas] Rogers, we have receiv'd with invo[ice]. and bill lading inclosed for 9 h[ogs]h[ea]'ds rum, w'ch we have receiv'd and shall follow your directions in regard to the remitting the neat proceeds when sold. But we are very sorry to inform you of the loss that there must be on it were we to sell it off at the price that is now given here for rum. More especially as this is the first consignment that you have honour'd us with, the bad consequences attending thereon may be the means of discouraging you from making any more attemps this way. It now sells at 12/ [shillings] 6 a [to] 13/9 p. gallon, and there

is such a quantity here that we see no prospect of its rising ([even] if there is no more imported) for these three mo[nth]'s to come, and to sell yours at so low a price as is now given we cannot think off. Therefore we are determin'd to lay up all the rum we have by us up, and not offer any for sale till we can obtain a better price than what is now given.

The most principal reason that no[rth]'ward rum is so low here is that we have had a vast q[uanti]'ty lately arr'd from your place, most of w'ch being consign'd to the masters of the vessells w'ch brings it to get [specie] dollars and get away soon, will even sell at 3/ and 4/ p. gallo. under the common price. This has reduced the price from 20/ p. gallo. to 12/6. Now had this rum been consign'd to good houses here [like ours, for instance!], they would have keept up the price, for rathar than to let it fall they woud have advanced two-thirds of the value and dispatch'd the vessell. This is a thing that we believe the people with you [up in New England where they make so much rum] are unacquainted with, and is the reason why so much has been consign'd to the [ship]masters and such losses been on them.

Rice sell here now at 37/6 p.ct[hundredweight]. and a great plenty at markett, but freights are very high and scarce. There is nothing you can send here from your place will answer at present, but we imagin a vessell with a little rum, cyder, appells, and a few horses, that can be afforded here at about forty and fifty dollars each, may do very well to arrive here in August.

We shall always be proud to render you or any of your friends any services in our power; interim, we remain with esteem, sir,

Your most hum. servants,
Da Costa & Farr.[45]

The Charlestown firm held on to the rum till December, almost nine months, but they finally disposed of it at a price of sixteen to seventeen shillings per gallon. Rum was only one of the several staples which DaCosta and Lopez sold one another. Other commodities were corn, flour, hardtack, butter, beeswax, rice, indigo, deerskins, tanned leather, beer, cider, and slaves. Prices on Negroes were quoted in the four categories of men, women, boys, and girls.

But all correspondents were not as satisfactory as Lopez. During the years 1761–62 the Charlestown merchant spent twelve out of the twenty-four months in Georgia, looking after the interests of his firm and investigating agents who had defrauded him. He suffered reverses in 1765 because of the economic revolt against the new laws of British mercantilism.

Bad times set in. DaCosta was very much concerned about the state of affairs. A fervent patriot, unlike many of his fellow-citizens in the South, he believed that the colonies could survive economically without England. The Southern planters, on the other hand, were heavily dependent on the mother country, which took their tobacco, rice, indigo, and naval stores and gave them, in return, finished products and luxuries.

Southern merchants, like DaCosta, wrote frequently to their friends and correspondents in the North. Every now and then they sailed north themselves, taking their families with them. Rarely if ever did they make the trip by land; the roads were too bad.

In 1774 DaCosta set sail for Newport. This town was not a sleepy little summer resort. It was then the third or fourth most important commercial center in all North

America, and it had a good-sized Jewish community. Jews from the South, like Philip Minis, for instance, found wives in Newport.

DaCosta reached his destination in nine days, very good time indeed, for often the trip took almost twice as long. The visit that year was a combination business and pleasure trip. Newport was the "Carolina Hospital" where the fever-threatened Carolinians and Georgians went to rest and to recuperate. The Harts, the Aarons, the Minises, and the DaCostas enjoyed coming.

Pastor Ezra Stiles and DaCosta met for quite a chat on that occasion. The well-known Congregationalist minister was always eager to interview the Jews who passed through Newport, particularly those who had some learning. Like many Sephardim, DaCosta had a good general education; in his latter years he moved in the best Charlestown circles, being a steward in the Palmetto Society. DaCosta was a loyal, devoted Jew; he had also received a good religious training under Hakam Isaac Nieto in London, and was apparently able to consult the rabbinic codes. At any rate, he owned, among other works, a copy of Maimonides' famous compilation of Jewish law. While in Philadelphia, in 1782, he was called in and asked for his opinion on the legality of the proposed marriage between Jacob I. Cohen and the proselyte, Elizabeth Whitlock Mordecai.

DaCosta told the Newport Christian Hebraist that he was still *hazzan*, although actually he was no longer the regular officiant. He had held that position until 1764, when he resigned, because of some misunderstanding, and was succeeded by Abraham Alexander. He probably still of-

ficiated occasionally, and a synagogue office certainly added
to his stature as an expert in Stiles's eyes anyway.

It was DaCosta who laid out the first Jewish cemetery in
the Carolina capital. Originally it was his own family plot,
but later it was turned over to the congregation (1764).
In 1775 he tried to build a synagogue and asked Shearith
Israel in New York for money, but *Parnas* Hayman Levy
and his trustees turned him down. The times were bad; the
country was on the threshold of revolution.

One day in April, 1764, DaCosta joyfully welcomed a
compatriot into his home. The guest was Aaron's brother,
Moses Lopez, who had just sailed into the harbor as super-
cargo with a shipment from Newport consigned by Aaron
Lopez and Jacob R. Rivera. He had intended to go to a
local tavern, but DaCosta had turned over to him the best
room in the house and had insisted that he remain. It did
not take much to persuade the New Englander. The voyage
had been a most difficult one; the ship had sprung a leak,
and the pumps had to be kept going. He was tired and sick,
and welcomed a good long rest. He hastily dashed off a
brief note on the Friday afternoon of his arrival. The approaching Sabbath prevented him from writing in detail.

After Moses Lopez recovered from the exhaustion of
the voyage, he had a chance to look around and see how the
town had changed. Evidently this was his first trip to
Charlestown since 1742, twenty-two years before. And
what changes had taken place! The town had doubled in
size, and he fell in love with it. Having just passed through
a typically severe New England winter, Lopez was de-

lighted with the mildness of the Carolina climate. Even the winters, he was told, were pleasant. Meat and fish were plentiful; vegetables were in season the greater part of the year.

Large and small shops and manufactories, many of them of brick and tile, were springing up everywhere. Still it was surprising how expensive rents were in the light of the large amount of building that was going on.

The harbor was large and protected, and ships kept coming in from the West Indies, from different parts of North America, and from Europe. The other southern ports were not worth considering, not because of their lack of facilities, but because of the people who carried on business there. St. Augustine, Pensacola, and Mobile were inhabited by the scum of society. Georgia? The country was growing and its agriculture was developing, but there was not a soul in the colony whom you could trust. They were a pack of pirates, and so envious of a man doing business that if a Negro peddled a handful of onions on the market they would raise a hullabaloo.

The best time to do business in Charlestown was in the winter and spring. Trade was so active then that the town resembled a fair going full blast.

There were plenty of opportunities to make money, particularly in the slave trade. In the back country you could secure fancy prices for goods from the Scotch-Irish settlers, who rarely came to town. The planters who did business in the city were loyal to their suppliers, and they would not buy from other merchants even if they could get the same goods for less money.

Back home, in Rhode Island, if you made any money, it was only by dint of hard labor and superior intelligence. But in South Carolina! The country was so rich you could not help but do well. Aaron, with the capital he had invested in Rhode Island, could live like a prince here. He was "murdering" his time by staying in Rhode Island. This was the country!

The Carolinas never had a "booster" like Moses Lopez. Moses had been charged by the family back home to get in touch with DaCosta and to sell the ship as well as its cargo of hay, candles, oil, and other commodities. This was much more easily said than done, for so many ships were unloaded at the port, and their captains were so eager for a return load, that the rate for outgoing freight was quite reasonable. The merchants, therefore, had no real need to own their own craft, Moses wrote, explaining to brother Aaron the difficulty he experienced in selling the ship. As a result Moses Lopez did not get a satisfactory offer for his brother's boat. The price he asked was £1,200, and even though Moses was willing to give up his own commission of £50, and shave the price another £50, the best offer he could get was £1,000.

Aaron had directed Moses to advertise for a load of freight for London if the ship could not be sold. Here Isaac DaCosta's help was invaluable. The chief merchants in town—all Gentiles at this early date—respected and admired him, for he was a "gentleman of generous principles and known character."

The hay was disposed of to good advantage. But the other wares were sold at auction or left with commission agents. From Henry Laurens, one of Charlestown's most famous merchants, DaCosta secured several hundred barrels of pitch and tar destined for London, and this freight was supplemented by about 300 barrels of rice which the Lopez family shipped on their own account.

With the passage of time and the failure to sell all his cargo advantageously, Moses began to lose his enthusiasm for the golden opportunities of the Carolinas. Ultimately, in June, he was glad to return to Newport.

Among the Charlestown businessmen whom DaCosta saw frequently was Moses Lindo. He was probably the most significant figure in the South Carolina indigo industry, the second most important staple in the province.

Back in London, where he had lived the greater part of the first half of the century, he had been a merchant, a broker on the Royal Exchange, and an expert in grading indigo, which was so important as a dye in the English textile industry.

He loved his native England, he once confessed, yet he could not have been deaf to the hysterical shouts of the rabble crying, "Christianity and Old England forever," as they forced the revocation of the emancipatory Jew Bill of 1753. He knew that in the colonies he would enjoy a larger measure of political and civil rights than was accorded him at home.

Certainly he must have weighed these things, for he was a man of some education and culture. He wrote well, had gone to a good English school, had a practical, if elementary, knowledge of chemistry, and frequently engaged in scientific experimental work in dyes. In the course of this research, he sent a communication, dealing with a vegetable dye, to a coreligionist, Emanuel Mendez da Costa, a clerk at the Royal Society of London, and had the pleasure of seeing his letter published in the *Philosophical Transactions* for 1763.

Lindo, we know, was the type of man who appreciated liberty and freedom, and the promise of America may have meant as much to him as the contract in his pocket when he took passage on the "Charming Nancy" with his German Jewish clerk, Jonas Phillips. He arrived in South Carolina in November, 1756.

The specific reason why he came was that he had a contract to buy indigo and to send it back to his principals in England. The English mercantilists were very eager to encourage its growth in the American colonies, and South Carolina was fast becoming one of the important sources for the dye. In 1748 the British placed a substantial bounty on indigo, hoping that the developing industry in the colonies would emancipate them from the superior product of the French, with whom they were almost constantly waging war. Even before he had emigrated, Lindo, ever a protagonist of Carolina indigo, for which he prophesied a great future, had praised its value and quality before a committee of the House of Commons.

Here was a developing source, and he realized that with his knowledge and capacity he could become a person of importance in the field. The thought that he might play an important part in a young branch of trade and commerce flattered his vanity. Moses Lindo had a high respect for

Moses Lindo's knowledge in all matters touching on indigo. For twenty-five years before coming to Charlestown he had worked at sorting and grading the plant. Once he modestly implied that he was one of the best judges of the product in America and in Europe, by which he meant to say that he had no peer anywhere. And, strangely enough, he was probably right in spite of his boasting.

Indigo culture in this country owed much to him because he encouraged its growth and bettered its quality. He was in constant touch with the dyers in London. Although he was only a middleman, he was the prime channel for the flow of the dye stuff from Charlestown to the continent across the Atlantic. He foretold correctly that the colonies would grow hundreds of thousands of pounds annually. During the eighteen years that he lived in the colonies, he saw the trade develop from an annual production of about 300,000 pounds to one of about 1,200,000 pounds, and Lindo himself handled millions of pounds of it. He lived to see the indigo industry employ 10,000 slaves, enrich the rice planters with a supplementary income, and bring to the hungry Charlestown markets large quantities of finished British goods in exchange. It was a source of pride to him that he was helping to build the commerce of the British Empire. It was an act of patriotism to perfect a colonial dye that could compete with the best that the French enemy had created!

Lindo was a one-man Chamber of Commerce, bent on promoting South Carolina indigo. He was so active in the trade that it was inevitable that his influence would evoke envy and slander. To combat those who were attacking him, he once offered a reward of £500, currency, for sub-stantial information about the people making malicious in-sinuations. But the best people appreciated his efforts; they accepted him socially and respected him as a "noted Jew."

The following letter to *The South-Carolina Gazette* characterizes and documents his interest in his work. It was addressed to the owner and editor, Peter Timothy.

Mr. Timothy:

I have made trial of two crimson dyes lately discovered in this province, and in justice to Mr. John Story of Port Royal, carpenter, I am obliged to declare that I find his crim-son, called John's blood, answers all the purposes of cochineal, for it dyes a fine crimson on cotton so as to stand washing with soap-lees, and it is my firm opinion will likewise dye scarlet.

I have sent samples of it home, via Bristol, that, when ap-proved of in London by Mess'rs George Farmer and George Honour, two eminent dyers there, the said Mr. Story may be entitled to part of the reward offered, by the society for en-couraging arts, to such as can fix a scarlet or turkey-red on cotton.

And as there are many roots and weeds to be found in this province and Georgia that will dye reds, I shall be obliged to all who will meet with such in their way to send me a pound dried in the shade, that I may make trials of them. And if the discoverers be persons in middling circumstances, and what they produce to me be proven a dye, I will reward them with fifty pounds currency, and use my best endeavours to obtain for them further gratuities from the Dyers Company in London.

I am sensible, Mr. Timothy, you are a well-wisher to the interest of this province and the mother-country; therefore, hope you will not omit publishing in your gazettes any hints tending to the advantage of both whenever such are offered you, and thereby, amongst others, oblige

Your constant reader,
Moses Lindo.

Charles Town, July 16, 1759.[46]

By 1762 the tradesmen, merchants, and planters of Carolina were quite willing to petition Governor Thomas Boone that Lindo be appointed Surveyor and Inspector-General of Indico. It is of interest, but not surprising, to note that there was not a single Jewish merchant or planter among the forty-eight men who signed the request. Individual Jews owned farms and plantation lands in the Carolinas, but agriculture was not a Jewish vocation. Francis Salvador in the next decade was one of the exceptions. The Jewish merchants who had begun to immigrate in larger numbers since the 1750's had not yet acquired wealth; they were on the way up, but had not yet arrived financially. With wealth they would seek larger social recognition as plantation owners.

Being Surveyor gave Lindo the opportunity of establishing those high standards of quality which were bound to create a receptive market for American indigo. There was no salary attached to the position, but he made a good living through the commissions he secured for buying, selling, and judging the finished product. His certification on a hogshead carried weight with prospective purchasers, and he wishfully, if naïvely, pointed out that counterfeiting a certificate was a capital crime back home in England.

In 1769 he met the Reverend Hezekiah Smith of New England, who had come to Charlestown to raise money for

Rhode Island College—later to be called Brown University —which had opened four years earlier. Smith found Charlestown Jewry liberal, and Lindo the most generous of all. Lindo was very much interested in the new college because of its broad policies, its prohibition of any type of religious tests, and the complete freedom accorded every individual to follow the dictates of his conscience. He recalled with great pleasure his own student days back in London, but probably also remembered that he was never matriculated because he was a Jew, and that he was admitted merely as an auditor or unregistered student. Surely a new day was dawning for the Jew in this country, and in a burst of generous enthusiasm—truly characteristic of the buoyant enterpriser—he promised Smith and the trustees that if the school would admit Jews without discriminating against them religiously, he would make substantial gifts to it. Suiting the action to the word, at least for this one contribution, he sat down and wrote his New York correspondents:

Charlestown, 17 April, 1770.

Mess'rs Sampson & Solomon Simson,
Gentlemen:

You will be so kind as to order your correspondent in Rhode Island to pay unto the Trustees of the new college the sum of five pounds York currency on my account, and to transmit me th'ir receipt in my name.

As the Rev'd Mr. Smith will inform th'm, the reason th't induces me to be a benefactor to this college is th'ir having no objection of admitting the youth of our nation without interfereing in principals of religion. If so, my donation shall exceed beyond the bounds of th'ir imagination.

246

I presume this college is like Merchant Taylor's School in London where I went every day for three years, as well as two of my brothers, from 9:00 to 1:00 o'clock. There was at th't time about 800 boys, sons of the principal merchants and trading people in the city. I have lived to see two Lord Mayors and seven aldermen, and many toping [excellent] merchants my school-fellows, which, I assure you, was no small service to me when I was a broker on the Royal Exchange.

I have sent yo' by the bearer two of our gazettes wherein I believe there is more news from London than at y'r place.

I sincerely wish you well, and remain, with regard, gentlemen,

Your obliged humble serv't,
Moses Lindo.[47]

A true copy of the letter to the Simsons was given to Mr. Smith as an evidence of good faith, and after the trustees and fellows of the College had studied its contents, they sat down at the next annual meeting, at Providence, and fortified their charter with the statement "that the children of Jews may be admitted into this institution and intirely enjoy the freedom of their own religion, without any constraint or imposition whatever." Accordingly, on January 1, 1771, this action of the trustees was communicated to Lindo. They informed him, in addition, that they would exempt Jewish students from attending Christian religious services, that they would provide a Jewish tutor if the number of students justified it, and, if the Jews so desired, they could establish their own chair of Hebrew, with a Jewish instructor of course. It was also pointed out by the eager trustees that there was a Latin School in town which might well serve as a preparatory department for those young Jews who wished to acquire the rudiments that would fit them for matriculation. And, finally, and most important, they enclosed a subscription book for the Charlestown merchant and his friends.

As far as we know, Lindo sent no more money. No doubt he had been carried away by enthusiasm. He had no wealth. Though we do have an advertisement of his in which he offered to buy a five hundred-acre plantation with about sixty to seventy slaves, this advertisement may merely have been a form of publicity with him.

Lindo liked to keep his name constantly in the public eye. In 1772 he surrendered his appointment as Surveyor-General of Indico, but he was still using the title when he died two years later, in April. He left a modest estate, the most important items of which were some silver plate, a few books, and a gold watch.

Perhaps it was just as well for him that he died that year. In just twelve months the Revolution broke out. For rebels there would be no bounty on indigo; without it the industry was doomed to decline. Indeed, in the post-war emergent United States, the royal blue of indigo was to give way before the immaculate white of King Cotton.

Moses Lindo, as far as the record shows, had no correspondence with the omnipresent Aaron Lopez, but after all he was not a merchant. Apparently they did not know each other, yet they had one thing in common: their gifts to the new Rhode Island College. Lindo, as we read, gave £5; Lopez and his father-in-law, 10,000 feet of lumber. But if Lindo did no business with Lopez, there were plenty of others in the South who did. Among the Charlestonians whose letters are now to be found in the archives of The Newport Historical Society, there were few on more friendly terms with the New England merchant than Joshua Hart.

Persons by the name of Hart were numerous and widespread in colonial America and, as we know, were not necessarily related. They were scattered all the way from Canada to St. Eustatia in the West Indies. There may have been some "Spanish" Harts, but most of the Jewish Harts were descendants of Germans.

The Harts complicate our study of history in the colonial period, for we are not always sure that we are dealing with Jews. The name was a very common one, borne by both Gentiles and Jews in early America. Henry Clay of Kentucky married a Hart. Though it was reported that Mrs. Lucretia Hart Clay was of Jewish stock and owned a Hebrew Bible which had belonged to her paternal grandfather, there is no real evidence that this pioneer family of Kentucky was Jewish.

This whole business of "Jewish" names is quite confusing. There was a definite tendency on the part of the immigrant Jews in those days to drop their Spanish and their German Jewish names, as they passed through England, and to appropriate English names. Thus it is that we find them in the seventeenth and eighteenth centuries with such names as Phillips, Brown, Rice, Hays, Henry, Laney, Simson, Jones, and the like.

We can be sure that Joshua Hart was Jewish. He had been in business in Charlestown at least since 1762, when we first run across his advertisements. He was a friendly soul, apparently, for he liked to mix a little sociability with his business, and on occasion he took time out to drop Lopez a friendly note:

Charles Town, 15th February, 1771.
Dear Sir:
Your kind and obliging favour of the 20th ulto. which was handed me by Capt. Earl, I have now before me, and am happy to find your goodself and family continue enjoying a perfect state of health. May the same be long attended with every other desireable felicity.

You'l please accept of a small cask sour oranges as a token of our sincer friendship. Mrs. Hart joins me in our sincer thanks for your kind favour of the salmon which came in due season. Mrs. Hart and family joins me in wishing you and family, your brother Abram and family, the widow Lopez and children, and Mr. David Lopez, and the rest of your worthy family, a merry Purim, and may the Good [God] of Israel set a blessing on you all, and am, with sincerity,

Your assured friend and most obedient servant,
Joshua Hart.
P. S. You'l please excuse my curtailing [this note], being Friday afternoon [right before the Sabbath], therefore not able to enlarge.[48]

Rarely in his letters did he fail to extend greetings for the coming Jewish holyday, whichever it might happen to be. Frequently, when writing to Newport, he included a good word for the "rabbi," Isaac Touro.

The following letter is another example of his bluff cordiality and of his not unpleasant admixture of rice and religion. We may infer from this note that Hart had married a widow whose maiden name was Allen, and that two of her daughters by her first marriage lived with Grandfather Allen in Newport. Although there was a well-known family of Allens in the Philadelphia synagogues in the early nineteenth century, the Newport Allens were very probably Gentiles.

Charles Town, 27th March, 1772.

Dear Sir:

It's with satisfaction and pleasure I acknowledge the receipt of your esteemed favor of the 5th ulto. which now lays before me, and note the contents. Am extream glad to find that you and every branch of your family injoy'd a perfect state of health, the continuance of which shall be my daily prayers to God to continue.

Inclosed you have bills of loading and parcells for three barrells of choice rice, marked and number'd as per margin, which I wish safe to your hands. And as you'l find there's a ballance due—as per account at foot of £5.6.6, our currency—to me, I beg and intreat you'l give it to my wife's two daughters, Rebecca and Sarah, who lives at Father Allens.

I should have sent you some ground nutts or potatoes for your acceptance, but none being come to market that was any way good I would not purchase any.

Having not of moment to add, but that I wish you and every one of your family a merry Pascua de Pesah [Passover], and that you may see many of them with felicity and happiness.

Mrs. Hart and [my] daughters joins me with my friendly salutations to you, Mrs. Lopez, and dear children, and, believe me to be with pure and disinterested regard, dear sir,

Your esteemed freind and humble servant,

Joshua Hart.

P. S. Please give my best respects to your sister Lopez and her good family, to Mr. Ab. Lopez and his family, to your brother, David Lopez, to Domini Truro [Hazzan Touro], to Father Allen and his family, and all inquireing freinds.[49]

It is interesting to note in the following letter that £26, South Carolina currency, was worth only about $17 specie. Inflation had already set in, and because of it—and the insistence of creditors abroad—the New England merchants were always glad to get Spanish dollars or Portuguese gold johannes from their customers. Inflation was to assume severe proportions in the next few years with the outbreak of the Revolution and the flood of paper money. The declining value of Continental currency was in turn accelerated by the appearance of counterfeits. Some of the Charlestonians must have felt sure that their paper money could not be counterfeited because they adorned it with letters of the Hebrew alphabet to baffle would-be imitators.

Charles Town, 8 Feb'y, 1773.

Mr. Aaron Lopez,
Dear Sir:

I have your much esteem'd favor of the 8th ultimo covering an account and bill of lading for eight quarter-casks of white, and two of red Lisbon [wine]. The red might answer very well here, but the people in this province are quite unaquainted with it, and the white comes to[o] dear for this markett, as I might have bought better here for less money. And about three months since I purchased a quantity of much the same quality as yours from Uriah Woolman, a merchant of Philadelphia, at twenty dollars. Since then I have been offer'd to be imported from the same city any quantity I liked at eighteen dollars.

The four kegs of cordials your brother [Abraham] sent me I have sold to some of [my] country friends for the great price of £26.17, this currency, to pay which I have sent by Capt. Earl, sixteen dollars, which—with seventeen/[shillings] I paid for freight and wharfage—is the amount. I should not

have been able to obtain so large a price but bye my connections in the country and selling them for a long credit.

I am very sorry to be oblig'd to inform you that I cannot
undertake a commission trade. You well know my incapacity,
and haveing no clerk to keep my accounts, I must therefore
decline it. But I shall in the propper season for cordials send
for a sufficient quantity of anniseed [cordial] as will answer
mine and my friends' purpose. In the mean time please to inform me how he [your brother Abraham] will sell the same
p. gallon.

I should have sent you rice for the cost of the wine, being
238 5/8 dollars, but it's now at 60/[shillings], and, by the
account I have, it can be bought for less with you. I have
therefore defer'd it, hoping that in a short time it may fall in
the price, when I shall execute your order, but if that does
not happen, I will send you dollars or johannes's which[ever]
will be most agreable.

I thank God that my family is well and, particularly, that
my daughter Hester is restored to a good state of health. You
will please to make all our kindest salutations acceptable to
your lady and every branch of your worthy family, and believe me to be very sincerely, my dear sir,

Your oblige friend and very h'ble servant,
Joshua Hart.[50]

In the fall of that year Joshua Hart made the long trip
by boat to Philadelphia to see a good physician. (The only
two medical schools in the country then were in New York
and in Philadelphia.) He may have taken time out while in
the latter city to run over to New York to see his friend
Jonas Phillips, who was just getting out of some sort of
serious trouble. When Phillips had first come to the colonies, he had stayed for a while with Hart in Charlestown,
and a friendship had sprung up between the two.

While Hart was up North his eldest daughter, Esther, carried on the correspondence with Lopez, whom she had met the preceding year while on a visit to Newport. Esther pops up quite frequently in the letters to the Rhode Island merchant, as Esther or Hetty or Hester, but, apparently, in spite of the change of name, she is the same girl.

Charles Town, 3d Sept., 1773.

Mr. Aaron Lopez,
Sir:

Your much esteem'd favour came safe to hand with the assurances of your kind wishes towards my papa and mama and family, which you have our greatfull acknowledgements in return for them. If my papa was presant he would with a great deal of pleasur answare his worthy friend's esteem'd favour, but as he [is] not, is deprived of that satisfaction, as [he] is gone to Philadelphia for the benefit of his helth, for he has been very much indisposed this summer.

My papa had thoughts of paying your place also a visit if he found himself better, which I hope kind providence will grant him. I hope my friend will excuse the liberty I have taken in addressing him with this scrall, but as papa being absent was the reason of my being so bold.

My mama joines with me in congratulating you and my dear Mrs. Lopez on her safe delivery. It also renders us happy to think she is so brave with all your dear branches. A continuance of that blessing we sincerly wish you all.

Good sir, you will pleas to make mama and seflf respects acceptab[l]e to Mrs. Lopez and Mrs. Mendez [your daughter], and Miss Ester [Lopez], and the rest of the family. You will pleas to accept the same from one that subscribes herself,

Your obliged humble serv't,
Esther Hart.[51]

Like her father, Esther referred to children as "dear branches," no doubt reflecting the words of Psalm 128:3, "Thy wife shall be as a fruitful vine in the innermost parts of thy house; thy children like olive plants, round about thy table." Esther sounds like a very sensible person; it is a pity that we know so little about her.

We are fortunate in knowing a little more about one of the sisters of Esther, the one next to her, Richea or Ritcey, as she was called. (The youngest, Shankey, was only a child then.) In November, 1777, Ritcey married Abraham Mendez Seixas of Georgia, and we are informed by the Charlestown *Gazette of the State of South-Carolina* that she was "a young lady of the most amiable qualifications." We would not dare to question Ritcey's charm, but our confidence in her amiability would be immeasurably increased had the newspapers of that day not used that adjective for so many of the girls whose marriages they announced.

Ritcey's Abraham, then twenty-six years old, was one of the numerous sons of Isaac Mendez Seixas of Newport and thus a brother of Benjamin and "Rabbi" Gershom. Although his family followed the Spanish ritual, and his paternal ancestors were indeed pure Sephardim, he obviously had no objection to marrying a "German"; his mother was of Ashkenazic descent. Such marriages were very frequent in those days for, as we have seen, the majority of the Jews in all the "Spanish" congregations were of Ashkenazic origin, but only in America. On the Continent Portuguese noses were still uplifted.

For part of the war, Abraham M. Seixas lived in Charlestown. Later he made his home permanently in that city.

He was a merchant. Like others, he advertised his wares, but, unlike most of his competitors, he preferred poetry to prose in appealing for custom. Here are a few of his verses from the *South-Carolina State-Gazette* for September 6, 1794: (Incidentally, we learn from the rhyme how to pronounce his name.)

> ABRAHAM SEIXAS,
> All so gracious,
> Once again does offer
> His service pure,
> For to secure
> Money in the coffer.
>
> He has for sale
> Some negroes, male,
> Will suit full well grooms.
> He has likewise
> Some of their wives,
> Can make clean, dirty rooms.
>
> He surely will
> Try all his skill
> To sell, for more or less,
> The articles
> Of beaux and belles,
> That they to him address.

During the Revolution, Seixas had served as an officer in Georgia and South Carolina, and, like many another veteran, he went into politics. But he had little luck. He ran for office in the 1790's and was defeated. Nothing daunted, he resorted to his favorite weapon, poetry, to hack out a victory for himself. In the following verse he asked the electors where they stood; he asked them to commit themselves:

> The man I love, who will avow
> He is my friend or is my foe;
> But he who comes with double face,
> I do despise as being base.

The people did commit themselves; in the next election he ended up at the bottom of the list.

Chapter 12

North and South Carolina, 1776 — 1790

ANOTHER Southerner who threw in his lot with the Continentals was Francis Salvador, a nephew of the English financier, Joseph Salvador. The elder Salvador had purchased about 100,000 acres, in 1755, in the northwestern part of the colony, in what was later to become Ninety Six District. Joseph Salvador lost much of his great fortune, possibly through the decline of the Dutch East India Company and as a result of the earthquake in Lisbon, and in order to keep his head above water he was compelled to sell some of his lands. Among the purchasers—and his creditors—was his own nephew and son-in-law, the twenty-six-year-old Francis Salvador. This young settler immigrated into South Carolina in December, 1773, and soon became one of the important landowners in Ninety Six District.

It took only a few months to change him into a planter administering a large estate of some 6,000 acres, manned by at least thirty slaves. He grew indigo.

Salvador's choice of this frontier area was, of course, dictated by the fact that his father-in-law had large holdings there, but, whether involuntary or not, the choice was an excellent one. This was the fastest growing area in the colony; settlers were pouring in to take advantage of the Indian trade, which consisted primarily of barter for deerskins. At the time Salvador took over his new plantation at Coronaca Creek, his election district was the second most populous in South Carolina.

Very shortly after he settled in Ninety Six, Salvador became a fervent patriot. It is fair to assume that family experiences may have contributed to make of him a Whig. Back in England, in 1753, Francis' father-in-law had been one of the leaders in the struggle to secure the passage of a naturalization act for the Jews of England. Wealthy Jews like the Salvadors, who had negotiated huge loans for the British state and who had helped to maintain its credit during acute political crises, felt that they were entitled to the benefits of a naturalization law which at best made of them only second-class citizens. During the agitation for the passage of the 1753 bill, Joseph Salvador had pointed out to the Duke of Newcastle that leading Jews had encouraged some of their coreligionists to improve themselves by going to the American plantations, but, ironically enough, when these protégés returned to England, after having been naturalized in the colonies, they actually had more rights than the very patrons who had sent them! After the English Naturalization Act of 1753 was finally passed, Joseph Salvador was booed in a theatre and compelled to withdraw. Soon afterwards the law was repealed.

There was every reason, therefore, for a man like young Francis Salvador to be anti-British in America; here he stood a good chance of speedily securing complete political equality.

Despite bitter Tory opposition Francis harangued his neighbors in defense of American liberties. On one occasion he and his Gentile friend, Richard Andrews Rapley—the lawyer for the Salvador interests in America—dared to present themselves at a pro-British gathering and were almost mobbed. The notorious Tory, David Fanning, who reported this incident, angrily stigmatized Rapley as a Jew. Perhaps the device was not new even then. It was Fanning's method of denouncing a rebel who was leading the people away from the mother country.

In spite of the fact that Salvador had been living in Ninety Six for only about twelve months, he represented that district in the First Provincial Congress in 1775. It is doubtful that he was ever elected formally, even by a Whig minority. It is more probable that he was selected and appointed by the patriot leaders in Charlestown. Later he served in the Second Provincial Congress of South Carolina (November, 1775). When this latter congress became the first General Assembly of the rebel colony of South Carolina in 1776, he naturally remained a member. He was thus the first unconverted Jew to serve either in a provincial or in an "American" legislative body.

The Whigs in his district respected him for his opposition to British aggression—and they were impressed also by the fact that he was a wealthy man. Most of them were small holders, and they were willing to follow the traditional

Southern pattern of electing their officers from among the rich planters. But what of the Carolina law which permitted only Christians to vote and to hold office? Obviously they ignored it. It was a virtue to flout laws which had been enacted under the British regime. Almost anything could happen in the colonies in those troubled times.

Colonel Charles C. Pinckney and his fellow-deputy, Francis Salvador, were appointed a committee to examine the 1776 constitution after it had been engrossed and to compare it with the original draft. Apparently Salvador voiced no objection to the action of the Provincial Congress, which provided that the president of the colony take an oath to "maintain and defend the laws of God, the Protestant religion, and the liberties of America." He realized—if he thought about it at all—that this proviso was directed not against Jews, but against Catholics. After all, he had been accepted as a member of the Congress; back in England such rights were not even in prospect.

Beginning the last week of June in that summer of 1776, the British launched an attack on South Carolina, front and rear. The army and navy attacked in the front at Charlestown on June 28th; the British-incited Indians and Tories attacked in the back country on July 1st. Salvador joined up immediately as a volunteer with his fellow-congressman, Major Andrew Williamson. The latter was in command of the district militia; it was their duty to defend the outlying settlements from the raiding Cherokees. The civil war between the Tories and the Whigs heightened the terror. There were hatred and cruelty on all sides. In a fight at Lyndley's Fort, near the Saluda River, during the night of the 14th–15th of July, some of the captured "Indians" turned out to be painted Tories. Ten days later, Chief Justice William H. Drayton wrote Salvador bluntly that Williamson and his men were to punish the Indians mercilessly. Their cornfields were to be cut up, captive Indians were to be enslaved, their towns burnt, their land confiscated, and the nation extirpated.

As the following letter testifies, Salvador was in constant touch with the aggressive Drayton, keeping him informed of the situation on the northwestern frontier. It was written at a little settlement just four miles away from the Cherokee boundary line.

Camp near Dewett's Corner, 18th July, 1776

Dear Sir:
. . . . You would have been surprized to have seen the change in this country two days after you left me [June 29th, at my plantation, Coronaca]. On Monday morning one of Capt. Smith's sons came to my house with two of his fingers shot off and gave an account of the shocking catastrophe at his father's. [The Indians had killed his parents and two of his brothers and sisters.]

I immediately galloped [twenty-eight miles] to Major Williamson's to inform him but found another of Smith's sons there, who had made his escape and alarmed that settlement. The whole country was flying—some to make forts, others as low as Orangeburgh [over halfway to Charlestown].

Williamson was employed night and day sending expresses [couriers] to raise the militia, but the panic was so great that the Wednesday following, the Major and myself marched to the late Capt. Smith's with only forty men. The next day we were joined by forty more and have been gradually increasing ever since, tho' all the men in the country were loth to turn out till they had procured some kind of fancied security for their families. However, we had last night 500 men, but have not been joined by any from the other side of the [Saluda] River. I rode there last Saturday and found Col. Williams and Lisles [Lisle] and two companies from Col. Richardson's regiment, amounting to 430 men.

They were attacked on [early] Monday morning, July 15th, by Indians and Scopholites [Tories and partisans], but repulsed them, taking thirteen white men prisoners. The Indians fled the moment day appeared.

I will not trouble you with more particulars, as Major Williamson will send a circumstantial account to his Excellency [John Rutledge, President of South Carolina].

I am afraid the burthen of the war will fall on this regiment, and that the people over the [Saluda] River [to the north] will do nothing. They grumble at being commanded by a Major; and, I fear, if they join us at all, which I doubt, they will be very apt to prejudice the service by altercations about command. I cannot help saying that if Williamson is fit to conduct such an expedition, he certainly ought to have a much higher rank than any of these chaps, who don't object to his person but his rank. I likewise think it an omission that the colonels on the other side the River have no written orders to put themselves, or their men, under his command.

On the last accounts from town [Charlestown]—that [Robert] Cuningham and his companions [suspected Tories] were set at liberty—we were very near having a mutiny in camp. And it [this release] is really a measure which, though certainly intended for the best, [is] very alarming to all ranks of people. The ignorant look upon it as turning their enemies loose on their backs in the day of their distress. And the sensible part consider it as a dangerous exercise of a dispensing power, assumed contrary to the express determination of [the Provincial] Congress and a corroborating resolve of the succeeding House of Assembly. . . .

Our men seem spirited and very much exasperated against our enemies. They are all displeased with the people over the River for granting quarter to their prisoners, and declare they will grant none either to Indians or white men who join them. We have just received an account that two of the Cherokees' head warriors were killed in the late skirmish at Lindley's Fort. 19th July.

. . . .We have just heard from over the River that the white people in general [the Tories] had quitted the Indians after the repulse at Lindley's and were delivering themselves up to Col. Liles. He has sent all these to Ninety Six jail against whom there is proof of having been in the action.

I hope you will pardon the freedom with which I express my sentiments, but I look upon it as an advantage to men in power to be truly informed of the people's situation and disposition. This must plead my excuse, and believe me to be, with great respect, dear sir,

Your most obedient humble servant,
Francis Salvador.

P.S. We, this day, increased to 600, all from the same regiment. Capt. [James] McCall, with twenty men, was sent by Major Williamson to the Cherokees at Seneca [Essenecca] to make prisoners of some white men [Tories], by the encouragement of some Indians who had been at the Major's. When the detachment got near, the Indians came out to meet them, spoke friendly to them, and invited the captain, lieutenant, and another man to sup with them, leaving three of their own people in their room. And, in a few hours after, in the night, the Indians returned and suddenly attacked the detachment which fled as fast as possible. They are all returned but the captain and six men.

This happened immediately [before July 1st] before Smith's family was cut off, who lost five negro men, himself, wife, and five children [Three of these five were later found alive]. . . .[52]

In the early morning of August 1st, Williamson and his men were ambushed in the village of Essenecca. Francis Salvador, shot three times, fell from his mount, and was scalped while still alive. He died within an hour. When informed in his last moments that the enemy had been defeated, he said he was satisfied, shook Williamson's hand, and died.

He was probably the first Jew to die in defense of the new United States. On the plaque dedicated to his memory in City Hall Park in Charleston, South Carolina, these words are inscribed:

> Born an aristocrat, he became a democrat,
> An Englishman, he cast his lot with America;
> True to his ancient faith, he gave his life
> For new hopes of human liberty and understanding.

Less than two years after the death of Salvador, the South Carolina Assembly framed a constitution that made it impossible for a Jew to hold office. The constitution made Protestantism the established religion of the state. No man could be elected to the state House of Representatives, to the state Senate, or to any high office, unless he was a Protestant. Only those church bodies that believed in the Christian religion were eligible for the privilege of incorporation. Beth Elohim, the synagogue, could thus not hope for legal recognition. However, as a society which believed in God and His justice, it was to be freely tolerated. These religious disabilities were not removed till 1790.

Salvador had served his country as a fighting man. Other Jews participated in the war in other ways. Some were merchants supplying civilians and the army at a time when the English blockade, the attacks of guerrillas, and the absence of a satisfactory medium of exchange made it very difficult to carry on commerce and trade.

Not all these businessmen lived in Charlestown. There were a few in Georgetown, Camden, Black Mingo, and Beaufort in the late eighteenth century. Within a decade after the Jewish community was organized in Charlestown, Jews began to move up the coast. No later than 1761, some of them were already settled in Georgetown on Wynah Bay, a town of less than one hundred houses. In some instances Charlestown Jews established branch businesses there with resident partners. One of the first Jewish settlers in this port was Abraham Cohen, the son of the Moses Cohen who was the first "rabbi" of Charlestown. After the Revolution, Abraham, a veteran, became Georgetown's first postmaster.

We are able to gain some insight into the typical problems which confronted the Georgetown merchants in doing business during the later days of the war from some letters addressed to General Francis Marion. The most famous of the South Carolina guerrillas, "Swamp-Fox" Marion, was particularly busy in 1781 harassing the British. His constant tactics consisted of wearing down his opponents by cutting their lines of communication with their base at Charlestown. During the summer and autumn of 1781, the Americans, despite repeated maulings by the British lion, continued to improve their positions. The Continental cause was in the ascendancy. But the American troops were in bad shape. Many were wounded and malarious, medicines were scarce, and equipment and supplies were hard to get, not only for the army, which had no money, but also for the merchants, dependent for stocks on almost inaccessible northern and foreign markets.

With Charlestown in the hands of the enemy, Marion and his commissary officers were only too happy to secure what they could from nearby Georgetown, out of which Marion had finally succeeded in driving the British in the spring of that year. One of the merchants with whom he did business there was the fifty-four-year-old Mordecai Myers. If we may judge from his advertisements, he had been in town, engaged in trade and coastwise shipping, in the early 1770's.

Myers was eager to do business with General Marion, his aid, Colonel Horry, and others, bartering merchandise for indigo. This staple would find a ready market in the North, where people were making their own cloth and needed a good dye. But the Georgetown merchant—like the others in town—wanted the assurance that after he got the indigo, Marion's officers would not seize it, "press it," for the needs of the army and the state. While submitting an invoice for goods supplied to one of Marion's commissary officers, Myers explained his financial problems to the General:

Honored Sir: Georgetown, Oct. 6, 1781.

Agreeably to your letter by Capt. Mitchell of the 15th September, and your order of the first inst., I have supplied Commissary Swinton with the following articles as per bill enclosed. I can assure you I have charged the goods at the same rate I sold them last fall for cash to the inhabitants of this part of the country, which any of them can testify.

The indigo you were so obliging as to promise me in payment for these articles you receive for the public use, I should be glad to receive when convenient, as there is now a trade commenced between this post [port?] and some of the northern states, that I may be able to supply the public as well as individuals with necessaries. But it will be of little consequence for me to receive indigo in payment, unless your Honor would be so kind as to give me a protection for it, as Major Vanderhorst is here at present "pressing" all of that article that he can lay his hands on.

Your Honor must be sensible that unless the traders of the place are indulged to keep what produce they have on hand, or what they may receive from time to time, they cannot barter with those masters of vessels before mentioned, and of course [the masters] will not come to this post. [This] will be of infinite disadvantage to the people at large, as well as the public. And as I have no other dependence, must of course perish unless your Honor will take this matter into consideration and give me some relief.

I have also supplied Col. Peter Horry's Regiment of Light Dragoons to a considerable amount, also Capt. Ransom Davis, which I should be glad to receive payment for in indigo, as it will enable me to give you further assistance in supplies, as I intend being concerned in a vessel to trade at present to Nerbern [Newbern, N. C.], there being at present a large quantity of captured goods there.

And if your Honor should think me worthy, I should be happy in importing any articles from thence that your Honor or the public may stand in need of.

I am, with the greatest esteem and respect,

Your Honor's very humble servant,
Mordecai Myers.

P. S. I delivered your handk's to Capt. Mitchell some time ago.[53]

268

So far as is known, Marion's reply to Myers' letter is not extant.

We have just read, a few lines above, that Myers was trading with North Carolina. Jewish shippers were constantly in touch with merchants and planters in that province, but very few Jews lived there.

An apparent exception was a planter-shipper in the Albemarle region, a man by the name of Cullen Pollok. It would seem fairly obvious that this Pollok was a Jew. (A Pollok is a Polack!) He was a correspondent of Aaron Lopez; his wife, Ann, was a close personal friend of Mrs. Lopez; and the two names, Cullen and Pollok, remind us of Cushman Polock, whom we know as a contemporary Georgia and Pennsylvania Jew.

Cullen sounds suspiciously like a variation of the good old Jewish Calman. Yet we know beyond the slightest doubt that Cullen, the grandson of a North Carolina governor, was no Jew.

Or take the case of another old settler, one Laney. To judge by his name, he was definitely not a Jew. But names do not always bring anonymity. When he testified in 1784 at the trial of a member of the North Carolina Assembly accused of theft, the minutes naïvely refer to him as "Mr. Laney, a Jew."

Why was it that no Jewish community developed in North Carolina in pre-Revolutionary days? Was it the lack of political and religious rights which kept Jews out?

It is true that the Church of England was established in the colony and that it made every effort to dominate the religious life of the settlers. Teachers in the different schools were expected to conform to the doctrines of the Anglican Church. Protestant Dissenters were taxed against their will to support the established church. Some of the Dissenters apparently were disfranchised: it was not until 1766 that Presbyterian clergymen were permitted to perform marriages, although even then the fees went to the clergymen of the Church of England; Baptists were not allowed to officiate at marriages till the Revolution; and it was not until 1778 that all ministers of the gospel were legally accorded that privilege. This last law would still have prevented a rabbi from marrying a Jewish couple.

Under the establishment—as in Virginia—there was little room, officially, for the Jew as a religionist, although his presence as an individual might well be overlooked. It might be argued, though, and with justice, that the establishment of the Church in North Carolina was no real deterrent to Jewish settlement, because the Church was always weak, always under attack by the vigorous, recalcitrant, Protestant Dissenters. But the Dissenters, though themselves fighting for religious liberty, were more illiberal than the Anglicans. That freedom which they so earnestly sought, they had no desire to accord to others.

Typical was the attitude of the people of the Mecklenburg district. When they sent their delegates to the state constitutional convention in 1776, they instructed them to insist on the free and undisturbed exercise of religion for all professing Christians. No Christian was to pay any tax for the support of any denomination other than his own. This emphasis on "Christian" was not accidental or formal.

It was deliberate. To be sure, there was probably not a single Jew at that time in that part of the colony—and they obviously did not want any.

The Mecklenburg delegates were instructed specifically to disqualify Catholics and Jews, among others, from holding office in the new state. In spite of strong opposition, they were successful in their effort. The first constitution of North Carolina allowed no place of trust to those who denied the truth of the Protestant religion and the divine authority of the New Testament (1776).

Later, when the adoption of the federal constitution was being debated in the state, David Caldwell, the distinguished Presbyterian clergyman, who was credited with prime responsibility for the above anti-Catholic and anti-Jewish clause, fought also to reject the federal constitution because it contained no religious test. It was his fear that unless such a test were imposed, Jews and pagans would come to North Carolina and endanger its character. However, the majority of the state leaders did not share Caldwell's fears and they finally approved the federal constitution as enlarged by the Bill of Rights. But it was not until 1868 that a North Carolina constitutional assembly—in which thirteen Negroes took an active part—finally enfranchised the Jews of that state.

There was, then, an absence of political and religious liberties for Jews, among others, in colonial and Revolutionary North Carolina. But it would be wrong to maintain that these were the factors which deterred Jews from settling in that province. Originally, South and North Carolina shared a common charter. Yet one sheltered a flourishing Jewish community, while the other had none.

As we saw, the Church of England was established also in South Carolina. Disabilities were imposed on Jews in the latter province limiting their right to vote and to hold office —yet they came and continued to come in in ever increasing numbers all through the eighteenth century. The Jews of Charlestown were certainly conscious of the disabilities under which they labored—but they were just as conscious of the statistical fact that the tonnage which poured in and out of their colony was larger than that of New York. Ultimately, South Carolina—Charlestown—sheltered the largest Jewish community in the South.

The fact is—and this is basic—that few Jews came to North Carolina for the same reasons that few Gentile merchants came: the coast was bad, the proprietors were negligent, the government inadequate, and pirates abounded. There were problems of land holding, there were few towns and markets, and, what is most important, there were more attractive opportunities elsewhere.

Nevertheless, by the middle of the eighteenth century, individual Jews were found scattered in the principal towns. One of them was Michael Levy of Edenton.

Levi or Levy was a common name in the eighteenth century. Many were Gentiles, though it is not improbable that a more or less remote ancestor was of Jewish stock. In North Carolina the name occurs as early as the 1760's.

Michael Levy was probably a Jew; we know of a Jew of that name who lived during this period in South Carolina. He might well have migrated north of the border seeking

272

new fields. In some of his letters this Levy of North Carolina referred to his friend Henry, who was about to embark for the West Indies, probably Joel Henry, a German Jew from Fuerth, and the father of a Jacob Henry who was later to become a member of the North Carolina legislature. In view of the fact, too, that Levy was a merchant, one is fairly safe in numbering him among the children of Israel.

During the fall and early winter of 1780, Levy was carrying on a correspondence with the planter-merchant Colonel John Walker, who had commissioned him to buy coffee and rum. In his letters to this well-known patriot, Levy reported on his purchases, and, of course, retailed the latest war gossip when he had any. He and his friends were, at the time, caught right in the midst of Cornwallis' maneuvers to capture the Carolinas with the aid of the loyalists. Ever since the spring the English had been working their way north from Charlestown toward the Virginia border. Fortunately, the battle of King's Mountain had just been fought, ending in a decisive victory for the riflemen from the hills, who succeeded in crushing Major Ferguson's loyalists and regulars. However, in Virginia to the north, the English position had been strengthened by the addition of 3,000 troops. Edenton and Newbern, the scene of Levy's activities, lay between these two grinding millstones of the English.

In the following note he briefly described the trials that faced him and his fellows during those difficult days.

Edenton, Oct'r 31th, 1780.

My dear Frind:
I supose yow think I have for got yow, but was yow to see me yow woold pity me. I have not got strength to walk.

I have the fever evry day from twelve at noon to twelve in the night. However, I have mindid my busnis. Yow have seen in one of my letters thet thair has been three wesels cut out of this harbur [by the British] and ware retaken. Also some of the merchants wanted money, and I have purchased four hog[hea]'d of rum at 135 doller p'r gallon. The[y] contain 466 gallons. I had likwise tew hog'd by me wich I give 130 doller p'r gallon. The[y] contain 246 gallons. The [w]hole contain 712 gallons.

We have bad news hiar. The enemy are landed in Virginia, with abowt 3000 mam [men]. We ware much alarmed hiar for fiar of coming hiar. But we this day [had] news thet thair is but 250 men at Suffolk [in Virginia]. The rest are the other side of James River.

Dear frind, I have taken care of the rum. I lodge in a privet [house]. The owner of it is a vidue and a great Tory, and my selfe so sickly thet if in case the[y, the British,] shoold come, my figure will keep thaim from hurting me.

Mr. Henry is gone to sea. Pray give my complimants to Mrs. and Miss Henson, and let thaim know thet thair rum is safe and in the same place ware my own is.

I have no more to adde, but remaime, with respect,

Yower humbl ser't,
Michael Levy.

Pray let me knew how rum sales with yow.[54]

North Carolina had no continuous Jewish history till the nineteenth century. South Carolina, as we have seen, had a synagogal organization in Charlestown ever since the middle-eighteenth century. But the attempt begun in 1775 to buy or to build a synagogue was not to be successful for another seventeen years. Charlestown's struggle to have its own house of worship was typical of the history of almost every American Jewish community of that period. In the years between 1749 and 1794 the members of Beth Elohim moved from one rented place to another, four in all, before they built a synagogue. The fourth building was a remodeled cotton gin manufactory, and was called the "Old Synagogue."

By the 1780's there was a well-rounded communal organization in the city. Its influence extended far beyond the confines of the town. Charlestown was destined to dominate Jewish spiritual life in the South until the War of 1861. Since the earliest days there had been an officiating *hazzan*, paid or voluntary, and soon they had a professional beadle. (Abraham Jones, who was *shammash* in the 1790's, had taken on the job in his eightieth year; the position was usually the financial refuge of a decent but unsuccessful businessman.) By 1798 there were already three Jewish cemeteries there.

We know that there were religious teachers in the congregation in colonial times. There may even have been a religious school. By the late eighteenth century, The Hebrew Benevolent Society (*Hebrah shel Gemilut Hasadim*), an immigrants' aid, sick-visiting, and burial society, became the social welfare arm of local Jewry. It may have started as a mutual-aid association. Prior to its establishment in 1784, such work was undoubtedly carried on by the congregation itself. Before the dawn of the nineteenth century the Charlestown Jewish community was known for the care it provided for orphans and indigent widows.

During the Revolution the city sheltered a number of newcomers who were not at home in the established synagogue with its Sephardic ritual. It may be, however, that it was not so much the ritual and prayers of the older settlers as the cultural distance between the two groups that made it difficult for the newer immigrants to feel comfortable in the synagogue. A generation of American tradition and Anglo-Saxon culture separated the newcomers from the original Jewish inhabitants.

Some of these more recent arrivals had come in with the British during their occupation of the city. Most, if not all, of them were German and Polish Jews, and some had been sutlers and commissaries with the Hessians before going into private business occupations. There must have been enough of these Yiddish-speaking immigrants to form a little religious group of their own. And we may assume that it was to help this "German Jewish Congregation" that Joseph Salvador, the philanthropist, left them a legacy of £20 in 1786.

There is, unfortunately, no other contemporary reference to this German society. No doubt, as soon as they became more Americanized and felt more at home in their environment, they joined the older, more socially desirable congregation. By 1794, when the "New Synagogue," the largest and most impressive in the Western Hemisphere, was built, there was but the one synagogue-community in town. Beth Elohim had succeeded in assimilating all its Jews.

CHARLESTOWN, SOUTH CAROLINA, ABOUT 1750

GENERAL FRANCIS MARION IN HIS SWAMP ENCAMPMENT

Chapter 13

Georgia, 1733 – 1768

THE basic facts of the history of the Jews in Georgia are soon told. They came in 1733, held services, laid out a little cemetery on the Savannah Common, but were not successful in keeping the little community together. With a small nucleus they started again to rebuild in the 1750's, participated actively in the War for Independence, and, finally, in 1790, established a permanent congregation in Savannah.

These are the skeletal facts. What is the story behind them? What induced a group of Jews to settle in the marsh lands and pine barrens between the Savannah and the Altamaha Rivers? What brought them to this southernmost outpost of the British?

Three reasons motivated the creation of the colony of Georgia. One was the desire to protect the Carolinas and their frontier by building a buffer settlement that would also threaten the Spanish in Florida and the French on the Gulf and on the Mississippi. The second reason was that the English industrialists, merchants, and shipbuilders were continually hungry for new sources of raw materials and new markets for their finished products. They were tired of enriching the silk and indigo countries of southern Europe. (Silk alone cost England, in some years, £500,000.) They hoped that in the Carolinas and in Georgia they could produce naval stores, flax, hemp, silk, wines, and indigo

> Till Georgi's silks on Albion's beauties shine,
> Or gain new lustre from the royal line;
> Till from the sunny hills the vines display
> Their various berries to the gilded day.

Through the aid of far-flung colonies they hoped to become commercially self-sufficient and to enrich themselves. The third reason was that the "philanthropists," the reformers, confidently expected that such a strategically located commercial colony would also contribute to the solution of the pressing social problem of poverty.

The early beginnings of the province were rooted in religious and humanitarian ideals. The Society for the Propagation of the Gospel in Foreign Parts, the Society for Promoting Christian Knowledge (which desired to further the Church of England and to convert the Indians and the Negro slaves), and the Associates of Dr. Bray, the educator and missionary—all three groups supported Colonel James Oglethorpe in his plan for creating a home for the English poor and underprivileged classes. The Anglican Church worked closely with the trustees of the colony in this program of "ecclesiastical imperialism."

It was an age of enlightenment and of a growing social consciousness. Philosophers, statesmen, and littérateurs were preaching the gospel of rationalism, deism, and tolerance. Anglicans and Protestant Dissenters began to concern themselves not only with the immortal souls but also with the perishable bodies of their congregants, and so the proposal for a colony in Georgia met with approval on all sides. It is true that religious diversity was a problem, but that was solved by tolerating all religions except the Catholic.

The practical Jewish businessmen of London were also attracted by this utopian scheme of mass resettlement. English Jewry in the eighteenth century, like the larger England itself, was confronted by the problem of pauperism. Influenced by the same half selfish, half humanitarian ideals, their leaders also were led to believe that a solution to poverty lay in large-scale emigration overseas.

A number of Jews made liberal contributions to the Christian clergymen who collected money to send Christian poor to Georgia. Jacob Mendez da Costa, Sr., who had given the New York synagogue a school building in 1731, was only too happy, four years later, to make a contribution to settle impoverished Christians in Georgia. The English Gentiles wanted to provide colonial homes for their impoverished—and for persecuted German Protestants. It was only logical that Jewish philanthropists should also seek new homes for their own poor.

The idea was not new. Less than a century before, in 1642, about six hundred Jews had migrated from Amsterdam to Recife in Brazil.

And others had ideas like that too, for just about the year in which John Law of "Mississippi Bubble" fame died (1729), a Scotsman, Sir Alexander Cuming of Culter, came forward with his immigration project. Because of services which both he and his father had rendered to the House of Hanover, he asked for a large sum of money. With these funds he hoped not only to pay off his debts but also to establish a giant bank in the Cherokee mountains, in the back country of Georgia and the Carolinas. The bank would serve as an inducement for 300,000 Jewish families to settle there and to improve the lands. Under the authority of the British and God—the true King of Judah and Israel—the Jews would become honest, industrious subjects. With the aid of the bank—and the Jews, of course — £80,000,000 of the national debt could be paid off in a decade or two—and both Cherokees and Jews would be converted to the purity of the Christian faith. It is not surprising that nothing came of this quixotic scheme of a man who could charitably be called impractical.

The English in London, however, encouraged by Sir William Keith, former governor of Pennsylvania, did make a treaty with the Cherokees. It was the hope of the Board of Trade that the tribe, like the Iroquois in the North, would serve as a western buffer against the Spanish and the French.

It was also Sir William Keith who encouraged American promoters to settle German and Swiss Protestants in the Virginia back country to serve as a more reliable shield against the French threatening from the north. But there was this difference between the two proposed settlements. The Germanic Protestant colony was to tolerate no Jews; the Cuming-Cherokee colony was to be built on Jews. (Maybe Sir Alexander was not crazy after all.)

All through the 1730's and the 1740's the rich Sephardic Jews of London attempted to send their poor coreligionists into the American wilderness. They thought in terms of close settlements and hundreds of thousands of acres. For a while they even considered Nova Scotia, which had just been taken from the French. It is well to recall that the Rhode Island courts, in refusing Aaron Lopez' plea for naturalization, told him that there was no room for him in Newport and that even good subjects (non-Jews!) of His Majesty had been compelled to go to Nova Scotia.

To effect their purposes, the London Sephardim in 1732 appointed a standing committee to further emigration and colonization, and in 1748 negotiated with the land promoter John Hamilton, who hoped to secure 200,000 acres in South Carolina for a Jewish colony. Jewish settlers were to produce naval stores in the proposed settlement; Jewish merchants were to finance them. Obviously these London merchants thought to combine philanthropy, profit, and patriotism. As far as we know, Hamilton never got the grant he sought from the government, and that specific scheme to transport Jews to the new world was dropped. Yet, as we have already seen, Joseph Salvador, the financier, bought 100,000 acres of South Carolina land and, curiously enough, from Hamilton (1755). In all likelihood, Salvador's purchase was purely speculative, unconnected with any plan to establish Jewish colonies. It is not improbable, though, that that hard-headed businessman was also caught in the web of the "Go West" propaganda which swept England in the second quarter of the eighteenth century.

It is easy to understand, therefore, why the London Sephardic leaders were interested in newly established Georgia. The London Jewish committee on colonization sought and obtained a commission from the trustees to raise money to send (Christian) poor to the new colony, and there is some evidence that in 1732 the Jews even broached the subject of sending some of their coreligionists there. At least two of the trustees were sympathetic to the suggestion. But before a decision could be reached, the Jewish committee stole a march on the indignant worthies by sending two boatloads of Jews to Georgia. This was in 1733. Back home in London the Christian philanthropists looked askance at this Jewish migration because of religious prejudice, their traditional distrust of the Jew as a tradesman, and their fear that if the rumor was noised abroad that the Jews were coming in, rich Christians would not support the colony and poor Christians would not settle there. "Georgia will soon become a Jewish colony," wrote Captain Thomas Coram.

The trustees urged that the utmost endeavors be exerted to remove the Jews who had already arrived (1733), but time brought more sober counsel (1734). Though annoyed by their arrival, Oglethorpe did not press for their departure; he knew that these Jews, many of them from the Mediterranean lands, were especially adapted to the climate and its forms of agriculture—and that they were not an obstreperous lot. Furthermore, the Charlestown lawyers whom he consulted advised him against sending them back home. Thus they were permitted to remain.

Who were these first Jewish settlers, and what do we know about them?

The first group to come to Georgia arrived on July 10th or 11th. Theirs was one of the first boats to dock following Oglethorpe's arrival at Savannah in February, 1733. About forty Jews were in that group; within the year, in all probability, another forty or more came in. All told, there were between seventy and ninety Jewish men, women, and children in the settlement within a year after its establishment.

The patrons of the colony, a contemporary declared, did not pay for the transportation of a single Jew. None of them came over "on the charity," that is, at the trustees' charge. (As we shall see, there was one exception, a convert to Christianity.) It is very probable, however, that most of them were sent over at the expense of the London Sephardic community, which used the fund collected by the three Jewish commissioners. A few of the Jewish families that came had some money of their own and paid their own way, for they brought with them Jewish and Christian indentured servants. Most of the Jewish immigrants of that year came by boat from England; others may have come from Charlestown, from the West Indies, and directly from Portugal.

This was the only "mass migration" of Jews in colonial North America. Judging by the land grants allotted by Oglethorpe in December, 1733, about fourteen per cent of the householders or responsible settlers in Savannah were Jews. They came in at the very beginning and grew up with the colony; they were "Founding Fathers."

In a pamphlet which a group of malcontent Georgians published in 1741—*A True and Historical Narrative of the Colony of Georgia in America*—this sentence occurs: "No wonder, then, that great numbers of poor subjects, who lay under a cloud of misfortunes, embraced the opportunity of once more tasting liberty and happiness; that Jews, attracted by the temptation of inheritances, flock'd over, etc." These were not rhetorical flourishes. That they had real meaning was amply demonstrated in London by the case of *Da Costa* v. *de Paz*.

Elias de Paz was a shipper and a commodity broker on the Royal Exchange. Like many of his associates, he did a considerable business with the North American and West India colonies. In 1729 he and another member of his family owned the "Friendship," built and outfitted in New England. It was engaged in the trade between Boston and Barbados until finally captured by Spanish privateers. The following year he owned the "Diligence" of Philadelphia.

When de Paz died in 1739 he left a trust fund in his will, to establish a study hall or school (*yesiba*) in order to further Judaism. The will, in the course of time, came before Lord Hardwicke, the Chancellor, in whose honor the Georgia town of Hardwicke on the Ogeechee was to be named. The problem that confronted the judge was twofold: was the legacy good and, if not, what was to be done about it?

The Lord Chancellor decided that the legacy was not good, for the intent, through the bequest, was to advance Judaism, and Judaism was in contradiction to Christianity, to the law of the land. The Jewish religion was not recognized, legally, in England; it was only connived at by Parliament.

With respect to the second question—what was to be done with the legacy—Hardwicke decided that since this was a charitable bequest, it was to be disposed of by the Crown for a charitable purpose. The money was ultimately turned over to the Foundling Hospital to support a Christian minister and to instruct young children in the Christian religion. Indeed, the principle laid down by the Lord Chancellor, that bequests left to further Judaism are invalid, was followed for decades in England.

By far the majority of the Jews who came to Georgia were people of Spanish-Portuguese stock. To judge from the records, this was one of the most Sephardic of the continental colonies, at least in its beginnings. Some of those who arrived in 1733 were Italians; at least five or six families were of German origin. Within a year a large family of Levis came down from Carolina; they were probably Gentiles of Jewish origin. In 1736 the tailor and laborer Johann Gottfried Christ arrived with some Protestant Salzburgers and settled at Ebenezer. Before his conversion to Christianity his name had been Salomon Levi. There is no evidence that the Jews associated with him or other converts.

Jews were hardly a curiosity among the settlers; the colony was one of the most motley in all America. It was a Noah's ark of English, Germans, Irish, Salzburgers, Moravians, Scotch Highlanders, and Catholics. Jews were not noticed—at least not too much. By 1735 there were more foreigners than British in Georgia.

The first Jews to arrive, so a contemporary chronicler recalled, brought a Scroll of the Law and soon received an additional scroll, a Hanukkah candelabrum, cult utensils, and Hebrew prayer books. A circumcision kit had also come over on the first boat. It is not known who acted as circumciser, but there was a trained physician in the group, a Dr. Nunez, who arrived just in time, so Oglethorpe reported, to stop the ravages of a deadly epidemic.

The rather numerous assembly held services, acquired a plot of ground as a cemetery, and possibly established a formal religious organization. According to our contemporary Jewish chronicler, one of the Sheftalls, the congregation called itself Mikveh Israel. If this statement is correct —and we doubt it—we may assume that the celebrants of 1733 named this, the second or third Jewish congregation in the country, after Mikveh Israel in Curaçao, then America's oldest synagogue, established in 1656. It is more probable that the name came late in the eighteenth century, after the community was resuscitated, and was in honor of the Philadelphia congregation where some Georgia exiles of the Revolution had assembled for worship.

A demographic study of the immigrants reveals that they were about equally divided between single men and family men. There were about twenty families. One family came in with seven children. Some of the householders, it seems, brought Christian wives with them; others later married Christian girls in the colony, and one Jew, Oglethorpe wrote, was desirous of being baptized a Christian. Most of the newcomers were relatively young, but a few of the settlers were not; Dr. Nunez' mother came with him, and he was over fifty. The travelers came in as clans, related groups.

Some of the Jewish colonists settled in the village of Hampstead, but by far the majority remained in Savannah. Here the Jews congregated together, by choice we may be sure, on the west side of the town. Many were granted lots and farms. Some made good farmers; others could not or would not work at clearing the land. Two men were later punished for scandalous conduct; a third was fined for assault and battery; another was involved, in 1739, in a suit for mistreatment and nonsupport of his illegitimate child. Still another was friendly with the malcontents who were dissatisfied with the colonial administration, but on the whole, the Jews seem to have been a law-abiding lot. John Wesley, the Methodist, was ready to testify to their good character (1737): "I began learning Spanish in order to converse with my Jewish parishioners, some of whom seem nearer the mind that was in Christ than many of those who call him Lord."

They all started out as farmers, but in the course of the next year or two a number of them drifted into shop-keeping and the coastal trade. On occasion the traditional dislike of Jews found expression. When the freeholders wrote a "saucy memorial" in 1738 asking for the right to use Negro labor, to import rum, and to buy and sell land, they refused to allow their Jewish fellow-settlers to sign the petition with them: "We did not think it proper to join them in any of our measures." But on the whole, the relations between Jews and non-Jews were quite cordial. Jews were certainly accorded all civil rights and served in the militia. They managed to get along with their Christian neighbors; they reserved their quarreling for their own group, and internal squabbles were frequent, perhaps constant. Some sort of permanent synagogue organization might have been established if the Sephardim and Ashkenazim could have agreed on the details of ritual. But in this insistence on their own parochial customs and in their determination not to yield an inch to one another, these Jews were typical of their age. No agreement was reached, yet in the meantime many of them met for a common service in a shack, where a competent young man served as a lay cantor.

By 1740 what there was of a community had disintegrated, but entirely from economic causes. At the most, three or four families remained, with one exception all Ashkenazim. The flight of the Jews from Georgia was part of a general movement that almost destroyed the colony. In 1741 there were only about forty-two families in all Savannah. The Jews left for the same reasons the others did: Negro slavery was prohibited, the liquor traffic was forbidden, land tenure was hedged in, the lots were often swamps—and utopia had failed to materialize. And—this was equally significant—there were just as many opportunities in other colonies and no hampering legal restrictions. The Indians in the outlying areas were still a menace. Two months after a number of Jews had left, in 1740, a group of Indian marauders attacked an isolated post on the Ogeechee River, killed the servants on the place, and even cut the throat of the family watchdog.

Life in a border colony like Georgia was hard; a study

of the little Jewish community in its initial years reveals a heavy incidence of infant mortality. A large percentage of all babies born in America died in infancy, and the Jews were no exception.

There were hazards enough for the grownups, too. Men were shot, or drowned, or killed by disease. In 1740 the threat of the Spanish coming in from St. Augustine, from Florida, was a real one; the Portuguese Jews were frightened, for the Inquisition was still a reality. Some of these refugees, who had been baptized as Catholics in the Spanish Peninsula, might well have been burnt at the stake as heretics if caught and convicted for their lapse. It is true that Jews and Marranos still managed to live in or do business with Catholic Mexico, Venezuela, and Cuba, but Jews who had just risked everything to escape from the Portuguese Inquisition had no desire to expose themselves to the very uncertain mercies of Spanish captors. Among those who fled was Dr. Nunez. Seventy-eight years later, his great-great-grandson, Major Mordecai Manuel Noah, wrote of a member of his family, a grandaunt who died in this country, that she carried with her to the grave the marks of the cords with which she had been bound to the torture rack. This family tradition should not be cavalierly dismissed as a typical Noah romancing. As late as the 1770's, while in St. Eustatia, Janet Schaw, the "lady of quality," met a victim of the Inquisition so disfigured by torture that he barely resembled a human being.

Yet how strange and how powerful is the love of fatherland! Some of these Portuguese Jews fled Georgia for fear of the Spaniards and the Inquisition, but others, it was recorded in 1741, left the English colony to return to Portugal where, rumor had it, the Inquisition had been instructed not to disturb them. And this only a year or two after the Portuguese poet Antonio José da Silva had been burnt alive as a Jewish heretic.

Whatever their destination, the fact remains that these former crypto-Jews left the province. Some fled to the English and Dutch West Indies; others, we know, went north to Pennsylvania and to New York, carrying the Scroll of the Law with them. A number of them, of course, took refuge in neighboring South Carolina.

The first settlement of the Jews in Georgia was a failure. It almost disappeared, but such failures occurred in many early colonies. The same thing happened with the first settlements of Jews in New York, Newport, and Charlestown. In all four towns the first group came, struggled a while, and then disappeared, except for a family or two. On the ruins of the first attempt a more permanent continuous settlement was built later. It is not surprising that the Jews of Georgia left after six or seven years; it is surprising that they held out as long as they did.

From then on the history of Georgia Jewry was the history of individuals and families, until the decade of the Revolution, when real community life began again.

Among those who landed in Savannah in July, 1733, were the Oliveras: father Jacob, mother Judith, sons David and Isaac, and daughter Leah. Isaac was accidentally shot and died in November, 1734. By 1741 Jacob probably had moved to Charlestown where, sometime after his arrival,

Leah married the enterprising merchant Joseph Tobias, who later became the first president of Congregation Beth Elohim. (Just two hundred years later his descendant, Thomas Jefferson Tobias, occupied the same office.) Jacob Olivera made out his will in 1751. In this document he wrote: "In primis, I commend my soul to the Almighty God of Israel, Creator of Heaven and Earth, imploring His most gracious pardon for all my past sins and transgressions of which I most sincerely repent. And, hoping His infinite mercies will extend to me also, I most vehemently and sincerely invoke His Holy Name, saying: 'Hear, O Israel, the Lord our God, the Lord is One.' "

These are words of one who had lived as a crypto-Jew and suffered under an Inquisition state.

The will ended with the following injunction to his son David, who had shared the hazards of life with him on the Iberian Peninsula, in England, on the Georgian frontier, and finally in the safe haven of Charlestown: "I also recommend to my said son to walk in the fear of God and in the path of virtue which is the last and best legacy I can leave him. I conclude with imploring the divine mercy of my Creator to receive my soul with pity on my frail nature, saying, 'In Thy hands I will deposit my spirit; Thou has rescued me, O Lord God of Truth.' "

The Minises were one of the Jewish families that remained in the colony. Abraham Minis had arrived in July, 1733, with his wife Abigail, two daughters, and a younger, unmarried brother, Simon. Abraham's son, Philip, born on July 12, 1734—according to another record, in 1733—survived to become a Revolutionary War veteran. The contemporary tradition, therefore, that he was the first white male person born in Georgia may well be correct. Abraham Minis was a hard-working farmer who did the best he could on his swampy lot. By 1743 he was prepared to farm on a larger scale; he then petitioned for an additional grant of 500 acres.

But long before that time he had come to the conclusion that he ought to supplement his scanty income as a farmer by engaging in commerce. No later than 1736 he already had a shop, and was doing business as a merchant-shipper in the coastal trade. He thus became one of the first men in the colony to engage in commerce. The firm was known as Abraham Minis and Company or Minis and Salomons, the latter concern being dissolved in 1739. Minis' partner Coleman Salomons is not to be confused with the Salomons of Charlestown and London, close kin of the Frankses who were also in the Georgia trade.

In 1738, Minis ran athwart the all-powerful judge and keeper of the public stores, Thomas Causton. Apparently Causton was discriminating against Minis in purchasing supplies for the colony, although the two had done business together the preceding year. The Jewish merchant had brought in an assortment of goods from New York and offered them to the storekeeper cheap, but Causton would not even nibble. Later Minis brought in another load, which was rejected with the laconic statement that no more supplies were needed. Yet only a few days later a strange sloop sailed up the Savannah with a load of goods, and the captain had no trouble disposing of it. William Stephens, the colony's secretary, reported the incident to the trustees in London. He implied that Minis was not being given an equal chance with others in spite of the fact that he was industrious and honest, and enjoyed a good reputation. As far as we can determine, this was not a case of anti-Jewish prejudice; Minis was obviously not an intimate of the severe Causton, who was suspected of financial irregularities.

The business activities of Minis, who was only a small entrepreneur, can best be understood against the background of the American and European political conjuncture and of the expanding commercial activity of the Franks family of England and America.

Jacob Franks had come from London to New York during Queen Anne's War (1702–13) and had, no doubt, gotten his share of business in the long conflict that won for the British, Hudson Bay, Newfoundland, Acadian Canada, greater power in the West Indies, and a monopoly on the importation of Negroes into the Spanish colonial lands. As the British-American colonies grew, the Frankses grew with them commercially. Almost immediately after the establishment of Georgia—in Spanish-claimed Florida territory—the Frankses were sending supplies to the colonists and to Oglethorpe's troops, either through Charlestown or through Savannah agents. Of course, Jacob Franks was not the only New York merchant doing business in the border colony. Rodrigo Pacheco of New York and London employed some of the Georgia Nunezes as his correspondents, but Franks's enterprises were far more extensive. In Charlestown his agents were Samuel Levy and

Moses Salomons. The mother of Moses Salomons was a sister of the numerous Franks brothers.

Queen Anne's War was only a phase in the long struggle between England and France for world hegemony. The battle began again in 1739 in the Anglo-Spanish struggle known as the War of Jenkins' Ear. Oglethorpe, a year later, led his troops in an unsuccessful attack against the Spanish at St. Augustine, and in 1743 he made another raid into Florida, again unsuccessfully, and this new war, King George's, dragged on to its indecisive end in 1748. The army purveyors were kept busy.

The increased interest of the Franks family in Georgia and their participation in its expanding peace and wartime economy are reflected in the fact that they registered the sloop "Oglethorpe" for trade with that colony as early as 1738. In 1743, during the first year of King George's War, they sent the twenty-three-year-old David Franks to Charlestown and to Savannah as a "trouble shooter." Moses Salomons, his cousin, had fallen into debt in Charlestown and was practically, or actually, a prisoner in town; one of the Franks boats, consigned with a cargo to Oglethorpe, had sunk, and there was a question of insurance and protested bills of exchange. As late as 1754 the firm was still supplying Georgia with goods.

Abraham Minis, to return to him, had been a correspondent of this far-ranging firm since 1736. The Frankses were certainly his chief source of supply, and he made periodic visits to New York, to the market, to see them. (On these occasions he would go to Shearith Israel—the only congregation with its own synagogue building in

British North America—and enjoy the pleasure and honor of being called up for the reading of the Law.) Though a correspondent of the Frankses, he frequently purchased goods from them on his own account. Minis' financial agent in London, Simpson Levy, was also close to the Franks and Salomons commercial clan in that city.

Minis was particularly busy during the years 1740-43, the period which included the two attacks of Oglethorpe on Spanish Florida. The British base was at Frederica, and one of Minis' boats plied between Savannah and Frederica, shuttling supplies.

In July of 1740, Captain Tingley, the officer in charge of the "Oglethorpe," returned from Frederica after unloading its cargo. While at Savannah, on this return trip to New York, he picked up two of the Jewish "Founding Fathers," the Bernals and the Abendanones, who were leaving Georgia. A few months later the records of Shearith Israel report the presence of the latter family in the synagogue where, no doubt, they had gone to express thanks for their safe arrival. Not many months passed before the congregation paid their passage out of town, probably to Charlestown, where the family was found in the next generation.

A Mr. Clee, a non-Jew, was Minis' agent with the English troops at Frederica during the war years. He was a salesman and a partner, but, primarily, the bookkeeper for the firm. Minis, not a person with any education or training in finance, was constantly having trouble with his accountants. He certainly did not understand the mysteries of single and double entry.

Clee was originally employed by Minis at a salary of
£40 a year and keep. Later he became a partner until
Minis discovered—or believed—that he was being cheated,
at which time the partnership broke up, with Clee staying
on as an employee. Minis next sent Clee to New York to
straighten out his financial affairs, for he had apparently
fallen behind in payments. Clee took with him £400, but
instead of paying Minis' debts, he used the money to buy
a stock of goods in his own name and went into business
for himself at Frederica. When he refused to account for
the money or the goods to Minis, the latter sued him but
lost the case in the Georgia courts. Undaunted by this set-
back, Minis threatened to appeal to the trustees of the
colony in London. The decision of the court against Minis
was not executed, and Clee, for some undetermined reason,
fled to Jamaica. This was about the year 1744.

The life of a petty colonial merchant was certainly not
all gravy. By 1754 Abraham—farmer, merchant, and tavern
keeper, too—was a very sick man, but lingered on till January of 1757, when he died.

Two years later Isaac Levy, apparently a member of
the Franks-Levy clan of New York, Philadelphia, and London, presented a petition to the Privy Council in London,
protesting that he had been illegally dispossessed of property in Georgia through collusion between Governor Ellis
and Thomas Bosomworth. The latter was an Anglican
clergyman, a power among the Indians through his marriage with Mary, "Queen of the Creeks." He was known

to be a dangerous, ambitious adventurer and anything but an honest man.

After slavery was permitted in the colony and other restrictions were removed, economic life began to flourish, and Levy had seen fit to make an investment in Georgia lands. (He himself never seems to have visited the colony.) As early as 1754 he had purchased from Bosomworth a half interest in two of the three Georgia Sea Islands, later famous for their cotton. In 1760, the clergyman relinquished his claim to the two islands, surrendering them to the Crown, in total disregard of the claim of Levy. That unfortunate speculator, who thought that he had made a wonderful bargain, appealed several times to the Privy Council in England for redress. In one of his later petitions, in the year 1768, he expressed his willingness to compromise his claim if the British would grant him the right to exploit a coal mine on Cape Breton Island in the Gulf of St. Lawrence.

The use of coal, contended Levy, would benefit both the American colonists and the English shippers. If the colonists could be induced to try it, they would soon find out how much cheaper than and superior to wood it was as a fuel. The colonial shippers could not compete with the English for this Cape Breton coal, for the Americans had no cargo to deliver at the Island. It would not pay them to make a round trip just for the sake of bringing back coal on the return voyage. However, English ships sailing for the colonies could head for Cape Breton and pick up a load, and after the colonials would become dependent on the superior fuel, the price could be advanced so as to make it a very profitable venture.

These suggestions were totally unacceptable to the Board of Trade, for its members pointed out—and they were right —that if the Americans could be supplied with coal at a moderate price, they would be able to rival the English in the manufacture of iron. Levy argued that the colonists could never become competitors because labor costs here were twice what they were in England, and, what was decisive, an Act of Parliament had forbidden the establishment of forges, mills, and furnaces on this side of the Atlantic. But all this expostulation was in vain; the Board of Trade was adamant. This, however, it did do: in 1768 it recommended a small monetary compensation, and in the following year the case was closed.

In 1765 Bosomworth, who had still retained St. Catherines, the third island, sold it to Button Gwinnett, a Georgia signer of the Declaration of Independence. Five years later, Gwinnett borrowed £500 from the Sheftall brothers of Savannah on a second mortgage and conveyed the island to them as security for the loan, subject to the prior rights of the first mortgage. As the brothers witnessed the signature of Button Gwinnett in 1770, they may have wondered if they would ever get their money back; their eyes would certainly have popped out of their heads had anyone whispered to them that in 1927 the bibliophile Dr. A. S. W. Rosenbach, a fellow Sephardi, would pay $51,000 for a letter bearing Gwinnett's signature and those of five other "Signers." In 1779, two years after Gwinnett died, his debt to the Sheftalls had not yet been liquidated.

Charles II, after whom the Carolinas were named, had hoped to develop the wine, oil, and silk industries on the North American mainland. His coronation robe, it is said, was made of silk reeled in Virginia. The very first boat that landed in Georgia brought in men who were supposed to be competent vintners, vinedressers, vintagers, and wine coopers—to say nothing of wine drinkers. But there is no evidence that any of these specialists did anything to create a wine industry in Georgia.

A few months later a more productive expert arrived. This was Abraham DeLyon, who came in with the Jewish contingent from London in July, 1733. There is some evidence that he and some other members of his clan, the Nunezes, came from Portugal, via England, with the intention of settling in the new American colony and specifically to plant vineyards. DeLyon was a practical farmer, and in a few years had a successful truck patch on which he grew peas, some grain, and rice. He was a viniculturist by training, having learned the art in the vineyards of Portugal, and he brought some choice cuttings with him from the homeland. After four years he succeeded in raising beautiful, almost transparent grapes, as big as a man's thumb. Some bunches weighed as much as two pounds. Planting more and more cuttings, he increased his vines to hundreds and confidently expected that by 1740 or 1741 he would have many thousands. He employed a number of men to assist him in his vineyard, a forty-five-acre plot, and later claimed that he had spent £400 of his own money to get started. He asked the trustees in 1738 for a loan of £200, and they ordered Oglethorpe to advance him the

299

money. But here, too, nothing was accomplished. The money lent him came in driblets of £5 and £10, too little to do any good. White help was expensive; Negro slave labor, much cheaper, was prohibited.

In 1741 "that industrious man Abraham DeLyon, on whom were all our expectations for cultivating vines and making wine" left the colony. In the spring of that year his relatives, the Nunezes, had already gone, taking his wife with them. DeLyon started to send out his goods, but the authorities stopped him, because he was indebted to them for loans; they knew he was getting ready to leave. By the summer DeLyon had slipped away, and his languishing vines were turned over to one of the German Protestants. (More than twenty years later a member of his family, probably a son, returned to the colony in which he had been born.)

In 1738, while DeLyon was still making an effort to create a wine industry in Georgia, two men, also Jews, approached the trustees in London with proposals for raising cochineal, a dye. One of the two promoters was a Marrano who had learned the business in Mexico and had fled the country when his religion was discovered. Although the trustees were eager to create a dye-stuff industry in the colony, they could do no business with these entrepreneurs. Their demands of £2,000 were entirely too extravagant, and the negotiations which went on for almost two years came to naught.

Great Britain never succeeded in making of Georgia a "Mediterranean" colony, a source of wine, olives, oil, and indigo. However, a native silk industry was begun and had a small measure of success, but by the time the Revolution broke out it, too, had died out. In the very first days of the colony much effort and money were spent to develop this industry. The first boat that brought over vinedressers and the like brought over also silkmen, silk throwsters, and silk weavers. A number of them were Italians bred to the business; they did produce some silk. Within a year after the first landing, Oglethorpe carried some native raw silk to England. In the following decade spun silk was manufactured, and in 1741 a sample was sent back to London and submitted to the criticism of Simpson Levy. By 1750, however, many engaged in the production of silk began to drop out; farming paid more money.

It was at this time that a man arrived who was to identify himself closely with this work for the next ten or fifteen years. He was Joseph Solomon Ottolenghe, an Italian Israelite, connected by blood and by marriage ties with some of the most distinguished Jewish families in Europe.

The story of Ottolenghe reads like a tale out of Balzac. Apparently fiction has a long road to travel before it catches up with life.

Our hero was born of pious, poor, but honest people in Casale, in the Italian Piedmont. He was given a better-than-average Hebrew education: by the time he reached the age of twenty-one he was invited to become the teacher and *shohet* in the community of Mondovi. Meir Bachi, the rabbi, signed his Hebrew certificate as a competent ritual slaughterer of cattle; Joseph had studied under one of the Bachis in Casale.

It was during that year (1732) that his whole life's course was changed by the receipt of a letter from his mother's brother, Gabriel Treves, a snuff merchant in London. The uncle, a widower, was angry. His daughter Deborah was about to marry a Judah Toby (Tubi) against her father's wishes. You come over, he wrote; I'll pay your way, teach you the snuff business, and you can marry Deborah and become my heir.

This was not an opportunity lightly to be cast aside. The ambitious young man sailed for England, and arrived, very probably in November, only to find Deborah married and already separated from her husband before the marriage had even been consummated. Gabriel was trying to secure an annulment on the ground that Toby had been seen doing business on the Sabbath.

But who can know the heart of a maid? Deborah crossed her father by going back to her husband, and Gabriel then spited his daughter by finding another wife. Unfortunately, this left Joseph out in the cold—no wife and no heritage.

When Ottolenghe demanded recompense for the loss of his job in Italy and asked to be sent back to his native land, Treves placated him with a series of promises. The nephew was to accompany the family to Exeter in Devon, and there help Gabriel in the snuff business. After everything was running smoothly, Joseph was to receive £50 worth of goods and passage back to Leghorn. With this understanding, the embittered young Italian went to Exeter in the spring of 1733, becoming, with his uncle and step-aunt, the first permanent Jewish settlers in town.

The step-aunt, the second wife, is, in the most approved

classical style, the villain of this piece. According to Ottolenghe—and we have only his side of the story—she was
jealous of him, resenting the fact that he had once been
the heir of her husband. So she set out to poison her husband's mind against the nephew, and she succeeded.

While Gabriel traveled around in Devon, peddling his
snuff, young Joseph tended shop and occasionally slaughtered cattle for the family. Some additional income came
to him through lessons he gave in Hebrew and in Italian.
Joseph's resentment against his uncle continued to grow.
There is no doubt that he felt aggrieved that the promises
made to him while still in Italy had not been, could not
be, kept; the new wife and her father—who also lived in
the house—abused him. The snuff business, it would seem,
did not appeal to him. Instead of looking after the trade,
so the Treveses said, he spent much of his time reading
Christian theological literature and studying the New Testament. He began to mingle socially with the townsmen,
and his Christian friends provided him with conversionist
literature, especially the tracts of the Society for Promoting
Christian Knowledge. One sometimes wonders if his orthodoxy had not already been tainted by his association with
the Bachis in Casale. One of the distinguished members of
that well-known rabbinic family was a devoted follower
of Shabbethai Zebi, the seventeenth-century Jewish pseudo-
Messiah.

Finally, after about a year, in the spring of 1734, Ottolenghe broke with his family. In the accusations which the
two parties hurled at one another Gabriel charged that his
young clerk neglected the business, that he was lewd, that

he threatened violence, and that he was not the true nephew but an impostor!

It became increasingly evident to Treves that Joseph, who was by then studying with a local clergyman, was on the verge of conversion. Some of the Jewish peddlers who were staying at the same tavern with Ottolenghe cursed him and spat at him. One of them, hoping to prejudice him against Christianity with its trinitarian teachings, sent him Hebrew quotations from the Old Testament emphasizing the unitarian nature of God. Treves himself went to the clergyman and asked him to discourage Joseph. He wasted his time; Joseph would not give an inch.

When Uncle Gabriel saw that his nephew was determined to go ahead with his plan for conversion, he called him in and coerced him, without resorting to actual violence, to sign a bond of indebtedness for his passage to London and Exeter, for his clothes, and for his schooling. It did Joseph no good to protest that everything his uncle had done for him was in the nature of a gift which he could prove by his uncle's letters sent to Italy. When called upon to show the letters, he could not find them; his uncle and aunt had stolen them while he was still in London.

Finally, when all his threats and cajolery failed, Gabriel sold the note to Judah Toby, with whom he had become reconciled, and the son-in-law pressed for payment. When it was not forthcoming, Joseph was thrown into Southgate prison in Exeter. This was in September, 1734.

Joseph maintained that Uncle Gabriel had him jailed to keep him from competing in the snuff trade, to induce Joseph's Christian friends to pay the note for £28, and to take revenge upon him because of his imminent conversion. Gabriel, however, soon found that sending his nephew to jail was a double-edged weapon. People looked askance at the man who had imprisoned his own flesh and blood. In spite of the fact that the snuff merchant bore a good reputation in his trade, the rumor that he was persecuting his nephew because of the latter's Christian sympathies could have proved disastrous to the newly-established business. To protect himself, therefore, Treves published his side of the story—in a pamphlet no copy of which has survived—*A Vindication of the Proceedings of Gabriel Treves against Joseph Solomon Ottolenghe, Now a Prisoner in Southgate, etc.* Later he inserted notices in a newspaper explaining his position in the cause célèbre, and published still another defense—no longer extant—which he entitled *An Advertisement, etc.* The Treves pamphlets appeared in the autumn of 1734 while Ottolenghe was languishing in the debtors' jail.

In the meantime, Joseph's Christian friends were working to free him, short of paying the amount of the bond. But they did intercede with Treves, who finally relented and agreed to release his nephew. Ottolenghe had been in the prison for less than four months when he came out on December 28, 1734. Six weeks later he was baptized into the Anglican Church.

Fifteen years after he became a Christian this Piedmontese succumbed to the alluring propaganda that was creating the Georgia "boom." Though no longer a young man, he was eager to go and was ready to exploit his knowledge of the manufacture of silk. He was a skilled worker, quite at home in the trade for which his parents had trained him in his native Italy.

The trustees of the colony paid his way over, gave him a monetary subvention, and finally a salary for his work in the silk industry. He also received the usual fifty acres of land. His parcel later became the nucleus of the Hermitage Plantation of Savannah.

Within two years after his arrival he was already in charge of an establishment for reeling silk, and for many years he devoted himself to the job of furthering that industry in the colony. He had his setbacks, of course, the worst of which occurred on July 4, 1758, when a fire broke out, destroying not only the silkhouse, but also his correspondence files, his records as a local tax collector, and various public and private funds which had been left in his care. It was a severe blow. Yet the very next year, under his superintendence, the colony exported 10,000 pounds of silk. When he came, in the year 1752, total production and export did not exceed a few hundred pounds.

Working in the filature was only one of his jobs, not unimportant to him financially, for after a while he derived from it an income of about £70 a year. More important was his work as a teacher among the Negro slaves. It was this task, rather than the silk business, that had made it possible for him to come to Georgia originally.

When, in 1749, the bars against Negro slavery were finally lifted and dozens of slaves were brought in, two religious organizations which had been associated with the trustees in establishing the colony felt called upon to educate and enlighten those unfortunates. These two were the

Society for the Propagation of the Gospel in Foreign Parts and the Associates of the Late Dr. Bray. This latter organization, like the Society for Promoting Christian Knowledge, was devoted to the furtherance of the Christian religion among Indians and Negroes.

There was a strong agitation to Christianize the slaves; there was no desire to emancipate them. The trustees of the colony, and the two religious organizations which together sent Ottolenghe to Georgia, thriftily used one stone —one missionary—to kill three birds. Ottolenghe was not only to work at the filature, but he was also to train Negroes in the industry and at the same time to convert them to Christianity.

Here is Joseph Ottolenghe's first appeal for work in the colony:

[January, 1750.]

To the Hon'ble and Rev'd Society for the Propagation of the Gospel in Foreign Parts:

The humble petition of Jos. Ottolenghe sheweth that your petitioner is going to settle in Georgia, and hearing that a number of Negroes to the amount of 300 and upwards were fix'd in that colony, in pursuance of a late regulation of the trustees, your petitioner makes an humble offer of his service to the Society to instruct the said Negroes in the Christian faith, promising, if accepted by this Hon'ble Board, to use his best endeavours, with the divine assistance, for the conversion of these ignorant people, so as that the honour of Almighty God, the good of his fellow creatures, and the designs of this venerable society may be answered by his undertaking.

J. Ottolenghe.[55]

307

Ottolenghe got this job as schoolmaster in February, 1750, although it was some time in July, 1751, before he arrived to begin his work. He was well-qualified to do a good job, for the former Italian was now thoroughly Anglicized and wrote a good English. There was no question that he was a cultured and refined person, and, according to reports, well versed in Oriental tongues. Some of the Ebenezer Germans thought he had once been a rabbi. The two religious organizations gave him a starting salary of £40 a year.

Shortly after his arrival Ottolenghe began his work as schoolmaster to the Georgia Negroes. He wrote a series of letters to one of his sponsors in England, the "Associates," reporting on his successes and failures in the work which he had undertaken. Here is one of his earliest reports. It was addressed to the secretary, the Rev'd Mr. Smith, who was rector of Allhallow, London Wall:

Rev'd Sir:

In my last sent you by the "Charming Martha" I took the liberty to acquaint you with my safe arrival to Georgia. I shall now proceed and lay before you the method which I have taken to discharge the awfull office which God was pleased to call me to, and the Honorable Associates [of the late Dr. Bray] to place me in.

As soon as the fatigue of the voyage permitted it, I desir'd the Rev'd Mr. Zouberbuyler [Rector of Christ Church] that he would be so good to give the people notice in the church that I would instruct their Negros three days in the week, viz., Sundays, Tuesdays, and Thursdays, which he accordingly did. And that I might make it easie to the masters of these unhappy creatures, I have appointed the time of their coming to me to be at night when their daily labour is done.

When we meet I make them go to prayers with me, having compos'd for that purpose a few prayers, suitable (I hope) to the occasion. Having thus recommended our selves to the protection of Heaven, and for His blessing on our undertaking, I instruct them to read that they may be able in time to comfort themselves in reading the book of God. . . .

And in order to get their love, I use them with all the kindness and endearing words that am capable of, which makes them willing to come to me and ready to follow my advice. And as rewards are springs that sets less selfish minds than these unhappy creatures possess, on motion, I have therefore promis'd to reward the industrious and deligent, and I hope thro' Xt's grace that 'twill have its due effect. . . .

I should be very thankfull to you (if my petition is reasonable, if not to let it die) to use your interest with the Hono'ble, the Trustees [of the colony] to make me a present of a couple of horses. The granting of my petition would be of great service to me, and no great detriment to the Hon'ble Body since that I understand that they have a good stock of them. . . .

I intend also, God willing, to visit gradually the plantations in this colony in order to spur them on as well as to advice them how to carry on the silk-manufactory which, if well attended to and rightly managed, will by God's blessing be of great moment to this colony, so well situated for it, as also to introduce among them, as God shall enable me, a little more sense of religion than they have at present. And I hope so to demean my self in this last particular as to give no offence.

I should have petition'd but for one horse, but as 'tis impracticable for a single person and a stranger to travel thro' woods without danger, I shall be oblig'd to have always a person to guide me. . . .   Your most obedient humb. se't,

J. Ottolenghe.

Savannah, Dec'ber 4th, 1751.[56]

From all indications, Ottolenghe did a good job as an educator. Certainly his attitude toward his charges was a most sympathetic and an understanding one, and he appears to have been an excellent pedagogue. His religious superior, the Rev. Bartholomew Zouberbuhler, thought well of his work and characterized him as a schoolmaster who discharged his duty with great care and diligence.

The following letters describe his accomplishments in this particular field of endeavor and the almost insurmountable obstacles which he encountered. These reports, like the others, were directed to his employers back in London.

Savannah in Georgia, Nov'r 19th, 1753.
. . . . It is true that their number [the slaves I teach] is not so great as I could wish, by reason of their penurious masters who think that they should be great loosser should they permit their slaves to learn what they must do to be saved, not considering that he would be a greater gainer if his servant should become a true follower of the blessed Jesus, for in such a case he would have instead of an immoral dishonest domestic a faithful servant.

Others again, especially those who resort to us from the West Indies, will upon no account whatever suffer their slaves to be instructed in the X'n religion, alledging that 'tis a just observation (of the devil's framing, I suppose) that a slave is ten times worse when a X'n than in his state of paganism. . . .

Savannah in Georgia, Nov'ber 18th, 1754.
Rev'd S'r:
. . . . Again, slavery is certainly a great depresser of the mind which retards thus their learning a new religion, proposed to them in a new and unknown language, besides the old superstition of a false [African] religion to be combated with. And nothing harder to be remov'd (you know) than

prejudices of education, riveted by time and entrench'd in deep ignorance, which must be overcom'd by slow advances, with all the patience and engaging means that can be studied to make them fall in love with the best of all religions, and so to captivate their minds as to give all their very little leisure to the study of it.

And I have so far gained this point in drawing the Negroes to it with the cords of love, that if their unchristian masters would but suffer them to come to me, they are willing and ever ready to be with me. But I bless God that there are many in town who have not bended their hearts to gain only, but think it highly necessary to have their slaves instructed, and careful in sending of them, insomuch that at times a large room that I have for that purpose is as full as it can hold. Tho' I must own that it is not the third part of the Negroes that are about us. . . .

Had all those Negroes which began their instruction at the begining of my coming to this colony continu'd with me to this time, some of them would by this time have been forward enough for an admittance into the Church of X't by the holy sacrament of baptism, but they are most of them remov'd to remote plantations or sent into other colonies. However, I have several now who are gone thro' their catechism and can repeat it by heart, together with such prayers suitable to their conditions, necessities, and capacities, and am labouring now to make them sensible of the meaning of what they have been learning. . . .

Rev'd Sir:

. . . . I have also pointed out some of those principal difficulties which create the impediments in the instruction of Negroes, and am almost certain that I have at large given you a particular detail of them. Therefore, shall just touch on them, to prevent repitition.

And first, possessors of slaves purchase them for hard labour out of which an annual profit is propos'd, to obtain which a daily task is allotted them and severely exacted from them. And as the Mahometans look upon their women to have souls of an inferiour nature to those of men, so our Americans look upon their slaves to have no souls at all, and a favourite dog or horse meet with more humane treatment than they. Add to this that if it be consider'd what little sense of religion is retained by the inhabitants of these parts of the world, . . . 'twill be no wonder that those who have so little concern for their immortal souls should not attempt the salvation of those whom they believe to have no souls at all!

As for the Negroes of these parts, they are mostly Africans born and are as ignorant of our language as we are of theirs, and consequently no impression can be made on them untill they are capable of understanding what it is that is offered to them in order to forsake paganism and embrace X'ty. It require[s] length of time, great patience, and much industry before they can have a sensible idea of our language and the strong riveted prejudices of education can be remov'd. Stupidity, the concomitant of a hard-felt everlasting slavery, the little time allow'd them for instruction, and the few or no opportunities to converse with such as might produce an improvement in their learning, together with other causes of the like nature, are great impediments in their way of instruction, and not well known but to those that experience them.

However, all these difficulties on the part of the slaves would throug God's assistance be overcom'd with diligence and patience, provided that their owners would suffer them to be instructed. . . .

Your very much oblig'd humble se't,
J. Ottolenghe.

Savannah, October 4th, 1759.[57]

Ottolenghe was entrusted with this special educational task until 1758 or 1759 when, largely because of a misunderstanding about his salary, the Associates ceased to employ him. It is worthy of note that he had continued to teach that long in spite of the fact that the colonial legislature had decreed, in 1755, that slaves were not to be taught to write. (It may be that he taught them to read and to recite only.)

By 1769 he had retired as Superintendent of the Silk Culture on an annual pension of £100, his full salary. The pension was practically a bribe to induce the apprehensive and closemouthed Ottolenghe to prepare a successor for his highly skilled work. The British were afraid that the old man would die any day without having trained anyone to carry on the work.

However, after he gave up his teaching post and the supervision of the filature, he still had plenty to do nourishing a flourishing political career and extending his plantation holdings. He began, as we saw, with a fifty-acre tract of land. Through purchase and grant he gradually built up a series of farms and plantations totaling about 2,000 acres in Savannah, in Christ Church and in neighboring parishes. (It is not improbable that he sold some of these holdings; certainly he did not farm them all.)

Two years after he landed he began to build a home for himself. All told, there were four rooms in it, and he expected it to cost £200 sterling. This was more money than he had on hand at the time. The largest room in the house was to serve primarily as a schoolroom for the illiterate whites and Negroes whom he taught. It had a large fireplace for the slaves who came in, for they were always cold even on the warmest days. By 1754 he owned two

slaves of his own, a young married couple. He reared them
in his own home, as he would have his own children, and
made every effort to improve and educate them, but he
found to his dismay that they were not quick to learn.
Later he owned twelve slaves. Yet the spirit of kindliness
and consideration which he applied to Negroes whom he
owned or taught was, apparently, not extended to slaves
when he concerned himself with them in an official capacity. As a Justice of the Peace—he had been first appointed
about 1757—he, together with his colleague on the bench,
tried a Negro for theft and ordered the execution of the
offender. The case was appealed by the owner, who recommended "transportation" for the condemned man, but
the reviewing authorities sustained the verdict of the jus-
tices. Ottolenghe was also on committees which dealt with
the Negro problem; judging by the recommendations in
which he concurred, and the activity in which he engaged,
he shared many of the prejudices of his day with respect
to Negro slaves.

Ottolenghe was a very active public servant. He rapidly
became a person of some consequence in the young colony.
In 1755, only four years after he landed, he was elected to
the colonial House of Representatives, probably the first
born Jew to occupy such a position in an American colony.
He remained in office almost until his death in July, 1775,
except for a brief period in 1766 when he was expelled
from the House for some act of insubordination against
that body. A study of the records of the legislature reveals
that he served on a number of important committees. He
was a collector and assessor for the town of Savannah and

Christ Church parish, a commissioner for erecting and building fortifications, and a trustee to purchase a "White House" for the colonial governor. In 1757 he was first appointed Clerk of the General Court; five years later he became a judge in a court of superior jurisdiction, and this by no means exhausts the list of the jobs and appointments of public trust that marked his career. In 1762 he was made a member of the committee to instruct and to supervise the activity of Georgia's colonial agent or representative in London.

Twelve years before this he had humbly besought the trustees to transport him to Georgia at their expense!

His was quite a career for a humble Jewish convert to Christianity, for an impoverished alien who had known the bitterness and filth of a debtors' jail. In Italy, in Piedmont, as a Jew, he would have found it difficult, if not impossible, to purchase a piece of ground; he would have been compelled to live in a ghetto, to listen to Christian conversionist sermons. It is extremely doubtful whether this Italian convert could have made a career for himself even in contemporary England where, as late as the second quarter of the nineteenth century, even *baptized* Jews were denied some of the basic economic privileges.

For him, Georgia and America had become the land of unlimited opportunity. But it became a land of promise, in spite of his Jewish origin, only because his more-than-average ability was recognized and given full play in a pioneer economy where men with his capacities were sorely needed.

It was while Ottolenghe was a colonial legislator that he stood out as one of the leaders in the fight against the Dissenters and the anti-religionists, a struggle which resulted in the establishment of the Anglican Church in the province of Georgia.

It has been found among Jews, since the days of St. Paul, that converts are usually very zealous for their new faith. Whether Ottolenghe made any religious approaches to Savannah Jewry is not known to us. He may have hesitated, fearing a sharp rebuff, for some of the Jewish settlers were crude and tough. This the Lutheran pastor, Henry Melchior Mühlenberg, discovered in 1742 on his first visit to Georgia. While in the village of New Hannover, the peacefully disposed minister volunteered to serve as an arbitrator in a dispute between a Jewish itinerant merchant and a German cabinetmaker. Later, when the pastor reproved the Jew for his offensive language, the latter refused to accept the reprimand in good spirit. He sourly told Mühlenberg that he, the pastor, did not know the manners of the country.

Mühlenberg's friend, Pastor Bolzius, the leader of the Salzburg Germans, was eager to proselytize the Georgia Jews, but had no illusions about the task that confronted him. When he offered the Savannah Jews some conversionist literature, in 1738, they rejected his evangelical advances, indignantly and vigorously. John Wesley, as we have read, courted the society of the Savannah Sephardim, and George Whitefield, another pioneer Methodist, preached, on occasion, to audiences in which it is known that there were Jewish auditors.

In August, 1770, not long after Whitefield left Georgia for the last time, he preached in Newport, Rhode Island. Among those who listened with rapt attention to the great evangelist was one of the Polock girls. This young lady—she was about fifteen years of age—was already predisposed to Christianity. Sometime before, she had been sent to a private school where the master had taken advantage of her presence to harangue the classes on the virtues of Christianity. This went on till her shocked parents took her out of school, but she had by then developed an interest in the religion, had read the New Testament surreptitiously, and had declared publicly more than once that she wished she were a Christian.

Ezra Stiles, the source of our information about the Christian sympathies of the Newport Jews, also recorded the receipt of a conversionist pamphlet from John Joachim Zubly, the minister of the Independent Presbyterian Church in Savannah. The pamphlet was *An Account of the Remarkable Conversion of Zachial Heishel from the Jewish to the Christian Religion*, published in Savannah in 1770.

Zubly was a native Swiss, born in St. Gall. No doubt he had purchased or seen a copy of the 1768 edition of John Caspar Ulrich's *Collection of Jewish Stories* dealing with the history of the Jews in Switzerland. There he had read how the Jew Heishel had come to accept Jesus, and in a thirty-two-page English pamphlet he retold the story for the edification of his American countrymen.

Briefly, the "remarkable" story was as follows. Zachial Heishel—more correctly, Jechiel Hirschlein—was a Jewish teacher from Württemberg, who wandered about from town to town in South Germany and Alsace, trying to make a living. By the time he was twenty, in 1726, he was already married. Ultimately he was to have four children. About three years after his marriage, he tells us, his eyes were opened by careful reading of the fifty-third chapter of Isaiah, where it says that the promised Messiah was to be distinguished through his suffering. When Jechiel told his thoughts to his Jewish friends, they suspected that he had heretical leanings, and asked him to do penance.

Contritely, the sinner took a vow to wander for three years and never again to discuss doctrinal matters. However, several years later, after living a pious and exemplary life as a Jew, he became more than ever convinced, through his reading of the New Testament, that the Messiah had come and was none other than Jesus.

Going home, he told his wife and children of his convictions, and when they refused to share his lot, he bade them a tearful good-bye and betook himself to Switzerland. There, in Zurich, in the presence of a great throng, he was baptized on May 26, 1746, taking the new name of Christian Gottleb. When Ulrich's book was published, Jechiel was still alive, a pious Christian, living honestly—so we are told—as a small shopkeeper.

This is the story which Zubly published and which, we may be sure, he sent to some of the Savannah Jews, who, we may be even more sure, ignored it.

Jews resented Christian conversionist literature. Christianity was the established faith of the body politic that denied them equal rights. Individual Jews respected and loved their Christian friends but had little respect for a

religion whose civilization did not square with its preach-
ments. They indignantly resented and rejected Christian
conversionist literature because of the implication that
Judaism was inferior to Christianity; they were unwaver-
ingly convinced of the superiority of their own teachings.

In Rhode Island or in Georgia or in another colony, the
Christian leaders were pathetically eager to make converts.
Ostensibly they were motivated by the earnest desire to
bring salvation to the individuals who were otherwise
eternally and spiritually damned. There was probably a
deeper reason for their avid interest in conversionism. The
refusal of the Jew to become a Christian was a rejection
of Jesus as the divinely begotten and divinely sent Messiah.
It was a curt declaration that evangelical Christianity was
built on a false foundation, that Christianity was not the
one true religion. Until the Jews accepted Christianity
pious Christians could never be sure that the Jew was
wrong! It is a very disturbing thought.

Chapter 14

Georgia, 1768 – 1777

SLOWLY, very slowly, the Jewish community of Georgia rose again. In 1746 a contemporary clergyman reported that there were thirteen Jews —families?—in Savannah. By 1760, when there were but 6,000 people in all the colony, newcomers had begun to swell the ranks of the handful who had never left. At this time Jews were found in different forms of enterprise. Practically all of them owned land; some farmed. A number were merchants; one was a tavernkeeper. Others became Indian traders, consorting with red women and begetting children by them. One became a butcher, taking a Salzburg German as his partner. In due course some of the Jewish settlers prospered, and their womenfolk, to the horror of the German Pietists, began to wear expensive clothes. Rising in the social scale, the men sought the company of their more enlightened and liberal neighbors by joining the Masonic order.

Most Christians and Jews were united in their neglect of religious observances. Very few of the families, possibly only one at first, held on to the old Jewish customs. Yet in spite of this religious indifference, individual families did pay lip homage to diverse Jewish rituals.

The work of assimilation went on apace. One of the Nunez Ribieros became a Rivers, a Marcus appeared as Marks, and the New Yorker of 1729, Collman (Coleman) Salomons, emerged in Georgia as Solomon Colman.

Among the merchants in Savannah in 1768 was a man named James Lucena, apparently a refugee from the Portuguese Inquisition, who had come to Rhode Island in the early 1750's, just about the time that his cousin Aaron Lopez arrived. Lucena was naturalized by the General Assembly on the last day of December in 1760, taking the oath on "the true faith of a Christian." This same legislative body refused to consider Lopez' application for naturalization about a year later.

In February, 1761—still in Newport—Lucena applied for a ten-year monopoly on the manufacture of Castile soap, the "secret" formula for which he had learned back in Portugal. His petition was granted, for he promised to employ many poor people, to increase exports to the West Indies and the continent, and, after the decade was up, to reveal to the public his method of soapmaking. Evidently he did not remain in Rhode Island to exploit his monopoly, for he migrated a few years later to Savannah, where we find him engaged in commerce, shipping mahogany and deerskins to the market at Bristol, England, on the account of Rivera and his son-in-law, Lopez.

Lucena was interested also in the slave trade, which certainly began to flourish in 1749 after the decision of the

Georgia trustees to allow the importation of Negro servants. Savannah itself never became a center for the traffic in colonial days. Overshadowed by metropolitan Charlestown to the north, it was never a great port. The South Carolina capital, no doubt, also helped provide for the slave needs of Georgia.

In 1755 Solomon Isaacs, of the New York family of that name, imported some slaves into Charlestown, but he was not a large dealer in the commodity. Among the Jews in the South, Isaac DaCosta was the only one to operate on a large scale. In 1760 he and his Gentile partner, Thomas Farr, Jr., brought in 200 slaves out of a total annual import of 3,573. Three years later the same company imported 160.

By the early 1770's the firm was out of business but had not yet settled all its old accounts. One Friday afternoon the future president of the Continental Congress, Henry Laurens, the largest slave importer in Charlestown, sought to collect from DaCosta an old bill due on an earlier slave deal. The Jewish merchant agreed to see Laurens that afternoon, but failed to appear. The latter was, of course, aware, as the afternoon passed, that DaCosta would do no business on the Sabbath. "I must not obtrude business upon him on this day," he wrote tolerantly to Farr, the partner of the old firm, asking him to settle the account.

Isaac Lyons of Savannah and his two Gentile associates imported eight slaves in 1763, but the Jews of Georgia do not seem to have engaged in this traffic after that until 1768, when Lucena dispatched the following letter to Cousin Aaron Lopez:

Savannah, in Georgia, 28 June, 1768.

Dear Sir:

This will be delivered to you by Captain Nathaniel Waldron. He is to proceed from this port to the Windward Islands [in the West Indies], there to procure a cargo of molasses and other produce. And then he is to proceed to Rhode Island and deliver to you what cargo and money he may have belonging to me, to be invested in rum, and what you think proper for the intended voiage to the Coast of Affrica.

If Captain Waldron proceeds the voiage round, he is to have from the time he first takes in any part of the cargo, the customary wages and privelege [of a number of slaves for himself] given in general from Rhode Island to a master of a vessell of the burthen of myne. The mate, John Brown, is also to have the customary wages and privelege of Rhode Island, to begein from the time the molasses cargo is delivered.

And neither of them are to receive of you any wages for the West India and Affrica voiage, being agreed the whole to be paid here. I desire of you to let me know the time when the alteration of their wages takes place, as the wages they now go for are very high.

As this letter will not come to hand this long while, I will take other opportunity to write more at large, and remain, sir,

Your affectioned cozen,

James Lucena.

P.S. As we are not acquainted what are the customary wages and privelege to the Coast of Affrica, [it] is left to you to determine it.[58]

This letter offers another excellent illustration of the classical triangular traffic: West India molasses was traded for Newport rum, which in turn was traded for African slaves to be delivered in the West Indies or in Savannah.

These slaves were, in turn, bartered in the West Indies for more molasses or for specie.

We do not know whether Lucena intended to employ any of the slaves whom he imported. Two years later he received a grant of 750 acres in Christ Church Parish, but there is no indication that he actually became a planter and farmed with the nine Negroes he then owned. A year later his slave holdings increased to twelve, and he put in a request for a thousand acres of land on the south side of the Altamaha River. Knowing that this sprawling patch of uncleared country would require an even larger complement of workers, he sent a vessel to Jamaica for a parcel of Negroes. By 1771 he owned twenty slaves whom he worked, but his major effort was still devoted to business. He was essentially a merchant, and he supported his wife and three children through commerce.

That year, at least, Lucena was rather glum about Georgia's economic future. It was a young undeveloped country of about 30,000 people, half of whom were slaves. Business opportunities were limited. The planters could not keep their books in favorable balance; they were always buying more than they could pay for. When they got a good bill of exchange they used it to buy more slaves, rather than to pay old debts, and so Lucena discouraged his Newport friends from shipping too much to Georgia.

In January, Captain Daniel Cornell, who had only recently finished a voyage to Quebec in the "Mary," sailed up the Savannah in the same sloop, carrying a small cargo belonging to his Newport friends, Lopez and Rivera.

Lucena handled the goods. A certain amount of business

could be done by bartering New England candles, cheese, oil, and rum for barrel staves, shingles, horses, and rice.

In a long letter, in Portuguese, to Cousin Aaron, Lucena pointed out that hay was one commodity which would do well in Georgia. There were plenty of horses to be had in the back country, and if hay could be sent down from New England, the animals could be well-fed on their way to a West Indian market. There was a good profit in this staple. Send us hay.

By 1772 James's son, John Charles Lucena, was in business with his father under the firm name of James Lucena and Son. During that particular year the son, then about twenty years old, traveled between Providence and Newport, working for Aaron Lopez and serving as the Rhode Island resident agent for his father in Savannah. In December, John placed an order with Lopez for cider, cheese, spermaceti candles and rum, 6,000 gallons in all, but "please to let as small a quantity of gall[on]'s of rum be mentioned in the clearance as possible"! It was considered proper—and certainly profitable—to fool the king's customs' officers in the stirring days that ushered in the Revolution. Lopez knew exactly what the Lucenas wanted. Four months earlier, up in Newport Harbor, one of Lopez' crews had attempted to run in forty-one quarter-casks of wine in the dead of night, but the inept smugglers were seized in the act by the British patrols. It was not a major calamity, however, for the Newport shipper stood in well with the government officials. Lopez' friends were convinced that though the vessel and wine would be condemned, he would be able to buy back the boat and its cargo for less than the actual customs involved! Nobody would bid against him.

The Newport merchant might well have excused himself on the ground that it was an act of patriotism to defraud the king's officers. John Charles could certainly not have salved his conscience with the same comforting thought, for he, like his father, was a self-sacrificing loyalist. When the break with the mother country came, the Lucenas maintained their loyalty to the English crown at the cost of proscription for the son. The father returned to Portugal, where the fires of the Inquisition had almost been smothered by this time, and young Lucena sailed for London, where he ultimately married a Gentile, became a consul general for the Court of Portugal, and died—as he had been born!— a Catholic.

In a January (1771) letter of Captain Daniel Cornell to his employer Lopez, there occurs this postscript: "Lett my wife be informed of my being well. Mr. Moses is well after being see sick. Mr. Moses gives his compliment to Mr. Rod. Revere and both your famileys." (Mr. Revere was no relative of Paul Revere; he was none other than our Sephardic friend, Jacob Rodriguez Rivera.)

The "see sick" Mr. Moses was Philip Moses. There were two by the same name in Georgia-South Carolina at the time, one of whom was a cousin of Haym Salomon. Our Mr. Moses had come to Savannah from Newport with a small load of goods. After a few weeks in business he was confident that in the small town at the southern end of the American colonies it would not be too difficult for a man with little capital to get a start. "I finde this place suitable for a man in my circumstances."

After opening his shop he wrote Lopez, offering to act as one of his agents in town, asked for a consignment of goods on credit, and set about disposing of nine kegs of cordial which Cornell had left with him.

Evidently the cordials sold well, for in April, Moses paid for them with raccoon and fox skins. Two years later he was still doing business with Lopez, still paying for shipments with Georgia skins and furs.

Moses was a religious man. This we infer from the fact that he scrupulously paid for the offerings which his friends continued to make on his behalf in the Newport synagogue, even though it was two years since he had left that community. He was also a charitable man. A thousand miles away from Newport, with little means of his own, he did not forget to ask his rich sponsor Lopez to apply part of his modest balance to aid the impoverished Myers family of Newport. (Apparently this was the Benjamin Myers or Myer Benjamin family. Benjamin, a Hungarian, could speak "all the living languages" and served as a Hebrew and Yiddish interpreter for the more prosperous Sephardic Jews in town, but he seems to have had difficulty in making a living for his eight children—and more to come. His most distinguished son was Major Mordecai Myers, who deserves to be remembered for his wry comment to a journalist during the War of 1812: "Some must spill there blud, and others, there *ink*.")

Philip Moses later migrated to Charlestown, where he continued to be active in business. Moses seems to have done pretty well; the Lucenas were, in all likelihood, even more successful. However, these people were the exception, as Abraham Sarzedas could well testify.

This Sephardi had come to New York in the 1740's, and was later made a freeman of the city. Sometime in the 1750's he had married Caty, the sister of Moses Michael Hays. Obviously the father, Judah Hays, a well-known merchant, could not have been happy with that marriage. Sarzedas certainly, at that time, had no luck as a businessman. For a time Judah Hays had to pay the rent of the young couple, and they had taken a house more expensive even than his!

In his attempt to make a living and support his family, Abraham wandered as far south as Savannah where, in 1757, he was at least successful in his Masonic activities. Four years later he was back in Newport, Rhode Island, a member of the rather exclusive Jewish club of that city, playing whist and piquet with the Riveras, the Harts, and the Polocks. In 1764 he was once more in Georgia, where he secured a grant of 500 acres on the promise that he would register it, pay the proper quitrents, and, of course, undertake cultivation. It is doubtful that he ever applied himself to the task. The three Negroes he owned were far too few to do a good job of farming. He kept wandering; Haiti, the Mole St. Nicholas, was his next stop. But that excursion ended only in a debt to Rivera and Lopez, and in 1771 he was back again in Savannah, still stumbling after Dame Fortune—and worried. By this time he had not only his wife but at least four children to support. He was determined to return to Haiti for another try, and wanted Lopez and Rivera to bear with him.

Savannah in Georgia, 25th July, 1771.

Gentlemen:

My last to you per Capt. Peck cover'd a recipt for two tierces of rice on your account to pay for the error of the accounts remitted from the Mole [Haiti], which I hope is safe to hand.

Notwithstanding my firm resolution of [n]ever more plowing the ocean and absent my self from my dear family, I find (allthough very desagreable) that nessesity obliged me ones more to go and reside at the Mole St. Nicholas to enable me to provide them confortably. As my children advances in age, so I find the wants the greater. While life doath last it's my duty to do my best for their aducation, etc., etc.

Influenced by these motives which must in the eye of every good man appear laudable, I am to quit my family within a fortnight for the Mole for one year at least. If God grants me life and health, it's probably much more [longer], which must cheafly depend on the business I shall have. It's boath my duty and interest to offer you and your friends my sarvice dureing my residence there.

Should you think me worthy of being intrusted with your consignement, depend that my study shall be ponctuality and dispatch so as to merit your aplause.

This being the nedfull, permit me to take my leave and to wish you and good family health and felicity, and to subscribe, gentleman,

Your most obliged humble sarvent to command,
Ab'm Sarzedas.[59]

Abraham Sarzedas apparently never found the long life and felicity which he sought for himself and wished for his friends. He was back in the colonies during the Revolution, but had already died by the time his daughter Rebecca was married in Charlestown in 1779.

It might well be wrong—even in this particular instance—to imply, as we have, that Sarzedas was incompetent because he wandered all through the colonies and to the West Indies in the attempt to wrest a living from a stubborn fate. The fact that his wife Caty had four Negro servants in Newport, in 1774, would seem to imply that he was by no means impoverished. In general, it is true that most Jews in colonial times just managed to make a living; many of them were merchants who never acquired any real wealth. This fact is brought home to us when we study the monetary gifts for the building of Mikveh Israel in Philadelphia in 1782. By far the largest portion of those donations was made by Jewish merchants from the different colonies. There were 61 contributors; nine of them gave about £664, approximately 74 per cent of a grand total of about £897.

Sarzedas had a son, David, who was a lieutenant in the Georgia Continental Line. What was the status of a Jew in Georgia at that time which made it possible for him to become an officer in the American army?

In order to understand what political rights the Jews of Georgia then exercised, it is necessary to go back to the colonial charter of 1732.

The original grant by George II gave the Jews, together with all Protestants, the right to worship God as they saw fit. (Catholics were excepted.) This privilege of the free exercise of their religion was not circumscribed in 1758, when the Church of England was established in Georgia. That the Anglicans were determined, however, to secure the emoluments due them as the only recognized church is made evident in an action which they brought in 1769. A suit was entered against a Protestant Dissenter to make him pay a funeral bell-tolling fee to an Anglican sexton even though the bell in the Anglican church had not been tolled. (The Dissenters had their own bell.) The case came before a court in which Joseph Ottolenghe was the presiding judge; the jury brought in a verdict against the Dissenter. Judge Ottolenghe made it quite clear "that the Dissenters had no right to the use of a bell at all, and that the Rector of the parish was to blame that he had not pulled it [the bell of the Dissenters] down."

The Jews of Georgia had to pay church taxes, a disability which they shared with all non-Anglicans, but then, as taxpayers, they were accorded the right to vote for Church of England vestrymen!

Nothing was said in the charter of 1732 about Jews' holding office. "Foreigners that are willing to become our subjects" were to be admitted. Their native-born children were to be free denizens. It is very probable that they voted for candidates for office but could not themselves accept one. As Jews they could not submit themselves to the Christian religious tests for officeholders. And there is no record that they were permitted to omit the phrase, "upon the faith of a Christian."

But it has been pointed out, by way of refutation of the above statement that Jews did not hold office, that Daniel and Moses Nunez were customs officers for the Port of

Savannah and also government interpreters. (Daniel was serving as a Spanish interpreter as early as 1736; Moses was an Indian interpreter in the 1760's.) David Emanuel, who was later to become governor of the state, was a justice of the peace in 1766; James Lucena was a justice in 1773, and his son, John Charles, was an officer in the militia the following year.

None of these men can be accepted as observant Jews. There is, indeed, no proof that David Emanuel was even of Jewish stock. The Nunez brothers and the Lucenas, all of whom had once been Marranos, crypto-Jews, found it easy to assume the outward forms of Christian society. In fact, as we have seen, the Lucenas were born Catholics and died as Catholics—at least nominally. The Nunez brothers did not hesitate even in Georgia to attend Christian services as auditors, and we know that Moses Nunez, in 1775, took the oath on the New Testament, the "Holy Evangels of Almighty God."

Jews, as Jews, in colonial Georgia could hold no office which required the taking of a Christian test oath. They were no better off—and no worse off—than their coreligionists in all the other colonies.

David Sarzedas was able to accept a commission as an American officer during the Revolution because, we may be sure, no religious test oath was imposed. Soldiers and officers were needed too desperately at the time to cavil about their religious affiliation.

The constitution makers of the new state in 1776-77 were more cautious, more traditional. They established the Protestant Church, continuing the officeholding disability for both Jews and Catholics. A law of 1785 gave the Catholics recognition by establishing "Christianity," not Protestantism, as the religion of the state. It was not until 1789, under the influence of the Federal Constitution, that the Jews of Georgia were given political rights, and it was not until 1798, under a new state constitution, that they were finally accorded complete political and religious freedom. By the terms of the revised constitution of that year no one could be compelled to support even the institutions of his own religious profession. It had taken over twenty years before the state of Georgia accorded full freedom to its white citizens, irrespective of their religious beliefs.

During the period of the Revolution the Jewish community, like the larger general community, was divided between Whigs and Tories. To express it somewhat differently, there was no Jewish community in which there were not some Jews who remained loyal to the established British government. Georgia was no exception in this respect. Moses Nunez was one of those who in 1774 protested against the anti-British mass meetings in Savannah. The quondam Anglican missionary, Joseph Ottolenghe, and the Lucenas were Tories. It is worthy of note that all four "Jews" were proselytes to Christianity or crypto-Jews. They had no interest in opposing the old regime because it denied religious equality to Jews.

As a customs officer on the watch for smuggling, Moses Nunez was certainly no favorite of the colonial merchants. But he was no out-and-out loyalist. During the war he served as an Indian agent for the Georgia revolutionary forces, and when the Whigs had the upper hand in 1782 he was not attainted as a Tory. He was a real pioneer who had come in shortly after Oglethorpe, in July, 1733. In the course of the years he became a man of some wealth, owning property, land, notes collectable, and slaves. Oglethorpe and Nunez belonged to the same Masonic lodge, and when the latter died, David Montaigut, a Gentile friend who once had been Speaker of the House of Assembly, preached the funeral sermon.

The first wife of Nunez—her maiden name was Abrahams—was a Jewess. His second "wife" was a mulatto. By his first wife he had one son; by the second, three sons and a daughter. Nunez made no distinction in his will between his first-born and the other children, but to protect the quadroons he emancipated them formally in his will. During his lifetime he also saw to it that they were given some schooling, to judge from the fact that one of them, who qualified as an executor, wrote a good hand.

A man by the name of Pollock—was this Cushman Pollack, the Jewish merchant?—protested the will, but the jury that studied the case decided to uphold the wishes of the testator. The foreman of that jury was Mordecai Sheftall. We shall soon have occasion to know him better.

It is very difficult to discover anything "Jewish" about Moses Nunez, the son of that Dr. Nunez who had sacrificed much of his fortune and had certainly risked his life to flee from Portugal and its Inquisition in order to live as a Jew in the freer Anglo-Saxon lands. In Georgia, the son viewed, at best with indifference, the ideals and folkways for which his father's generation had died at the stake. This is not to imply that he denied his family; he provided for many of them, brothers and sisters, in his will. One of the witnesses to it was a Jew, probably his brother-in-law; and after his death the court appointed three Jews to appraise his estate.

We know of two sisters of Moses: Esther, a native Georgian, had married a DeLyon; Zipporah, the other, was a young lady nineteen years of age when she arrived from abroad with her father. Zipporah had been born in Portugal, a Catholic, and she grew up in this land to marry a "rabbi," Mr. Machado, the *hazzan* of Shearith Israel. Her contemporaries agreed that Zipporah Machado was an unusual woman, charming and cultured, mistress of six languages. Her charity, which she bestowed as her means permitted, was "unbiassed by national or sectarian prejudices." She was the mother-in-law of a Revolutionary veteran (Jonas Phillips) and the great-grandmother of a commodore in the United States Navy (Uriah P. Levy) and of a Grand Sachem of Tammany Hall (M. M. Noah), all Jews.

John Charles Lucena, a fervent defender of the status quo, was ousted from his post as lieutenant in the militia because he refused to side with the anti-British party. In August, 1775, together with others, he protested that his civil and religious liberties had been subverted because the pro-British rector of Christ Church had been silenced. Lucena did not hesitate to add his signature to those of the other signers who pointed out that the chairman and one or more of the members of the county committee of rebels were persons professing the Jewish religion, and that they had appointed "a layman and of doubtful religious character to perform divine service in the church." We are "oppressed . . . in our civil and [Anglican] religious rights," thundered Lucena along with the rest. "We think it our duty . . . to express our abhorrence of those unlawful proceedings. . . ."

Why were there Jewish Tories? Why were there Jewish Whigs? The attitude of the Jewish Whig in relation to the political struggle was a twofold one: as an American he sought emancipation for himself from English domination; as a Jew he insisted upon complete political equality with his Gentile neighbors. There is little evidence, if any, that Jewish Whigs fought solely because they wished to improve themselves as Jews. Practically all the evidence seems to point to the fact that they sought a larger measure of freedom for themselves both as Americans and as Jews. The Jewish patriots identified their struggles and aspirations with those of their fellow-patriots. They pinned their hopes as Jews on the outcome of the larger struggle for freedom, confidently expecting that independence would bring them complete civil, political, and religious equality.

What was it, for instance, that prompted a man like Abraham M. Seixas, a veteran of South Carolina and Georgia campaigns, to take up arms against England? Why did he react differently from some of the Harts and Polocks whom he knew so well in Newport? It is very difficult, if not impossible, to fathom the motivations that prompted individuals to rebel or to forebear from rebelling. It is probably correct to state that the differences—in so far as they related to American and Jewish liberties—between Jewish patriots and Jewish Tories were those of strategy, of approach. The goals, as both groups envisaged them, were close, if not identical. (And this is certainly true of many of the non-Jews of the time, too.) A Tory like David Franks of Philadelphia was just as much opposed to the British pre-war restrictive commercial regulations as was a Sheftall of Georgia. Some of the Jewish Tories—again this was true of the Gentile Tories—signed the anti-English boycott or nonimportation resolutions. We may be sure that a Tory like Isaac Hart of Newport wanted political equality for himself as a Jew just as much as did the Whig, Abraham M. Seixas of Georgia. But there was this difference between the Whig and the Tory, certainly in so far as the rights of Jews were at stake. The Tory Jew was willing to work and to wait for improvement. He was well aware of the fact that he was making progress. Religious freedom was his; economic opportunity was practically unlimited. Even Jewish Whigs—as far as we know—were not distressed or downcast because of existing political disabilities, even though they were increasingly resentful of such injustices. The Jewish Tory was confident of the future. He believed that political liberty, under England, was on the way. The Naturalization Act of 1740 was the first breach in the wall of political disabilities. A parliamentary statute of 1773 permitted naturalized citizens—apparently Jews would also be included—to assume crown offices in the colonies. Time would bring equality. He was willing to wait. The Whigs wanted immediate action; they supported the Revolution.

There were other factors, too, that determined the pro-independence or the anti-independence sympathies of Jews during the Revolution. As legislators and public servants, men like Ottolenghe and the Lucenas were closely bound to the English regime. They benefited by its continuance. Loyalism was strong in the country around Savannah. As late as May, 1775, after the battles of Lexington and Concord had been fought, the Second Continental Congress urged an economic boycott of Georgia because the colony had not espoused the Revolutionary cause.

To be sure, it is not always easy to stamp individuals as Tories or as Whigs. The very terms are relative. There was a large segment of the general population in the South which was eager for a peaceful solution of its difficulties. In the interval between 1774 and 1781, one and the same individual might veer, under the stress of conscience or circumstances, to the revolutionary or to the loyalist side. The Savannah Presbyterian, the Reverend John J. Zubly, represented Georgia in the Continental Congress in 1775, but in 1777 he was banished from that very state as a Tory.

Savannah and Charlestown were both in the hands of the English for a number of years. Merchants and others who wished to remain in a city or colony under British control had to conform to the demands of the armed rulers. They had to take an oath of allegiance. Many who took "protection" or "addressed" themselves to the occupying authorities were convinced that the Continental cause was hopelessly lost and were ready to make peace with the enemy. They wanted to save their property, to support their families.

Levi Sheftall, a Savannah rancher (diamond LS brand), butcher, and American commissary, fled British-occupied

Georgia in 1779 and was disqualified in 1780 as a Whig. He lost his political rights because he was a rebel. Two years later, the State Assembly of Georgia denounced him— even if only temporarily—as a Tory! He was doubly damned! A Revolutionary patriot like Philip Minis also fled in 1779 from Georgia to Charlestown. There, in May, 1780, he signed a petition asking the besieged General Lincoln not to continue the hopeless war with the English invaders. This man was no Tory. Two months later he was deprived of his political privileges in Georgia by the British because of his known devotion to the "audacious, wicked, and un- provoked rebellion" of the Americans.

However, unreconstructed Jewish Tories like the Lu- cenas were in the minority. Like most of the dissenting Protestant sects, the Jews, with few exceptions, were sym- pathetic to the American cause. Not a single Jewish name is found in the lists of South Carolinian loyalists who were banished and lost their property.

The Jewish rebels of the South—that is, of Georgia and South Carolina—evidenced their sympathies in different ways. Levi Sheftall served as a guide for Count d'Estaing in 1779 when the attempt was made to recapture Savannah from the British. Had he been caught, he probably would have been executed. Isaac DaCosta, an uncompromising Whig, bought "certificates" at the State Loan Office. Others, like the Pollacks, the Minises, and the Sheftalls, were commissaries or purveyors to the militia and to the Continental forces.

Some of these men served as soldiers in Georgia, but later, after the British conquest of the state, they went into exile into South Carolina. A number of the Georgia and Carolina Jews were members of Captain William Lushington's Charlestown company of militia. When thirteen of the officers and men served as a board to pass on the loyalty of their fellow-townsmen, two of the Jews in the company were co-opted.

One of the most active of the southern patriots seems to have been Israel Joseph, a merchant in King Street, Charlestown. Like many others, this German Jewish immigrant had come to America via England, and one of his brothers was still living in that country after the turn of the century. When Joseph immigrated to New York City at the time of the French and Indian War, he was a young man of about twenty-one. The close of the war found him in Charlestown; by 1775, he was a well-known member of the Jewish community. Evidently he was something of a troublemaker in the synagogue, for the DaCostas were instructed by the congregation to reprimand him, diplomatically, for some breach of which he was guilty. Ultimately he became the perennial president of the congregation, earning that honor by substantial gifts to it during his lifetime. When the "new synagogue" was built in 1792 he was probably the most liberal donor, and was given the honor of laying the first cornerstone. His kindness also expressed itself in a contribution to Rhode Island College (Brown University). The wealthy childless businessman may have been captious, but he was certainly generous. After providing for his wife and relatives, he left legacies for Jewish and Christian charities in Charleston, and for the synagogal community in his native town of Mannheim.

From a letter sent to him by Rawlins Lowndes, who had been President (Governor) of South Carolina, we are in a position to understand the part Joseph played in the war during the years 1778–79. All indications are that he was an outstanding Whig, for the enemy deprived him of his property. Lowndes expressed the pious hope that it would not be long before his correspondent would be restored to his possessions and to his "country." Joseph might well be assured that Lowndes would help him to this end.

The Charlestown merchant's efforts were centered in the attempt to mobilize all resources in defense of the upper Savannah River area, the back country of South Carolina and Georgia. In December, 1778, the British had taken Savannah and were marching against the settlements up the river. The American general Robert Howe was in retreat. During that critical turn of affairs, President Lowndes wanted Joseph to help collect the scattered inhabitants of the borderlands and to co-operate with General Williamson in opposing the enemy's move on Augusta. The whole interior of South Carolina and Georgia was threatened by the advance. The Tories had to be frightened off from joining the British. In order to forestall the approaching enemy, and to prepare for a counterattack, General Williamson had seized whatever boats he could lay his hands on. President Lowndes hoped that Joseph would agree on the propriety of the measure.

It is a pity that we know so little of Joseph's activity during that period. Judging from the deference which President Lowndes showed him, he must have been a striking personality.

Chapter 15

Georgia, 1778 – 1783

THE Sheftalls were the best known, if not the outstanding, Jewish family in early Georgia. Benjamin Sheftall had come over from London with the first batch of Spanish-Portuguese Jews in July, 1733, but he was not of Sephardic ethnic stock. He was a German Jew, a native of Bavaria or Frankfort-on-the-Main, who spoke English and a fluent German Yiddish, which he even taught to his oldest son, Mordecai, who was born in the colony in 1735.

Mordecai's mother died the following year. Pioneering life on the frontier was hard on women. Many of them died giving birth to children. After two years as a widower, Benjamin married again, this time a woman named Hannah Solomons.

The first of the Sheftalls in the colony, he never acquired much wealth. After a generation in Georgia he owned but two slaves, and, sometime before his death in the middle 1760's, his slaves—who may serve as an index to his fortune —had increased to about five.

It was soon obvious that Mordecai Sheftall, the son, was

CATTLE BRANDS OF THE MINIS AND THE SHEFTALL FAMILIES, 1755–72

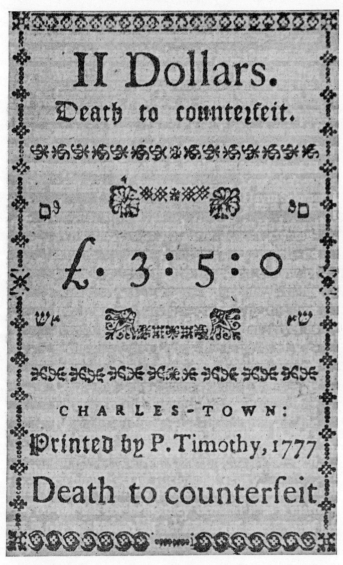

CHARLESTOWN PAPER MONEY WITH HEBREW CHARACTERS, 1772

to be more successful than his pioneering father. He started acquiring land by grant and purchase at twenty-one, and by the time he was twenty-five, he owned a warehouse and wharf lot "under the bluff" on the Savannah River, where he stored and shipped merchandise. Few of the successful Georgians limited themselves to one field, so, like his neighbors, he also went into ranching and had a cowpen on the Canoochee. Soon he was the owner of five slaves, a married man, and the father of a growing family. At twenty-six he had wed Frances Hart, The Hague-born daughter of a Dutch Jew, Moses Hart, who may have lived in Charlestown for a time. Frances Sheftall wrote a rather good English letter—assuming that she wrote the letters signed with her name—but when she subscribed her own will at the age of seventy-five, in the early nineteenth century, she employed the Hebrew script.

Following the custom of the time, Mordecai made provision for his wife immediately before the marriage. This was not a marriage settlement but an indenture in the form of a release. It appointed Isaac DaCosta, the Charlestown merchant, trustee of certain properties to be held for Mrs. Sheftall in the event of her husband's decease. The items included were 650 acres of land, two Savannah town lots with the houses and other improvements on them, and three Negro slaves. (Obviously Mordecai had done well for himself, and was now determined to do well by his bride.) The indenture also protected Mordecai. As long as he lived he received the income of the specified items; if he got into business difficulties, the creditors could not touch these particular assets; they belonged to his wife. One might call this trust a sort of insurance policy against hard times.

When Mordecai was twenty-seven years old he owned 1,000 acres and nine Negroes. Though not wealthy by colonial standards, he was certainly a substantial citizen. (Governor James Wright, a little later, owned 19,000 acres and 500 slaves.) Sheftall was a farmer, rancher, tanner, shipper, storekeeper, and sawmill owner. Taking advantage of the laws of the colony, he later gave his three young sons five slaves and sought grants of land for them for a cowpen. The place was stocked with black horned cattle that grazed on free range. Hay or grain was also grown, for winter feeding, no doubt. A supplementary income was derived from dairy products and hogs. About the same time his five children—two of them were girls—were entered into the brands book as the owners of the 5S ranch (1772). The oldest of the boys, Sheftall Sheftall, was then about ten. No doubt they actually were put to work at a very early age. By the time the first-born was fourteen or fifteen he was already an experienced, trained merchant.

Mordecai's friends in the colonial assembly recognized his ability—at least as a judge of hides and leathers—and they appointed him inspector for tanned leathers for the Port of Savannah. They were eager to maintain the quality of their exports and to prevent the sale abroad of unmarketable goods of that type.

The enterprising merchant was very active in the life of the larger Georgia community. He was one of the incorporators of the non-denominational philanthropic Union

Society which at that time did much to support widows and poor children.

It is interesting to note, moreover, that his position in the community at large was not purchased at the price of indifference to his religion. Throughout his life he was an observant Jew. When only a boy in his teens, living in Charlestown, he had helped his coreligionists there organize their first synagogue.

In 1762 the handful of Georgia Jews—Mordecai was certainly among them, if not the leader—sought in vain to have the ownership of their little cemetery on the Savannah Common confirmed by the legislature. A similar attempt, eight years later, also failed. The Anglicans would not tolerate the legal existence of a dissenting Christian (Presbyterian) cemetery on the Common, let alone one owned by Jews who had "imbibed principles entirely repugnant to those of our most holy [Christian] religion."

The Savannah freeholders and inhabitants who objected to the recognition and the extension of a Jewish cemetery on the Common questioned whether Oglethorpe had ever made such a grant in 1733. They declared that a Jewish burial ground in town was a "nuisance" and that it would have "detrimental consequences." Those Savannah "boosters" insisted that it would stop the town from spreading in that direction and that it would cut down the value of lots. No one would rent or buy a house looking out on a cemetery, particularly a Jewish one!

In 1770–71, in a general population of 1,175 whites, there were six Jewish families with a total of twenty-seven male adults, certainly enough to reconstitute the community.

Three years later, Sheftall gave the little Jewish group in Savannah a few acres in town to serve as a burying ground and as a building lot for a synagogue. On the eve of the Day of Atonement the following year he invited his fellow-Jews, probably not more than ten households all told, to worship with him in his home, in a room which he had furnished as a chapel.

The congregation of 1774 was the third effort to organize permanently—and there was to be at least one more resurrection before the present existing synagogue received its charter in 1790. No building was erected till 1820, almost ninety years after the first Jewish service was held in town.

When the war started in 1775 there was not a more determined patriot in all the colony than Mordecai. Most Georgians, as we have seen, refused to be hurried into rebellion against the mother country, but Mordecai was in the van of those opposed to British rule. As an American Jew of German Jewish origin—who knew England only through a business visit in 1766—all his loyalty and affection were centered in the land of his birth: Georgia and the America about him. He knew only that this land had given him and his father opportunity and freedom which were denied him everywhere else in the world, and that freedom was worth preserving in the face of what he considered to be English tyranny.

Sheftall was made chairman of the rebel Committee of Christ Church Parish, probably the most important county in Georgia because it included Savannah. The Parochial Committee dominated the life of the county after the imperial government broke down during the Revolution. It implemented the Whig regulations with respect to English imports, broke into the old customs office to seize the records, and assumed control on behalf of the revolting colony. It was the *de facto* government.

Mordecai Sheftall, his younger brother Levi (Lewis!), and Philip Minis were very active in the Savannah uprising. The indignant Tories of the time stressed the fact, in their complaints to the English authorities, that members of the Jewish persuasion were the leaders in that work of revolt. When Governor Wright fulminated against the American troublemakers in a letter to the Earl of Dartmouth, he wrote that "one Sheftall, a Jew, is chairman of the Parochial Committee, as they call themselves, and this fellow issues orders to captains of vessels to depart the king's port without landing any of their cargoes legally imported. And fresh insults continue to be offered every day. . . ."

Whenever the opportunity presented itself, the English and the Tories struck back at the Sheftalls. One of the notorious McGirths raided Sheftall's ranch during the war and carried off some of his slaves to British Florida. Years later, shortly before the war came to an end, when Wright was temporarily restored, the governor wrote to England about the part played by Georgia Jewry in the American Revolution. In that letter—sent probably to Sir George Germaine, His Majesty's Principal Secretary of State for America—Wright informed the English that he had approved of a bill authorizing the arrest and expulsion of rebels and disaffected persons. He took pains to explain that Jewish *émigrés* from Georgia should not be allowed to return and that other Jews should be prevented from migrat-

347

ing to that colony: "For these people, my lord, were found to a man to have been violent rebels and persecutors of the king's loyal subjects. And however this law may appear at first sight, be assured, my lord, that the times require these exertions, and without which the loyal subjects can have no peace or security in this province."

In 1777 Sheftall was appointed to the general staff of the Georgia Brigade with the titular rank of colonel. He became Commissary General of Purchases and Issues to the militia of his native state. That was a state, not a "federal," appointment. The next year he became the Deputy Commissary General of Issues to the Continental Troops in South Carolina and Georgia. The latter appointment was made by General Robert Howe, but before it could be confirmed by Congress, Mordecai fell into the hands of the enemy.

It was his principal duty to see that the troops had food and clothing and other necessaries—and he insisted on a receipt for everything he gave out. (Mordecai had been well-trained by his father Benjamin.) Mordecai's oldest son, Sheftall Sheftall, who was already (January, 1778) an Assistant Commissary of Issues, became his father's deputy. He was only fifteen or sixteen years of age but evidently a boy of parts, as we shall have occasion to see.

In November, 1778, the British sent out two invading expeditions northward from St. Augustine. The advancing forces were to be met by a sizable British contingent coming down from New York. Between the two forces Georgia was to be squeezed into submission. Thereupon, some of the Jews of the state, in order to spare their families the horrors of warfare, sent them on to Charlestown, to safety, but remained themselves to fight and to oppose the enemy coming up from Florida. To their astonishment they read, on the first of the month, a vindictive attack on them that appeared in *The Charlestown Gazette*, a paper owned by a Mrs. Crouch. The article was signed *An American*. Two days later an answer to the libel appeared in *The South-Carolina and American General Gazette*. It was addressed to John Wells, the publisher.

Mr. Wells:

On perusing Mrs. Crouch and Co's paper of the 1st instant [December 1, 1778], I was extremely surprised to find, in a piece signed *An American,* a signature sufficient to lead every honest and judicious man to imagine that whatever was said in so publick a manner should be ingenuous and true, assertions directly contrary. Here are his words:

"Yesterday being by my business posted in a much frequented corner of this town, I observed, in a small space of time, a number of chairs [chaises] and loaded horses belonging to those who journeyed, come into town. Upon inspection of their faces and enquiry, I found them to be of the *Tribe of Israel* who, after taking every advantage in trade the times admitted of in the State of Georgia, as soon as it was attacked by an enemy, fled here for an asylum with their ill-got wealth, dastardly turning their backs upon the country, when in danger, which gave them bread and protection. Thus it will be in this State if it should ever be assailed by our enemies. Let judgment take place."

I am apt to think, Mr. Printer, that the gentleman is either very blind, or he is willing to make himself so. For I am well convinced had he taken the trouble of going closer to the chairs he would have found that what he has thus publickly asserted was erroneous, and a palpable mistake, as he might have been convinced they were of the female kind, with their dear babes, who had happily arrived at an asylum where a tyrannical enemy was not at theirs or their dear offsprings' heels.

I do, therefore, in vindication of many a worthy Israelite now in Georgia, assert that there is not at this present hour a single Georgia Israelite in Charles Town. And that so far to the contrary of that gentleman's assertion, I do declare to the public that many merchants of that State were here on the 22nd ult. [November], and on being informed of the enemy landing, they instantly left this [town], as many a worthy Gentile knows, and proceeded post haste to Georgia, leaving all their concerns unsettled, and are now with their brother citizens in the field, doing that which every honest American should do.

The truth of this assertion will in the course of a few days be known to gentlemen of veracity who are entitled to the appellation of Americans. The Charlestown Israelites, I bless Heaven, hitherto have behaved as staunch as any other citizens of this state, and I hope their further conduct will be such as will invalidate the malicious and designing fallacy of the author of the piece alluded to.

> I am, sir, yours, etc.,
> A real *American*
> and
> True hearted *Israelite.*

Charlestown, Wednesday, December 2, 1778.[60]

Less than four weeks after the above letter was written, Mordecai and his son, Sheftall Sheftall, were captured by the British when Savannah was taken. Mordecai's wife, then in Charlestown, was frantic with worry about them. The other children, an increasing brood, were with her. About four or five days after Colonel Campbell's Highlanders and

Hessians took Savannah, Joshua Hart brought her the following letter which had been sent through him:

Savannah, January 1st, 1779.

My dear Fanny:

I am now to inform you of my being a prisoner and confined in the white gaurd house where I am fully as well treated as I could expect, as it is the duty of every honest man to give praise where it is due. I must acknowledge that I have met with much [more] genteel treatment from the officers than I was formerly led to believe we should receive. Our son Sheftall, thanks be to God, has escaped unhurt and is with me. We are reduced to the cloaths on our back and when we shall get a shifting, God only knows.

I must recommend to you to take care of the rest of the children, as I mean not to quite [quit] the boy that is with me, if it's in my power to prevent. I hope our son Benjamin is or will in a short time be with you.

I have met with the kindest treatment from some of our old friends and neighbours, which I hope I shall ever retaine a greatfull sense of. When it will be in our power to see you and the dear children, God only knows. Therefor recommend to you to keep up your spirits, as I and the boy do ours, and wish that the Great Disposer of all things may take you all under his immediate protection.

And I am, my dear Fanny, your affectionate husband,
Mordecai Sheftall.

Sheftall gives his duty to you and joins me in love to the dear children; give mine to our friends.[61]

Mordecai and his son had attempted to escape as the British were overrunning the small Savannah garrison. The father might have gotten away by swimming Musgrove Creek, but Sheftall could not swim and Mordecai would not dream of deserting him. Mordecai and about 185 offi-

351

cers and privates were trapped. As a notorious rebel the Commissary General was given special treatment: a sentry with drawn bayonet watched him constantly. The British commissary officer—Mordecai's opposite number—started quizzing him about the town's supplies, and when he refused to talk, he had him taken out of the guardhouse reserved for whites and thrown into the rooms where Negroes and drunken soldiers were locked up. Three times during that night a drunken soldier tried to bayonet him, and only the intervention of a Sergeant Campbell saved his life. For two days he was given nothing to eat, until a Hessian supply officer, finding that Mordecai spoke his language, took care of him. All this happened before he wrote home, but he omitted these harrowing details when he sent his letter to Fanny, for he did not want her to worry about him and the boy.

On the second day of January (1779) he was taken to headquarters, where one of the naval commanders, Captain Stanhope of the "Raven," pitched into him viciously for refusing to supply the king's ships with provisions. "I made a point of giving Mr. Stanhope suitable answers to his impertinent treatment and then turned from him," wrote Mordecai as he later recounted the trials of those unhappy days.

He suffered for several months on board a prison ship where, so a contemporary historian wrote, his captors evidenced their contempt for him as a Jew by feeding him pork. Finally he was paroled under the watchful eye of the British at Sunbury in Georgia. His friends in Savannah did not forget him. William Jones sent him some fine sugar and three gallons of the best Jamaica rum, no small comfort for an exile.

While he was in that town, there were enough members of the Union Society among the prisoners to constitute a quorum, so a meeting was held and Mordecai was elected vice-president. One of the prisoners with him was Lieutenant Laban Johnson, and when the lieutenant was exchanged and went north to Charlestown, a free man, he carried the following letter to Mrs. Frances Sheftall:

Sunbury, 6th April, 1779.

My dear Fanny:

The pleasure I received at the receipt of your favour of the 26th Feb'y can be easier conceived than expressed. The happiness of hereing from you and my dear children is the only happiness I can injoy in my present sittuation.

I am happy to here that you are once more become mistress of your own house, as I very well know that, notwithstanding the kindness of our freinds, home is home, as the old saying is.

I must beg you will put the poor children to school that they may not be intierly lost in this corroupt age.

I arrived at this place yesterday but have not the happiness of haveing our son with me. He still continues on board the prison ship "Nancy" where my freinds from Savannah will endeavour to make his life as comfortable as their circumstances will admite.

If you see Miss Patty Wright and finde that she stands in need of your assistance, pray give it her, as it never will be in my power to requite her marm [mother] for the many favors received at her hands during my confinement. Therefore could wish her child made as happy as one of my own.

I am obliged to live at an expence here rather higher than my present circumstances can well admite off, but I must endeavour to make the best of a bad market and keep a good flow of spirits in hopes of once more seeing you and my dear children, whom I pray God to take under his immediate protection. And that you may be a comfort to the dear children whilst I am kept from them, is the sincere wish of, my dear Fanny,

Your affectionate husband,
Mordecai Sheftall.

Pray give my blessing to the children and compliments to all my freinds, and let me hear from you as often as possible.[62]

Mordecai was more worried about his imprisoned son than he was about himself. Just a few days after he wrote the above letter, he appealed to a number of Georgia's most distinguished patriots to use their influence to secure the liberation of young Sheftall from the "Nancy." Sometime in May or June, the boy was released under parole and joined his father in Sunbury.

While Mordecai was busy writing to men such as Colonel Samuel Elbert and Major John Habersham to intercede for his son, his wife, Frances, was writing from Charlestown to persons in authority, asking them to arrange for the exchange of her husband. She wanted him back, she wrote, because she could not support herself; her family was in distress. Her husband could have escaped but remained behind because General Robert Howe had ordered him to stay. Howe, continued the embittered and unreasoning woman, wanted her husband taken! The son could have escaped, too, but he would not desert his father.

Mordecai Sheftall was still in the hands of the English in January, 1780, when his friend Mrs. Abraham Minis, who was under the mistaken impression that he had been released, addressed a letter to him in Philadelphia, asking him to collect a bill for her from the Continental Congress.

The two families were close to one another, enjoying a friendship that went back to the first days of the Georgia settlement when Abraham Minis and Benjamin Sheftall had come over on the same boat. Abraham had died in 1757, leaving his horses to his three sons, Joseph, Minis, and Philip, his cattle to his five daughters, and the rest of his estate and his business to his sturdy wife, Abigail. Joseph and Minis died soon after their father, leaving Philip the only son to carry on his father's work.

It is not difficult to trace the career of this second-generation Georgian. Since he lived in Savannah, his business was naturally oriented toward the south, the West Indies, and in 1772 he was traveling in Jamaica and writing letters off the coast of Cuba. He corresponded with Aaron Lopez, but did business primarily with the Newport firm of Hart and Polock. In 1774, then a mature man of forty or forty-one, he married one of the Newport Polocks, a spinster of twenty-nine.

When the war broke out, he threw in his lot with the rebels in spite of the fact that his commercial interests should have made him favor the English. In the fall of 1776, while Acting Paymaster and Commissary General, he advanced a total of almost $11,000, Georgia currency, to the North Carolina and Virginia troops fighting in his native state, and was fortunate enough, two years later, to get some of it back. In September, 1779, he and Levi Sheftall were picked by Count d'Estaing and General Benjamin Lincoln to serve as guides in the landing on the Georgia coast, in the attempt to recapture Savannah, which then had been in the hands of the British for almost a year.

When, finally, the American troops and their French allies landed and attacked Savannah, they needed supplies and provisions. Among those to whom they turned was the vigorous Abby Minis, then a woman of at least eighty, but still active in business. She did not disappoint those who turned to her, but after the disaster which overtook the allied expedition she found it difficult to remain in town. Charges were preferred against her as a Whig, and no doubt measures were taken also to confiscate her property. Under the circumstances, she found it advisable to go to Charlestown. Accordingly, she and her five daughters sent the following petition, in October, 1779, to Governor Wright and the Royal Council:

To His Excellency Sir James Wright . . .
The humble petition of Abigail Minis of Savannah in the said province, widow, and her daughters, Leah, Hester, Judy, Hannah, and Sarah Minis, sheweth that your petitioner Abigail Minis is seized and possessed in her own right of a small plantation near the town of Savannah and of a house in said town, some Negroes and other personal property. And your other petitioners are seized and possessed of some lots of land and premises in said town and personal property,

That some prosecution of late has been entered against your petitioners, [who] are desirous the same may be withdrawn, and [they] be permitted to go to Charlestown, South Carolina, to reside for some time, and carry with them their personal property,

That your petitioners desire permission to appoint one or more attorneys or attorney to rent out or otherwise manage their said real property in Georgia for their sole use and benefit,

That your petitioners hope by means of removing to Charlestown the same will not be deemed or looked upon as forfeiture of any part of their said real property.

Your petitioners therefore most humbly pray your Excellency and Your Honorable Board will be pleased to grant them the several matters stated and set forth in this their petition, and that you will be further pleased to grant or order a proper vessel to carry them and their personal property with a flag [of truce boat] by water to Charlestown.

And your petitioners as in duty bound will ever pray.

> Abigail Minis, Leah Minis, Esther Minis,
> Judy Minis, Anna Minis, Sally Minis.[63]

It is worthy of note that in the body of the above petition three of the girls used the Hebraic and European form of their given names: Hester, Hannah, and Sarah. When they signed their names, however, they employed a more colloquial American form: Esther, Anna, and Sally.

In spite of Abigail's known Whig leanings, the governor and his cabinet approved of her petition, promised not to confiscate her property, and permitted her to leave for South Carolina. Obviously she must have had influential friends in the governor's mansion.

Though secure in the safety of Charlestown—for a few months at least—Abigail and her five daughters needed money to live. They were eager to secure payment for the staples supplied the government during the siege of Savannah. Abigail wrote to General Lincoln, to whom she had surrendered her original receipts, but he never got her letter or he ignored it. She next appealed to Colonel Wylly, the Acting Quartermaster General for the Southern Department, but he would do nothing without proper certification. Apparently he, too, did not have the records, which must have disappeared during the Savannah debacle. Her last resort was her old friend Mordecai Sheftall, to whom she wrote in January, 1780.

Abigail appealed to him to dig out the necessary documents, and she further instructed him that when—and if—he secured her money he was to lay it out for her in goods to her best interest. She was always ready to do business. She had to make a living for her five girls!

Abigail was, we believe, a matriarch in the best classical style, with all that it implies: not one of her five daughters married during the lifetime of the mother; her son took no wife until he was forty. Surely this looks suspicious, although we may be doing Abigail Minis a grave injustice. It implies "too much mama." Even though her son Philip was still living, she, in all likelihood, ran the business, or she had a lot to say.

What is more to the point, she was successful. She owned seventeen Negroes and added at least a thousand acres to the family holdings. Until her death she also managed a small cowpen or plantation, but her prime source of income seems to have come from commerce.

The type of woman who was ready to gird her loins and help keep the pot boiling was common in German-Polish Jewry of the eighteenth century. Abby—of Ashkenazic origin—was very obviously that kind of woman: intelligent, clever, aggressive, unschooled in the academic sense, for her writing, apparently, was limited to Yiddish.

Even that she wrote haltingly. Her signature, in the Hebraic script, is almost illegible, but part of her name in Yiddish appears to have been Voegele, "Birdie." Her boy's name in Hebrew was Uri Phoebus or Feibush, which emerged in English as the traditional, homonymous Philip. At least the initial consonants sounded alike!

Abigail lived very comfortably in the city. If the house she occupied was the one which her husband left her, it was a seven-room building containing four bedrooms, a sitting room, a kitchen, and a business office. The large "hall" of her home was covered with rugs and a carpet; ten mahogany chairs invited tired callers to rest; a mahogany rum case and three bottles brought them all the comfort they craved against the penetrating dampness of a wintry day. The fireplace was adorned with firedogs and fire screens; looking-glasses softened the broad expanse of the walls, and there were glassware and cutlery in abundance for all occasions.

Evidently the Minises encouraged company, for all rooms were liberally supplied with chairs. The "parlour" had twelve chairs, again of mahogany; there were card tables, a sofa, some more looking-glasses, tables, plated candlesticks, a silver mug, other silverware, a grate fender, and a profusion of table and bed linen. Mahogany bedsteads studded the rooms liberally; there was probably a bed for each one of the girls so that they did not have to double up.

If the kitchen was as well furnished as it was in the days when Abraham Minis was still alive, then it contained an assortment of vessels and utensils that must have delighted the heart of the most finicky of housekeepers. There were firedogs, tongs, gridirons, spits, frying pans, hooks, skillets, and flatirons. Of pots there was a variety: of iron, brass, copper, and pewter. There were brass kettles, tin fish-kettles, and teakettles. To furnish light—and darkness—the kitchen boasted of candle molds and candlesticks as well as candle snuffers. There were pint and half-pint measures, a bellows, an assorted lot of bottles, a funnel, a brass mortar, and a warming pan, to say nothing of stools and benches, teaspoons, sugar tongs, and a tea strainer—and three cots. There were so many beds in the house that one is constrained to think—and there is evidence for this—that the Minis home served also as a tavern.

There was a chaise whenever Abigail decided to take the air accompanied by Sue or Lizzy or Sandy, her Negro servants. And even though none of the girls were married at that time, there was plenty of noise around the house, for there were six Negro children in the yard. Abby lived to be about ninety-six, lived to see her son president of the congregation and one of the seven wardens of the city of Savannah, and she lived to bury him. We suspect she held the reins in her own hands till her very last breath.

We are not quite sure what happened to Mordecai and Sheftall Sheftall while they were in the hands of the British. Both left behind detailed but conflicting accounts of their imprisonment and travels, written, in one instance at least, some fifty years after the events described.

According to Sheftall Sheftall, the troubles of both father and son were by no means over at the time they were

360

paroled to Sunbury. When, in the autumn of 1779, the allied American and French forces attempted to recapture Savannah, the British garrison at Sunbury withdrew, and the Tory irregulars moving in began to abuse and even to kill their Whig enemies. To save themselves, the Sheftalls and other paroled Continentals fled on a brig to Charlestown, only to be retaken on the way by the British frigate "Guadeloupe." It carried them to Antigua, where they remained under English surveillance until the spring of 1780. In May, Mordecai learned that he was to be paroled and wrote to tell his wife the good news. Here is her answer:

Charls Town, July 20th, 1780.

My dear Sheftall:

I have now the pleasure to inform you that I received your letter on the 19 instn., dated May the 5, and sincerly congratulate you and my dear childe on your enlargement, hoping that we may once more meet again in a great deal of pleasure, for I can assure you that we have been strangers to that for some time past. But I still hope that our troubles will now be soon at an end.

I make not the least doubt, but ere thise comes to hand that you have herd that thise place was given over to the British troops on May 12th by a caputalation after three longe months sige. During that time I retier'd into the country with my family, and a great many of our people ware at the same place. During the sige thare was scarce a woman to be see[n] in the streets. The balls flew like haile during the cannonading.

After the town was given over, I returned to town and have hierd a house in St. Michael's Alley belonging to Mrs. Stephens at the rate of fifty pounds sterlinge a year. And whear the money is to come from God only knows, for their is nothing but hard money goes here, and that, I can assure you, is hard enough to be got.

I am obliged to take in needle worke to make a living for my family, so I leave you to judge what a livinge that must be.

Our Negroes have every one been at the point of death, so that they have been of no use to me for thise six weeks past. But, thankes be to God, they are all getting the better of it except poor little Billey; he died with the yellow fever on the 3 of July.

The children have all got safe over the small pox. They had it so favourable that Perla had the most and had but thirty. How I shall be able to pay the doctor's bill and house rent, God only knowes. But I still trust to Providence knowing that the Almighty never sends trouble but he sends some relife.

As to our Adam [a free servant?], he is so great a gentleman that was it to please God to put it in your power to send for us, I do thinke that he would come with us.

I wrote to you about three weeks agoe by way of St. Austatia to Antigua whare I mention every particular to you, but must now refer it untill it shall pleas God that we see you again. You[r] brother Levy went out of town during the sige toward the northward and has not returned as yet. Thise day his youngest baby, Isaac, was buried. The poor baby was sicke for about three weeks and then died.

We have had no less than six Jew children buried since the sige, and poor Mrs. Cardosar [Cardozo], Miss Leah Toras that was, died last week with the small pox. Mr. DeLyon has lost his two grand children. Mrs. Mordecai has lost her child. Mrs. Myers Moses had the misfortune to have her youngest daughter, Miss Rachel, killed with the nurse by a cannon ball during the sige.

Perla begs that you will excuse her not whriting by thise oppertunity as she has been with her Aunt Sally for several nights and is very much fatigued, and the flag [of truce ship]

goes immediately, but hopes that she will be the bearrer of
the next [letter] herselfe. But havinge so favourable an oppertunity as the flag [I] was willing to let you no [know] some
little of our family affairs.

I have nothing more at present but wish to hear from you
by the first oppertunity.

The children joine me in love to you and their brother, and
I remain

> Your loving wife,
> Frances Sheftall.[64]

Although still under parole, the two Sheftalls were set
free, and by June had arrived in Philadelphia. Six months
later they were formally exchanged and thereupon released
from all obligations of parole.

Before the end of the year, however, Mordecai set about
straightening out his accounts with the Continental Congress. In a series of letters which he sent, Mordecai begged
its members to pay him what they owed. "I must entreat
the Honob'e Congress to have some consideration for a
man who has sacrificed every thing in the cause of his
country. I want nothing but justice. . . ." The phrase "who
has sacrificed every thing in the cause of his country" was
not a patriotic flourish. His capture and his inability to
remain in Georgia to look after his many business interests
were a severe economic blow. Senator James Gunn told
Alexander Hamilton that Sheftall had lost all his property
during the Revolution. Mordecai pleaded earnestly that
his accounts be settled. His bill for back pay and rations
alone ran to $139,800, Continental, or, in hard cash, $2,330.
Being in straitened circumstances, the Georgia exile asked
for relief, but not in paper currency. The government

settled with him in July for pay and subsistence, giving him $7,682—in paper money of course.

But almost £1,900, sterling, was due him for financing an expedition against the Indians, for his share in a brigantine burnt by the British, and for a hogshead of rum supplied to the troops. Here is one of the petitions he submitted after his arrival in Philadelphia, asking for relief:

To his Excellency, the President and the
Honorable Members of Congress:

The memorial of Mordecai Sheftall humbly sheweth that your memorialist was appointed Deputy Commissary General of Issues in the State of Georgia,

That his attention to the wants of the army in that quarter led him to make advances for their support at those times when no Continental money was sent by Congress for the support of the troops there,

That your memorialist had also a considerable sum due to him which in the present state of depreciation would amount on receiving the same to a literal nonpayment,

That a long and painful captivity has reduced your memorialist to very distressed circumstances which are still heighten'd by having a wife and foure children in Charles Town deprived of every means of subsisting.

Your memorialist humbly subjoynes an acco't and submits his situation to Congress, requesting they will pleas to take his case into consideration and afforde him such relief, in the whole or in part, as the wisdom and humanity of the Honorable Congress will thinke expedient, to assist him in removing his family from the miseries the[y] now labour under.
And your memorialist will every pray.

Mordecai Sheftall.

Philadelphia,
Aug't 21, 1780.[65]

As late as 1792 he was still petitioning for a settlement. Secretary of the Treasury Alexander Hamilton was polite to Sheftall Sheftall when he called to further his father's cause, but made no promises. Exasperated because nothing was accomplished, Mordecai wrote his son: "I can only say that if my account is not allowed me, I have faithfully served an ungenerous publick, which I hope will not be the case, as I still thinke that theire is virtue enough in Congress to take care of their old faithfull servants and adherents." But he was mistaken; there was not enough virtue in Congress; the accounts were never settled, at least not to the satisfaction of the Sheftall family.

While Mordecai Sheftall was still in Philadelphia, in December, 1780, his son was called in by the Board of War and given a special assignment that might have turned the head of a much older man.

He had been his father's helper, an Assistant Deputy Commissary General in Georgia; he had gone through the attack on Savannah, suffered on a prison ship, and now, only eighteen years old, was sent on a mission of mercy by the all-powerful Board of War. Young Sheftall was ordered to take the sloop "Carolina Packett" through the British blockade under a flag of truce to Charlestown. After Sheftall accepted the appointment his father bought him a new suit and an overcoat. Mr. Hillegas, the Treasurer of the United States, had just given Mordecai $20,000; the clothes cost $12,800.

Sheftall Sheftall's job was to deliver money and food to the sick and hungry American prisoners there and to their leader, General William Moultrie. (The invoice of the gold and silver forwarded by the Board of War was eloquent testimony of the variety of coins then circulating in the young republic. The commissary officer carried with him: guineas, Spanish pistoles, moidores, johannes, carlins, pistareens, and silver dollars.)

When Flag Master Sheftall reached Charlestown, after a long, laborious voyage, one of his men deserted. Sheftall, thereupon, appealed to the imprisoned General Moultrie to have his man sent back or to supply him with another hand. Here is his letter:

> On board the sloop, "Carolina Packett,"
> Flag of Truce, March 2nd, 1781.
> Hon'ble Brig. Gen'l Moultrie:
> Sir:
>
> A sailor belonging to this flag [of truce ship] deserted from her the 27th of February in attending upon some of the guards on shore. I wrote a letter yesterday to the [British] commandant requesting that the said fellow might be delivered up, as we are only allowed to carry six private men by [the British General] Sir Henry Clinton, and have not received an answer. I therefore thought it my duty to inform you of it, and hope that you will demand him or send a man out of the prison ship in his room [place], as we shall be very weak handed. Our detention is owing to our anchor and cables being in the river which we cannot get without assistance, and likewise our ballast [because we are now weak handed].
>
> You will be pleased to get any dispatches that you have to send as soon as possible, as the Honorable, the Board of War, pays demurrage. My instructions from the Board is that in case of any detention, that I must bring proper testimonials for the justification of myself. You will therefore be pleased to notify to the Board the reason of my detention.
>
> Sheftall Sheftall, Flag Master.[66]

Sheftall accomplished his mission and set sail on the return trip some time during the early part of the month of April, 1781.

Most of the Jewish merchants of this time, like other merchants, lived in the coast towns and were close to the sea, both in body and in spirit. Shopkeeping and shipping were closely intertwined. It was but natural, therefore, that the Sheftalls in Philadelphia should venture the last of their slim stock of capital in privateering, preying on enemy commerce. It was a chance to make money, "big" money, in a hurry. (Be assured the many losers said little of their losses.) Everybody knew that on one voyage alone the sloop "Peacock" had hauled in prizes worth hundreds of thousands of dollars. It was an alluring gamble. Patriotism and profit here went hand in hand; the best men were in the business: Robert Morris, and a host of others. Among the Jewish element no man was more active in the field than Isaac Moses, the New York merchant who was then also a refugee in Philadelphia—and Moses was a good friend of the Sheftalls.

Mordecai in his office in Front Street—where no doubt he had a chance to make the acquaintance of that brilliant businessman, Haym Salomon—decided to try his luck at the game. It is true that he had a job as agent for purchasing clothing for the State of Georgia, but it is doubtful if that was sufficient to provide for his needs.

It was early in 1781, probably, that he purchased the schooner "Hetty" and outfitted her as a privateer. The expense of equipping the boat was reduced by selling shares of the anticipated prize money; "tenths" were offered to venturesome businessmen. The list of arms carried by the "Hetty" demonstrates that her cruises were not pleasure jaunts. There were muskets, bayonets, blunderbusses, pistols, howitzers, cutlasses, and boarding pikes. On one occasion she also carried "tommyhaks." At least one of the voyages was a success, for the schooner brought in a prize, the sloop "Swift."

In June, 1782, Sheftall received a sharp note from his new master, Captain Thomas Deburk, requesting his sailing orders. The captain, lying at anchor at the top of Chesapeake Bay, at the Head of Elk, was eager to set sail. One of his men, tired of waiting, had already left him, and to add to his irritation, there were a number of bills to be paid, with no money forthcoming. Mordecai had not even advanced a farthing for expenses. He probably could not spare it. When his wife and children had finally arrived from Charlestown the preceding year, the captain of the ship that brought them seized their clothing for passage money. The baggage was not released until Mordecai had signed a note payable in three days, although the harassed Georgian did not have the slightest idea where he could raise the money. The following spring (1782) he turned also to Robert Morris at the Office of Finance, asking him to settle some old accounts, and got a beautiful letter of sympathy but no cash. Obviously the cruise was undertaken on a shoestring.

The orders came through from Philadelphia the following day; the two letters had crossed each other on the road.

Philadelphia, June 5th, 1782.

Capt. Thomas Deborke,
Sir:

You will with the most convenient speed proceed to sea with the privateer schooner "Hetty," now under your command, and proceed with every necessary caution to Egg Harbour [off the coast of New Jersey], out of which port you will continue to cruise at such times and at such places as you shall thinke will be most for the benefits of all concerned. As it is impossible for me at this distance to provide or caution you againste casualtys that may occure, I shall therefore leave the direction of your cruising ground to your self, only recommending it to you to be as cautious as possible and not run to great risques with your small bark, as you are sensible she is my all in this part of the world.

If you are so fortunate as to take a prize, I would recommend it to you to get her into the first safe port and advise me thereof by [courier] express—if no other immediate oppertunity offers—that I may come and do my own business myself, provided the prize is worth the expences that will attend the express and my coming.

You will be sure to advise me of your arrival at Egg Harbour as soon after you arrive as an oppertunity offers, and be sure to keep me constantly advised of your proceedings, as I shall take care to keep you advised of any thinge that may offer that I shall thinke will be of advantage to the cruise.

You'l send me your shipping paper, that is, the duplicate of what you keep by you. You'l allso signe the duplicate of these orders which I now send you, and send them to me by the first safe oppertunity.

I shall conclude with wishing you a prosperous cruise, a safe and happy return, and recommending prudence, caution, and vigilance, and am

Your humble serv't,
Mordecai Sheftall.[67]

The "Hetty" finally sailed on the 10th, with a short-handed crew consisting of the captain, a carpenter, a Negro slave, and one other crew member, a physician, all out to get themselves a fat share of prize money. But they had no luck this time. In August the ship ran aground and had to undergo extensive repairs. After the "Hetty" resumed her voyage she was attacked by a British barge, was captured, and scuttled. Was the captain discouraged? By no means! He wrote Colonel Sheftall that he was repairing the boat once more and looked forward to a good cruise. Let us hope that he was not disappointed.

While waiting for reports from his schooner, Mordecai might have sauntered over to Cherry Street to watch the building of the new synagogue. He had given Jonas Phillips £3 as a donation, not much compared to the £340 Haym Salomon had subscribed, but it was the best he could do. (After all, you can't expect a German to compete with a Polack!) He might well have recalled that of the five synagogues in the country he himself had been present at the formal establishment of three: Savannah, Charlestown, and, finally, Philadelphia. That September he attended High Holyday services in the new building, and the next month, with a pass from the British, he, Abraham Seixas, their children, and a number of Gentile fellow-exiles sailed back to Savannah to start all over again. They embarked on the shallop "Pearl," which Sheftall had purchased with the aid of generous friends. As the light open boat headed toward the Atlantic, it was loaded to the gunwales with furniture, bedding, 100 barrels of flour, and adequate provisions for the voyage. There were five barrels of pork and ten firkins of butter nestling side by side—in the tally. Be assured, the pork was not eaten by the Sheftalls.

Sheftall Sheftall, now, in 1783, an old veteran twenty-one years of age, made periodic visits to Charlestown. The Savannah Jews were always traveling to the Carolina capital. It was their metropolis, the business, social, and religious center of the hinterland in which they lived. When in town, he boarded with the Mottas but received his mail at Uncle Levi Sheftall's on Broad Street. (Uncle Levi also kept up his Savannah business connections.)

In a long gossipy letter of this period we can see that Sheftall was always on the lookout for a girl for himself and a beau for his sister. For the benefit of Perla he dutifully reported on the two Judah boys: Baruch (Barry)—well, Perla knows him; his brother, a fine manly young fellow, was apparently more attractive. Mr. Lopez was a tall young man "with the same colour of myself, but as much of a gentleman as any Jew I ever seen." (This, apparently, was the highest praise.) Joshua Hart's daughter Shankey wouldn't tell him if she was going to marry Abey Jacobs: "She gave an evasive answer. She is so wild and giddy that in my opinion she does not know her own mind." (But she did! She married "Mr. Abraham Jacobs of the Jewish nation" that same year.)

Sheftall was mildly interested in the Misses A. . . . .; he didn't have to spend any money on them; evidently they weren't very exacting; they weren't very pretty. "I should not like either of them for a wife," he wrote to his father—and then proceeded to make a ribald remark. Evidently the spirit of gallantry, so characteristic of Georgian England, was not without its influence on provincial America.

He had a line of news or a tidbit of gossip for almost everyone in the family. He hoped that mammy's stock would increase—evidently mother had some cows and calves of her own which father had picked out of the cow-pen for her. Mother had better watch her chestnut tree, for Perla, Benny, and Moses, the younger fry, are "great snookers [thieves]." "Tell Perla people is here balloon mad; tell Moses I shall bring when I come home a glister (enema) pipe." (Moses was destined to be the doctor in the family.) And as for father—"Honor'd Sir"—let him beware of a load of dry goods consigned to Uncle Levi at Savannah. They may be offered on credit, but don't touch them. I suspect there's some swindle here. They probably belong to Mr. DeLyon. Watch him. "Old DeLyon has a sweet mouth and will, I know, try to come over you." Thus Sheftall to his father.

But one day Mordecai Sheftall had some very interesting news for his son:

Savannah, 13th April, 1783.
My dear Son:

Allthoe I wrote you on Friday last, yet so happy an event haveing taken place, [the declaration of suspension of hostilities between Great Britain and the United States,] as the inclosed will communicate, since my writing, I could not help giving it to you and all my freinds by the first and earliest opp[ortunit]'y.

What my feelings are on the occassion is easier immagined than described. For it must be supposed that every real well wisher to his country must feel him self happy to have lived to see this longe and bloody contest brot to so happy an issue. More especially, as we have obetained our independence, instead of those threats of bringing us with submission to the foot of that throne whose greatest mercies to Americans has been nothing but one continued scene of cruelty, of which you as well as my self have experienced our shares.

But, thanks to the Almighty, it is now at an end. Of which happy event I sincerly congratulate you and all my freinds. As an intier new scene will open it self, and we have the world to begin againe, I would have you come home as soon after the [Passover] hollidays as possibly you can. As I shall plan a voyage for you to execute which will requier dispatch.

If you have not purchased the linen directed, don't buy more than one peice, as goods must be very low in a very short time. Let Mr. Jacobs have this news as soon as possible, as the knowledge of it for a few hours, befor 'tis published, may be of the outmost consiquence to a man in trade. And I really wish I could be a means of his and Mr. Cohen, in particular, benefitting by a knowledge of it in time.

Your mother, brothers, and sisters are all well and give theire love to you and compliments to all freinds. I am

Your affectionate father,
Mordecai Sheftall.

Give my love to your Uncle Levi and family. Hetty says she fears that you have spent her money instead of buying her scisars, as there are none come to hand for her. For fear that I forgot to mention the arrival of the things you sent by George, I now inform you that they are.[68]

"An intier new scene will open it self, and we have the world to begin againe," Mordecai had said. This was the simple but eloquent statement of a man who was deeply conscious of his ancestral heritage and fully aware of the promise of American freedom.

373

SURVEY
AND RETROSPECT

Chapter 16

The Coming of the Immigrants

BACKGROUND FOR EMIGRATION

THE seventeenth century—when American Jewish history begins—was an age of mercantile and commercial expansion. Shipping and world commerce grew rapidly; the merchants, the middle class, acquired wealth and political power.

Spain and Portugal were building up their resources abroad. France, Holland, and England were laying the foundations for their colonial empires. Colonial development and growth were accompanied by an expanding money economy and rising industry. The older "feudalism" was supplanted by what historians call "mercantilism," the desire to increase the wealth of a country by encouraging the import of raw materials, and the export of industrial products, and by the re-establishing of a favorable trade balance that would bring in a reassuring flow of gold and silver.

The first half of the century witnessed a series of devastating wars in practically every country of Europe, all the way from the Polish Ukraine to the British Isles. Much of the warfare was bound up in religious conflicts. The price of peace included the cost of tolerating dissenters, heretics, and infidels. Religious and political tolerance grew in Germany, Holland, and England. Men began to assert the authority of reason in the conduct of states, and of conscience in the conduct of the individual. Philosophers spoke of the dignity of man, of the idea of progress. Superstition and bigotry gave way to Enlightenment, and modern science was born.

The rationale of tolerance was harnessed to the political and economic needs of new national states and man-hungry colonies. Even convicts and foreigners could serve the need for manpower in the overseas settlements. In this context, the American colonies of the Protestant European states were open to the Jews.

Did the Jews need those lands of refuge?

*   *   *

At the close of the Polish, Cossack, and Russian wars in the 1650's, East European Jewry was shaken to its very foundation. The massacre of thousands upon thousands by the ruthless Cossacks, the ensuing economic distress, the continuing political anarchy in the country brought a change for the worse in the status of the Polish Jew.

In Austria, the Counter-Reformation—the Catholic response to Protestantism—was in full swing. For Jews the typically medieval picture of political, civil, and economic disabilities, of expulsion and exile, was characteristic of large parts of the Austrian Empire. In Alsace they eked out a miserable existence under a French regime which was barely tolerant. Most of the German states had already expelled their Jews. Some had accorded them but a grudging right to live. However, the new Prussia after the Thirty Years' War (1648) sensed the economic utility of Jews, and welcomed a limited number of Jewish businessmen. But even in the German lands of paternal despotism progress was slow. In Portugal and in Spain, the Inquisition was still at its grim task of ferreting out Marranos, "underground" secret Jews. Many of them were imprisoned; some were burnt at the stake.

The prospect for Jewry in Europe was anything but pleasant. There was a comforting hope that time would bring an amelioration to political and economic discrimination. Actually, the eighteenth century did bring a large measure of improvement for Jewry in practically all European lands, even in Poland.

In the seventeenth century most Jews stayed where they were. This was hardly the result of choice. It was difficult to get away: the cost was beyond the means; and even with the means the journey was enormously difficult. And if the goal was somewhere else in Europe, little gain would accrue simply from moving. There were few countries in Europe that would tolerate them.

WHERE THEY WENT—OUTLETS IN EUROPE AND IN THE NEW WORLD

Accordingly, most Jews remained where they were. But there were ambitious young Jews who were too impatient to listen for the footsteps of a tarrying improvement. These were the individuals who girded their loins and emigrated.

Jews have nearly always been able to crawl into the interstitial spaces. Many a Polish Jew wandered west to Germany, Alsace, and Holland. The German Jews moved from villages into towns. With the rise of industries in eighteenth-century Germany and Austria, they moved to the new manufacturing centers.

It was obvious to all men that the economic star of the Dutch, freed at last from Spanish domination, was in the ascendant. Many Jews crossed the German border into more hospitable Holland, where they were later followed by East European émigrés. Those German, Polish, and Lithuanian Jews found a comfortably ensconced community of Marranos who had filtered north from Spain, from Portugal, and from France and had reverted to Judaism. Some of those Sephardim had kept on moving and had crossed the channel into the England of the Stuarts and of Oliver Cromwell. By the second half of the seventeenth century, Jews sensed that the English also were to be of increasing importance in the North Atlantic economic sphere. Trade and tolerance flourished together.

A few Jews—underscore that they were not many—went to the colonies in the Americas. There was no "mass" Jewish immigration across the Atlantic until the 1880's. For colonial days the "mass" movements are two: twenty-three Jews came to New Amsterdam in September, 1654, and almost eighty years later, in 1733, something less than a hundred Jews—many of them subsidized by the London Sephardic welfare agencies—landed in Savannah, Georgia.

The Jew rarely leaves the land of his birth except under the stress of utter compulsion. For seventeenth- and eighteenth-century European Jews, America was the end of the world. Europe was the great center of Jewish and general culture, of the world's economy; and conditions, as we intimated, were constantly improving. Tomorrow was likely to be better than today. The possible commercial advantages in the colonies did not seem to outweigh the disadvantages of colonial life. Aside from the hazards of the ocean crossing, North America grimly held out the threat of savage Indians and the ever-present danger of disease. Moreover, one would have to go from an atmosphere of intense religious life to a virtual wilderness.

Marranos were the first Jews in the colonies. Some of them accompanied Columbus in 1492. Spanish and Portuguese crypto-Jews went to South America, to Mexico, and to the West Indies, the colonies of Spain and Portugal. No doubt many of them reasoned—unfortunately, falsely—that the Inquisition and its agents would not be effective in those distant territories.

By the first half of the seventeenth century the Jewish Iberians were joined in the West India Islands and in South America by other European Jews. Tolerant Dutch Brazil (1624) sheltered German, Polish, and Hungarian Jews. Dutch Guiana and Curaçao had publicly recognized Jewish communities in the 1650's. After 1655 Jews were found in Barbados, in English Guiana, and in Jamaica. In one of the Guianas—we are not quite sure whether it was English or Dutch—Jews were offered unusually favorable "minority rights" in the best medieval tradition. People were desperately needed, and almost no price was too high to pay for manpower.

THE JEW COMES TO
THE NORTH AMERICAN MAINLAND

As we have seen, individual Jews were found in some of the North American mainland colonies in the first half of the seventeenth century. The first group, which arrived in New Amsterdam on the Hudson in 1654, consisted of refugees fleeing from Brazil after its reconquest by the Portuguese. For the next century and a half individuals kept arriving from the Dutch and English West Indies and from the Guianas. On occasion, Marranos sailed into American ports, coming directly from Spain and Portugal. Many, if not all of them, had fled from the mother country to escape the Inquisition. However faithful a Christian one might be, a Jewish origin was grounds for suspicion, and suspicion could entail numerous and arduous difficulties. Some of the fugitives had no interest in Judaism; but others—members of the very same family—had fled because of their love for the ancestral faith and because of their desire to practice it openly.

It is a popular misconception that all colonial Jews came from Spain or Portugal. But Jews came from many European lands. Though conditions here and there on the Continent were indeed improving, they were by no means congenial, judging even by the standards of that age. In many countries and principalities Jews were not even tolerated. In lands from which they had not been expelled there were harsh laws delimiting their exercise of political, civil, and economic rights.

Moreover, within a land practice was not uniform. In the

Prussia of Frederick the Great, and in many of the smaller German territories, the rich Jew was benevolently accepted and encouraged. The poor, however, the unskilled, or the itinerant refugee encountered cruel laws prohibiting settlement, trade, the purchase of a home, and marriage. Such laws were an invitation to leave, and individuals headed toward the English North American mainland colonies, stopping over in England briefly in order to begin the process of Anglicization.

In sum, it was the inhospitality of the European scene which sent Jews to these shores in the colonial period. The tone of inhospitality ranged from the constant physical danger of Spain and Portugal through the occasionally relieved but arduous vexations of Western and Central Europe. The East Europeans enjoyed the right to worship, but were exposed to sporadic persecution and, on occasion, to massacre. But European Jews—all of them—were second-class citizens by virtue of their religion. The right of franchise was not accorded them in any European land, not even in the Netherlands.

Jews were not alone in hoping for more opportunity in the colonies. The hundreds of thousands of Christians who came here wanted "cheap" land, the right to marry, and the privilege of worshipping God as they saw fit. Jews especially were conscious of their need for a larger measure of political liberty. They cherished the hope that they would enjoy freedom in the colonies. And this political freedom they did achieve in the later Republic, in the course of a process which took a full century to complete.

WHERE THE IMMIGRANTS SETTLED, AND
THE RECEPTION THEY RECEIVED

The Jewish immigrants settled where everyone else settled, in the tidewater areas. There was this difference, however. The Jews were a trading class and practically all of them remained in the towns. We have seen that the first place in which they established themselves was New Amsterdam, and we will recall that their settlement there was accidental, rather than deliberate. They were Dutch-Brazilian refugees who had been forced to start over again, seeking another refuge, or perhaps on their way back to the Netherlands. Wherever their intended goal, it was quite evident that the rulers of that Dutch outpost were not prepared for their coming, nor were they friendly.

The political, civil, and economic climate in which the New Amsterdam Jews found themselves was characteristically medieval. At first they were forbidden to purchase homes, to practice a craft, to sell at retail, or to trade with the outlying settlements and the Indians. The newcomers were not to stand guard with the militiamen, and were not to hold public religious services; they were not to vote, and not to hold office. The imposition of most of those disabilities came arbitrarily from the governor, without authority from his superiors. It is practically the only body of "medieval" restrictions which the Jews experienced in the North American colonies. Indeed, it surpasses in rigor the legislation in European lands. As a matter of fact, there were singularly few communities in the medieval world which labored under disabilities as severe as those above described. Had the restrictions persisted for any length of time in New Amsterdam, the Jews could not have existed economically. They would have been compelled to leave. It is patent that Stuyvesant nursed that hope.

The Company was more realistic than its director-general. It wanted to further its settlement. Moreover, the prime interest of the directors was profit. That the English in the West Indies offered larger opportunities to settlers—even Jews—was known to them. Hence their disposition to allow the Jews to remain. But more determining in the Company's commands to the stubborn Stuyvesant was the intercession of Amsterdam Jewry. The intervention of that influential Jewish community—then the most powerful in Europe—and the spirited, dogged, and repeated remonstrances of the handful of New Amsterdam Jews turned the scale against Stuyvesant and brought an improvement in the position of the little Jewish group. Under the Dutch they gained at least the right to stand guard with the others, to trade, to own lands, and to become burghers. These were privileges already enjoyed in the mother country. These were the basic rights needed for existence.

The Dutch in New Amsterdam never permitted the Jews to hold public religious services. The West India Company's permission to trade was construed in its most narrow sense: the Jews were not allowed to sell at retail or to practice crafts. Though they disregarded the last two prohibitions, they were not happy with the treatment they received. Many, if not most, of the Jewish immigrants went back to the West India Islands or to Holland. They were better off there.

Under the English—New Amsterdam was renamed New York—conditions improved. By the year 1695, at the latest, the Jews were worshipping in a synagogue, selling at retail, and practicing crafts. They labored under no overt economic disabilities. The English colonial government was tolerant; New York became the largest Jewish community in North America prior to the outbreak of the Revolution.

Unlike New Amsterdam, the settlement in Newport, Rhode Island, was probably deliberate; the coming of the Jews there was due to no accident. Newport had one of the largest and busiest harbors in the country. In New England, it was second only to Boston. If the tradition is true—there is no sure evidence—the first Jews came to Newport in the 1650's, at a time when the Dutch were still in New Amsterdam. Some of the Jews, therefore, may have by-passed the Dutch city because basic economic and religious liberties were not assured them. In the Rhode Island to which they turned, where Roger Williams was still alive, they were assured of complete religious equality and hopeful of political freedom. With the exception of an unsuccessful attempt to disable them economically as "aliens," there were no limitations on their right to do business.

We know—and this fact is documented—that there were at least the beginnings of a Jewish community in Newport in the 1670's. It may well be that these settlers, probably Barbadians, were welcomed for their island connections. In 1677 Newport Jewry had already purchased a cemetery.

But the first congregation there was not to enjoy a long life; it seems to have been dead by 1690.

The three other cities in which Jewish communities were established in the pre-Revolutionary days were Charlestown, Philadelphia, and Savannah. (Though Lancaster Jewry held services on occasion, it is very doubtful that it was ever truly a Jewish "community.") Jews did not hesitate to settle and to remain in these towns because from the very first they enjoyed economic liberty and religious freedom. Individual Jews had come to the South Carolina city as early as 1695. They were welcomed in that small town on the exposed Spanish frontier. But it was not until the decade 1730–40 that Jewish settlers in any appreciable number began to come to Charlestown. The arrival of the Jews in Savannah in 1733 was resented by the Georgia trustees and, to a lesser degree, by Oglethorpe himself. It was their hope that the colony would be Protestant. Catholics were certainly not wanted; Jews at first were only grudgingly tolerated. When the entire colony began to disintegrate in the face of colonial hardships and of land and slave restrictions, the Jews, too, slipped away, like most of the other settlers. The initial Jewish community was not to last a decade; by 1740 there were only a few families left. It was to be a generation before the congregation was re-established.

Not all American Jews lived in the five cities where there were organized communities. A Jew was "warned out" of Boston in the late 1640's, at a time when some of the Pilgrim Fathers still walked the streets of Plymouth. (A Moses Simonson, who came over in the "Fortune" and landed in Plymouth in 1621, was not a Jew in spite of his name.) There were individuals in other towns and in other colonies. When more intensive research is done in the early records, we shall probably find that there were Jews in every one of the thirteen colonies.

But why were there no communities, no group settlements, in some of the other colonies? Surely Boston should have sheltered a community in the early eighteenth century. It was then the largest city on the British-American mainland. Was the absence of a synagogue due to Puritan intolerance, to the denial of basic religious liberties? It is difficult to answer with any assurance, but it is improbable that religious intolerance was the determining factor in hindering the rise of a Jewish community in that city. The Jews, had they wanted to settle there, would not have been deterred by men like Increase Mather, who preached against the "hideous clamours for liberty of conscience." It is equally doubtful that the existence of an established, a privileged, church kept the Jews out of New Hampshire, Massachusetts, Connecticut, and North Carolina. The motivation that determined Jewish settlement was not a greater or lesser degree of religious tolerance or freedom, but rather economic advantage. Shall we assume that the Jews did not make of Boston a Jewish center in the eighteenth century because that city was losing out economically to New York and to Philadelphia? Moreover, Newport with its tiny Jewish community was nearby and probably more attractive to incoming Jews.

The economic life of early Virginia and Maryland was characterized by a plantation economy. There were no large towns, no merchant class of any size; hence there were few opportunities there for Jews who wanted to engage in business, nor was there a Jewish urban community.

Charlestown dominated much of the business life in North Carolina. To be sure, Charlestown and South Carolina, Savannah and Georgia were under an Anglican establishment. Along with Christian Dissenters, Jews had to pay taxes to support a church that was alien to them, but economic advantages induced them to remain.

The five large towns in which the Jews lived had their miniature diasporas; they had their Jewish hinterland. Individuals and families lived in the hamlets and rural districts that were within easy traveling or sailing distance of the established communities. The village Jews went to their metropolis to attend religious services—and to replenish their stock of goods. All of New England, until the 1750's, was part of the back country of New York City Jewry; New Jersey and western Pennsylvania up to the Blue Ridge were tied, spiritually and commercially, to Philadelphia. (Delaware had few if any Jews.) North Carolina, South Carolina, and all of Georgia were spiritual dependencies of the Jewish mother city Charleston.

WHO CAME?—ETHNIC STOCK AND RITUAL AFFILIATION

Of what "ethnic" stock were the Jews who came to America? What was their ritual affiliation? After the first quarter of the eighteenth century the Spanish-Portuguese Jews were never a majority in New York City. They were numerically the largest group in the short-lived Newport

Jewish community of the 1670's and 1680's, although the entire group at that time did not exceed a dozen Jewish families. In Georgia, too, in the 1730's, the Sephardim were most numerous, but never after that. Philadelphia and Charlestown had Ashkenazic majorities from their very beginnings as communities. Most immigrants after 1735, at the very latest, were of Ashkenazic stock both ethnically and ritually. This means that they or their forebears originally stemmed, for the most part, from Central and Eastern Europe, that they followed a German or Ashkenazic ritual, and that they or their parents spoke Yiddish, a German dialect.

Who came over: the rich, the successful, the learned? Hardly; such persons can nearly always carve out a niche for themselves even in an unsympathetic environment. Rather, some incompetents, seeking a world of lesser competition or greater opportunity, found their way to these shores. Some poor were sent over by the London charities. Generous relatives brought over members of their families. Sutlers came in with the English troops at the time of the French and Indian War. Those who accompanied the English in their conquest of Canada remained to establish a community in Montreal (about 1775). A number of sutlers came in the 1770's with the German (Hessian) mercenaries and remained to become American citizens.

Indeed, a few economically well-established merchants did come to trade in this country. Some of the Amsterdam Jewish merchants were here as early as 1655. In the next century the Frankses and the Adolphuses and the Salvadors—some of them native-born Englishmen, all of them excellent names in the City, in London—came to these shores. If their names mean anything, we must assume that most of them brought some capital with them. But by far the largest number of Jewish immigrants who sailed into American harbors in the eighteenth century were economically venturesome businessmen, weak in capital, but strong in ambition. Many of them were competent.

THE SIGNIFICANT 1750's

The generalization may be repeated that the European Jew of the first half of the eighteenth century was close to medievalism. Intolerance was still strong; anti-Jewish disabilities were still severe; men's minds were still closed against their neighbors of different religious faiths.

By the middle of the century there were some marked changes. The despised money lender was being transmuted into a respected banker. Industry and manufactures were beginning to play a more significant role in the mercantilistic state. The rationalism of the Enlightenment was no longer a distinction of the philosopher and the humanitarian; it was beginning to influence states and their peoples. Many began to be ashamed of their religious prejudices; superstition was a word that made people squirm. Accordingly, the economically useful Jew was given more consideration in nearly all European lands.

This new European society, with its new horizons, had no desire to burn or destroy the Jew. There were many who were brash enough to admit, at least to themselves, that they did not even care to convert the Jews. Their desire was to use them, economically.

The Jews who came to America in the eighteenth century were mostly of the 1750 background, children, or at least neighbors, of the Enlightenment; they were well on the road to modernization. The new arrivals found a very acceptable environment here.

The larger American community was, as we know, not untouched by the spirit of the European Enlightenment or the economic rationalism of the age. The country was beginning to show the results of a long century of material progress. The roads were better, the Indians had been pacified or pushed back, the frontier had moved forward to the mountains, the French and Indian War and its troops had brought a measure of prosperity to the colonies. It was just at this time that the American Jewish communities emerged or experienced a rebirth. Newport was reborn; even the almost century-old Jewish community of New York pulsated with new life. The decade of the 1750's was particularly significant for the growth of American Jewry.

POPULATION AND MOBILITY

Many of those who had landed here were Jews from the German villages, accustomed to a rural, one might almost say a colonial, economy. Most of them were young and unmarried. It was only on rare occasions that they came in with families. The first group in Georgia, in 1733, was exceptional in this respect.

There can be no question that some of the businessmen came to make their fortunes (or at least to get a good start) and then to return home. A few, making good, did return, but the majority of those young men who came liked the country, found themselves wives here, and remained. It is difficult, exceedingly difficult, to determine how many came and how many were born here. For the population figures prior to 1790 we are dependent on the very scanty records of the Jewish congregations, occasional secular tax lists, and estimates of the number of Jews in the different towns and colonies. The first United States census was taken in 1790. The inhabitants of seventeen states were polled, but, unfortunately, the census lists of six of those states, including four of the original thirteen, were destroyed when the British burnt parts of Washington in 1812. But even the records which are extant are incomplete and marred by typographical errors.

The problem of counting Jews becomes further complicated by the difficulty of determining who were Jews. "Good Jewish names" are frequently misleading. By the eighteenth century Moses and Levy and Cohen were already good Christian names. Different individuals frequently bore the same name—Isaac Moses, Levy Marks, Ezekiel Levy, Hyman Solomon—and it is not always easy to determine whether we are dealing with several different men or with one man who has hopped about from one community to another.

In the seventeenth century there were probably not more than 250 Jews, natives and immigrants, in the colonies; by 1790 there were probably no more than 2,500 in the United States and in Canada. It would be hazardous even to guess the proportion of immigrant Jews to natives. The general increase in population from 1650 to 1790 was about 7,700 per cent; the percentage of increase among Jews was obviously less, approximately 1,000 per cent.

The colonial Jew was constantly moving about. Mordecai Campanell was in Brazil in 1654. Its capture by the Portuguese made him a refugee, and we next find him in Barbados in 1678. That same year he is documented in Rhode Island, and he may have moved on from there. His wanderings were typical.

Jews moved about not because they liked to travel, but because, frequently, they had little choice. Most of them were in commerce. In the seventeenth century this meant that they were merchant-shippers, though frequently in modest circumstances (sea-peddlers). Throughout the century they shuttled their wares back and forth on the "royal highway," the Atlantic Ocean, moving between England, the West Indies, and the North American colonies.

In the next century they continued to make numerous trips to the West Indies as supercargoes, but they also began to travel the land highways. The roads were better, regular stagecoach schedules were established, and coastwise transportation improved perceptibly. By the dawn of the nineteenth century, the Jews began to move by boat and by coach from New York to Savannah and the West Indies and back. It is not always easy to follow the individual in his wanderings.

Chapter 17

Economic Activity to 1790

AGRICULTURE AND RANCHING

IT may be useful for us, having glimpsed individual Jews in various economic pursuits, now to turn to a larger perspective of colonial Jews. In this chapter we bring together the vocational and commercial endeavors of early American Jewry. Since the over-all picture is composed of details we have already encountered, we need not stop on each occasion for a full description of the economic matters touched on.

There is little question that most of the Jews who came here in the early days gravitated to towns. Few of them were wilderness pioneers; not many were colonists in the literal sense of the word. It is true that the Jewish leaders in London toyed with the idea of close settlements in South Carolina. The first Jews in Savannah did come as a body within a few months after the arrival of Oglethorpe, but that was exceptional. Unlike the Puritans, the Salzburg Germans, and the Moravians, the Jews did not establish separate colonies. They came singly.

Few Jews were farmers, for reasons which go far back

into European history. Ever since the early medieval period, Jews were excluded from the agrarian feudal system, which was saturated with Christian ritual and religiosity. Later, Jews were actually forbidden, in many lands, to own farm lands and estates. This was true even in the eighteenth century.

Conditions, of course, were different in the American colonies. They could go back to the soil with impunity, but they had no desire to do so. They were not interested in becoming farmers when they had the choice, as they did, of remaining in a city and enjoying all its amenities. They had no urge to head for the edge of the frontier, to plunge into its dark forests, and to begin life anew as hunters and trappers. There were, probably, individual Jews who did just that very thing, but most Jews were unequipped for that type of life, and disinterested in it. Those among them who had religious interests—and the majority had—knew that they could not survive as Jews, rear Jewish families, and enjoy traditional home life unless they were close to a Jewish community, to a school, to a religious teacher, to Jewish associates. They could always make some sort of living in the city or, at the worst, in the villages of the metropolitan back country.

Consequently, there were very few Jews who were petty farmers; some, however, became larger farmers and plantation owners, although the total number of Jews engaged in agriculture was minimal. Francis Salvador, a highly-respected South Carolinian, was a plantation owner in the best Southern tradition. The Minises and Sheftalls of Georgia combined farming, ranching, and commerce on their not inconsiderable holdings. Abraham Minis operated the A.M. ranch in the 1750's, and after his death his wife retained the brand. But those were exceptions. Economically, Jews were rooted in city life and city occupations. Moreover, in their scale of values, a city dweller was better off than a farmer.

CRAFTSMEN

Colonial Jews were found in practically all the trades. They were tallow chandlers, watchmakers, soapmakers, saddlers, bakers, shoemakers, wigmakers, engravers, snuff-makers, distillers, and indigo sorters. Many of these artisans were anything but poor, struggling workers. Master craftsmen like Asher and Myer Myers—one was a brazier, the other a competent silversmith—were also merchants; Isaiah Isaacs, also a silversmith, was one of the richest Jews in Richmond.

THE PROFESSIONS

The only profession followed was that of medicine. There were no professional Jewish attorneys before the Revolution. The Levy brothers of Philadelphia, Moses and Samson, who began to practice law after the secession of the colonies from England, had nothing to do with the Jewish community. Their parents were buried in a Christian churchyard. Moses and Samson married Christians, and their children followed the faith of their mothers.

Jews in this country were, doubtless, influenced by the English attitude of not encouraging Jews to enter the legal profession. It was not until 1770 that the first Jew was admitted as a solicitor in England; the first Jewish barrister was called to the bar there in 1833. There was nothing, of course, to stop competent businessmen in this country from serving as amateur attorneys, and on occasion Asser Levy (seventeenth century) and the Gomezes of New York (eighteenth century) acted in that capacity.

But the practice of medicine had not yet been standardized; for many it was only a craft. Jews had been engaged in it professionally ever since 1656, beginning with Jacob Lumbrozo of Maryland, "the Jew doctor." Most of those men had acquired their skills as apprentices; some may have studied in European medical schools; a few were probably quacks.

One of the most interesting of those medical practitioners was Dr. Isaac Levy of Cahokia, on the Mississippi. He had lived so long among the people there that he had become a typical Frenchman. The Doctor probably had a French wife and had no hesitation in taking the oath on the Holy Gospels. He was a merchant, an Indian trader, a banker, a purveyor to the Virginia troops in the Illinois country—and a physician. In 1782, Dr. Levy sued a man named Buteau for not paying a medical bill of 400 livres. The sick man seems to have had a venereal disease, and refused to pay because, he said, the doctor had not cured him. The court thereupon ordered "the plaintiff to continue attending the defendant until he should be cured, on condition that the defendant acts according to orders and does nothing that can counteract the medicines of the plaintiff." Levy continued to attend Buteau, but still could not cure him. The doctor then complained that Buteau disobeyed orders; Buteau countered that he was most cooperative and that he had taken the prescribed sixty-seven pills in two days in order to get well in a hurry. Dr. Levy informed the court dryly that had the patient taken all the pills in that short time the dose would have killed him. Levy finally secured a judgment against Buteau.

INDUSTRY

There were not many Jews in industry; there were as yet few industries and industrialists in the country, although the merchant who hired men to prepare barrel staves, castile soap, or potash was in some sense of the term an industrialist. A large merchant like Mordecai Gomez was also a snuff manufacturer. Aaron Lopez, the Newport businessman, probably distilled some of the rum he sent to the West Coast of Africa. He certainly manufactured his own candles.

Candlemaking was one of the notable products of the whaling industry. Lopez and his father-in-law, Jacob R. Rivera, were important men in that field. Jewish merchants had been active in the whaling industry at least as early as 1726, when Mordecai Gomez and Isaac Jacobs petitioned for a monopoly on the porpoise fishing in Connecticut for a period of ten years. By 1761 most of the Jewish candlemakers of Newport had become an important part of the United Company of Spermaceti Candlers who were banded together in a monopolistic corporation to control the production and sale of their product.

COMMERCE AND TRADE

Though Lopez manufactured candles on a large scale, he was essentially not an industrialist, but a merchant. Commerce and trade were the most characteristic forms of Jewish economic activity in the pre-Revolutionary and in the Revolutionary generation. Actually, most of the Jews who landed on these shores in those days had been merchants and traders at home; they continued the same occupations here.

The merchant was a very important figure in colonial commerce. The export of raw materials and the import of consumers' goods were among the basic needs of the country. The mercantilistically-minded English at home were bent on this type of economic life; colonial commercial life prospered under it. In a young, undeveloped country like British North America, businessmen were at a premium; Jews, consequently, were in a favorable position.

Not all merchants were alike, economically. They constituted a hierarchy. There were peddlers, clerks who engaged in "adventures" of their own, small shopkeepers, larger merchants, and finally, the merchant-shipper.

PEDDLERS

There were Jewish peddlers here almost from the time of their first coming to New Amsterdam. We know that New York Jews, itinerant merchants, bartered goods and products and traded in horses in the Connecticut of the seventeenth century. The colony of Pennsylvania issued licenses to Jewish peddlers in the days before the Revolution. It is strange, however, that we know so little about their manner of doing business and about the goods they handled.

SHOPKEEPERS

Because we know so little about the peddlers, we are inclined to believe that there were very few of them. If they followed the pattern of their nineteenth-century fellows, they were quick to exchange their peddler's pack for the chance to open a little shop in a likely village or town.

Most shopkeepers were men, but not all. On rare occasions we find women in business—a Hannah Moses of Philadelphia or, on a far more impressive scale, an Abigail Minis of Savannah. Abigail was a widow who doubtless took over her husband's business during the long period of his fatal illness. The pattern of a woman making the living was not uncommon in the Jewish communities of Europe, particularly of Eastern Europe. There the wife kept the shop and the husband devoted himself to talmudic study. There was no talmudic study in this land; husbands in this country were expected to work, not to gather merit for the world to come.

The shopkeeper who waited patiently for customers only too often had a small stock and a still smaller capital. At times his first dab of capital may have been the loan of a few pounds from the local synagogal charity fund. As a rule, a clerk got a line of credit from an indulgent employer who might well give the new merchant his first stock of goods at prime cost. (If the man succeeded, he might some day become a loyal and lucrative customer!) Established merchants apparently had unlimited confidence in their fellow men who applied for credit—at any rate, people were glad to help a young beginner.

Those immigrant shopkeepers who feared the keener competition of the city took refuge in the towns and villages. There was an additional advantage in going into the country; one could learn the vernacular more quickly. And Jews did go into the towns. Across the border, in Connecticut, in Fairfield County, three of the twenty-two merchants in 1749 were Jews.

Locations favored by Jewish businessmen who settled in the interior were the outlying towns situated on navigable creeks and rivers. When possible, they chose fall line towns where they could tap the grain and furs brought in by the farmers and ship them down river to coastal ports or to distant markets. Individuals settled in Easton, Lancaster, Reading, and York in Pennsylvania, at Frederick Town (Winchester) and Richmond in Virginia, at Camden in South Carolina, and probably elsewhere where they left no traces.

MERCHANTS AND MERCHANT-SHIPPERS

Whether a man was a petty merchant or an important merchant-shipper, he stocked hardware, textiles, and food-stuffs. Nearly all stores were general stores. Cash was not plentiful; barter was common.

The larger city merchant was more than a mere retailer; he was also a jobber and wholesaler and, as we have described above, he was on occasion a manufacturer. He was a commission agent buying and selling for clients, a maritime insurance agent, if necessary, and a banker who discounted paper.

The more ambitious and enterprising businessmen in the port towns were merchant-shippers. Their boats plied the American coast from Montreal to Savannah; they sailed south to the West Indies and to the Guianas; and they crossed east to the African coast, to the Madeiras, to Spain, Portugal, France, England, and Holland. Shipping was the keystone of American colonial commerce. The merchant-shippers were often the intermediaries between the North American colonies, the West India planters, and the European distributors of manufactured goods. The chief imports from Europe were textiles and hardware, but this country was also thirsty for wines and liquors and luxury goods. Sugar and molasses came in from the Islands. The American merchants imported goods from the European markets on their own account, or served as agents for firms that sent over shipments on consignment or on a long-term credit basis. The exports from this land were raw materials: lumber, naval stores, furs and hides, grain, tobacco, rice, indigo, horses, cattle, and, occasionally, kosher smoked meats. This latter product was sent primarily to the West Indies and to the Guianas. Not infrequently, the captain of a ship was charged with selling his boat after he had disposed of its cargo.

A number of the merchant-shippers, like the Gomezes and Frankses of New York or Rivera and Lopez of Newport, owned their own vessels. A merchant did not have to be wealthy to own a ship. Partners could join together to

403

buy a small boat; they were relatively inexpensive. Frequently, merchants did not depend upon their own goods to make a load but freighted cargo for others.

Most Jewish merchant-shippers—and this is probably true for the general run of merchants—were dependent on the London market. (Some were in touch with the French and Dutch markets, particularly Amsterdam.) London was the central market for goods, money, and credits. The American merchants had agents and correspondents in that city who supplied them with goods and sold their bills of exchange. Larger firms had partners in England who served as resident buyers. In turn, the larger London Jewish firms had their correspondents and agents in this country. It was not uncommon to employ relatives for these purposes on both sides of the Atlantic. The Sephardim of Europe were not the only ones to have a network of friends and families scattered all over North America and the Islands with whom they did business. There was also an Ashkenazic diaspora of relatives and *Landsleute* who helped one another. Business was not always carried on in a formal fashion. Commercial letters often ended on an intimate social note. The Jewish shippers and merchants offered one another home hospitality, felicitated each other on the Jewish holidays, and exchanged gifts. Lopez sent New England salmon to Joshua Hart; that South Carolinian reciprocated with a barrel of oranges.

SLAVE TRADE

One of the best-known branches of colonial commerce was the slave trade. The classical form of this traffic was the "triangular" method of trading. A cargo of molasses was secured in the West Indies and carried to New England; there it was traded in for rum. The rum was then shipped to the African West Coast and bartered for slaves. The slaves were carried, in turn, to the West Indies, the chief market for this commodity, where they were then bartered for molasses and specie. There were, of course, many variations of the triangular trade. Sometimes other wares besides rum served as the medium of exchange on the African coast; on occasion, the slaves were brought back and sold in the mainland colonies. New York and Georgia Jewish shippers sometimes engaged in this business, but such voyages were exceptional for them. Isaac DaCosta of South Carolina was for a time active in the slave trade; numerous transactions of Aaron Lopez of Newport in this traffic are recorded. It is difficult to determine the extent of participation in the trade by Jewish merchants in relation to the trade as a whole.

PRIVATEERING

A common form of gainful enterprise in those days was privateering. Individuals fitted out armed merchantmen—usually on a share basis—to prey on the commerce of England's enemies. It was not until the French and Indian War (1754–63) that Jewish merchants began to appear among those who were licensed by the colonies to engage in that type of commerce. Many of them owned shares in privateers. Some of them, no doubt, made money, but there are also records of losses. There is no evidence that any Jewish merchant made a fortune in the hazardous traffic.

SUPPLYING THE ARMED FORCES

Privateering probably did not play too large a part in the economics of the colonial Jewish shipper. It was too speculative and could no more serve as underpinning for a sound commercial life than gambling in lottery tickets. Army and naval supply, however, played a significant role in the financial and commercial history of the American Jewish merchant and shipper.

At times army purveying was big business, very big business. Here, too, there was a hierarchy. It began at the bottom with the sutler attached to a military unit, and it was crowned at the top by important political and financial figures in London.

American Jewish merchants began supplying the armed forces with food as early as Queen Anne's War (1702–13). By the time of King George's War (1743–48), the Anglo-American Frankses of New York and London were operating on a large scale, sending supplies—among other places—to Georgia (Oglethorpe) and to the West Indies.

Jewish purveyors do not seem to have engaged, to any extent, in the supplying of arms and munitions, although they did, on occasion, provide armament for privateers.

Much of the supplies furnished the British government during and after the war for the conquest of Canada was sold to it by a consortium in which the Frankses were large shareholders. With high government officers as their associates in London, this army supply company did business in the hundreds of thousands of pounds.

The American representatives of this supply company

were Jacob Franks of New York and his son David of Philadelphia. During the struggle for the defense and conquest of Canada, the outstanding French purveyor was Abraham Gradis. He was the "opposite number" of the Frankses and, in many respects, more important even than they. It was due to his patriotic, almost superhuman efforts that the troops of Montcalm were equipped and were thus able to offer spirited resistance to the English.

Aside from his work as purveyor to the French armed forces, Gradis was the largest stockholder in a trading corporation that almost monopolized the commercial life of Canada, the Société du Canada (1748), which did business in the millions of francs. Earlier that same year Gradis hoped to establish a somewhat similar corporation to exploit the resources and to build up the strength of the French in Louisiana at the mouth of the Mississippi. The agricultural economy there was to be built on slave labor; commerce, on the exploitation of Mexico. It would thus appear that Gradis' plan was to maintain mercantile corporations at both ends of the Mississippi Valley, on the Gulf of Mexico and in Canada. By developing and furthering French interests in those two strategic areas, the whole Mississippi Valley and the Great Lakes region would be dominated and saved for the French Empire. It was a far-visioned scheme, but the Louisiana company was never organized.

In spite of the break with the mother country in 1775, David Franks continued to serve as an army purveyor in the American colonies and states, representing the English firm in providing supplies for imprisoned soldiers and Tories in the hands of the Americans. This, too, was big business, although ultimately Franks suffered severe losses because of difficulties in securing repayment from the British and because of his expulsion as a loyalist from the American lines.

Unlike Franks, quite a number of other Jewish merchants worked for the Continental forces. Those Whig army supplymen were of two categories. Some of them were quartermaster and commissary officers, like the Sheftalls of Georgia, who served the government directly, with at least quasi-military status. Mordecai Sheftall was "Colonel" Sheftall. Officers of that type, however, frequently operated with their own capital—and then spent years trying to recover from the government the money which they had advanced on its behalf.

Other suppliers were characterized by a completely civilian status, although they had state appointments as purchasing agents. It was their job, as in the case of the Gratzes in Virginia, to secure supplies for the state that employed them. Still others, among them Jews, had no "federal" or state appointments, but were simply merchants who sold goods to the states and to the national government for the use of the armed forces.

Most of the Jewish merchants of the Revolutionary period operated on a small scale. Their sales, whether to the military or to civilians, were not significant, but there were, of course, a few notable exceptions. Among the outstanding companies was the firm of Isaac Moses, Samuel Myers, and Moses Myers. Though Moses at times generously offered and sold the Continental Congress commodities which were otherwise almost impossible to secure, his firm does not seem to have had many dealings with the government. They were not army purveyors.

FUR TRADE

Businessmen who were sutlers or commissary officers or large-scale suppliers sometimes found themselves out of a job when war was over. This was certainly true of a group of Jewish purveyors who accompanied the British troops and naval forces in their conquest of Canada (1759–60). Many, if not all, of those commissary men made an important shift from army supply to Indian trading and fur buying. Levy Solomons, for instance, an erstwhile army trader, became one of the largest fur buyers in Canada (1770) after the period of the conquest.

The fur trade was one of the oldest forms of business in the colonies. Jewish merchants had dabbled in it, as had almost all others, since the seventeenth century. As early as 1717, the Gomez family had built a stone trading post in the Devil's Dance Chamber country, about sixty-seven miles north of New York on the Hudson River, strategically located on an important Indian trail.

The nature of the Indian trade, as we know, was the exchange of furs for cheap textiles, hardware (kettles, axes, etc.), tobacco, guns, ammunition, and strong drink. The liquor traffic was lucrative.

Like army supply, the fur trade was also a highly complicated business operation. Here, too, there were graded ranks commercially and financially. The goods, the supplies, were obtained in Montreal, Lancaster, New York, Philadelphia, and other large towns, where they had been shipped from London. The prime suppliers were the entrepreneurs, the capitalists, who shouldered the financial responsibility. These merchant-capitalists, whether in London or on the Atlantic seaboard, sold their goods to the men who carried them west to the frontier trading posts, among which were Detroit, Mackinac, Green Bay, Kaskaskia, and Fort Pitt. Jewish traders or their partners were present in all these western posts, and, like Ezekiel Solomons at Mackinac, or Jacob Franks—not the New York Franks—at Green Bay, trafficked with the Indians who came to the trading depot. As we have pointed out, few Jews, if any, were themselves trappers or hunters.

Fur trading, even more than army supply, was a hazardous and speculative business. Competition was frequently cutthroat. There was resentment against the merchant who gave an Indian more for his furs than his competitors. Overpaying was cheating! It was difficult and expensive, in the first place, to bring the Indian goods all the way across the Atlantic to a distant western outpost; it was equally difficult to transfer the furs to Europe. During the Indian wars (Pontiac's uprising, 1763) there was real danger of capture and death by torture. Indian depredations were frequent; credits advanced the Indians were often not collected; and the final load of prime fur, auctioned in an inauspicious moment on the London market, might not bring what the furs had cost.

LAND BUSINESS

There was a close relation between fur buying, Indian trading, and western land speculation and colonization.

Ambitious American planners and aggressive businessmen, since the first half of the eighteenth century, were eager to exploit the huge trans-Allegheny land area and to establish colonies there to be peopled by the land-hungry masses from Europe. Back in London the same powerful combination of merchants, capitalists, and political personalities, who were joined together with the Frankses in an army supply corporation, had high hopes of securing huge grants of land for colonies and settlements. They worked closely with numerous others, and with clever American lobbyists, including Benjamin Franklin, to attain their purposes. They were all eager to make money, in a hurry. When the fur traders at the western posts and the men who financed them in eastern Pennsylvania and in London lost a fortune in the Indian attacks which caught the traders off guard before (1754) and after (1763) the French and Indian War, these "suffering traders" sought to recoup their losses by securing huge grants of land as compensation from the Indians whom they held responsible. It was hoped that the British government would confirm these Indian land concessions once they had been secured. Other consortia, which had no excuse to demand punitive grants from the Indians, bought large tracts of land outright from them.

By the outbreak of the Revolution, several different groups of speculators had purchased land or staked out large Indian grants extending from the Forks of the Ohio (Fort Pitt) west to the mouth of that river, at the Mississippi, and then north on the Mississippi and the Illinois Rivers to the Great Lakes.

It was hoped that money would be made, not only through Indian trade, but also by the sale of land to immigrants, and then by supplying them with their needs. These were grandiose schemes, none of which was ever realized as planned. Here, too, the companies faced the hazards of hostile Indians; and the British hesitated to approve transmontane colonies distant from English influence. Rival companies had overlapping claims. Moreover, colonies like Virginia looked askance at corporations that proposed to carve up lands which Virginia considered part of her territory.

In many of those multi-million-acre enterprises, particularly the Indiana (West Virginia), Vandalia, and Illinois-Wabash Companies, American Jewish and Anglo-Jewish businessmen were heavily involved. They made little, if any, money in those ventures. Ultimately, after the Revolution, the federal and state governments, by legislative and judicial decision, outlawed the rights of the entrepreneurs.

Toward the end of the century, businessmen turned their attention to speculation in acreage within the confines of established state boundaries. A merchant and town builder like Aaron Levy (Aaronsburg), acting as an agent primarily for others, bought and sold hundreds of thousands of acres of land, primarily in Pennsylvania.

"VISIBILITY" OF JEWISH BUSINESSMEN

If a very substantial percentage of the Jews were in commercial and mercantile fields in the cities, then, we may assume, they evinced a high degree of visibility in the market places and on the main streets. To judge by Montreal, this would certainly seem to be true. If one computes from signatures to various petitions, it seems that about ten per cent of Montreal's merchants were Jews, a not inconsiderable proportion, and Montreal may be typical of the smaller-size cities like Newport, Lancaster, Richmond, and Savannah.

We are fortunate in possessing a list of the taxpayers in Newport for the years 1760 and 1775. In 1760, seventeen of the 954 taxpayers were Jews. That year, less than a decade after the Jewish community was reorganized, there were 21 non-Jews who were assessed higher than the most prosperous Jew in town. The Jews were not in the top bracket. However, the next bracket—still a high one—included almost half of the Jewish taxpayers in town (47 per cent), but only about 9 per cent of the non-Jews were in that same income class.

In 1775, of the 954 individuals and firms listed, eighteen were Jews. Though less than 2 per cent of the total number of taxpayers, they paid 8.25 per cent of the amount collected. If all those who are listed are divided into three categories, the top group, the broad middle group, and the lowest group, the following comparative figures emerge. They are interesting. Fifty per cent of the Jews are in the lowest category, but over 80 per cent of the non-Jews. About 39 per cent of the Jews are in the broad middle group, but only a little over 18 per cent of the non-Jews fit into that bracket. About 11 per cent of the Jews are in the highest income class, but only about 1 per cent of the non-Jews.

As the outstanding merchant in Lancaster—there were at the most five or six Jewish businessmen there—Joseph Simon was known to everyone in town. One is tempted to say that the Jewish merchants of Charlestown also stood out, but it is significant that in a list of South Carolina merchants and businessmen for the year 1762, not a single Jew was found, and this in spite of the fact that some of them had been in business there since the 1740's, if not earlier. (And Charlestown in 1763 was a city that sheltered 4,000 white inhabitants.)

Conditions were probably different in the two large cities of Philadelphia and New York. Many of the New York Jews had fled in 1775, and it is difficult to determine their participation in the business life of the city. In Philadelphia, in 1765, about 400 persons signed the nonimportation agreement; at most nine were Jews. That is two and one-quarter per cent. In that same city, in 1783, about 800 businessmen, merchants, and citizens petitioned the Continental Congress to return to Philadelphia. (There had been trouble with mutinous troops.) Eight of the signers were Jews; they numbered, thus, about one per cent. As we have just seen, their numbers in business ranged from one to two per cent—if we may judge from the Philadelphia examples cited above. Their percentage of the population in that same city during the Revolutionary generation was considerably less than one. Obviously, they had a higher percentage of business people than their ratio in the population. This was true of Pennsylvania and, we judge, it was equally true in all other colonies where they had communities. But the absolute number of

Jews in business in New York and in Philadelphia was inconsequential in relation to the large number of Gentiles engaged in commerce, in industry, and in trade. Jewish merchants in those two large cities had no "high visibility" in the America of that generation.

THE JEWISH BUSINESSMAN—HIS MEASURE OF SUCCESS

Were the Jews in business successful? It is almost impossible to answer this question with any degree of certainty. Individuals did make money. Some acquired considerable wealth. But, we suspect, very few acquired great wealth, judging by the standards of that day. In the first half and middle of the eighteenth century, Moses Levy, Jacob Franks, and the Gomez family of New York were substantial businessmen living in great comfort, if not luxury. They owned vessels; some of them had country homes, and apparently they denied themselves little. In the second half of that century, David Franks, the last of his branch of the family to retain associations with Jews, was still wealthy at the outbreak of the Revolution. But new faces and new wealth began to appear. In Canada, Aaron Hart stood out as a man of large fortune; in Newport, the merchant-shippers Rivera and Lopez were at their height in the years from 1770 to 1775. Aaron Lopez was a very wealthy man. In 1775 he was the highest taxpayer in town, paying more than all the other Jews combined; the next highest on the tax list in Newport—a non-Jew—paid a little more than half of what Lopez was assessed. The best index to his wealth is the fact that his personal entourage at Leicester, during the war, at a time when his fortunes were on the decline, numbered close to thirty people. Either he was very generous or very wealthy, or both.

Haym Salomon, the Philadelphia Whig, was certainly a fast money-maker. He acquired a modest fortune within a short period, from 1781 to 1785, but he died insolvent. The firm of Isaac Moses, Samuel Myers, and Moses Myers was very successful for a time, reaching its peak during the Revolution. There can be little doubt—although there is little evidence—that they were blockade runners. When the war was over they collapsed (1785), with debts amounting to £150,000 or more—it was only in New York currency, not sterling, but it was still a large sum.

As we have suggested, individuals here and there made fortunes rapidly, and lost them just as quickly. Of course, a competent person, with some degree of luck, could come back in a hurry. After his failure in business, Moses Myers landed in Norfolk in 1787 with nothing but a new wife and a cargo of goods purchased on credit. Four years later he began to build a beautiful Georgian home; it is still standing, one of the ornaments of the city.

In general, the road to financial success—and we shall leave that word undefined—was long, wearisome, and full of heartaches. Many of the merchants failed in business or made a settlement at some stage in their career. Yet, if we can judge at all from the biographies of many Jewish merchants, it would seem that most of them made a modest, or even a comfortable living.

Financial reverses were not matters entirely of lack of capacity, or of the recurrence of bad times, but lay rather

416

THE MOSES MYERS MANSION, NORFOLK, VIRGINIA

RICHMOND, VIRGINIA, ABOUT THE YEAR 1810

in the nature of the financial and commercial structure of economic society. The merchant who did business in the eighteenth century faced hazards not encountered by businessmen of later generations. There was no adequate workable banking system; there were constant problems with bills of exchange. Different colonies issued different monies. Hard money was nearly always scarce; inflation was a constant danger; paper money of fluctuating value proved a constant source of annoyance to the businessman who was always hoping for a stable, commonly accepted medium of exchange. Counterfeit money of the hard and paper variety was everywhere.

Chambers of commerce were just beginning. Sampson Simson was one of the eleven men entrusted with the task of securing the charter of the first New York Chamber of Commerce from Governor Cadwallader Colden in 1770, but an institution of that type could do little to stabilize the manner of doing business and bring order into the monetary chaos. Stockbrokers began to appear in the period of the Revolution. A number of Jews were found among them, dealing in Continental and state securities, in bonds, and in other types of paper.

It was difficult for a wholesaler to secure adequate credit ratings of prospective customers. Commercial information was hard to get in the days before rapid transportation and rapid communication. The chief sources for economic data, sailings, and prices were newspapers and personal letters, and frequently both came too late, or not at all. Because of inadequate knowledge of trade conditions—supply and demand—it was often most difficult to fix prices.

Nature frequently interfered. The small-size ocean-going ship of that day was not adequate to cope with the terrible gales and hurricanes of the Spanish Main. Pirates and privateers—the latter were often no better than the former—confounded the confusion.

It will be maintained, and quite correctly, that those were hazards which all businessmen had to face, and that if those difficulties contributed to the economic destruction of the Jewish merchant, they should have been equally fatal to Gentile businessmen. Still, the war and the postwar period may have been fortuitously harder on the Jewish merchants than on others. They were concentrated in five large towns, all of which, at one time or another, were occupied by the British. The Tories, among them Isaac Hart and David Franks, were either killed or banished, or hampered in doing business. The Whigs fled their homes with the coming of the enemy, leaving behind them their property and, no doubt, their stocks. The war ruined many of them, and consequently, in the late 1780's, there were very few Jewish merchants of any consequence in the country.

CRIMINALITY AND MALEFACTORS

Under the laws of the time, people who were bankrupt were often jailed by their creditors. Those unfortunates who were put into a debtors' jail were by no means criminals in our understanding of the word, and Robert Morris is the best example. Sometimes a Jewish merchant saw the handwriting on the wall and fled to escape prison; he feared he might never be released.

There were, of course, individuals who absconded with whatever goods they could lay their hands on; a few deliberately secured large shipments on credit and fled with the loot. Examples of the latter type are exceedingly rare. Now and then an unregenerate transported criminal appeared on the scene to take advantage of gullible fellow-Jews. And there is a record of one Jew in early eighteenth-century New York who was hanged for theft. He had stolen from one Jew; another witnessed against him and helped send him to the gallows. Under normal circumstances, a Jewish community would make every effort to save a fellow-Jew from execution, certainly if he had any redeeming qualities. This victim, a German immigrant who could not even speak English, must have been a confirmed criminal. It is interesting to recall that a statute of the chief Sephardic synagogue of the British Empire specifically declared that no effort should be made to save men of that type:

If it should be that the law seize any Jew for evil deeds, such as robberies, frauds, or other untoward things designedly done, or criminal acts of bad repute, and he dare to commit misdeeds of such sort in the thought that the Nation will endeavor to liberate him, it is firmly resolved that no time nor money shall be wasted upon such a one, nor shall the Mahamad endeavour to liberate him, but they shall consent that he be punished by the law according to his crimes, as an example to others, and that thereby the stumbling-block in our midst be removed and God's people be free (1663).

Probably a majority of all the immigrants who came to America in the eighteenth century were bond servants. A study of criminality in this country during that period would probably disclose that a large percentage of malefactors were from that class and from the criminals transported here. All those men and women were exposed to many hardships and temptations. There were a number of Jewish indentured servants—more than most students realize—but still very few. The European Jewish poor had no need to salvage their miserable lives by selling themselves for the cost of the voyage to America, for they could nearly always manage to survive physically by wandering from one Jewish community to another. A Jewish pauper was always taken care of by the local social welfare agencies before being transported to the next town. Unlike his Gentile peers in poverty, he knew that his coreligionists would not turn him in as a vagrant. In that respect he had nothing to fear; he did not have to escape to America.

Jews in this land do not seem to have produced an expectable percentage of criminals. The reasons are not far to seek. Most of them were engaged in some form of mercantile activity; as members of the middle class they enjoyed a relatively high social status; their needs were less desperate; and in a period of crisis the local Jewish community was always ready to provide for them. There was no necessity to resort to violence or to fraud in order to keep body and soul together.

THE CONTRIBUTION OF THE JEWISH ELEMENT TO AMERICAN BUSINESS LIFE

In the broadest sense it may be said of the Jewish merchants—whether it was an Aaron Hart in Canada or an

Abraham Minis shuttling supplies to Oglethorpe in Frederica, Georgia—that they participated in the contribution which the commercial and merchant class made to American well-being. In a predominantly agricultural country, on the outskirts of civilization and culture, they were, on the whole, competent and progressive merchants. They helped raise the standard of living by exporting the native products and by importing manufactures, necessities, and luxuries. Doing their jobs as purveyors of goods, they helped develop the trade, commerce, and civilization of the North American British colonies in the seventeenth and eighteenth centuries.

Until the Revolution, the Jewish merchants as a group had their counting houses in but six towns. (During the war, Richmond, a seventh city, began to shelter a growing Jewish community.) But the economic influence of those businessmen was not limited to the immediate environs of the towns in which they lived. Their affairs touched all parts of the continent, to say nothing of the West Indies and Europe. Lopez' agents were everywhere; he dealt with a Benjamin Lyon in Canada and a Philip Moses in Georgia. His correspondents transported his goods and executed his orders in all the colonies. In addition to his activity as a merchant with intercolonial and international contacts, Lopez was one of the important builders of the maritime prosperity of New England, especially in the fishing, whaling, and candle industries.

The isolated Jewish shopkeeper who opened a "Jew's store" and settled in the small towns from St. Denis in Canada to Georgetown in South Carolina was helping, through the goods he sold and through his commercial relations with the outer world, to make life more comfortable for the village artisan and the farmer. That type of tradesman helped build the town in which he lived. Aaron Hart was probably the leading citizen of Three Rivers in Canada; Myer Hart of Easton (no relation) was for a long time its chief merchant. (Both Harts might well have been the most successful men in their towns for years, even the most influential, in spite of the fact that they were denied political rights.) Mordecai Myers of Georgetown was not only an important cog in its little mercantile world but also the first postmaster in town.

In Pennsylvania the Simon and Gratz clan (often working together with the more powerful Frankses of Philadelphia and London) made their influence felt in the back country of Pennsylvania, Maryland, and Virginia, and they and others were active in opening up the West. Their commercial relations with the western outposts were part of that chain of events which linked the Mississippi Valley and the Atlantic Coast colonies. Their participation in that historic process was by no means unimportant.

The Canadian merchants tapped the fur resources of the North as far away as the Great Divide. They themselves, not their agents, traveled and settled in the trading towns as far west as Mackinac and as far south as the region about present-day St. Louis. They brought in supplies, took out the furs, and thus helped the country to grow and to develop.

What the Canadian Jewish traders accomplished was equally true of those south of the border. The eyes of the

Philadelphia-Lancaster group were fixed on the trans-Allegheny region. From the middle 1760's on, Joseph Simon and the Gratzes and the Frankses kept a stream of supplies flowing over the mountains into the Illinois country. As alert businessmen awake to their opportunities, they hoped to dominate the east-west river route from Pennsylvania to the Mississippi, and to control the river routes and portages that led up the Mississippi and the Illinois River to the Great Lakes. It was their intention, of course, to divert the fur trade from going up the Mississippi to Canada and to direct it to their own Pennsylvania seaboard area. Like many others whose eyes were fixed on the West, they, too, dreamed of establishing towns, villages, and colonies in the area between the Alleghenies and the Mississippi River. And, like the others, they failed, but the constant flow of goods they sent down the Ohio did in some measure prepare the ground for a more successful colonization in a later decade.

THE CLASS STRUCTURE

How many social classes were there in American Jewry during the period under discussion? Actually, there was only one: a middle class.

One might assume with some justification that there was a proletarian group. And it is true that there were cobblers and housepainters who were always at the bottom of the economic if not of the social ladder. We have said that there were indentured servants; we know that there were also free laborers. However, the people in this category—and who remained in it—numbered only a handful. But were there not also impoverished men in this class, men who were thrown completely onto the mercy of the local Jewish charities? There were a number of them. But they were men like Eleazar Levy, who had once been one of the leading merchants in Canada, or a man like Isaac Elizer, a merchant of some distinction in Newport. These were not proletarians, and in spite of their misfortune they enjoyed status in the Jewish community to their very last day.

Above those few impoverished Jews dependent on the philanthropy of their fellow-Jews came the employees of the Jewish community. They were in the lowest income group of the gainfully employed. The cantor, the *hazzan*, received a modest salary, supplemented on occasion by teaching youngsters Hebrew. In general, the cantors were not encouraged to augment their income by dabbling in trade. The ritual slaughterer and the beadle also received very small salaries, but on occasion they plied some trade or did a little business on the side. Typical, we suspect, were the economic activities of the schoolmaster Abraham I. Abrahams. The congregation gave him a subvention, but he was also a merchant, tobacconist, and distiller. All these men were respected members of the Jewish community.

If, on one side of the social scale, there was no real proletarian class, it was equally true that at the other end there was no body of wealthy Jewish planters, no great industrialists, no office holders, no established aristocracy of title, wealth, or lands. There was the beginning of an aristocratic group in the Levy and Franks clan of New York, Philadelphia, and Baltimore, but by the third quarter of the eighteenth century, those Jews were already out of the faith or on the way out. The one Jewish family whose members seem to have nursed aristocratic pretensions was the Gomezes. They had come to New York about the year 1703. They were proud and still enjoyed prestige as presidents of the New York congregation. But many, if not most of them, lost their wealth, and it was hard to be aristocratic on an empty pocketbook. One member of the family, a Whig *émigré* in Philadelphia, was well in the lower income bracket. His contribution to the building fund of the Philadelphia synagogue was just about one per cent of that of Haym Salomon, the Polish Jewish immigrant who had not yet been on American soil for ten years.

There was in fact only one social class in American Jewry, a large middle class. This is not to imply that those businessmen formed an integrated homogeneous whole without variation in social power and social status. Distinctions of wealth and poverty are not easily forgotten. Millennial peace did not shed its beatific glow over them. From time to time there was bitterness in the relations between natives and immigrants, even when they hailed from the same European country. This social distance was due to differences in wealth, knowledge of the English vernacular, and understanding and employment of the social amenities. But there were few, if any, differences that were unbridgeable. An analysis of seventy-one marriages, in which the man and woman were both Jews and at least one of the partners was of Portuguese-Spanish stock, discloses that forty-five—a majority!—were with Ashkenazim. Ultimately, the natives and older immigrants learned the age-old lesson that a newcomer ceased to be objectionable when he became a son-in-law.

On the whole, that large roomy middle class was fluid. Status within it was not easily frozen. Newer immigrants were constantly coming in, being accepted, and being integrated into the larger Jewish group. Jacob Franks, a native of Germany, was the wealthiest Jew, we believe, in middle eighteenth-century America. He knew Yiddish, of course, and had received a rather good Hebrew education. In the compact, small New York community he must have met the young German sutler or peddler, Manuel Josephson. This young immigrant was something of a Hebraist and a student. He was the kind of man whom Franks would respect, academically at least. It is very much to be doubted that rich Mr. Franks would snub poor Mr. Josephson.

There was a great deal of horizontal economic mobility in the Jewish community. It was not too difficult in that new world of few traditions to move from clerk to boss. The sutler, the *shohet*, the beadle, the petty storekeeper of the French and Indian War appeared a decade later—at the most two decades—as the president of Shearith Israel in New York or of Mikveh Israel in Philadelphia. It is an eloquent commentary on the fluid nature of American Jewish society to note that of the five Jewish leaders in trade—and leaders, too, in the Jewish community in the second half of the century—all were immigrants who had come here in the 1750's or later. These five were Lopez and Rivera of Newport, and Hayman Levy, Isaac Moses, and Haym Salomon of New York and Philadelphia.

Naturally, not all these men were on the same income

level. Within the class there were various income groups into which the men fitted as they started their climb from clerk to merchant-shipper. For convenience we can divide them into four groups: those in the highest, in the middle, in the lower, and in the lowest income brackets.

A study of the list of contributors to the New York cemetery in the year 1728 reveals that 45 per cent of the money was given by 15 per cent of the contributors. About 70 per cent of all contributors were in the lower and lowest brackets. A little less than twenty-four years later (1750), the members of Shearith Israel were assessed for their congregational seats. About 37 per cent of the money was given by 15 per cent of the contributors. About 66 per cent of the contributors were in the two lowest income classes. When contributions were collected in Montreal, in 1779, to purchase a Scroll of the Law, one man, 6.25 per cent of the congregation, paid about 16 per cent of the cost; 4 men, 25 per cent of the group, paid about 42 per cent; 11 men, a little less than 69 per cent of the congregation, also contributed 42 per cent of the sum raised.

A few years later, in 1782, Jews, mostly refugees, who were gathered together from all parts of the country, contributed according to their means to build a synagogue in Philadelphia. They represented a cross section of all American Jewry. A study of their subscription list provides an index to their wealth and generosity. A warning is in place, however. They were living under a war economy. Some of the members were making money fast; others, also refugees, had left everything behind and apparently were struggling to maintain themselves. It was a decade of extremes. Nevertheless, the subscription list is enlightening. There were 61 subscribers who gave a total of about £897. One man, Haym Salomon, gave £304, or a little over 34 per cent of the total. Three other men gave about 28 per cent of the total. The four together thus gave close to 62 per cent of all monies contributed. Forty-five of the 61 contributors, about 74 per cent of the givers, were in the two lower income brackets. Twenty-eight—46 per cent of the subscribers—were in the lowest bracket.

It is clear from the available figures that there was always a relatively small wealthy upper-middle class, and that the group in the lowest income bracket was large but not unduly so. It is important also to note that if the middle and lower—not the lowest—income groups are lumped together, they form a not inconsiderable proportion of the whole. One gets the impression that the American Jewish community—if we may judge from the synagogal financial records—was, economically, a healthy body.

Chapter 18

Religio-Communal Organization

WHY AMERICAN JEWS CREATED A COMMUNITY

I T was probably not very long after their arrival on these shores that the New Amsterdam Jews created some form of religio-communal organization. Why did they establish such a formal association? We may be sure that that was a question which they never asked themselves. They did not stop to rationalize their action. They acted almost automatically.

The community had been the core institution of Jewish life since the days of the developing Diaspora, from the first or second pre-Christian century. The community was typical, basic, in Jewish life. Thus when the first Jews came here they automatically transferred their European type of organization to this land, and recreated some of the religio-communal institutions.

There was no compulsion for the Jews who came here to remain Jewish. From the Christian side there was no objection to their integration as proselytes into the Christian social structure. There was no racial or ethnic rejec-

429

tion of converts. Individuals who were ready to surrender their Jewish ancestral faith were accepted even in the somewhat hostile New England villages.

Had the individual colonial Jew been stopped by a Dr. Ezra Stiles and asked by that inquiring clergyman why Jews created religious communities of their own, the individual Jew would not have been at a loss for an answer: He would not be happy as a Christian. The Christian faith was the religion of Europe, the religion of a hostile environment, of a world that had continually persecuted the Jew. It was the religion of the intolerant Inquisition, of the Central and East Europeans who had exposed Jews to social humiliation for almost a thousand years. It was the religion of the state that still tolerated physical abuse of the Jew in almost every country of Europe. The faith of the Christian was completely and utterly unacceptable to the Jew, emotionally and theologically. Even if he had no theological training or learning whatsoever, the average Jew, the man in the ghetto street, had no doubt whatsoever that Judaism was immeasurably better than Christianity. If his own personal experiences in Christian lands did not convince him of the superiority of Judaism, they did convince him of the un-Christian character of Christianity. The pragmatic philosophy of the average Jew was: "By their fruits ye shall know them."

Actually, this type of rationalism did not exhaust the motivations that induced Jews to remain Jewish. Basic with them was the desire to survive. They were conscious that they were a minority in a larger group that outnumbered them at least a thousand to one. The New England states,

430

with the exception of Rhode Island, were little less than hostile to the surviving children of Israel. No colony welcomed them with open arms; some were tolerant. All this the Jews soon sensed.

It was their religio-social need that impelled them to join together. And if they were to cluster together, it would be as a community. Apprehensive immigrants, far from home, from kin, from familiar sights and scenes, they wanted Jewish association; they could be happiest when they were with their own people. It was imperative that they have—and this as soon as possible—a synagogue and a cemetery. Thus they would be united both in life and in death. Even the thought of Jewish burial gave them a sense of security. They would always be with their own.

Once the community was established, it would persist, certainly as long as there was a trickle of immigrants to feed it. The newcomers would turn to it almost instinctively within an hour after they had landed. They knew they had nothing to worry about as long as there was a synagogue in town and a *sedaca* ("a charity fund") for pious works. A Jew who was willing to work would always be welcome, would always find a little niche for himself in any American Jewish community. There he would be at home; there he could win for himself that prestige, that status, which might well be denied him in the larger Gentile world.

No doubt it has already been noted by the reader that the Jewish fellowship which was established was not called a "church," a sect, a religious group, but a community, a religio-communal institution. The organizational structure that was to rise here was very much like the European *kahal,* or *kehillah,* or *Gemeinde,* "community," but there were differences, too.

The European Jewish community was a chartered corporation. It possessed specified rights. It was legally recognized by the state. The European Jewish *kehillah* had authority in relation to the state, and it had considerable power in relation to its component membership, an authority not inherent in the group but conferred and enforced by the state. The Jewish community in a European town controlled the privilege of settlement and the right to do business. It taxed the individual and transmitted the corporate taxes to the patron state. It had its own courts where rabbinic law was authoritative.

There was nothing like this in colonial America, except for intimations of it during the decade under the Dutch, in the statement of the West India Company that the Jews might "reside and traffic" in the country. That was, perhaps, a charter in implication. The only proviso was that they take care of their poor just as the Christian church provided for its poor. But nothing was said of the authority that the Jewish community was to exercise over the Jews themselves. The Jewish community and its basic institution, the synagogue, were not officially recognized by the Dutch. There can be no question that the omission was deliberate.

With the coming of the English in 1664 the condition of the *kehillah* was not worsened. As in the England of the Restoration, the status of the Jew was not fixed. Had a "charter of rights" been granted, it would of necessity have been medieval in tone; the position of the Jew as Jew would have been crystallized; in the "Christian State" he would have been compelled to remain a second-class citizen. But, having no status, he could, if he were given time, aspire to the same status as the Gentile citizen. There was thus no formal government sanction for the Jewish community. Perhaps disadvantageous at first, in the long run this was good, very good.

The English government frowned at the thought of a charter. The unitary concept of citizenship was beginning its slow labored growth in England and here. England had no desire to share its sovereignty and administrative authority with chartered enclaved groups. It tacitly tolerated the Jewish community, according it little or no recognition at law.

In the wake of this English precedent, the American Jewish town-community found that it had no corporate control over the individual Jew. He was free of the Jewish community; he was certainly not subject to it according to English law. The American Jewish community, following the typical Dissenter pattern, was a voluntaristic one. The Jew belonged to the Jewish group not because he had to belong—as in most European lands—but because he wanted to belong.

This last statement, however, requires a little modification. The Jewish community believed that every Jew in the area should affiliate by virtue of the fact that he was a born Jew. Social pressure made up for the absence of legal authority. In order to make sure that every newcomer would unite with it, the democratically created organic statutes of the organized community grimly informed him that if he did not join he would be denied the basic religious rites, both in life and in death. The fear of not receiving Jewish burial was a most effective argument.

When Montreal Jewry wrote its constitution in 1778, it gave all Israelites in town twenty days to sign, under the threat of the loss of all synagogue honors. Those fur traders who had gone into the wilderness were given a six-month period of grace. Two of the men, Chapman Abraham and Benjamin Lyon, were on a very long trip. Abraham, no doubt, was at his favorite post, Detroit; Lyon, at Mackinac. Those two traders were specially favored; they were given twenty days to sign after their return to town. If a man threatened to resign or actually resigned from the Montreal congregation, he was cut off from all ritual honors and religious privileges till he paid a fine of $40, the stiffest fine permitted.

Affiliation thus was to a large degree compulsory in every American Jewish community, and, we suspect, most Jews joined. When, on occasion, Jews refused to join, it was because of personal quarrels, not because of religious indifference. Actually, the individual immigrant who came to a town was very eager to become a member of the local Jewish association. He required no threat to quicken him; he believed that circumstances allowed him little choice. If he wanted to "belong" somewhere he had to associate with Jews, or with Christians. Jews fought one another vigorously, and, we suspect, cheerfully, but they rarely allowed themselves the luxury of a divorce from the community. It was possible but uncomfortable to straddle two worlds. There were few interstitial spaces between the two social spheres of Judaism and Christianity.

The American Jewish community was a folk-community, a religio-cultural community in which theology in the Christian sense played a very subordinate part. When a man joined a synagogue no theological tests were applied; indeed, none existed in the official records of the congregation. There was no catechism to recite; there was no confession of faith, no "covenant" when joining, as among the Christians.

Of course, this made it easy for any Jew to join the Jewish community. The deist, even the secularist, could become a member, and his conscience was not violated. He could believe or not believe and still continue his Jewish associations. Men of this type could even become active in the Jewish community as long as they were not too vocal about their convictions—or lack of them—and, what was more important, as long as they did not publicly flout Jewish traditional customs.

The ties that bound colonial Jews together were social, "ethnic," folkistic. The synagogue was more than a house of worship: it was the symbol of the community, the associative instrument. It was the institution through which an individual documented his Jewish identity.

THE RISE OF AMERICAN JEWISH COMMUNITIES

The laconic statement that the Jews created a community as soon as possible gives no indication of the difficulties which were experienced in accomplishing this.

435

Under normal circumstances many years passed before there were enough Jews in town to organize a permanent congregation. The first few individuals who came to town —if they stayed—frequently intermarried and disappeared Jewishly. Ultimately, holiday services were held when there were ten male Jews; finally, a community was established. New Amsterdam Jewry and Savannah Jewry were exceptions. They were sufficiently numerous to have held services the day they landed—and probably did.

As we have seen, the New Amsterdam, the New York, Jewish community was the first one to organize on the North American mainland (1654); it became the mother congregation. It is not improbable that there was a brief period under the Dutch and the English when no services were held because there were not sufficient Jews in town. But sometime in the 1680's, at the latest, the community was restored and began to grow. It was the only Jewry in the colonies to have any community life before 1728. The details of its history before that time are unknown to us because of the loss of practically all its earliest records.

The basic facts of the rise of the other congregations are soon given. After the original Newport community died out, there does not seem to have been any assembly for religious purposes there until about the year 1750. Jews settled in Charlestown and Philadelphia a generation or two before services were held regularly. In both cities community life began in the years between 1740 and 1760. The Savannah community experienced at least three deaths before it was permanently resurrected about the year 1790. Canadian Jewry, concentrated in Montreal, probably had sufficient individuals to hold services as early as 1760, but it was not until about 1775 that a formal community was brought into being. The Richmond community was established in 1789.

THE SYNAGOGUE

The synagogue was the primary institution in the American Jewish community. It remained basic down into the twentieth century. It is the synthesizing factor in the writing of the history of American Jewry; it is the spinal cord of American Jewish life. In this land the synagogue occupied a more important position than it did in the typical European Jewish community. In Europe it was also the most important Jewish institution, but it did not overshadow or dominate communal life. Every European Jewish town of any size had, in addition to its synagogues, philanthropic, educational, and other religious institutions and pious associations (*hebrot*). The Jewish communities in this country, even in a large city like Philadelphia, were comparable only to the European rural synagogue-communities. The colonial synagogue, practically the only institution of any significance, extemporized as it went along. The American Jewish congregations were "frontier" communities, frontier in relation to European Jewish culture.

The congregations in the early days were always too poor to buy their own buildings or to build. Invariably they began with a rented room or house, or met in the home of some leader who devoted himself to the task of keeping the faith alive in his town. New York finally built its first synagogue in 1730; Newport in 1763; Mont-

437

real in 1778; Philadelphia in 1782; Charlestown in 1794; Savannah and Richmond, not until the nineteenth century.

The worshippers in the American synagogue of the eighteenth century came from many lands. There is some evidence of a clash between the two ritual groups in Savannah, after they first landed in 1733, but the differences were dissipated speedily. The liturgic pattern followed in North America may have been set in Brazil in the middle-seventeenth century, since the Sephardic synagogues there assimilated Ashkenazim from the different European lands. Ritually speaking, the Jewish synagogue throughout history has been vigorous enough to assimilate and digest the most divergent types of Jews. In the final analysis, universal Jewish ties are stronger than ethnic or ritual differences.

There is no statement in the extant minute books of our period that any attempt was made to introduce German rituals, although there is some evidence that temporary Ashkenazic conventicles were established in Philadelphia and in Charlestown. (There was no permanent Ashkenazic synagogue in North America until about the year 1802, when one was established in Philadelphia. Today, American Jewry is overwhelmingly Ashkenazic, Germanic, in its ritual.) If the Ashkenazim, the Central European Jews, who constituted the majorities in the American Jewish synagogues, were not satisfied with the Spanish-Portuguese ritual, they were at least resigned to it. They accepted it as the current, typical "American" rite. The liturgy in the American synagogues was thus exclusively Sephardic. It was only natural, therefore, that Bevis Marks, the London

Spanish-Portuguese congregation, would exert considerable influence on them. In details of discipline, of administration, and even of synagogal architecture the Americans patterned themselves on that pioneer English institution. In 1784 Charleston declared that it was following not only the London but also the Amsterdam Sephardic synagogue in the matter of ritual. But the American Jews of those days were not wedded to one tradition. A study of The Great Synagogue of London indicates that the statutes of that Ashkenazic institution were frequently drawn upon by the congregants here when they wrote their eclectic constitutions.

The relatively tolerant attitude of American Jewry toward ritual differences and toward Jews of diverse ethnic origins was documented in 1774 when the leaders of Shearith Israel sought the appointment of trustees for their property. Unable to incorporate under the American laws of the time, the members of the congregation asked Naphtali Franks, the London merchant, a native American, to appoint new trustees to hold title to their properties. They suggested names to him, five men of Iberian origin and four of Germanic parentage. Franks, the man to whom they appealed, though a native New Yorker reared in Sephardic Shearith Israel, was a leader in the London Ashkenazic synagogue. This crossing of synagogue and community lines would not have been tolerated in London or Amsterdam. In those cities and in other European towns, ritual differences were crystallized; ethnic differences were fixed institutionally, nursed, and exaggerated. American Jewry was a melting pot.

439

THE SYNAGOGUE A SOCIAL CENTER?

The synagogue had auxiliary buildings—living quarters for some paid officials and a schoolhouse—in which the officials frequently met to carry on their deliberations. At times the officers and the members called congregational meetings in the synagogue auditorium itself. But there is no evidence that there were any social activities in the synagogue or in any of the adjacent buildings. For the Jew the synagogue was a house of prayer and, presumably, also a place for study. Actually, there is no evidence that *adult* education was carried on in it in colonial and in Revolutionary times. The community had no real social center. (This is not to deny that on certain joyous holidays the congregational leaders stepped into one of the anterooms and toasted one another—frequently!)

If the synagogue was not a social center, it was certainly an associative center. It was the place where the Jews met for services, during which they passed a friendly word, exchanged gossip—and kept up with the latest trends in business. A congregant would not admit it, but he expected to have a good time in the synagogue—and he did. It was no mausoleum with its hushed silences. It was a spot where social warmth radiated. With its noise and vitality it cheered and enriched the life of the Jew and comforted him.

Because most of the men who attended services were immigrants, they had special problems of their own. They were homesick, without family often, hampered by ignorance of the vernacular, struggling for a livelihood. Con-

440

stantly torn by frustrations, they vented them in the one place where they felt at home—in the synagogue. It was the place where they met most often as a group.

They quarreled there frequently; they squabbled in it and over it, for it was the physical seat of religious authority and power. It was thus the scene, but hardly the cause or source, of their difficulties. Control of the synagogue might, indeed, serve as a pretext for a struggle, but those quarrels, we repeat, did not stem from religious differences. More often their source was personal. Men sniped at one another because of economic envy and rivalry, because of the social snobbery of the earlier families and their fear of losing status. The roles they could not play, politically and socially, in the world around them, they could and did play in the microcosm which was the synagogue.

LEISURE ACTIVITIES

If there were no dances, no weddings, no feasts in the community buildings, this did not mean that people did not have a good time. Those who sought relaxation or edification in the larger Gentile community joined the Masonic fraternity or one of the clubs. There were clubs for every person and for every purpose: Irish, French, and Hungarian clubs, dancing associations, musical and philosophical societies, and private library groups. And, naturally, Jewish social clubs. The Newport Jewish club is the only one known, but it is difficult to believe that such pleasure-seeking groups did not exist in other towns, though no record of their existence has come down to us. The Newport club (1761) was purely social, exclusively for card-playing and supper. Congregational affairs could not be broached! Anyone bringing up such matters was fined the value of four bottles of good wine. Evidently, the New-port Jews took their congregation seriously—or wanted to insure themselves a peaceful evening at the card table.

In the larger cities the wealthy Jews had country homes in the suburbs; the New Yorkers liked Long Island—Flat-bush. Many of the Southerners sailed north to Newport to summer. Others found relaxation in visiting their Gentile friends and clients in the back country, where they com-bined business and pleasure. Most Jewish families enjoyed visiting one another in town. But the prime scene of leisure activities in those days was the home. It was there, and not in any public or religious institution, that marriages took place, circumcisions were performed, and convivial Purim parties (porter, ale, cider!) were held.

LEADERSHIP IN THE CONGREGATION

It is not easy to derive a coherent picture of eighteenth-century American synagogal organization on the basis of the extant records. The only minute books available before 1778 are those of the New York community; but even its constitutions and bylaws, with certain exceptions, have been lost.

A study of the minutes of that congregation reflects con-stant and frequent shifts and changes in methods whereby presidents and boards came to power. In general, select members (*yehidim*) elected the officers. But on occasion the officers appointed their successors. Sometimes an oligarchy made the selection, and at times the congregation as a whole elected its honorary leaders.

Those variations in elections and appointments are not an expression of the conflict between an oligarchy and the "democratic" masses, nor are they the expression of the victory of one political philosophy over the other, but rather, a study of the records shows that the appointments and elections were acts of constant improvisation dictated by expediency. The congregation did its best to function organically in spite of great difficulties. New electoral regulations were made only to be speedily discarded in favor of others, for the problem with which the synagogue had to cope was flight from office. Many men did not want to be president. The rich were too busy to take office; the others still had their fortunes to make. The job took time, much time; it required an outlay of money by the *parnas*, who often enough served as banker, advancing funds to the empty treasury. In Canada the incoming president had to repay, out of his own capital, the money spent by his predecessor. In addition to financial problems, discipline was nearly always a headache.

There was rarely a time when it was easy to get effective leadership. When the Revolution broke out, the New York City Jewish communal leadership evaporated. Not a single member of the newly elected board was willing to serve. They were frightened, disturbed by the impending political and economic upheaval; and they would assume no responsibilities.

There was never any clerical, "rabbinical," leadership in colonial America. In the first place, there were no officiating rabbis in the North American mainland congregations, and if there had been one or two they could hardly have asserted themselves. The rabbi in his prerogatives was certainly not comparable to the minister among the Protestants. The Anglicans and the hierarchical Dissenters accorded great power to their clergymen by virtue of the church organization; rabbis had little inherent authority vested in them by virtue of their appointment. After the Revolution, when New York state in 1784 gave status to the minister, Congregation Shearith Israel recognized its cantor as its minister. It was probably after this that Cantor Gershom Mendes Seixas began to develop prestige and status.

Prior to the nineteenth century, leadership was exclusively in the hands of laymen. Domination by the lay members, frequently men of wealth, was characteristic, too, of the European Sephardic congregations. New York Jewry had a number of prominent laymen who assumed office for more than one term. Jacob Franks was one; others were members of the Gomez family, Hayman Levy the Indian trader, Manuel Myers, and Solomon Simson. All of them were merchants. None was outstanding in his leadership—as far as we can determine—with the possible exception of Franks, in whose first administration the synagogue was built.

The other towns seem to have developed more leadership. Levy Solomons, apparently, dominated the Montreal congregation in spite of his quarrels with the congregants; the father-in-law—son-in-law combination of Rivera and Lopez ruled Newport Jewry; Manuel Josephson, the erstwhile sutler of the French and Indian War, emerged as the leader of Philadelphia Jewry during Washington's first administration; and Jacob I. Cohen seems to have been Richmond's outstanding Jew. Charlestown and Savannah developed vigorous leadership in both towns: Isaac DaCosta in the former; Mordecai Sheftall in the latter. DaCosta was the first cantor—it was a voluntary job—of Beth Elohim. It was he who established the first cemetery and tried to build the first synagogue. He was a known Whig leader who suffered proscription for his patriotism. Mordecai Sheftall's career was almost identical.

In a formal sense, leadership was vested in a board of officers known variously as the *junta, adjunta, junto,* or *mahamad* ("standing committee"). The board members served for one year. No limitations, apparently, were imposed on the candidates for re-election. In Richmond, where two of the richest Jews in town were partners, and where some of the members were brothers, no close relatives or business partners were allowed to serve at the same time on the board. This synagogue merely dusted off an old European communal statute.

The head of the *junta* was the *parnas*. All congregations agreed that the *parnas* or president was the "boss." And he was. The term *parnas* is still a synonym in Jewish life for an autocrat. The president gave out the synagogal honors, kept records, and maintained decorum with a firm hand and by constant resort to monetary fines. He assigned seats to transients, prescribed whatever regulations he considered necessary, and disciplined the congregational employees. As a rule, he consulted his associates on the board, particularly when giving large sums to charity.

New York annually elected two presidents; each served for a period of six months. In some places there were only three members in the *junta;* on occasion, there were as many as seven. They met monthly, working closely with the president. Some congregations had a volunteer, unpaid secretary, who might or might not be a member of the board. All communities, from the third quarter of the eighteenth century on, kept their books in English.

In most congregations there was no sharp division of function among board members. The organization of the *mahamad* to include a secretary, a treasurer, and committees. each with their own duties, did not become general until after the Revolution. The *parnas* and the community had not yet learned to delegate authority to individuals or to special groups. Montreal seems to have been an exception. During the Revolution it had an executive committee of two, a president, and a treasurer (*gabay*). The latter rendered a statement of the finances quarterly to the congregants. One or two other congregations, it would seem, also had a *gabay*. Among his duties was the job of recording the synagogal offerings. In Savannah, if a member bought an honor in the synagogue, he was to be billed quarterly; if a stranger wandered in and made a contribution, he was dunned for payment within a week, if not sooner—he might sail away on the next boat.

When a member was called up for the reading of the Law, he was expected to make an offering. The languages employed in making these voluntary gifts were Hebrew,

Spanish, and Portuguese; on rare occasions English also was used. Minimum amounts were fixed for these acts of bounty; there was, of course, no maximum limitation. In most synagogues the amount offered by an individual could be credited against his annual dues or seat charges. Actually, therefore, his generosity cost him nothing as long as his gifts did not exceed his fixed dues. A philanthropist like Aaron Lopez of Newport made munificent contributions. During the Passover service of the year 1772 he "offered" £160 Rhode Island currency, $20 in specie. Donations of this type by the wealthy and philanthropic members were an important source of income for the congregations.

PAID OFFICERS

There were ordained officiating rabbis in the West Indies and in Dutch Guiana, but none, as we have said, on the British North American mainland. The congregations here were too poor, or thought they were, to support a rabbi. The rabbis had little desire to "go into exile," to the frontier of civilization. The commodities they had to offer, knowledge of Jewish rabbinic law and instruction in the Talmud, had no market in the American wilderness.

The chief officiant in the American synagogue was the cantor, who gradually assumed an importance altogether out of proportion to his traditional status. Originally, all who served as cantors in the colonial communities were volunteers, as were all functionaries. Later, as the synagogue grew in financial strength, it paid salaries. It was the duty of the *hazzan* to chant the services, and to be present and to officiate at weddings and funerals, circumcisions, and similar religious affairs. Above all, he was to heed the orders of the *parnas*. He rarely preached, and then only by request. He was frequently, but not always, the teacher of the young.

Two other officers who received pay were the ritual slaughterer (*shohet*) and the beadle (*shammash*). The position of the *shohet* and that of the *shammash* were only too often occupied by the poor and the unsuccessful. The *shohet* was obliged to accept the counsel of the learned members (*bodekim*) who knew the laws of slaughtering and who made sure that there was a plentiful supply of kosher meat in town. The *shammash* served as the general factotum. He saw to it that the synagogue was kept clean, that the perpetual light had an ample supply of oil, that the brasses were polished, the candles made, and the congregants served in their hours of sorrow and joy. In some towns he also collected the dues. In Montreal he was instructed to remind delinquents that if they did not pay what they owed the congregation, they would be excluded from religious honors.

In New York, the houses owned by the congregation—there may have been more than one—were at different times occupied by the cantor, the ritual slaughterer, or the beadle. The latter two were expected by the *junta* to take in sick and itinerant poor. Their homes thus served as the communal hospice. Naturally, they were paid extra for this work. When quarters were not available for those officers, they were given rent subsidies and other grants of money, fuel, or meat.

The teacher, as we shall soon see, was not a communal

officer, nor was the *mohel* or circumciser. In some instances circumcision in the eighteenth century was a "paying" job. Grateful fathers, we may be sure, were generous in their gifts to those who performed this rite for their children. On occasion, the circumciser was a volunteer, frequently a businessman. After all, any one with skill could perform that operation. At times the *mohel* had to make extensive trips by boat to the next town, or to travel the primitive roads to a back-country village; and he was glad to go to the homes of friends and render this service; aside from the fee which he might or might not receive, he was eager to lay up a store of religious merit.

MEMBERSHIP

The man whom a New York *mohel* visited in a Long Island, Connecticut, or Rhode Island town was more frequently than not a member of or a contributor to Shearith Israel. Before 1750 the Jewish merchants of Boston and Newport were associated with that synagogue. In the next generation a Savannah shopkeeper was a regular contributor to the Newport congregation. In the larger cities of Philadelphia, New York, and even in Montreal, the board elected the members; in the smaller towns, it would seem, the members were elected by the congregation as a whole. Of course, in those places it was much easier to become a member: there were few Jews, and every man was needed. Complete democracy prevailed, if only through dire necessity.

There was probably no fixed age for admission to membership. Montreal admitted single men when they were twenty-one years of age. Younger men were accepted if they had a wife and family.

Certainly in the larger congregations membership was of two kinds, as among some of the Protestants, though based on entirely different criteria. In some of the Congregational churches, for example, a distinction was made between the pewholders who owned seats and the "members." These latter were men who had by God's grace been "converted." The pewholders had not yet reached that state of grace. Among Jews, however, the distinction between members seems to have been financial only, not religious or theological. The two types of members were the select (*yehidim*) and the sustaining members, or first-class and second-class. The latter group was sometimes referred to as "seatholders." Among the sustaining members there were, no doubt, individuals who, for reasons best known to themselves, refused to join the congregation in a formal fashion by subscribing to the articles of the constitution. It is unfortunate that we do not have sufficient information to determine fully the differences in degree and in prerogatives which characterized the two groups in the synagogue. Seatholders could not become officers, nor could they receive synagogal ritual honors until the needs of the *yehidim* had been satisfied. Those ritual privileges to which a *yahid* looked forward were: to be called up for the reading of the Law of Moses, to open or close the ark, and to receive special recognition for himself and his wife on the birth of a child. That was in the synagogue. At home, the privileged member could *automatically* expect the cantor and the beadle to minister to him at weddings, funerals, and circumcisions.

In Montreal, the original subscribers, the men who had organized the synagogue and signed its first constitution in 1778, stipulated for their right to a double vote and the privilege of transmitting that prerogative to a son when he reached the age of twenty-one. "Strangers"—the Jews who came in later—were not allowed any office in the synagogue for three years, and no vote for two years. Then they were accorded but one vote. The subscribing members were quite frank in justifying their own special privileges. They had gone to heavy expense, they pointed out, and they wanted more rights than strangers. They had built and paid for the synagogue. (It was *their* building!) Indeed, they went on to legislate that if at the end of a year there was more than £150 on hand, a dividend was to be declared and given to the builders to compensate them in part for their original expenditures.

This we do know, that although "select" members did secure preferential treatment when synagogal honors were handed out, the worship facilities, and frequently the honors, too, were available to any Jew who entered the synagogue. No man was denied any basic religious privilege in an American synagogue because of his poverty or social station. In line with tradition, women, of course, were not accepted as members, and in some congregations membership was denied to a man who had married out of the faith. Bond servants and slaves were not accepted as members: there can be no doubt that they were permitted to worship; there is no evidence that they were granted synagogal honors.

CONGREGATIONAL MEETINGS

Under normal circumstances congregational meetings were called but once a year, usually before the High Holidays in the fall, but the members could be summoned more frequently if there was trouble or some specific need. The new men elected took office during the coming holydays. In New York, at least, attendance at the annual meeting was compulsory.

A special meeting of the entire congregation might well be called to relieve its straitened finances. Communities were nearly always in need of money, and there were many ways in which it could be secured, though not all devices were employed by the same congregation. The income of the American synagogue was derived from initiation or entrance fees, from the sale or rental of pews, from assessments on the wealth or the income of a member, from memorial offerings on behalf of the dead (*escaboth*), from freewill offerings and vows made during the course of a service, from formal cash subscriptions, from legacies, from taxes derived from the certification on kosher meats sold or exported, and from the inescapable fines.

DISCIPLINE

Threats of fines sprinkle the minute books of almost every congregation. There were fines for all types of violations of the congregational bylaws, particularly for minor infractions of decorum. Rigid discipline had to be exer-

452

cised to compel individuals to assume honorary but onerous positions. The typical Jew in colonial days wanted an organized Jewish community, and he was willing to pay for it—within reason. He would not remain in a town that would not tolerate his institutions, but he preferred not to accept office. Compulsion in the form of fines was therefore frequently employed to make him accept appointments. Once an individual paid his fine he attained the status of one who had actually served, and he was thus eligible for honors reserved only for those who had been in office.

Financial penalties were the commonest and simplest form of punishment to keep the members in check. Money came hard, and the threat of a fine was, it was believed, a most effective deterrent. For instance, fines were employed in Montreal to keep the members from talking too much— about each other. In a typical community, where there were only a dozen or two families and where they were constantly thrown together socially, religiously, and economically, it was imperative that there be internal peace. A man was not to divulge what was said about another at a meeting. If he did—in Canada—he was fined 50 shillings. (In the American Baptist churches of a later generation, any one betraying "what is done in the church meetings" could be excommunicated.) The fines were actually collected, although they were by no means a substantial source of income.

Bickering within the congregation, as has been suggested, was a real problem everywhere. Preaching on one occasion to his members, Gershom M. Seixas asked them "to relinquish" their "prejudices against each other." Some men would not come to services because of personal enmities. The result, at times, was that the requisite ten men were not present for a religious service. In Canada the members were expected "to promote harmony" and "to assist each other." When disputes arose between them, they were not to haul each other into the civil courts before they had exhausted the arbitrational or advisory facilities of the congregational board.

Back in Europe, in the German and Polish synagogues—where the members felt very much at home—fist fights were not uncommon. In London, in the late seventeenth century, the members of Bevis Marks were enjoined not to enter the synagogue "with weapons of offence." The American Jew preferred lampoons and verbal insults to dirks and fists. The Montreal *junto* threatened those members who vilified their fellow-Israelites and thus brought disgrace upon the community. Conditions had reached such a pass in Montreal that in 1779 the members took a solemn oath and subscribed it to the effect that they would not defame one another. Unfortunately for our curiosity—purely intellectual, of course—we do not know the details of the quarrels. (And let it be noted at once that Montreal was probably no worse or better than any other congregation. Montreal, fortunately for our purposes, succeeded in salvaging some of its colonial minutes.)

We do know that in that year (1779) the president, Levy Solomons, "walked out" on his board and told it in no uncertain terms what he thought of it and the whole congregation. He refused to call a meeting of the board.

454

In response to his action, or inaction, his four fellow-junto-men suspended him from office for slandering the congregation. All this happened a few months after the adoption of a constitution. No wonder, then, that our Eleazar Levy, the Canadian pioneer who knew the community well, sniffed when its name was mentioned!

But let us not take these upheavals too seriously. Within a year after what seemed to be a major crisis in the synagogue, Levy Solomons was back again, once more an honorary officer.

Fines, as we have intimated, were not the only form of discipline. The Canadians had another form of threat and punishment for anyone who created a disturbance in the house of God. In the first place, that disturber was to receive no ritual honors till he had satisfied the indignant and ruffled board members by paying the financial penalty imposed on him. But, in addition, that others might be deterred, his name would be solemnly entered into the minute books in capital letters and, alongside of it, there would be inscribed the "crime" he had committed. Though the minutes speak of a "crime," be assured it was not one in reality. It was not a morals problem. It was probably nothing more serious than a nasty name or a Rabelaisian gesture directed toward the man who was dispensing synagogal courtesies.

The Christian churches of the time, and later, did concern themselves with moral derelictions. They set up courts to handle problems involving moral turpitude. They exercised formal social control. Some of the churches had discipline committees which operated by means of a carefully worked out procedure. They concerned themselves with religious transgressions, gross improprieties, and scandalous conduct. The punishments they applied ran the gamut from admonition and suspension from communion at the Lord's table to excommunication.

Among the Jews, there was no ostensible policing of morals. Congregations did offer arbitration facilities to members in conflict with each other or with the congregation, but they had no morals courts. The social pressure of the group was effective, it would seem, in keeping people respectable. If a serious wrong should be done, the state would know how to protect itself.

The synagogue limited its authority to matters of ritual and religious observance. Violators of the Sabbath and of the dietary laws were held to strict account. It insisted on decorum during services, and asked the worshipper not to raise his voice unduly in prayer, not to outsing the cantor. "Smart alecks" were fined for offering malicious or satirical public blessings. Every man at services was expected to wear decent apparel. In Savannah, where some of the members owned plantations or did business with the planters, no one was called up for the reading of the Law if he appeared in boots. In other congregations stubborn, fractious members who refused a ritual courtesy were to receive no other honor till they offered a satisfactory explanation for their strange conduct.

In the desire to maintain proper behavior at business meetings, some of the early American synagogues explained in considerable detail the basic principles of parliamentary law which were to be employed. For example, members

456

were to stand when addressing the chair, to keep their hats on, and not to leave the room without the permission of the chairman.

The most drastic disciplinary measure to which a congregation resorted was the denial of basic religious rights. An offender was refused the privilege of the ritual bath, of worship, of burial, of marriage, and of circumcision. The very threat of the denial of these rights, so vital in the everyday life of the Jew, was sufficient to control the recalcitrant and the fractious who would not pay their dues and debts, who married out of the faith, violated the Sabbath, ate forbidden food, insulted the officers, or disrupted the assembly. In effect, these threats, when carried out, were forms of religious ostracism, and were employed, on occasion, in pre-Revolutionary days. The ban was effective because the observant Jew had no place to go. He could not live happily outside of the synagogue.

Shearith Israel once expelled a man and forbade any member even to talk to the troublemaker. Every three months thereafter the congregation denounced him at a Saturday morning service. But this fellow was stubborn. He held out for five years, when he finally made proper submission for the injuries done the congregation. Then he was readmitted as a member. "Peace be unto Israel" was the laconic closing phrase of that entry in the minute book.

Sometimes, as a final resort, the board would take a stubborn member to court. No doubt the court assumed jurisdiction on the broad ground that the man was breaking the peace. Possibly the basis for court action, where no violence was involved, was the charge that the offender had violated a contract: most members had solemnly affixed their names in writing to the constitution and by-laws of the congregation as a pledge that they would observe their provisions.

From the vantage point of twentieth-century religious tolerance and the autonomy of the individual, the discipline employed in the Jewish community seems severe, if not arbitrary. Yet the discipline it attempted to exercise was not unduly harsh for its own time. It was an authoritarian, paternalistic, and monarchical age.

The communities were small, and every man available was needed for the requisite "ten men" to constitute a religious quorum. The average *parnas*, who had problems enough of his own, was not looking for trouble. The officers were probably long-suffering. The members were frequently vigorous, assertive, and tumultuous. It was a tough era in American history.

CEMETERY

For very obvious reasons, a cemetery was an important institution. The first cemeteries in Philadelphia and in Charlestown were originally the private burying grounds of an individual householder; the Savannah cemetery was the gift of one man, Mordecai Sheftall. Ultimately, all these served the community as a whole. Of necessity, the House of Life, as it was euphemistically called, was at times the first Jewish institution in town. This was true of Halifax, Boston, Newport, Philadelphia, and Baltimore. Sometimes a whole generation was to pass—even a century—before the appearance in the same city of the sister institution, the synagogue.

RELIGIOUS OBSERVANCE

Most of the Jews whom we know by name in the eighteenth century were observant to some degree. One of the chief sources for our knowledge of them is, of course, the congregational records. Jews who did not affiliate themselves with the Jewish community are very hard to identify at all.

Religious observance manifested itself in the traditional manner: no writing on the Sabbath after sundown Friday, no riding, no transacting of business. In a more positive sense, men went to the synagogue on the Sabbath and the holydays. The women went to the *mikveh*, the ritual bath; the congregation provided *mazzot*, unleavened bread, and the Passover dietary regulations were widely observed.

Every effort was made to see that there was an ample supply of kosher meat, and most people in town tried to keep a kosher kitchen. But there was always trouble in securing the right meat. The *shohet*—not always an efficient or competent person—had to be watched; the butchers who sold the meat were sometimes Gentiles who refused to take Jewish ritual requirements very seriously. The ever vigilant synagogal board kept a particularly watchful eye on housewives who ran boardinghouses. The itinerant or the foreign businessman who stopped with the Widow Hetty Hays was to be assured that her table was strictly kosher. Once, when she had purchased some lamb whose "ritual fitness" was in doubt, she was ordered to *kasher* ("clean

459

ritually") all her utensils, otherwise her house would be looked upon as a "treffo house." Rest assured she cleansed her spoons and pots and plates.

An observant Jew made every effort to keep kosher even when he traveled about in areas where there was not a single Jewish family. Sensitive Gentiles made every effort to co-operate sympathetically with them. Whenever Mordecai Sheftall visited one of his friends on a plantation, the latter would pen up a sheep—not a pig!—to fatten and would warn him to bring his "sharp knife" for the ritual slaughter.

Jews who were loyal to the ancestral traditions would not intermarry. A town Jew, living where there was a community, did not have much choice: he had to be "Jewish" or run the risk of a bitter conflict with his more scrupulous neighbors. In the city he was under constant surveillance. He had to be observant or face disciplinary measures. And let it be said in his favor that he cheerfully complied. Complaints about infractions of the ritual law were very rare.

Though there were occasional individuals who goaded the community with legalistic controversies, it was reasonable in its scrupulosity. Measured by its own code, it was considerate, if not lenient. Montreal Jewry buried the body of an uncircumcised—and probably baptized—son of Ezekiel Solomons, the fur trader, in its cemetery. It was mindful of the fact that Solomons was an important member and frequently an officer of the congregation.

Country Jews who went to the nearest synagogue on the holidays tended to be lax when they returned to the isolation of the towns and hamlets in which they lived. They traded on the Sabbath, ate forbidden foods, and committed other "heinous crimes." There was no one to watch them or to report them. In 1757, however, the patience of the New York *parnasim* was exhausted; something had to be done about this non-observance. To put a stop to these transgressions, the leaders of Shearith Israel threatened all violators with the ban, but the threat was soon recalled. Either it had an immediate salutary effect—which is very much to be doubted—or the congregation retreated from its position. In all probability, the economic and religious consequences for itself, had it carried out its threat and banned a number of families, would have been serious. In addition to depriving itself of revenue, it would only have driven lax Jews into the arms of the local Christian church.

Though second- and third-generation Jews still continued to conform while in the towns, there is evidence that many of them blithely ignored the dietary laws when traveling on the highways. After the Revolution the threat of the ban for ritual derelictions was not employed. The leaders saw fit, perforce, to take a realistic view of the situation.

From our vantage point the old congregations have acquired dignity, austerity, and the aura of aristocracy. Accordingly, we may be prone to romanticize about their beginnings. It is a frequent whim to think of the founders as supermen and supersaints. Actually, they were ordinary human beings, earthy and tough, sentimental and irascible. They were plain common Jews, just like the Jews of today.

461

Chapter 19

Culture and Philanthropy

JEWISH EDUCATION

OBSERVANCE of Jewish ritual and custom was conditioned by the training in the home and by formal Jewish education.

There were Jewish schools, as we know. New York and Newport had school buildings. How little did a Rev. Andrew Burnaby understand Jewish life when he complained (1760) that the outside of the Newport synagogue was "totally spoilt" when the community tacked a school onto the synagogue. In New York, in the early days, only Hebrew and religion were taught in the all-day school. After the year 1755, secular subjects were introduced; Spanish and the three R's were taught. It is not improbable that even then the language of instruction was English, and, by 1762, we are sure that English was used. There is reason to believe, however, that the congregational school functioned only sporadically.

We know practically nothing about classroom instruction in the communities outside of New York. That very silence is ominous. There is ample warrant for the statement that there were men with knowledge of rabbinics in almost every town, and we know that there were Hebrew teachers. Although parents occasionally taught their children, we suspect that most of the Hebrew instruction was given by a professional called a *reby*. This was true even of New York. Teaching, we believe, was limited to an introduction to elementary Hebrew. The Hebrew teachers taught the children both individually and in classes; the vernacular employed by some *rebies* was probably not English but Yiddish. In New York—and this was doubtless true elsewhere—the community intervened to subvention the teacher to instruct those children whose parents could not afford to pay. The teacher himself was not a paid officer of the community.

The schools and the teaching were frequently of an inferior order, but not altogether poor. There is evidence that natives like Gershom Mendes Seixas did receive a fairly good training in Hebrew lore, good for a frontier culture at least. Those Americans who had studied had a good command of biblical Hebrew and could consult the basic, simpler rabbinic codes. Some individuals like Isaac DaCosta and Manuel Josephson had small Hebrew libraries with rabbinic works, but these two, and others like them, had secured their education in Europe.

Haym Salomon had once written: there is no real interest here in things Jewish. But Salomon wrote to frighten off a religiously observant but impecunious uncle who was prepared to descend upon him. There was real interest, certainly among some, in perpetuating Judaism. When Rivera and Lopez and other Newport leaders appealed for help to build a synagogue in 1759, they stressed the prime importance of such an institution in educating Jewish children. A synagogue and its attached school, they said, would be of great help in preserving Judaism among the Jews of the hinterland.

Yet there was a measure of truth in what Haym Salomon had written. Despite the consciousness of the need for Jewish education, there were no serious attempts—as far as the records disclose—to cope adequately and profoundly with it. The various congregational bylaws, even in the post-Revolutionary generation, ignored it almost completely. The only explanation for this surface indifference is that education was not considered a congregational responsibility. Rather it was incumbent upon the parent to make adequate provision—and most of them did do something. There was not, to our knowledge, sufficient interest on the part of anyone to send a child to Europe to study in the Jewish academies. Indeed, there was not a man in the colonies whose rabbinical learning, piety, or religious authority was deemed adequate for weighty ritual decisions. When important problems of Jewish religious law arose, queries were referred to the authorities in Europe, primarily to the rabbis and sages of London.

CONTENT AND PROBLEMS OF
JEWISH CULTURE

It has been suggested that the general secular culture originally brought to America was modified slowly under the influence of the frontier environment, that ultimately the transplanted traditions and customs disappeared, and that finally there emerged a new, different, a changed way of life. This may possibly be true of some aspects of American culture; it is not abundantly true of early American Jewish life and institutions. The most that can be said is that if this imported Jewish culture was being modified in the eighteenth century—and it was—the process was almost imperceptible.

In political aspiration, the Jews here faced "West"; the synagogue-community, in matters of ritual and tradition and Jewishness, faced East. This European orientation was particularly strong among the Jews. They did not live on the frontier's edge; their settlements were urban, in constant contact with Europe. The tiny little Jewish communities here were always being reinforced and reinvigorated by newcomers. The immigrants coming from Europe, the reservoir of Jewish life, were invariably observant. Up to the Revolution, and even after it, at least one-half of the leaders, the *parnasim*, were immigrants whose spiritual and religious ties were European. At no time in the eighteenth century did the immigrants cease to be the important, the decisive, group in the American Jewish community. They were influential in every generation. The religious culture here was predominantly an immigrant culture, because the immigrants were dominant.

In a Jewish sense, very little in a cultural way was achieved. The group was too small and too busy getting established to concern itself about matters of the intellect and of the spirit. It was a small, struggling, isolated community, and it is rare in any group that the first generation or two is creative in matters of literature, religion, and education. They lost, in this land, the feeling of need for the isolated life they had lived in Europe; they lost much of the culture of the ghetto, but they were not sufficiently experienced in the new life of freedom to be able, as yet, to create in its medium. The little culture which they had, they brought in from abroad.

AMERICAN INTEREST IN HEBRAISM AND THE CONTEMPORARY JEW

There was, of course, a considerable amount of Hebraic culture in this country, particularly in New England, but let it be clear from the very outset, the colonial Jews like Judah Monis of Harvard were only in small part responsible for that interest. The New England Hebraists would have studied and taught Bible if there had never been a single Jew in that part of the country.

Hebrew, primarily biblical studies, were pursued in the colleges and private schools of New York, Philadelphia, and New Jersey in the eighteenth century. James Logan of Pennsylvania, the distinguished colonial administrator, owned a good Hebrew library, and Samuel Johnson, president of King's College (Columbia), believed that some knowledge of the holy tongue was part of a gentleman's education. And there is a contemporary story, for what it is worth, that some members of the Continental Congress proposed that the English language be prohibited and that Hebrew be used in its stead!

Even in the South, Hebrew books were not so scarce as one might be led to think. Back in the seventeenth century, the library of the Reverend John Goodborne (1635)

included a number of Hebraic works. As early as the
1720's, the Society for the Propagation of the Gospel in
Foreign Parts collected books for a library in Edenton—
"the metropolis of North Carolina," they called it—a town
of no more than 200 or 300 people. Among the volumes
obtained was a Hebrew psalter, probably Leusden's He-
brew-Latin edition dedicated to John Eliot, the Puritan
missionary to the Indians. Other works on Hebrew in the
Edenton collection were the elder Buxtorf's dictionary and
grammar. The publication in Boston of Judah Monis'
Grammar of the Hebrew Tongue in 1735 and of Stephen
Sewall's *Hebrew Grammar* in 1763 made it possible to
secure American works of this type. In addition, British
publications in the Hebraic field were nearly always available.

Men like Richard Lee II (d. 1714) studied Hebrew; and
instruction in the sacred language was available in 1763,
"agreeable to the most modern methods," at James Wad-
del's school in Lancaster County, Virginia. Chief Justice
Nicholas Trott of South Carolina (d. 1744) was a student
of the Old Testament in the original, and General Christopher Gadsden of Charlestown studied the language while
a prisoner of the British in St. Augustine. Even in distant
Ebenezer, Georgia, the Salzburger library had Chaldaic
and Hebrew works as early as 1751. Though Hebrew
linguistic studies were certainly cultivated more in the
North, they were definitely known in all the colonies of
the South.

The Hebraic tradition as reflected in the *English* Bible
was always present and strong in Virginia, in the Carolinas,

and in Georgia. New England had no monopoly on interest in the Bible; wherever there were Dissenters, "fundamentalism," based on a literal interpretation of Scripture, flourished.

Colonial presses reprinted books on the ancient Hebrews; they published editions of the ever popular writings of Flavius Josephus, to which they appended the stirring adventures of the heroic Maccabees and the account of Philo's embassy to the crazy Caligula. The revolt of the ten tribes of Israel against King Rehoboam became a precedent for the revolt of the thirteen colonies against King George III. Republican polity found its classical expression in the romantically conceived idyllic conditions of premonarchical Israel. The story of the Exodus from Egypt, of the escape of the Hebrew slaves from the despotic Pharaoh, was a source of inspiration to the dissident Americans.

These influences or concepts were common to many of the colonies in the days before the Revolution. And in 1776 the Hebraic ideal of freedom was reflected in the proposed design for a seal for the new United States. On the fourth of July, 1776, Congress appointed a committee consisting of Franklin, Jefferson, and John Adams to make recommendations for such a seal. Jefferson made several proposals, two of which were based on the Exodus theme. In one, the seal showed the children of Israel in the wilderness, led on to liberty by a cloud by day and by a pillar of fire by night. In the other, suggested by Benjamin Franklin, it portrayed Pharaoh, sword in hand, plunging into the Red Sea in hot pursuit of the escaping Israelites, with

Moses on the far shore, standing bathed in the rays of the pillar of fire, his arms extended over the Egyptians, overwhelming them in destruction. Around the edge of the design there ran the motto, "Rebellion to tyrants is obedience to God." The second suggestion, just described above, became the recommendation of the committee. But it was not accepted. It was not until 1782 that the present seal, so familiar to all of us from the one-dollar bill, was suggested by a totally different committee and adopted by Congress.

In the mind of the average Bible-reading Christian, whether in the South or in the North, there was very little connection between the heroic Hebrew of the Old Testament and his latter-day descendant in the streets of Richmond or Boston. Abraham, Isaac, and Jacob were regarded as proto-Christians. Many Americans were never in their whole lives to see a Jew in the flesh. Their picture of the contemporary Jew was frequently colored by the conversionist pamphlets that came off the presses as far north as Massachusetts and as far south as Georgia. New London, Connecticut—a town that never harbored a permanent Jewish settler in colonial days—published the weird tale of *The Wandering Jew*, the fabled shoemaker of Jerusalem, who was doomed to wander throughout the ages because he had taunted the crucifix-carrying Jesus on the road to Golgotha.

The intelligent, the learned, and the curious talked and debated with the Jews whom they met, or they read the apologetic literature of David Levi, a poor Whitechapel hatter who had once cherished the ambition of becoming a rabbi. In the course of a hard life he had turned to shoe-making, hatmaking, printing, and the publication of Hebrew and Jewish works. The year after the war was over, in 1784, he published his *Succinct Account of the Rites and Ceremonies of the Jews,* in London, and two years later he began to issue his three-volume *Lingua Sacra,* a combination Hebrew-English dictionary and grammar. These books were purchased by both Jews and non-Jews in the United States. (Manuel Josephson of Philadelphia imported a number of the Levi publications for resale.)

Gentile publishers in this country, not Jews, issued English and German editions of the famous sermon preached by the Berlin rabbi, David Hirsch Fraenkel, on the occasion of the victory of Frederick the Great over the Austrians at Leuthen in Silesia (1757). It proved very popular and ran into four English editions and printings in 1758. One religious publisher was motivated to reissue it in 1763 for "the Christian Reeder," to demonstrate God's providence in protecting princes, and to emphasize the loyalty of the German Jews, who invoked God's blessings on their Christian rulers in spite of the disabilities which they endured. Jews evidenced "the warmest gratitude to princes who have wisdom and humanity to protect and defend them." This particular edition was intended to be a plea for tolerance toward the Jews—and for their ultimate conversion. The reason why this pamphlet received such a cordial reception may well have been that Frederick was liked in the colonies, not only because there were so many German settlers, but also because he was an ally of the English during the French and Indian War. The sermon had first appeared in the colonies in Philadelphia in William Bradford's pro-British *American Magazine and Monthly Chronicle* for June, 1758. The head of the Sheftall clan in Savannah purchased a copy, and proudly displayed it to one of the Salzburg Germans.

JEWISH LITERATURE

Of the half-dozen or less Jewish books published in the colonies and states by Jews before 1790, two are of particular interest. The first was the *Evening Service of Roshashanah and Kippur, or The Beginning of the Year, and The Day of Atonement*. This work, printed in New York in 1761, is an English translation, without Hebrew text, of the Sephardic ritual for the evenings of the High Holydays. It was the first Jewish prayer book printed in America—as a matter of fact, the first Jewish prayer book (Sephardic-rite) in the English language printed anywhere in the British Empire. Though Spanish-Portuguese Jews had been in England for over a century, and though manuscript copies of English translations of the liturgy were in existence, the English Sephardim still used a Spanish translation made by Rabbi Isaac Nieto.

The New York translation was probably the work of Isaac Pinto, a well-known Whig and professional translator. Pinto may have hesitated to acknowledge his authorship for fear of being accused of undermining the study and the sanctity of Hebrew, the Holy Language. English was still considered a profane tongue; Spanish, like Yiddish, was almost a sacred tongue, and translations in those languages were tolerated.

Five years later (1766) a complementary volume, the *Prayers for Shabbath, Rosh-Hashanah, and Kippur,* the morning and afternoon services, appeared in New York, again in English translation. This time Pinto's name was given as translator and publisher. Evidently there had been no serious objections to the first volume.

Hebrew must be preserved, wrote Pinto in the Preface to the 1766 volume. It is sacred to us not only because God revealed Himself in that language, but because of our "firm persuasion that it will again be re-established in Israel." Unfortunately, he continued, there are some people who know no Hebrew. The Spanish translation will do them no good, certainly not in the British Dominions in America. That being the case, he attempted "a translation in English not without hope that it will tend to the improvement of many of my brethren in their devotion."

These editions of an English prayer book were significant. They document that the assimilatory influence of the American environment was largely limited to translating the prayer book. Some of the younger generation—both male and female—certainly had no knowledge of Hebrew, and it was felt that prayer in English was better than no prayer at all. But religious adaptations, broader than translations of the liturgy, are not recorded.

By 1766 Spanish was no longer being taught in the all-day (parochial) school of Shearith Israel, a Sephardic-rite congregation, and as early as 1728, it had required that its bylaws be read in English as well as in Portuguese. In 1762, Abraham Isaac Abrahams, the new schoolteacher hired by the congregation, agreed to teach ciphering, English writing, reading, and Hebrew, but not Spanish. The secular instruction in the New York Jewish school is to be ascribed not only to the high Sephardic standards—particularly characteristic of the Amsterdam Jewish school—but also to the influence of the American environment. Children of wealthy New York Jewish merchants went to the best American private schools; their parents had the opportunity of learning what was culturally necessary and adequate.

New York Jewry broke with its "Spanish" background almost a generation before the Sephardim of metropolitan London. David Levi's translation of the Sephardic ritual into English did not begin to appear in London until 1789. Despite the fact that English began to be taught in the London Sephardic "parochial school" no later than the 1770's, Bible instruction and preaching in English were not tolerated until about the middle of the nineteenth century.

In addition to the Pinto works, colonial Jewry published also two translations into English, a prayer-service celebrating the victory over the French in Canada (1760) and a sermon of Rabbi Haim Isaac Carigal, delivered in Newport in 1773, the former originally given in Hebrew and the latter in Spanish. This was practically all that the North American Jews had written or printed. It was certainly nothing to boast about. There was to be no American Jewish literature till the nineteenth century.

GENERAL CULTURE

It is to be assumed that the Jews, many of whom were clerks, shopkeepers, and merchants, men engaged in affairs, would possess the ability to read and write. Most of them could; there were very few, if any, businessmen among them who were not literate, but sometimes one was to be found who could not write. This was true even among the Sephardim. When Solomon Marache's mother, Estter, signed her son's indenture of apprenticeship to Isaac Hays in 1749, she had to make her mark. Abraham Depass, one of the founders of the post-Revolutionary Savannah synagogue, could not sign his name.

But not only were most of the Jews literate, many of them were bilingual and trilingual. Up to the period of the Revolution a very large percentage of the members of the Jewish community were, as we know, immigrants. Consequently they spoke their native vernacular and had some command of the English which they acquired either in England or in the colonies. Most Sephardim knew Spanish, Portuguese, and English; the Ashkenazim knew Yiddish, some German, and the English they had acquired here. Some of the Central Europeans had difficulty writing the Roman cursive script, but wrote that language using Hebrew letters. The English of the immigrant was generally written phonetically, full of misspellings, of course, but intelligible. He was not alone in his incapacity to deal with the vernacular; illiteracy was widespread in the eighteenth century, and there were not many natives who could write and spell properly. Conditions were even worse north of the border: Most of the French peasants in Canada and in the Illinois country were probably completely illiterate.

Many if not most of the letters dispatched by the Jewish merchants were written by their clerks, who carried on the correspondence for them and handled their books. The

Jewish businessmen seem to have had some knowledge of bookkeeping, finance, and banking. There were, of course, exceptions, who were at the mercy of their accountants, if we may judge from the fact that those merchants complained of mistreatment and fraud on the part of their employees.

The culture that the immigrant settlers possessed reflected, in large part, their background in the lands of their nativity. The Jews who came of Iberian stock seem to have possessed some general culture. This they had acquired in the Islands, in Holland, in France, or in their old homeland, the Spanish Peninsula. The Lopezes and the Riveras of Newport were families of intelligence and culture. Jacob R. Rivera was an active member of the Redwood Library. The records show that on occasion he shared his library privileges with a Jew of an inquiring mind. This was probably not an infrequent occurrence.

The education of the Germans and the Poles reflected the fact that they had fewer opportunities for study and learning in their European homes. But a few of them, seemingly, had gone to school somewhere or had taught themselves. Manuel Josephson was a cultured man with a beautiful script both in English and in Hebrew; Marcus Elcan and Joseph Marx of postwar Richmond were men who read widely of the best literature.

In those days when schools were few, and young immigrants had neither the time nor the opportunity to take advantage of what schools there were, many of them entered into the stream of American culture by associating with others, by speaking the language of the country, by

475

reading, and by joining various clubs, societies, and lodges. Unlike the different groups of Germans and French who lived in close settlements and spoke their native tongues almost exclusively, the Jews lived in the larger towns and always spoke English in addition to their mother tongue. There were no Jewish enclaves. When Sephardic and Ashkenazic Jews met together, we may assume that their common medium of communication was English, for the Sephardim knew no Yiddish and the Ashkenazim, as a rule, no Spanish or Portuguese. The Jews read the papers if only to keep up with prices current; and many of them possessed and read books.

A not unimportant source for communicating the culture of the land to them was the Masonic movement. Both immigrant and native Jews were very much interested in Masonry, and, as we have seen, individual Jews in many colonies were outstanding leaders in the local colonial or state lodges. If there were Jews in a community, even only a handful, it is safe to assume that they were active in a local lodge. Those societies were an important Americanizing influence of a liberal type. Politically, Masonry stood for tolerance if not for equality; religiously, it preached a gospel of deism and non-credal universalism which must have been acceptable to many of the Jewish members.

Communal and church schools were created primarily for the poor and the lower middle-class group. People in good circumstances either provided tutors for their children or sent them to private schools frequented by the rich, the influential, and the governing classes. When the all-day school of Shearith Israel assembled, the children

476

of the wealthy were probably absent. A Jewish merchant in a small town who had means sent his children to the nearest city, where the son or the daughter might acquire the knowledge and the amenities agreeable to the father's social station. Thus the children were taught to read and to write, to compose poetry, to dance, to paint, and to understand something of good music. There is little, if any, evidence that the children of Central European parents read German; some of the Jews read French.

Books, imported from abroad, were readily available to any man who could pay the price. The readers were found principally among the wealthy, or among those who made a good living; they had leisure. Most Jews, as members of the middle class, did some reading, if we may judge from the fact that their letters of administration frequently list books among their effects. Widows and older women, having less to do, liked to read. They too, had more time.

Rare individuals had good collections of books. The Franks women of New York, as their letters in the 1730's and 1740's show, were buying and reading the best that the English market afforded. Samuel Judah of Canada (1785) had an excellent library of English literature, and David Franks's collection of books (1780) must have been an unusually fine one. When he was banished from Philadelphia a bookseller printed a catalogue of his library and offered it for sale at auction. (It is a source of deep regret that no copy of this publication has yet been located.)

Francis Salvador of Ninety Six District, in South Carolina—he was educated in England and in France—owned a large library, if we may draw any conclusions from the fact that one of the best craftsmen in the province made him a series of bookcases. Moses Lindo of Charlestown wrote for the *Philosophical Transactions* of the Royal Society of London, and even in distant Savannah the Sheftalls, ranchers and merchants, knew of the most recent book imports on the latest boat from London.

It should occasion no surprise, therefore, to discover that Marcus Elcan, a merchant in the little town of Richmond, owned an excellent library. In his choice collection of books and pamphlets there were a number of works on the natural sciences, on the American Revolution, and on the life and letters of Washington, together with prints of Charles James Fox, William Pitt, and the Washington family. He owned James Monroe's *View of the Conduct of the Executive* and three volumes of *Virginia Debates*. A *Life of Chatham* and the *Letters of Junius* testified to his Whiggish and liberal sympathies. Classical history was well provided for; the English historians were represented by Hume, Smollett, and Gibbon; the eighteenth-century French and German Enlightenment shone in the writings of Helvetius and Rousseau, ánd in Lessing's *Nathan the Wise*. Along with a few volumes of gallant literature—which were invariably present in a gentleman's bookcase—there were Bolingbroke, Laurence Sterne, Samuel Johnson, Pope, Fénelon, and Chesterfield. Elcan read English, French, and German, knew Adam Smith's *The Wealth of Nations*, and, like Jefferson and Madison, leaned toward the deists, if we may judge from his copies of *Christ Unveiled*, Paine's *The Age of Reason*, and Priestley's *Letters to the Jews*. Elcan was a child of the age of reason

478

and read history and literature that preached a God of reason. Such books were generally popular among liberal Americans of the day.

Elcan's interest in the Hebrew language and Jewish literature was documented by a good collection of the apologetic writings of the London David Levi, an account of the controversy of Moses Mendelssohn and Johann K. Lavater on the claims of Judaism and Christianity, and a copy of the Passover ritual. He also possessed a well-known philo-Semitic novel, *Theodore Cyphon*, by George Walker; this book, first published in 1796, presented a Jewish money-lender as benevolent and philanthropic.

A comparative study of the two libraries of Samuel Judah and Marcus Elcan discloses that both were interested in history, biography, and travel, and in political science and law. There was little poetry and belleslettres, and very little fiction. Both libraries had a substantial number of dictionaries and other reference works.

In August, 1771, quite a number of years before Elcan and Judah had completed their collections, Elcan's fellow-Virginian, Thomas Jefferson, described a basic library in a letter to a friend. It is curious that a study of all three libraries reveals the fact that they had but one author in common: Pope. In addition, Judah and Elcan both owned Gibbon's *Decline and Fall of the Roman Empire*, and Jefferson and Elcan had seven authors in common, among whom were Bolingbroke, Lady Montagu, Hume (history), and Rousseau.

Were there many intellectuals among the Jews? Undoubtedly there were some men of intellectual capacity;

we have noticed that here and there some read widely, and we have reason to believe that every Jewish community possessed one or two individuals who cultivated an interest in literature if only in a very modest fashion. Yet it is obvious to the unjaundiced eye that American Jewry could boast of no leaders in the broader cultural areas. It might be argued that there were relatively few academic and intellectual leaders in general in the America of the colonies and of the Revolutionary age. But that was a generation which knew Franklin, Jefferson, Madison, Rittenhouse, Hamilton, and a host of others.

There were many Christian clergymen of real literary and academic distinction in the second half of the century, men like Jonathan Edwards, Jonathan Mayhew, John Woolman, Henry M. Mühlenberg, John Witherspoon, and Ezra Stiles. As far as we know, there was not a Jew in the country who deserved to be compared scholastically to those Christian worthies. The few Jewish "clergymen" in this country, we have seen, were cantors who "chaunted" the service. They had no substantial knowledge of the secular disciplines. The first American among them was Gershom M. Seixas, self-taught for the most part. His family was too poor to give him a good systematic education. He read a great deal, was intelligent, but was not an intellectual figure of any stature. The two published sermons of his which are still extant do not rise above the level of mediocrity.

In spite of the fact that the London and the American communities were equally old—both came into being in the 1650's—what a difference there was between the two! The

North American Jewish colonies had produced nothing in the humanities; English Jewry could boast of a number of competent Hebraists, preachers, apologetes, poets, and even devotees of science. But then, London was one of the great centers of world commerce and power; its Jews were numbered in the thousands. America was on the outer rim of culture and civilization; its Jews, for the larger part of the century, could be numbered only in the hundreds.

There was no Jewish academician of any standing in all of North America. The most that can be said is that here and there individuals participated in a modest degree in the cultural life of the general community. Jews played no role in American literary life.

CHARITY

Making provision for fellow-Jews who were in need was one of the basic concerns of every Jewish community. The feeling of a common fellowship, of mutual responsibility, of kinship among Jews, has always been strong, not only on a familial level, but also on a communal, national, and international level.

American Jewry was always conscious of the fact that other Jews in other lands were interested in them. But that was only right and proper! As the different communities here turned to building their synagogues, they confidently appealed to their fellow-religionists in this land, in the West Indies, and in England for aid. Frequently they got it. When a London Jewish family built the New York

Jews a schoolhouse in 1731, the leaders of Shearith Israel were grateful but not overwhelmed.

The fact that the American Jews were on the periphery of Jewish civilization did not lessen their interest in other communities, and they were always ready to respond to a call for help from any Jewish group. They felt as close to the impoverished settlements in distant Palestine as to another American Jewish congregation.

Over here, the feeling of mutual dependence was particularly strong; so many in the small settlements were tied together by bonds of blood and marriage. When, in July, 1779, the Tory raids took place on the Connecticut side of Long Island Sound, the Jewish exiles driven out by Governor Tryon did not hesitate to descend on Aaron Cardoza as a body and crowd into his village home. And when Aaron Lopez heard of the flight of the pillaged exiles, he at once dispatched relief to them. He did not have to be solicited for help.

The charities of Shearith Israel were usually included in the category of *obras pias*, pious works. At times there was a special fund for this philanthropic work; in general, however, the alms were paid out of the congregational treasury. The amount expended was sizeable; in the years 1730–45 it ranged anywhere from 19 per cent to 23 per cent of the entire community budget.

The investigation of the needs of those who petitioned for help and the giving of charity were functions reserved primarily for the *parnas* and his board. This took a great deal of time, and was probably the most onerous of all his

duties, which in itself may have deterred many a businessman from accepting the office of president.

It was the task of the local officials, as part of their
philanthropic work, to raise money for the "messengers"
from Palestine, to help impoverished itinerants who passed
through town, and to make adequate provision for the
local poor and the impoverished sick and aged. The elee-
mosynary pattern in America was a replica of that of the
European Jewish community.

Providing for different types of itinerants was a major
task. There were always poor Jews on the march; there
had been for hundreds of years. It was, indeed, a millennial
tradition, never forgotten in the Diaspora, to feed and
clothe the unfortunate, to give them a pittance, and to
transport them by cart to the next town where there was
a Jewish community. Jews may have resented the constant
drain upon them by the poor who straggled into their villages; they may have been severe at times in clearing them
out of town after a few days, but they never ignored them.
Every Jew who needed help was helped, if only modestly.
It is hard to find any reference in the minutes to a petitioner who was denied relief.

The "messengers" from Palestine, "apostles" if you will,
were emissaries sent out into the Diaspora to collect funds
for Palestinian scholars and schools, or to meet some local
crisis. (Under the rapacious Turkish pashas there was always oppression somewhere in the Holy Land.) The messengers were usually scholars, rabbis, and men of some
distinction. They were always treated courteously, generously, too, as far as we know, and given transportation

to the next port on their itinerary. Forwarding itinerants was a heavy expense; it was sometimes over a thousand miles to the traveler's destination in the West Indies.

The local poor were given grants for fuel and rent and food. The luckless in the debtors' jails were helped; the sick were given subsidies and the services of a physician. The impoverished and helpless aged, particularly respectable merchants who had come down in the world, were given pensions. There were no fixed rules for this aid; each case was considered on its merits. Burials were undertaken by the congregation, and apparently no charges were made either to rich or to poor. That was a religious service accorded every Jew.

Toward the end of the century, after the close of the Revolution, social welfare procedure patterned itself more closely on European models. The *parnas* and his board turned over much of the philanthropic work to a pious association or confraternity. That society, usually referred to as the *Hebrah Gemilut Hasadim* ("society for deeds of loving-kindness"), or the Hebrew Benevolent Society, was semi-autonomous, though still an integral part of the congregation. It became the social welfare arm of the community, a special committee dealing only with the charities.

At first glance, there does not seem to have been any attempt at the social rehabilitation of the poor and the unfortunate. Strangers got help, not only because they needed it, not only because they asked for it, but because they had a right to it. The Jewish poor were claimants, not suppliants. It was the privilege of a Jew to demand help; it was the sacred obligation of a fellow-Jew to provide it. Professional schnorrers ("suppliants") were not investigated; they were given money and sent on. But there were intimations of a sounder approach to the problem of poverty and the wandering beggar. Any man who wanted to work, and could work, was given money or a small congregational loan, clothes, or credit.

Were the Jews more generous than their neighbors? That is hard to say. The Baptists speak of the manifold duties of a Christian, "especially to the household of faith." They meant that one Baptist was expected to help another. We know that some of the German (Christian) Reformed Congregations of Pennsylvania had charity monies, received from Holland, which they distributed to schoolmasters, to widows of ministers, and to the blind. Because of the unavailability of detailed budgets of expenditures of colonial Christian congregations, it is difficult to determine to what extent the Christian churches "took care of their own." The Jews did.

* * *

The history of the American Jewish community through the period of the Revolution can be summarized in a few bold strokes. The Jews were loyal to their faith; they were determined to survive as an integral part of the world Jewish fellowship. The community organization which they improvised with their synagogue as the hub and the Sephardic prayer service as the new American rite gave them group cohesion. But they were not a dynamic body; they evidenced no great organizational skills comparable

485

to those of some Dissenter churches; their activity was modest; there was no clerical leadership, although Jewish lay guidance, especially in the South, was of a high order. As far as the records run, there were few examples of sacrificial devotion; real generosity occurred, but it was exceptional. American Jewry of colonial and Revolutionary days was a settlement on the outskirts of a Jewish cultural sphere. It can bear no comparison with an established Jewish community in Central or Eastern Europe, in the midst of Jewish mass settlement, nurtured by an intensive, living, Jewish religious culture. It would have been surprising had it been otherwise.

THE AMERICAN JEWISH RELIGIOUS COMMUNITY AFTER THE REVOLUTION

After the independence of the United States was recognized by the British (1783), there were changes in the Jewish communities. Some of the states permitted the Jews to incorporate their institutions. For the first time in American history synagogues and cemeteries were given legal recognition in the larger American community.

The long struggle for freedom was not without its influence on the internal organic structure of American Jewry. Under the impact of American liberalism and the French egalitarian doctrine, Jewish personalities in the synagogue began to preach the gospel of democracy. This was certainly true of New York and was, in all probability, equally true of the other Jewish communities. The Jewish towns from New York to Savannah were all officered and led by staunch Whigs and war veterans. Newport was the one exception, and even here Moses Seixas put on a bold front as a liberal and patriot.

As early as 1785, New York Jewry began to talk of a Bill of Rights for the congregation. Five years later one of the authors of the New York synagogal statutes seized the opportunity of preaching his own brand of democracy: Because of the civil and religious liberty that we enjoy, he wrote, we are free to adopt the best means of preserving our privileges; we can freely enter into a compact to order our internal affairs. All power originates and derives from the people, and they retain every right necessary for their own well-being; a group only complies with its duty to itself and to posterity when it covenants to create a congregation. They should not only have a religious Bill of Rights, but they should know what these are, and they must keep them inviolate. Hence, we who profess the divine law make this declaration of our rights and privileges!

This same affirmation of democracy is expressed in another paragraph of the New York regulations: Every free person who professes the Jewish religion is entitled to all congregational privileges. He must be treated in all respects as a brother and, as such, be subject to every fraternal duty.

It would not be hazarding a wild guess to surmise that the writer of these pro-democratic pronouncements was none other than Solomon Simson, a sturdy Whig of New York. He was then one of the two presidents of the congregation. The sentiments he expressed were in many men's hearts in those days. The French Revolution had broken out less than a year before; the first American Congress had already met and had adopted a Bill of Rights. A few years later Simson joined the pro-Jacobin group that organized the Democratic Society, and he became its president in 1797.

Undoubtedly, democratic advances were made in congregational administration, but we are not always able to determine the degree of progress. As we have pointed out, there are not sufficient earlier constitutional data to allow us to make valid comparisons with the new, postwar constitutions and bylaws which we do possess. (Fortunately, we do have some material of this latter type for Philadelphia [1782], Richmond [1789], New York [1790], and Savannah [1791]).

The new liberal political tradition that came in with the Revolution was mirrored also in the election of the once all-powerful board and in the limitations placed on its authority. In Richmond, Savannah, and Philadelphia, the congregation, in general assembly, elected the *junta*. Philadelphia would not even allow the board, the *mahamad*, to elect its own president; the congregation assumed this prerogative.

The advance, after the war, in New York, at least, seems to have been that it was easier, almost automatic, for a contributor to become a select member. However, before the candidate was accorded all rights there was a brief interval which ran from three to six months.

New York had a more conservative tradition which it hesitated to abandon. Back in the early eighteenth century, the congregation elected only the chief executive, the

488

parnas, and he appointed his associates. In 1790, the congregation elected three members of the *junta* of five, but these three had to be men who had once served or qualified as "juntamen." The three board members newly elected met with the old president and vice-president, and those five elected the two new presiding officers from former board members. Where, then, was there any democratic advance? It was permitted every year to elect two of the privileged members (*yehidim*) to serve the congregation as "bridegrooms." (The "bridegrooms" had the honor of closing the annual reading of the Pentateuch and of commencing it anew.) Although not members of the board at Shearith Israel, those "bridegrooms" enjoyed the status of officeholders. There can be no question, however, that even under this modified system electoral revolutions in the New York community were virtually impossible.

It was also in the increasing limitations placed on the power of the *parnas* and board to mulct the members and the "employees" that the developing American democratic process revealed itself. In some congregations a *parnas* could be held to account—while in office or after his term—for mistreating a member. The *junta* was not necessarily a creature of the president; it might serve as a check upon authority arbitrarily exercised. In Savannah, an excellent provision was made for arbitrating quarrels between the *junta* and a member of the congregation; three aggrieved members had the right to summon the congregation to hear a complaint. In New York, according to one bylaw, the same privilege prevailed; according to another contemporary New York statute, however, the three men might well ask the board for a general meeting, but the board reserved the right to refuse to assemble the congregation. Apparently, the right of a small number of individuals to appeal directly to the congregation was in dispute in that community. In no congregation did the *junta* have final authority to dismiss a paid official. That was the prerogative of the congregation as a whole.

All new laws adopted by the board had to be publicly announced in the synagogue on two successive Sabbaths. If there was objection, a congregational meeting was to be held, and the new regulations were to be ratified in general assembly. Provisions were made in all communities to amend the constitution and the bylaws.

Was the growing and expanding political freedom for the Jew—we shall soon touch on that—matched by a corresponding expansion of the spirit in religious thought and practice? Was there a theological change in line with the Enlightenment which still dominated much of American thought? Was there an intellectual attack on orthodoxy? Was there anything comparable in Judaism to the revolt in Boston against the old Calvinist theology? Was there anything in Judaism comparable to the rise of Unitarianism in Christianity (1785)?

There were Jewish political liberals and deists, men like Solomon Simson and young Moses Hart. Hart, a son of Aaron Hart of Three Rivers, Canada, consorted with deists in the States. He was influenced by the religious radicals of the French Revolution, and came out a generation later (1815) with a plan for a "modern religion" of a broad universalistic and deistic character. Yet, in spite of such postwar liberals, American Jewry was untouched theologically. The reason, as we have intimated, was that the congregations remained in the hands of immigrants with strong orthodox sympathies. After the war quite a number of newcomers arrived, mostly Germans, who fortified and reinforced the conservative tendencies of the older immigrants.

But what of the liberals, particularly in the New York congregation? How could they remain spiritually content in the light of the new American and French thought? They had no problem. They did not come into conflict with the synagogue. As we know, there never had been, nor were there ever to be, any religious tests for members. A Solomon Simson could not only remain in the synagogue; he could even become its president.

A NATIONAL AMERICAN JEWISH SYNAGOGAL COMMUNITY?

Why did the Jews of the 1780's not create a "national church," as did a number of the Christian denominations? Why not unite all Jews into one organic whole? The thought of union and nationalization was in everyone's mind. The hope and need for unity were slowly creating a strong federal government out of the body of confederated sovereign states. An American government was being born. To fit into this new national state, and to sever relations with the now alien British fatherland, national organizations were formed by the Christian churches of this country. They were at first somewhat hesitant in cutting themselves off from Europe and in establishing self-governing American organizations, but they finally did so. By the decade of the 1780's the hierarchical churches, such as the Catholics, the Presbyterians, and others, had begun to perfect their national structure. Why did the Jews not follow in the wake of the others and create a national American Jewish Synagogue? Shearith Israel, in New York, could have served as the core around which an all-American Jewish "church" could have been built. That historic old synagogue, then almost 150 years old, might well have assumed the leadership.

But no nation-wide American Synagogue was established. National community organizations had no deep roots in the past fifteen hundred years of Diaspora Jewry. The local community was characteristic of Jewish life everywhere. Spanish and German Jewry had never perfected national governments, though the attempt was made repeatedly in both lands. There were such structures in Poland and Lithuania, but even there the town community was dominant—and there were few East European Jews in colonial America. Hierarchy was always foreign and objectionable to European Jewry.

Though no attempt was made to create a permanent over-all Jewish body, there was an attempt at concerted action in 1789. Had it been more successful, it might have paved the way for a country-wide Jewish community.

Manuel Josephson, then of Philadelphia, a self-appointed American Jewish leader, appealed to the six American Jewish congregation-communities to join in one common letter of congratulation to the new president, George Washington. The attempt failed. There was, as we have just said, little historic background for such hierarchical, authoritarian action. Josephson may have been inadequate as a leader. The congregants and congregations had economic problems of a serious nature. Many of the merchants were only beginning to recover from the postwar economic depression. Mikveh Israel—that was Josephson's congregation—was so debt-ridden that it was about to be seized by those who held the mortgage. There was inertia, and, moreover, the communities—or their leaders—were jealous of one another. "Who made thee a ruler and a judge over us?" Savannah and Newport wrote independently. The letters from both towns were signed by men who, justly or unjustly, were tainted with the charge of Toryism. (Maybe this is why they wrote independently, making haste to document their loyalty to the new republic!) Josephson did succeed in presenting a joint letter to Washington on behalf of the congregations of Philadelphia, New York, Richmond, and Charleston. It was a beginning, the first faint stirrings toward a national Jewish religious community, a beginning that was not to find its realization even by the second half of the twentieth century.

Chapter 20

Acculturation

WE have already touched on the influence of European Jewish culture on American Jewry. Europe was the hearth, the center, the nursery, of all Jewish life. The men who came from that continent brought with them their old-world languages, occupational patterns, social habits, educational and philanthropic institutions, religious worship, home ceremonial, and ancestral traditions. All those factors tied them to the body of Jewry and helped keep them Jewish. Had they remained at home, they would have been bound closely to their faith by their distance from the Christian world, by their suspicion of a culture which still burdened them with political, social, and economic disabilities. Jews in Europe were frequently kept Jewish by resentment. To a large degree, this situation did not obtain in the American colonies.

There were anti-Jewish prejudices here, disabilities, too, but they were not crushing or keenly felt. Certainly the prejudices which Jews encountered here were not sufficient to throw them back into a ghetto frame of mind. They did not "suffer" as Jews in this land.

On the whole, the early American Jew was accepted by his neighbors. They associated with him and influenced him to follow their ways of living and thought. There was a continuing process of adaptation to the dominant Anglo-Christian culture. It may be called Anglo-Americanization or assimilation. The Jew was replacing his Polish, German, Iberian, or even British nationality pattern with an emergent Americanism.

To America, Jews as Jews were all alike. That is, it was not interested in the ritual and ethnic differences which characterized them. It made no distinction between Ashkenazi and Sephardi. The Iberian Jew as such had no superior status in urban society because of his origin. Most Gentiles were certainly not even conscious of the difference between Spanish and German Jews.

Jews had social contacts on all levels, ranging from the petty shopkeeper in a little village who married a local girl to a David Franks of Philadelphia who allied himself with one of the aristocratic Pennsylvania families.

Because of the letters they wrote, we know more about the Jews who moved in the better social circles. Phila Franks's marriage to Oliver DeLancey was not regarded as a *mésalliance* by those New York aristocrats. Fortified by letters of introduction, Moses Myers, the merchant, was received socially in good homes when he first visited Norfolk.

Social acceptance by the dominant Gentile group was determined by integrity (Darmstadt of Virginia), importance in the economy of the colony (DaCosta of Charlestown), and political activity during the Revolution (Sheftall of Savannah). These merchants and shippers seem to have been close to their Gentile friends of equal economic status.

Some of the wealthy Jews in this country—David Franks, for instance—had a tendency to seek the society of Gentiles. This was not quite true of English Jewry. There were a number of very wealthy Jews in England—members of the same Franks family, brothers, as a matter of fact—who had their own social clique. The English Jews did not have to leave their own group in order to mix with economic and social equals; they did not have to step out of their own circle to seek and attain status. Here in the colonies, the relatively few rich Jewish families, living on an economic and social plateau above their fellow-Jews, found it undesirable to descend for purposes of marriage. They would not step down, socially or economically, to marry with newer Jewish immigrants even if those stemmed from the very same areas as their own foreign-born parents. Those Jewish aristocrats preferred to associate with Christians of their own milieu. Ultimately, the Jewish womenfolk married Gentiles, or if their loyalties deterred them from marrying out of the faith, they did not marry at all.

Jews of wealth, in colonial and post-Revolutionary days, sent their children to the schools and tutors patronized by the aristocrats. They visited the same social clubs and dancing assemblies; they joined the same private libraries; they played in the same quartettes; and they, too, sat for Gilbert Stuart.

It was inevitable that they should also form business partnerships of a temporary or more permanent nature with Gentiles. Such Jewish-Christian commercial relations seem to have been more common here than in Europe. Partners and clients of different faiths accorded each other many personal courtesies. Samuel Jacobs of St. Denis, Canada, a Jew, entrusted his Christian daughter to a Protestant who saw to it that she went to the best school in town, to a Catholic convent. The freer social relations of colonial society, where classes and prejudices were not yet frozen, made it possible for Jews and Gentiles not only to dance together, and to do business together, but also to discuss more freely the theological problems which in those days loomed so large in the minds of thoughtful men. The well-educated Manuel Josephson and John Maylem, a New England poet, discussed immortality and the future life; Ezra Stiles of Newport made it his business to talk and to dispute theologically with every learned Jew who came his way. Back in London there was not the same give and take. At least the Sephardic synagogue, in its seventeenth-century constitution, had sternly forbidden its Jews to become involved in religious controversy:

No Jew may hold dispute or argument on matters of religion with Guim ["Gentiles"], nor urge them to follow our holy Law, nore may offensive words be spoken to them against their profession, because to do otherwise is to disturb the liberty which we enjoy and to make us disliked, since we are not bound to do so; wherefore it is enjoined with all earnestness. And if any should do the contrary, action shall be taken against him as may seem good.

There is not the least evidence that Jews here were asked to avoid arguments on matters of religion with their neighbors. There is ample evidence that they discussed intellectual matters of import with their Gentile friends and participated—to the extent of their capacities—in the cultural life of the community.

The Jewish newcomers found their niche quickly in the American scene. They exhibited a readiness, if not an eagerness, to adapt themselves to the life and culture about them. One phase of this integration was the adoption of typically English names. John Jones was one of the first members of the Savannah congregation! It is beyond question that the Jews were assimilated to the common culture more quickly than the French in the Illinois country or than the Salzburg Germans in Ebenezer. Some of the latter could speak no English after almost two generations in Georgia. The followers of the German Reform church, as late as 1785, refused to co-operate with English-speaking Christians in establishing a school at Carlisle, Pennsylvania, for fear that their German language might be neglected and that their German nationality might be suppressed. The distinguished Lutheran clergyman and botanist, Gotthilf H. E. Mühlenberg, was a native American, but the epitaph on his tomb was completely in the German language.

The Jews were less tenacious of their old vernaculars, although they, too, did not drop their Spanish, Portuguese,

German, and Yiddish with the celerity which one might have expected. Shearith Israel was still keeping some of its financial records in Portuguese as late as 1751, almost a century after the arrival of Jews on these shores. Some of the Gomezes of New York, native Americans, were able to write, and did write, Portuguese letters to Aaron Lopez. It may be maintained, quite correctly, of course, that the use of those languages does not prove a lagging assimilation. Every good countinghouse had a clerk who knew Spanish and Portuguese, because so much of the trade was still carried on in South America and in the West Indies. The Palestinian rabbi, Haim Isaac Carigal, preached in Spanish in Newport in 1773, and apparently the people understood him. (The Riveras and the Lopezes certainly did.) Perhaps Carigal knew no other European language. *Hazzan* Seixas of New York knew no Portuguese or Spanish. His father was a Sephardi, his mother was an Ashkenazi, and he loved Spanish meat balls, but he was ignorant of the paternal vernacular. Born in the middle 1740's, he went to school in New York in the period when English was just being substituted for the Iberian vernacular as the language of instruction.

The Yiddish-speaking Polish and German Jews, doubtless, never forgot their mother tongue; some even taught it to their children, but there were second-generation Ashkenazim in America who seemed to have no knowledge of it. One finds no intimation of an acquaintance with the language in the letters of Rebecca Gratz, but then this *grande dame* was a little on the stuffy side. She lived long enough to become a real Victorian. Most of the Yiddish-

499

speaking immigrants learned English rapidly, and tried to write it. Frequently, it was a gallant though not a very convincing effort.

It is probably no exaggeration to declare that the Jewish emigrants who came here fitted into American life not only quickly but happily. There was no attempt on their part to resist their environment. They became part of the community at large, emotionally. Back on the European continent, Rabbi Haim Isaac Carigal would have thought twice before going into a church to listen to the pastor; here, in Newport, he did not hesitate to accept Ezra Stiles's invitation to attend a Congregationalist service and to sit with the preacher's wife and children in the family pew. It was not difficult for Jews to contribute to the building of Anglican Trinity Church in New York, in 1711, or to help subsidize a Catholic missionary in Mackinac in the days of the Revolutionary War. They were probably not even conscious of the fact—or interested—that the Anglican church was vigorously opposed to Jewish emancipation in the colonies, or that the Catholic church could not conscientiously—and never did—urge equality for Jews in any Catholic land. These were communal charities, and they were members of the community. Men like Lopez in Newport and Lindo in Charlestown were not unaware that there were Christian institutions which were truly broad-minded, and when they gave gifts to a liberal school such as Rhode Island College, we may be sure that they made their donations with a special sense of satisfaction.

On the whole, Jews believed—and they were right—that

there was a widespread feeling of tolerance and of friendliness toward them. They reciprocated that attitude. Their identification with the town in which they elected to remain was without reservation. Aaron Hart, for example, was not accorded any political rights in Three Rivers, yet he was a devoted citizen. It was his town; he was to spend forty years there, to become, probably, its wealthiest if not its most eminent citizen. He was glad to work in the community for good government, better schools, better markets, better courts.

The surest indication that colonial Jewry was possessed of a sense of security, of a feeling of belonging, is documented in the freedom with which they turned to Gentiles, to Christians, and asked them to support Jewish religious institutions. When Mikveh Israel was in straits in 1788, it turned for financial support—and not in vain—to men like Benjamin Franklin, David Rittenhouse, and William Bradford. It was the conviction of those Jews—for this is what they wrote on their subscription list—that the enlightened citizens of Philadelphia would never be deterred from helping Israelites because of the fact that they worshipped the Almighty God differently from other religious societies.

But if the Jew of Mikveh Israel or Shearith Israel felt so much at home—and he did—how could he repair to his synagogue every Sabbath and pray fervently and sonorously for a speedy return to the Promised Land? How could he pray for restoration from exile? In his sermons "Rabbi" Seixas preached at some length on the return of the Jews to Palestine. There was no doubt of the sincerity of Seixas; he loved the ancient homeland and all that it stood for; he wanted it to rise again. The theme of the Restoration was integral in the theology of Judaism, and had been solemnly discussed by Jewish preachers and theologians for over 1,500 years. But—no matter what they said—it was not an immediate problem; it was a hazy hope floating mistily somewhere on a distant horizon. For the present it was an old and beloved liturgical phrase. Though Gershom M. Seixas and his generation spoke about and calculated the date of the coming of the Messiah, they were no more sanguine of it than the Church was of the Second Advent. The Jewry of eighteenth-century America did not actually believe that it was in "exile," even though it was conscious of the deprivation of certain rights and resentful, by the time of the Revolution, that such disabilities still persisted.

The Revolution gave the Jew more privileges. He was now an American citizen. Because he had fought for his country, he was more vigorous in asserting his rights in common with all others. Typical of his demand for equal treatment was the almost belligerent confidence of the Jewish war veteran that he would be taken care of. By that he meant that he, too, was entitled to a political job, a federal appointment. Colonel Solomon Bush had no sense of inferiority because he was the son of an immigrant Jew. Having acted the part of an amateur and, apparently, successful diplomat in London, the Colonel cheerfully importuned the federal authorities for an appointment as the representative of the American government in London. He did not specify ambassadorial rank—he would have been content with the job of consul general—he wanted a job. He even sought appointment as postmaster general in Washington's cabinet. Delusions of grandeur? By no means! He was just another citizen who took the democratic phraseology of his day seriously. He was conscious of his worth and convinced that the new republic connoted equality of opportunity for all.

Let it not be thought that, in this land where toleration for the Jew prevailed before the Revolution and where equality and justice began to manifest themselves after the Revolution, it was easy to remain Jewish. It was not quite that simple. The small Jewish group seldom found it easy to hold its followers together in the face of a dominant mass of Christian believers. Many a Jew was overwhelmed by the Gentile-Christian world about, and ceased to survive religiously. It has never been a light thing for Jews to maintain a steady balance between the social, cultural, and economic attractions of a tolerant Gentile world and the demands of Jewish folkways. The measure of this balance is determined by the degree of resistance or surrender to conversion and to intermarriage.

Converts found it easier to achieve wealth and social acceptance. Political office and financial opportunity were furthered by religious integration, by the adoption of Christianity. The inroads that conversion and intermarriage made into the Jewish communities of America were not inconsiderable. Church lists of marriages and baptisms in Philadelphia, Charlestown, and other large towns not infrequently record typically Jewish names. The 1790 United States census of heads of families is studded with names which point to undoubted Jewish origin. Who can doubt the ultimate Jewish provenance of Cohen, Levy, and Israel?

It is only a rude guess, but it may be ventured, that possibly ten per cent of the Jews in the cities married Gentiles. Intermarriage, of course, is not necessarily to be equated with conversion, or even with lack of devotion toward Judaism on the part of the Jewish partner. Jewish men who married Gentile women were frequently observant Jews, active in the affairs of the Jewish community of which they were a part. This might be true even if the wife and children adhered to Christianity. On rare occasions, the wife in the intermarriage became a convert and reared a family of loyal Jews, as did Elizabeth Whitlock Mordecai.

The Jewish community was totally unsympathetic toward the Jew who married out of the faith. It refused to recognize marriages between Jews and unconverted Gentiles.

Traditional Judaism, from the vantage point of religion, has never sanctioned such marriages, although it is today cognizant of their civil validity. In accordance with rabbinic law, the Synagogue frowned upon Christians who became proselytes in order to marry Jews. Such conversions were, of course, suspect. Proselytes to Judaism were from ancient times carefully scrutinized lest the ruling power apply punitive sanctions to the Jewish community collectively for engaging in conversionist activity. Since the fourth century, the conversion of a Christian to Judaism had been a capital crime. The Jew who converted a

Christian girl to Judaism in order to marry her was subject
to the death penalty. Jews in eighteenth-century Poland
were literally cut to pieces, while alive, for encouraging
conversion to Judaism. The English Sephardic Jews who
had crept into England in the second half of the seventeenth century—many of them had just escaped from the
Inquisition—had no desire to incur the wrath of the English government and to go into exile again. They decreed
that

No person who is not of our nation, Portuguese and Spaniards [crypto-Jews], may be circumcized . . . under pain of
herrem [the ban] . . . and under the said penalty is included
any one who may bathe [baptize] a foreign [Christian]
woman, because it is not meet that they be admitted into our
congregation.

This *ascama* or constitutional article was undoubtedly
known to the American Jews and influenced them. Like
their English co-religionists, they were not looking for
trouble. Once a Jew had married an unconverted Christian
woman, the community penalized him—if they could afford
to do so. They clearly and markedly expressed their dis-
approval, for they were fully conscious of the fact that if
the practice became prevalent, the Jewish community
would die out, since the children of intermarriage almost
invariably followed the faith of the mother. New York
Jewry could grimly point to Jacob Franks, its *parnas* for
many years, as a classical example of the effects of intermarriage. Franks himself was pious, observant, and, apparently, learned in rabbinical law. But he lived to see his
daughter Phila elope with a Gentile in 1742, and his son

David marry out the following year, and he survived to hear of the baptism of his grandchildren and of a great-grandchild. Two of his sons, when young, had been sent by him to the large Jewish community of London. Certainly, one of his motivations was to make sure that they would marry in the faith. He was vigorously opposed to intermarriage. (These two sons did marry Jewesses—but some of their children married out!)

Much that has been said above about the assimilation of the Jew to American life was true not only of the city and town dwellers but also, to an even greater degree, of those who lived in the villages. A family like that of Aaron Hart was exceptional. Although his was the only Jewish family for many years in Three Rivers, he succeeded in maintaining the old traditions, and reared sons and daughters who remained in the fold. In general, the village Jew, exposed to the full blast of an overwhelmingly non-Jewish environment, did not survive religiously. It would appear that every eighteenth-century Connecticut Jew who settled in the colony, permanently, married out of the faith. One might venture the theorem that assimilation was in direct ratio to distance from an organized Jewish community. Individual Jews, not many, strayed as far west as the edge of the frontier. Some lived as squaw men and probably never returned to civilization. Jacob Franks of Canada—and there were others who lived like him—settled in Green Bay, sired a number of children (breeds?), but returned to spend his declining days in Montreal with his Canadian wife, Mary Solomons.

Connecticut was no exception; nearly all Jews who settled permanently in the villages ultimately married Gentiles, if they remained. Some of them kept kosher kitchens, circumcised their children, and tried to visit the nearest Jewish synagogue whenever the opportunity presented itself. And even when the Christian wife baptized the children, sometimes the father, nostalgically, would give them typical Hebrew or even Yiddish names. Michael Judah of Norwalk, Connecticut, circumcised his son David, but all to no avail. The lad grew up to become a Christian, even though the mother predeceased the father. David's son was an Episcopalian minister. Two of the preacher's sons were notable men. One, Henry Moses Judah, was a general in the Civil War. The other, Theodore Dehone Judah, was the promoter primarily responsible for planning the first successful railroad across the Sierra Nevadas; thus he helped make possible the building of a transcontinental railroad.

One can trace the struggle of some immigrants as they advanced reluctantly along the road of the complete surrender of their religious identity. In the North it was not uncommon for the isolated settler to live with his housekeeper. On occasion, when she bore him children, he married her. Ultimately, he might join her church; but even when he did, he was still known as an Israelite—even on his tombstone. This was not a term of reproach by his neighbors; it was merely a form of identification. Down South he might have a Negro concubine and in his will set his mulatto or quadroon children free. There were times, too, after the isolated settler had achieved a competence, when he went to the big city and brought back a wife from one of the old-line families.

In spite of conversion and intermarriage, the majority of American Jewish settlers succeeded in overcoming the hazards of religious assimilation. They gradually sloughed many of their foreign characteristics and succeeded in fitting themselves into this new cultural world. Most of them assimilated, with relative rapidity, to the evolving, common American type, but retained their own religious customs and practices. In the correspondence even of good friends, both Jews, it is frequently impossible to find indications that the writers are of Jewish origin. The majority had succeeded in striking a very satisfactory balance between ritual observance and participation in the life of the larger community. They survived as Jews and became Americans, ceasing to be Germans, Spaniards, Poles, and Britons. Many of them, as they became increasingly Americanized, were not necessarily de-Judaized. Some played an active part in the life of the Jewish community. Practically all were at least emotionally attuned to their fellow-Jews, if not to Judaism the religion.

Jewish types ran the gamut all the way from the undeviating traditionalist, who reported his fellow-Jew whenever he caught him shaving on the Sabbath, to the wealthy merchant-shipper—we have David Franks in mind—whose children ate ham and went to church.

There were interesting variations even in the life of a single individual. David Salisbury Franks, a distant cousin of the above, was the president of the Montreal synagogue in the opening days of the Revolution, but after he became a patriot he seems to have cut himself off almost entirely from Jewish associations. Still another member of the same family, Isaac Franks, encouraged his children, in his will, to be good Christians. None of these three Frankses, as far as we know, ever withdrew from Judaism by accepting Christianity.

In spite of the almost overpowering assimilatory influences of the environment, of social acceptance on all levels, the Jew remained in the fold through the appeal and the discipline of the organized Jewish community. It is interesting to note his sensitivity with respect to the noun "Jew." He avoided it. As one who had in his own lifetime emerged from the ghetto, he was only too conscious of the fact that the word "Jew" was used by many people as a term of reproach. He preferred to be known as a Hebrew, as an Israelite. Sometimes he substituted the adjective "Mosaic" for "Jewish." At times he referred to himself as a "follower of Judaism."

Christian and secular concepts of reverence and of the amenities made their impact felt on the religious service. The church in the larger urban communities of America was for many of its devotees a house of awe; through the Host, the Deity was even physically or symbolically present. As the colonial Jew came more and more in contact with Christians, he took over their concepts of reverence and decorum and legislated to attain that end. (It was the beginning, in a modest way, of the "Protestantization" of American Judaism.) Even the Jews who had come in as immigrants and had grown up in a tradition of an exuberant and noisy religious service were among those who helped re-establish the Philadelphia synagogue, which was known for its decorum. The more closely the Jew came in touch with his Christian fellows, the more he became sensitive to the need for order. The demand for more reserve and tranquillity in the service is thus an expression of Americanization, although it is by no means characteristic of this country alone. Back in the Middle Ages, even in the Orient, the religious leaders sought for quiet and peace in their worship, and in this endeavor Sephardic London, also, significantly established standards for colonial Jews. The London *junto* declared that

> To those who are reading their prayers it shall not be permitted to raise their voices in . . . impeding others who are praying and giving ground to strangers [Gentiles] to be able to blame.
>
> No person may talk in the synagogue . . . nor likewise may they go out after the raising of the Law . . . it causes much scandal and disturbance. . . .

That the evolving synthesis of Americanism and Judaism was a development which met with Gentile social approval is documented by the fact that frequently the best known and most highly respected Jew in the general community was the man who was the leader of the Jewish *religious* community.

Jews here succeeded in making the transition from an orthodoxy nourished in a European world of lagging medievalism to an American orthodoxy that flourished in the soil of liberalism and freedom. Take the case of Michael Gratz. He had been born in the town of Langendorf, on the Polish-Silesian border. Surely as a child he wore the

earlocks and the traditional garb of an East European lad.
He wandered as far as India, but came, as a young man, to
these shores. Years later, Michael Gratz, the merchant-
shipper and land entrepreneur, but always an observant
Jew, was a well-dressed American in knee breeches and
buckles as he sat for his portrait with Thomas Sully. Or
consider the case of Moses Myers. By the late eighteenth
century many of the younger generation who still frequented the synagogue—on the holydays, at least—were
Americans of the third generation. Such a man was Myers,
a liberal donor to the Philadelphia synagogue building
fund, a major in the Virginia militia, and president of the
town council in post-Revolutionary Norfolk.

For Jews and Judaism, the transition from the old world
to the new world was not an easy one. The new environment stirred up many problems, though they are seldom
reflected in the sober and cautious statements of the men
who kept the congregational records. The transition had
been made through the hazardous but successful transporting of old-world institutions and spiritual values to this
new land. But it was to be expected—one might almost say
it was inevitable—that the Jew would change or modify
the old, that under the influence of the new America he
would modify his religious regimen in order the more
easily to make his adjustment to new scenes and to new
demands. Interestingly enough, as congregations, they did
not do so.

But as time passed, the Jew who was loyal to the old
traditions found himself nevertheless changing. There was
a cultural lag between his American political and spiritual

world and his age-old faith. An adjustment between the new and the old was called for. The congregational leaders were not conscious of this need, or else they chose to ignore it, to their own hurt. Some of the younger generation—how many we do not know—left Judaism, for they could not reconcile it with the American culture which was dominant in their spiritual economy. It was to be expected, logically and chronologically, that the land which was the first to emancipate its Jews politically would also be the first to witness their enlargement spiritually. But there was no attempt, as far as we know, in eighteenth-century America to cope with the conflicts of traditional observance and with the liberalistic demands of American thought and attitude. Was Carigal in his Newport sermon (1773) referring to American liberals when he attacked the critics who declared that Jewish precepts need not be observed if they can not meet the challenge of reason? The first rumbling protests against the old order were not voiced until the second decade of the nineteenth century. When changes in religious practices did come, they stemmed from Europe.

Yet, in some respects, American Jewry was to serve as an exemplar for Europe's Jews. The group on this side of the Atlantic demonstrated that a whole community could receive enfranchisement, could live in a monolithic political world of strong Christian overtones, could participate intimately in it, and yet remain Jewish in a traditional sense. Historically, this vanguard American community could offer the encouraging news to fearful, apprehensive lay and rabbinic leaders of Europe, many of whom denied the possibility of harmony between modernity and Judaism, that they, too, could survive as observant Jews in a new liberal world when the sun of emancipation rose to shine upon them.

Chapter 21

The Struggle
for Political Equality

AFTER the Declaration of Independence the original rebelling American colonies became states: Each adopted its own constitution or made arrangements to govern itself independently. Only one state, New York, in its original constitution, granted the Jews political equality. With that exception, therefore, the *status quo* was maintained, and Jews did not receive full political rights. Apparently, as far as political rights for Jews were concerned, the Revolution had little beneficial effect.

As far as we know, the colonial Jews did not come here with the express purpose of securing political rights. It is true that they came over to avoid annoying political disabilities and to worship freely, but they came primarily to make a decent living and, above all, to be left alone.

The man who landed here found little trouble in securing religious freedom. No colony drove him out because he was a Jew. Through the grant of the freedom of the city, through letters patent of denization, through acts of naturalization, or through administrative connivance or indifference—by virtue of all or of any one of these reasons, the Jew received the right to establish himself in those colonies which appealed to him. But what he wanted, had to have, were economic privileges: the right to buy land, exercise a craft, trade at retail and wholesale, and carry on business with the British colonies in other parts of the world. These economic rights were his no later than the year 1700. But political rights did not claim his overwhelming attention.

The home government in London attempted to deal with the political status of colonial Jews—among others—by passing the Naturalization Act of 1740, a law motivated primarily by the desire to advance the wealth and the strength of the colonies by encouraging immigration. The statute of 1740 gave Jewish aliens the right to be naturalized in the British-American colonies after seven years' residence there. None of those naturalized citizens, Christians or Jews, were, however, to hold an office or place of trust, civil or military, in England or abroad. But apparently the different colonies did not consider the Act of 1740 compulsory or automatic, and Aaron Lopez was refused naturalization in Rhode Island in 1761.

Less than two hundred Jews sought naturalization under that act; none, apparently, in the decade immediately before the Revolution. Possibly one of the reasons why so few took advantage of it was that the rights and privileges offered by it were already being exercised *de facto* by both Christian and Jewish immigrants. The immigrants settled where they wanted, did business, bought and sold land, and many managed very well without the benefits of naturalization. Many persons did not bother to go to court, pay their two shillings, and pocket their naturalization certificates. The records available—and they are not complete—indicate, however, that Jews were formally naturalized in the colonies of Massachusetts, New York, Pennsylvania, South Carolina, and, possibly, Maryland.

In 1773 another parliamentary statute gave naturalized immigrants the right to hold office in the colonies. It is difficult to determine from the wording whether the law contemplated the inclusion of Jews in its provisions. Most of the American provinces had established churches, either Congregational or Anglican. It is very much to be doubted that Jews would have been permitted to hold office in those colonies. Commonwealths with established churches expected their officials to be communicants of the established religion. That new statute was probably of no significance, as far as Jews were concerned. In general, it may be asserted that there was no advance beyond the provisions of 1740, no amelioration of political privileges, no right to office anywhere in the British colonies in the eighteenth century.

The privileges of the Jews were determined in practice, then, not by the imperial British government but by the individual colonies. What was their status in the different colonies prior to the Revolution?

As we have read, the Jews of New Amsterdam (1654–64) were rigidly delimited in their rights. The West India Company, in reality no more sympathetic than Stuyvesant, exercised common sense. It was quite conscious of the fact that a trading company engaged in peopling a wilderness could not afford the luxury of ethnic and religious prejudice. Motivated by purely mercenary considerations, it decided to allow the Jewish newcomers to remain.

About ten years after the first Jews landed in New Amsterdam, the English, we recall, took possession and named the city New York. In the course of the next generation the few Jewish settlers who remained or who came in received, or assumed, the privileges which were denied them by the Dutch. About the turn of the century, they began to exercise political rights by voting for candidates for the Assembly. On occasion, this right to vote was challenged. At no time were they permitted to hold honorary offices.

On the whole, conditions for New York Jewry throughout the eighteenth century were quite satisfactory, though they were now and then marred by untoward incidents. It is curious that those expressions of anti-Jewish prejudice found their record only in contemporary newspapers and other non-Jewish sources; the synagogal minutes ignore them. The instance of the governor's brother, Oliver De-Lancey, married to a Jewess, was a drunken escapade. DeLancey broke into the house of a Dutch Jewish immigrant and made insulting proposals to his wife. A more serious incident, for it bore all the marks of religious bigotry, was a brutal assault on a Jewish funeral cortege. The incident is described in the May 16, 1743, issue of Zenger's *New-York Weekly Journal*. The shocked witness, a Christian of some theological learning, said that the rabble interfered with the burial and "even insulted the dead in

517

such a vile manner that to mention all would shock a human ear." But those were isolated incidents covering almost a century. In general, there was very little anti-Jewish feeling that expressed itself in violence.

Like New York, Rhode Island had admitted Jews in the second half of the seventeenth century. But the reception accorded them there was much more cordial. Unlike Stuyvesant, Roger Williams and his friends vigorously affirmed the principle of religious freedom. But whether political freedom for Jews was also contemplated is difficult to determine. It is by no means improbable that the authors of the law of 1665 did not have Jews in mind when they enacted it, and would not have accorded them its political rights had they sought them under the terms of its provisions. Although Williams wrote of the right of Jews to religious freedom, nowhere did he declare, or even intimate, that they were entitled also to political equality. It is a fact, however, that the law of 1665 unequivocally offered political rights to all men of proper "civil conversation." It may be that their awareness of that statute induced Jews from Barbados to migrate to Rhode Island in the late 1670's. In Barbados bloody Negro revolts, the yellow fever and elephantiasis, hurricanes, the exorbitant cost of land, the high cost of a patent of endenization, without which no one could carry on commerce—all these factors doubtless played their part in encouraging Jews to emigrate and to go to Rhode Island. Jewish immigrants were encouraged to remain there and to do business. They remained, but not for long.

Sometime between 1705 and 1719 the law of 1665 was

altered or amended to exclude Jews and Catholics specifically from the rights of citizenship. Jews could neither hold office nor vote, and in that respect they were worse off in religiously free Rhode Island than in some other colonies where there was an established church. After 1719, Protestant Christianity was in fact, though not legally, the established religion of the colony of Rhode Island.

After the Revolution the Jewish community of Newport was reduced in size; some had died, and others never came back. A comparison of the census of 1782 with the tax lists for 1772 and 1775 shows that about two-thirds of the Jewish names had disappeared. There were not ten males over sixteen years of age in town. The Jewish community was moribund. There was no one to lead a fight for political liberties; Rhode Island Jewry was not to secure equal rights until 1842.

In the rest of New England, in New Hampshire, in Massachusetts, and in Connecticut, there were no synagogues, only scattered families. In those states where the Congregational church was established, other Protestants were taxed against their will to support religious institutions in which they were not interested, which were objectionable to them. Certainly no concessions would be made to Jews; they were not even Christians. The New Englander felt a great spiritual kinship with the ancient Hebrews, but very little with their latter-day descendants. Let it be clearly understood that interest in the Hebrew language did not imply affection for Jews. Even Ezra Stiles, who associated intimately with Jews over many years and counted Aaron Lopez as a good friend, metaphorically smacked his lips as he recorded that the Newport shipper had been refused naturalization. "Providence seems to make everything to work for mortification to the Jews and to prevent their incorporating into any nation, that thus they may continue a distinct people." Preserving a solid front against the Jews, and others too, the New England states gave Jews no full equality until the nineteenth century. Like the three New England states we have just described above (Massachusetts, New Hampshire, and Connecticut), New Jersey, Delaware, Maryland, and North Carolina were also without Jewish communities. And, like those New England states, Maryland and North Carolina both sheltered an established church, in these instances the Anglican, not the Congregational. There were very few Jews in New Jersey, still fewer, if any, in Delaware. Baltimore, in Maryland, had a handful; there were only a few scattered families in North Carolina. The paucity of Jews in North Carolina did not deter some of its citizens from the attempt to make sure that the number would remain small. Some of them protested against the federal constitution because it prescribed no Christian test. The Dissenting Protestants, who had just been freed from their disabilities, had no desire to grant rights to Jews either in North Carolina or in the American republic. Delaware removed all religious tests from its constitution in 1792; New Jersey and Maryland gave equality to their Jews in the first half of the next century; but it was over eighty years after the federal constitution was written before North Carolina made it legal for Jews to accept office (1868).

The Struggle for Political Equality

In addition to Rhode Island and New York, Pennsylvania, Virginia, South Carolina, and Georgia could each point to a Jewish community in its midst.

Pennsylvania and Rhode Island had this in common: Both had no official religious establishment, yet in both, Protestantism had been, at least *de facto*, the recognized church and religion ever since the early eighteenth century. Political rights were reserved for Protestants only. When the Pennsylvania state constitution of 1776 was being written, Lutheran and other religious leaders were concerned lest the Jews and other infidel and heterodox groups be placed on the same footing as orthodox Christians. While General John Peter Gabriel Muhlenberg was fighting to secure freedom for this land, his distinguished father, Pastor Henry Melchior Mühlenberg, and other Christian leaders fought with equal vigor and success to keep Jews from enjoying the fruits of that freedom. The Pennsylvania constitution of 1776 allowed office only to those who believed in the divine inspiration of the New Testament. The pastor of the Philadelphia German Reformed Church, who had been imprisoned by the British for his American sympathies during the war, permitted his congregation, even before the war was over, to protest against the close presence of a proposed Jewish house of worship. Bigotry did not die easily.

Virginia, South Carolina, and Georgia denied political liberty to the Jews not only before the Revolution but even for a decade or two after the start of the war. There were so few Jews in colonial Virginia that they were completely ignored, but the Protestant Dissenters there were

521

not so fortunate. Many of them were vigorously fought and even mistreated by the authorities, who sought to suppress them and to assert the supremacy of the established Anglican church.

Whether they had the right or not, Jews were reported to be voting in South Carolina in the first decade of the eighteenth century. After 1716 only Christians were permitted to hold office. The people, anti-Catholic and pro-Protestant in their sentiments, attempted to reserve all political rights to Protestants only, but the English authorities at home vetoed such legislation. The government in England was more liberal—with respect to the colonists— than the settlers themselves. It is a fact that a Jew, Francis Salvador, served in a provincial legislature, but he had, no doubt, been appointed to office extra-legally by a Whig group. His appointment was no indication of a growing liberal sentiment on the part of the people of South Carolina.

During the early days of the settlement in Georgia the Jewish pioneers were permitted, as in the colony to the north, to participate in political life. We may assume that the Jews who arrived in Savannah a few months after Oglethorpe were permitted to exercise the franchise in the first decade or two of the colony's existence. But here, as in South Carolina, when the territory became more secure, it was less eager to invite new settlers and more ready to support the newly established Church. Then it attempted to limit the rights of infidels. No Jews could hope for appointment or election to office. They may have, however, retained the right to vote.

The Struggle for Political Equality

Apparently, antiquity in settlement, or even priority, provided no immunity against attack. Georgia Jews met opposition from the very first day. Even before the first ships sailed for that colony some of its trustees had objected to the inclusion of Jews among the prospective settlers. Jews, they believed, would only hurt the young colony and damage its reputation. They would impede its growth. Years later (1774) one sardonic writer put Jews in the same class as Indians, socially; another wanted to deny them all civil and political liberties (1784). During the war the Tory governor, James Wright, denounced Georgia's Jews as Whigs, disloyal to the mother country. At the same time a South Carolinian attacked the very same men as Tories and slackers.

In these brief references to anti-Jewish prejudice in the American colonies, it is fairly obvious what happened. In the early days, as the colonies struggled desperately merely to survive, prejudices were played down, either by the settlers themselves, or by those in authority. Every man was needed. The settlers huddled together for comfort and protection. The colonies granted Jews some rights by default, or the Jews, conscious of their equal sacrifices and efforts, assumed certain political prerogatives, particularly the franchise. But as security developed, as the frontier was pushed back, inherent, historical, traditional prejudices reasserted themselves and found expression in a tightening up, or even in a revocation, of political rights tacitly assumed in an earlier period. After the wilderness was somewhat subdued, "home" was transferred to these shores.

But let it at once be interjected here: prejudice was not

directed solely against Jews. It was as sharply directed against the Christian Dissenters: the Baptists, the Presbyterians, the Methodists, the Quakers, and, of course, the Catholics. By the time the Revolution broke out only three colonies gave Protestant Dissenters equality with all others: Rhode Island, Pennsylvania, and Delaware. No colony gave Jews and Catholics political equality with others. Jews and Catholics were really not much worse off than the Protestant Dissenters. The latter had no political equality in ten colonies; Catholics and Jews, none in thirteen. It was a matter of degree.

Let us now return once more to the subject of anti-Jewish prejudice. (We have deliberately avoided the use of the term anti-Semitism. That word should be reserved for the late nineteenth century philosophy which advocated the disabling or annihilation of Jews on racist grounds.) It would not be difficult to assemble a collection of anti-Jewish statements, actions, and incidents from the earliest colonial times down through the Revolution. It is not surprising that these exist. The settlers, coming from Christian lands, did not wipe their minds clean when they first set foot on American soil. They brought their prejudices along with their intellectual baggage; stereotypes weighed them down. Concepts that had been growing and developing for centuries, almost for millennia, on Europe's and Asia's soil, cropped out here, too. Old literary traditions in which the Jew played the part of a villain were transferred and nurtured here. English folk ballads of the alleged ritual murder of Christians by Jews could be heard in this land also. If, in the year 1752, a young Virginian had never seen a Jew in the flesh, he would know how to recognize one if he ever met one, for had he not been to the theater in Williamsburg and watched Mr. Malone perform the part of Shylock the Jew "before a numerous and polite audience with great applause"? Jews were rich, and by inference dishonest. Arthur Lee, who could not suppress his surprise that a Jew should have fair coloring and blue eyes, said that Robert Morris had taken advantage of his position to become as rich as a Jew. In the very month when Director-General Peter Stuyvesant could have looked out of his window and watched the auction of the household goods of Jewish refugees who had risked everything they owned, even their lives, in defense of Dutch interests in Brazil, he declared that Jews as a class were usurers. Many a good Christian, from the Mathers on down, resented the fact that Jews blindly refused to accept Christianity as the only true faith. A pious Christian missionary, after he had been aided by a Jew who was meticulous in observing the Sabbath, made a self-righteous reference in his journal to Pharisaic hypocrisy. The Jew was the coward who ran away from danger; the Jew was the merchant who set out to exploit Christian craftsmen. All these are notes taken from a colonial scrapbook.

About four years after the first Jewish community was established in New Amsterdam, a Dutch settler, Vervelen, made the following remark to one of his Jewish neighbors: "You are a Jew. You are all cheats together." This statement is interesting but not historically important. What is significant and symptomatic of the future is the fact that, thereafter, Vervelen denied making the statement.

It is not too difficult to assemble a body of anti-Jewish remarks. But it is easier to assemble a larger corpus of pro-Jewish acts of personal friendship between Jews and Gentiles.

Occasionally one can find an imported medievalism in legislation—which was only on the books and never implemented—such as the Virginia statute that Christian servants were not to be employed by Jews. In reality, there was probably not a single law in the land, in the eighteenth century, that had been enacted for the purpose of imposing a disability on Jews alone. (The Pennsylvania and Delaware constitutions, which required officeholders to affirm belief in the divine inspiration of the New Testament, were not directed solely against Jews; they were aimed also at deists and atheists.)

No Jews in the colony ever had to defend their existence as Jews; they were never beaten because of their religion, like the Quakers or the Baptists. In many places they were more acceptable socially than Catholics—and they knew it. They were quite content with the economic rights accorded them; they owned homes, farms, and slaves. Civil liberties were always accorded them; occasionally they were granted some political rights. Many of them were respected members of a common colonial society. They enjoyed social status among their Christian peers. There was no ghetto or ghetto spirit in the land. If the times are taken into consideration, their economic, social, religious, civil, and political status was good, excelled by conditions in no land of Europe. They could not have been unaware that, aside from certain creature comforts and Jewish religious associations, they were better off here than anywhere else in the world.

Before the Revolutionary generation, before the non-importation days of the 1760's, the American Jew was passive politically. He was, of course, conscious of the fact that there was considerable room for improvement in his political status, but he did nothing about it. It may be that he was content with the measure of economic and civil rights which he possessed and was willing to bide his time. But his desire for more political freedom for himself flared up in the decade before the outbreak of war. Strange as it may appear, the very fact that he had so many rights and privileges made a Whig of him. Had he lived in Europe, he would have been very content to receive the rights enjoyed by American Jews. Not so here; liberty feeds on itself. He was not satisfied with a partial liberty; he wanted it whole.

Moreover, it was no deep wrench for the Jews, native or immigrant, to align themselves in opposition to Great Britain. Few of them were British-born; they had no deep roots in England. Many of them were of German and Spanish-Portuguese stock. By the time the year 1775 rolled around, and people were beginning to declare themselves, they knew where they stood. Certainly the Sheftalls and Minises in Georgia, and others like them, were conscious of the fact that their fathers had been here since the earliest days, that they had built this country, had helped lay its very foundations. They had no sense of inferiority as aliens or immigrants. They knew what was their due; they wanted equality.

The Jewish Americans must have been thrilled when they read the Declaration of Independence. They had more to gain than the average Gentile American who already possessed all rights, or at least was potentially entitled to them if he only paid the requisite taxes. For the first time since their settlement in the colonies, Jews envisaged the hope of full liberty. By implication, at least, the country had committed itself to political and religious equality—for all whites. Before this time there had been little intimation of this here. The Revolution was to become a sharp dividing line in the history of the American Jew. Old-world prejudicial legislation would have to go. The idea of liberty was to be stronger than prejudice itself.

Even as, on the one hand, there were church forces which feared the new liberalism of 1775, and rallied to defend the old concept that only a trinitarian could become a good citizen, so, on the other, there were Christians who encouraged the emancipation, the enfranchisement of the Jew. Those liberals, if they may be so called, had a tradition that went back over 150 years to the days of James I. As early as 1614, the Baptist Leonard Busher argued for the readmission of the Jews to England, from which they had been excluded since 1290. He pleaded for religious liberty for the Jews, pointing out, incidentally, that such an act of historic justice might aid their conversion to Christianity. When Roger Williams preached his doctrine of complete religious freedom, he, too, may have been moved by a similar desire of winning the Jews to his faith. But it is only fair to him to add that nowhere does he predicate his promise of religious freedom on the hope of conversion. The tolerant Lockean constitutions for the Carolinas—whether they are all of Lockean origin or not— are definitely evangelical in motivation, and by the time the Declaration of Independence was published many Christians favored enfranchisement for the Jew, not only because of its intrinsic justice, but also because it offered the hope of finally Christianizing the Jews. Freedom for the Jew is the surest evidence of Christian charity. Probably the following statement, which appeared in *The South-Carolina Gazette and General Advertiser* of August 30, 1783, was motivated by conversionist expectations. It certainly reflects the spirit of true Christian love for the Jew:

He who hates another man for not being a Christian is himself not a Christian. Christianity breathes love, peace, and good-will to men. The Jews have had a considerable share in our late Revolution. They have behaved well throughout. Let our government invite the Jews to our state and promise them a settlement in it. It will be a wise and politic stroke and give a place of rest at last to the tribe of Israel.

The Jews must have been further encouraged by the turn of events even before the signing of the Declaration of Independence. As early as May, 1776, Virginia, in the Bill of Rights of its new constitution, had declared, by implication at least, that religious differences were not to disqualify any man for political equality. That principle was not fortified at once by any supporting legislation, but it was a beginning. A year later, the state of New York made it possible in its constitution for a Jew—though not for the pious Catholic—to become a full citizen. That was the first act of its type in North America. In the sense that Jews were granted the same rights as non-Jews, it is the first emancipatory law in modern history, the most significant legislative deed since the Roman enfranchisement act sponsored by Caracalla (the *Constitutio Antoniniana*) in the year 212. That the New York constitution makers of 1777 had the Jews in mind is documented in the records of the constitutional convention: The Jews as such were to be enfranchised.

And because of these provisions, made with Jews in mind, the American concepts of toleration and of liberty were perforce expanded to include all religious groups. As early as 1655, Stuyvesant had irately written to the West India Company regarding Jews: "Giving them liberty we cannot refuse the Lutherans and Papists." The logical and humanitarian compulsion to emancipate the Jew broadened the spiritual horizon of the people of the new state of New York and established a precedent for other states, even for the national government, to grant greater rights to Jews, Catholics, Negroes, and others. Because of the need to provide for the Jew, the larger America was to become more liberal, more true to its own profession of political principle. The mere passive existence of the New York Jewish citizen, his hope that justice would be done him— and it was done him—helped teach the entire country that a man's religion must be no bar to citizenship. Eventually every advance toward freedom made by the Jew was a victory for American political democracy.

Although there were Tories among the Jews at the time of the Revolution, the communities as a whole were

Whig. The one exception was Montreal. Canada was overwhelmingly loyalist, and its Jews also sided with the pro-English element. But here, too, there were a number of outstanding Whig patriots. Among them was David Salisbury Franks, who was to achieve some recognition, and notoriety, as a staff officer during the war and as a consular agent in Europe in the postwar period. In some states, as in Georgia, where many of the settlers refused to ally themselves with the Continentals, the Jewish majority persisted in their Whig sympathies.

American Jewry was later conscious of the fact that it had been overwhelmingly patriotic at a time when many others were neutral, and when only a minority of Americans had openly proclaimed their belief in the justice of the Continental cause. Proud of their record, the New York Jews, for instance, did not hesitate to write Governor George Clinton: "We flatter ourselves that none has manifested a more zealous attachment to the sacred cause of America in the late war with Great Britain."

The Jewish communities as a whole were Continental; random individuals here and there stood out as vigorous patriots. To men like Colonel Solomon Bush and Colonel Mordecai Sheftall the Revolution was more than a political incident; it was an act of faith. In a modest way such soldiers manifested qualities of leadership. Other Jews who rendered little military service—although almost everyone had a short tour of compulsory duty in the militia—were helpful as merchants, supplying the army and the civilian population. Often among the leading businessmen of their towns and villages they were very active in keeping open

the arteries of trade and supply. It is difficult to over-
estimate the strategic importance of the merchant. In an
agrarian land starved for consumers' goods, and at war
with a powerful empire that had at its disposal an ample
supply of manufactures and wares, the contribution of the
enterprising merchant to victory must not be minimized.

As we have said, in the early days of the Revolution
(1776) Protestant Dissenters in a number of southern
states achieved either tolerance or actual equality; yet some
of them set out to withhold that very equality from Catholics and Jews. South Carolina, North Carolina, and
Georgia, in their early constitutions, succeeded in making
Protestantism the only legally recognized church in their
states. Many Virginians engaged in a vigorous campaign to
establish Christianity as the state religion. It was fortunate
in Virginia that a number of the larger Dissenter groups,
particularly Baptists and Presbyterians, threw their weight
behind the liberal forces in the struggle to prohibit all
religious establishment. They knew that an established
church, no matter how broad and inclusive, made for intolerance, fighting, and quarreling between churches and,
ultimately, for the persecution of Christian by Christian.
It was the courage and the vision of the Dissenters that
prevented the establishment of Christianity in Virginia in
1784, and it was largely due to their support of Madison,
Jefferson, and Mason that the Bill to Establish Religious
Freedom, for all, was passed in 1786. Thus there were two
states out of the thirteen that had already enfranchised
their Jews when the federal constitutional convention met
to begin its deliberations in 1787.

The franchise, we will recall, was dependent on the individual state as well as on the federal government. While the constitutional convention was deliberating, some Jews nursed the hope that the federal government would assume the authority to regulate civil and political liberties in the individual states. The convention had adopted Article VI, which provided that no religious test should ever be required as a qualification to any office or public trust under the United States. Some weeks later, in September, 1787, the Philadelphian, Jonas Phillips, petitioned the convention to alter the Pennsylvania test oath, this for the sake of the Jewish citizens who "have been true and faithful Whigs . . . and have bravely fought and bled for liberty which they cannot enjoy." Why did Phillips petition? It may be that he did not know of the inclusion of Article VI in the proposed new constitution—the deliberations were held in secret. Or, if he knew, he took it for granted that under its terms the government had the power to alter and change all discriminatory test oaths and disabilities of a religious nature found in state constitutions, and the purpose of his petition was to invite attention to the discrimination still in force in his state, and thereby to end it. Phillips was a "federalist" with a vengeance—in that respect at least. He, and other Jews, too, were probably very impatient at the slow progress being made to liberalize the state constitutions.

When, finally, the federal constitution was ratified by a majority of the states, a huge federal parade was held in Philadelphia on July 4, 1788. The Jews were elated. The younger fry who were present must have been torn be-

tween floats depicting "Independence" and "Union" and
the kosher snack-bar at Bush Mill where there was an ample supply of salmon, bread, crackers, almonds, and raisins.
The older folks were happy that a federal government had
been created which gave them the franchise in all national
elections and equality in the realm of appointments. Possibly some of them, the more astute among them, may have
been aware that they paid no religious price for the rights
they received; they made no sacrifices, no implied promise
of surrender of practice or of principle, to gain the ballot
or the privilege of office. No American-Christian religio-
nationalistic sentiment had developed which by its very
nature would vent itself against the Jew because he was
"different." Because there was no dominant culture here,
no pressure and no compulsion could be exerted to force
the Jew to harmonize his faith and practices with it.

The satisfaction of that generation with the turn of
events was dramatically documented by a strange sight.
Surely, nothing like it had ever been seen before in any
community in Christendom: the rabbi of the congregation
marching in the parade arm in arm with two Christian
clergymen! There could be no question—the millennium
was just around the corner.

But if it was, something delayed it. During the year 1788
there were no changes in any of the state constitutions
that might have removed existing religious and political
disabilities affecting the Jew. While the first amendment
to the federal constitution was being considered in Congress in 1789, James Madison introduced another in the
House of Representatives, that no state be permitted to

violate the rights of conscience. (Jonas Phillips knew what he wanted!) The amendment passed the House, but failed in the Senate, probably because of the fear that the federal government was assuming too much authority. Had the action of the lower house been approved by the Senate, Jews and Catholics, agnostics, deists, and atheists would have received equal consideration under the law in all states, a hope that has not yet been realized in this land.

The proposal of the first amendment by Congress in 1789 was, very probably, an important factor in influencing some states to modify their constitutions with respect to test oaths and other religious requirements. Early that year, Georgia had already given its Jews all political privileges. The very next year, in 1790, Pennsylvania and South Carolina emancipated their Jews from all disabilities. Wherever there was an active Jewish community, the Jews had by that year succeeded in securing the constitutional changes needed to insure them full freedom.

Through the adoption of Article VI and of the first amendment as finally framed, the United States expressed its determination to maintain the separation of church and state, in its national government at least. Like some liberal leaders in the state constituent assemblies, the makers of the national constitution realized that the rivalries of the various Christian church bodies made such separation imperative. It was the necessity for religious peace, as well as the positive appreciation of tolerance and liberty, that moved them to make that decision.

It is well within the realm of probability that if the Jews had been the sole minority religious group, they would not have received complete equality in the federal constitution and in some of the state constitutions. The Jews rode to equality on the coattails of the Dissenters.

In 1790 the Jewish communities wrote Washington, congratulating him on his inauguration as President, and seized the opportunity to emphasize the importance of religious liberty in the United States. Washington was well aware of the uniqueness of this country as a pioneer in the field of political and religious freedom: "The citizens of the United States of America," he wrote to the Hebrew Congregation in Newport, "have a right to applaud themselves for having given to mankind examples of an enlarged and liberal policy, a policy worthy of imitation. All possess alike liberty of conscience and immunities of citizenship."

The Catholics and Protestant Dissenters were also among the churches that wrote to the President. In the back of the minds of those three religious groups—all of whom were still laboring under constitutional disabilities in several states—was no doubt the hope that the liberties proclaimed by the national government would some day find a responsive echo in the constitutions of all the American states. When Moses Seixas of Newport wrote to George Washington, he referred to the national government as one "which to bigotry gives no sanction, to persecution no assistance, but generously affording to all liberty of conscience and immunities of citizenship, deeming every one, of whatever nation, tongue, or language, equal parts of the great governmental machine." Was there in this description of the nature of the new federal union a wistful hope that his own lagging state of Rhode Island

536

might one day pattern itself after the example of the national government? Even in 1790, there was still room in this land for the extension of political and religious liberties.

In 1792 Delaware removed those religious tests which affected Jews; of the remaining eight states which still retained discriminatory clauses, seven modified their constitutions in the course of the nineteenth century. One, New Hampshire, still holds fast to phrases which, by implication, limit the rights of its Jewish citizens.

Chapter 22

Retrospect

THE "typical" American Jew of the seventeenth and eighteenth centuries can be described in a sentence. He was a courageous enterpriser. This is the whole story. All the rest is commentary.

Courage—or was it only desperation?—was essential in the make-up of a man who dared to come to these shores in the seventeenth and eighteenth centuries. More so probably than his Christian neighbor, the Jew was compelled to become self-reliant. There were few people to whom he could turn. In his first ten years in New Amsterdam, for instance, he had to fight every inch of the way. The alternatives were either constant struggle or return to Europe. Stubbornly he persisted, and won out.

At some point in his early career, in the latter part of the seventeenth century, the Jewish immigrant decided to make a home for himself in America.

The immigrant was almost invariably a businessman of modest means. He was enterprising, speculative, and daring in spirit, persistent in his economic ambitions, determined to get ahead, unafraid even of the challenge of huge and grandiose plans. Whether he trained his sights on the sea, the town, or the forest, he was willing to venture. If, from the bastion of his countinghouse in town, he turned toward the sea, his speculative spirit made him a merchant-shipper willing to hazard his fortune and the fortunes of others in the attempt to win the grand prize. His addiction to lotteries, the hope for great gain, was typical. As a merchant he might go down, but he was determined to rise again. He was nearly always willing to take a chance, though his speculative courage was tempered with responsibility, reflection, and careful planning. He was not a reckless speculator. Yet, if he did not throw caution to the winds, he was at least possessed of a profound optimism, or of an imperturbable fatalism, which permitted him with equanimity to send his vessels to distant ports and to new and untried clients. As a slave entrepreneur he gambled on the hazards of the voyage, the African supply, losses by death in the "middle passage," and the fluctuating West India markets. As a whaler he risked his fortune in a voyage to the southern seas and to distant lands thousands of miles away. Any investment that promised a huge return interested him; that is why he was happy to take a share in a privateer or, when the ship was his, to invite his friends to share the gains—and the losses—with him.

For the merchant-shipper, new times—the rise of the American Republic—brought death to old-style ventures and invitation to new. But the "type" remained: an aggressive eagerness for new opportunities. After the Revolution, the Newport beginner who had once shipped mahogany from Honduras Bay or had sought a consignment from a larger jobber might well go to Boston and become a pioneer in the insurance and banking business. His counterpart in New York might outfit a boat for India or China.

A merchant might have begun his career in this country as a sutler. He traveled with the troops, he ate and lived with them, and at times fought shoulder to shoulder with them against the common enemy. A man who consorted with colonial troops and mercenaries could be no namby-pamby. The barracks, the bivouac, the colonial outposts, and the forest encampment demanded a courageous and tough person, and if he became hard, he had little choice. He might be shrewd, but he was not courtly. He was a rough-and-ready individualist out to do well for himself.

The sutler or merchant who became a western fur trader was merely switching from one hazard to another. He would try his hand at anything, as long as there was a reasonable chance to make money. But that chance had to be there. Not infrequently, the determined entrepreneur accompanied his pack train to the frontier himself. From districts which he was never to see, which would not begin to shelter white settlers for another hundred years, he reached out for furs. He was willing to risk almost anything, not only because he saw a prospect of gain, but because he saw his competitor make the attempt. What they could do, he could do. Competition did not frighten him. In the European school of business where he had matriculated at twelve or thirteen with a small pack on his back, he had known real competition—and with picayune profits. Here in America was a chance to really do things. So he sent his packhorse convoys into the trans-Allegheny country, into Kentucky, before that name appeared on an American map. He was alert to opportunity. Aggressive, forward-looking Jewish firms twice gave credit to the Indian agent George Croghan when he needed goods immediately to pacify sullen and resentful Indians. It was good business to keep the Indians quiet—and at the same time to sell some goods. Croghan was a decent person; we'll get our money. And the same spirit of "take a chance" prompted another firm (Gratz and Gibson) to outfit George Rogers Clark on an expedition against threatening Indians or a distant British post. Keep the goods moving. You'll come out all right. Help your friends; they'll help you sometime.

The bigness of America did something to the Jew. It enlarged his vision; his hopes were not limited even by the edge of the horizon. In his mind's eye he dreamt of thousands of settlers streaming across the Alleghenies to the Forks of the Ohio, going down the river to its mouth, turning up at the tributaries on their way down to settle and to build. Here was real opportunity on a grand and gigantic scale. For a whole long generation the Jewish merchants of Philadelphia and of Lancaster planned great colonial settlements in the new American West. They struggled, schemed, and poured their money and effort and hearts' blood into the hope of western empire. They contemplated settlements of millions of acres. It is immaterial that they failed; important is the vision of the Polish and German Jewish peddlers and clerks who, under the spell of the unending forest and its broad streams, matured into responsible merchants dreaming dreams of colonial greatness.

Is this early American businessman, who essayed anything and who tackled everything that offered a chance at speedy gain, typical only of the Jews? He was not. The Jewish urban businessman who tried his hand at any and all commercial ventures had his counterpart, maybe even his prototype, in his Gentile neighbor. The characteristics which the Jewish entrepreneur displayed were typical of the America of that day. The American merchant, shipper, whaler, and slaver was aggressive, courageous, and speculative. But is it not possible that the Jew, the European immigrant, more eager to get ahead because he had been so often left behind, was more daring, more venturesome? It is possible, but we have no way of knowing. Every act of boldness in business, of courage in enterprise, can be matched by equally numerous examples among Gentile fellow-merchants. This we know: men with the over-reaching and vaulting ambition and capacity of a Robert Morris are not documented in colonial Jewish history. Had he lived, Haym Salomon might have made a name for himself as one of the great merchants of the postwar New York to which he was moving, but he died in his middle forties, in Philadelphia, before he had a chance to test his mercantile mettle.

The Jewish settler was nearly always a refugee, if not physically, at least spiritually. In the seventeenth century he fled from Portuguese-controlled Brazil with its constant threat of Inquisitional spying and even death. In the next century many of those who came were not driven out

542

from their native lands by violence, but they were still exiles. Immutable Canon Law, the unyielding, mean, petty, craft- and merchant-guild spirit, harsh anti-Jewish legislation, the crushing inertia of the unprogressive feudalistic domination in town, hamlet, and countryside, the throttling power of Europe's age-old authoritarianism—all these and more made an exile of the European Jew. He was hopeful of a larger opportunity here. The very American soil made him free; there is no trace of Oriental and European servility in him. In relation to the political authorities of the day he may have been courteous; he was never obsequious. This was a new world, and he sensed it. The very first batch of newcomers in 1654 met the onslaughts of Stuyvesant with coolness, dignity, and courage. Maybe that was their urbane Spanish and Portuguese training; maybe it was a new American spirit of spiritual independence which they had acquired in the freer atmosphere of Dutch Brazil; maybe they were cognizant that Stuyvesant and the West India Company needed them as much as they needed a home. Whatever it was, they parried blow with blow, thrust home when they could, and compelled the Dutch to give way, to make room for them.

The seventeenth-century immigrant Jew fought to secure what rights he could, but he was wise enough to realize that there were political barriers which could not be surmounted in a hurry. In the next century, the very immigrant who optimistically bought himself a wet slice of the Dismal Swamp or who recklessly hazarded his hard-won dollars on a transmontane colony was, in matters of politics, a cold, calculating realist. Fourteen hundred years of intimate association with the Christian State had taught him to be grimly wary in matters of political and civil liberty.

That political realist believed—and he was right—that he had squeezed what rights he could out of England and the semi-autonomous colonies. His notable political passivity prior to 1775 was not motivated by cowardice, but by two positive considerations. The one was that he could always live without the vote or office as long as he was allowed to do business. The second consideration was the sober reflection that the times were not ripe for further concessions. The colonists, as they grew in strength, had no desire to share their rights with others—unless they had to. Thus it was that the Jew who weighed his chances made no move as an individual or through his community to secure more rights and liberties. But when the opportunity came, he reached out for it. He threw in his lot with the minority of active rebels on the chance that victory would make him a free man. Maybe he saw more clearly than his Gentile fellow-Whigs what was at stake. Many of them saw in the Revolution no radical political eruption, but merely an emancipatory act which permitted the Americans to remain what they were, but without British control. The Jew sensed, to the dismay of his more conservative fellow-patriots, that this was a political *revolution*. He sensed it and he took advantage of it.

It is not improbable that the Jew was more sensitive to the real impending changes in America because he had been the classical victim of Europe. The realist who had tacitly stood by for generations now snatched vigorously at new opportunity. A case in point was Joseph Salvador. Here was a man who had been one of the great bankers of the British Empire. A Dutch Jew originally, he had become a power in the English financial world. A contemporary tradition relates that at the time of the rebellion of Bonnie Prince Charlie in 1745–46, he raised a million pounds sterling on two hours' notice to help the state at a critical moment. Such a man certainly had the right to expect gratitude from the land in which he lived. He was one of the chief sponsors of the "Jew Bill" of 1753 which was to offer naturalization—in limited form—to foreign-born Jews living in England. It was his hope that naturalized Jews in England would at least have as many privileges as their clerks and agents who had received naturalization in the American plantations. They, the patrons, were inferior in political status to their own employees! Yet the anti-Jewish sentiment aroused by that bill was so inflammatory that Salvador was hooted out of a British theatre. The bill to naturalize Jews in England was passed, but only to be repealed the same year. Though he became a Fellow of the Royal Society, a governor of several hospitals, and the first Jewish member of the board of directors of the East India Company, Joseph Salvador was never permitted to become a citizen in England itself. Over a generation later, after he had lost his fortune, this man of almost seventy came to these shores, where his nephew Francis had died in defense of American liberties. At the earliest possible moment he forswore allegiance to England and became an American citizen.

Joseph Salvador, though born in Holland, was symbolic

of the new type of Jew who desired complete equality and had no fears of its effects on Jewish religious loyalties. A decade after his death, the Amsterdam Jewish leaders, when offered emancipation through the French Revolution, refused to accept the bid if it meant the loss of Jewish communal autonomy. They refused to surrender their "minority rights." They were afraid to exchange their chartered privileges for a unitary type of common citizenship.

The American Jew never had any "autonomy" here. In spite of the fact that he had come from a Europe where the legally recognized Jewish religious community was distinguished by its cultural apartness, there is no evidence that he wanted to transfer that kind of institution to these shores. America was no place for any type of ghetto or segregation. This land was different; here he would not lose his Jewishness even when he assimilated himself, likened himself, to the large body of American citizenry. His own experience convinced him of that.

Enfranchisement was a logical continuation of a process that had been going on for over a century. The American Jew had already become so intimately integrated into American life that complete acceptance by his Gentile fellows was most desirable, rejection of full political rights and responsibilities was unthinkable. It is doubtful that an American Jew ever thought that emancipation was a hazard to his religion. But if it did occur to him, there was no question what his answer would have been. Believing that emancipation was precious, this transmuted European Jew, this new American, was willing to risk the hazards of freedom and assimilation. He was optimistic enough to believe that he could work out a satisfactory synthesis of Americanism and Judaism, one that would do justice to both.

One is almost tempted to say that the Jew of the Revolution and of the post-Revolutionary generation was a changed man. The common political and military struggle after 1775, the common suffering, unleashed something in his psyche. Before the war his prime interest was his livelihood. To be sure, the economic avenue was the only road then open to him. Another, the political, was closed to him because of his religion. He preferred obscurity; he had little to say. But with the Revolution the wellsprings of hope within him gushed forth and with it the desire, the intention, to fight for personal and communal recognition, for freedom and for equality. This man was different, or reborn; he was insistent on his rights, proud, firm in his resolution to receive his political due. He was a new man.

In 1776, then, the colonial Jew stepped from out the circle and shadow of second-class citizenship into the new world of modernism and freedom. He was already different from his own fellow-Jews in Europe. He was different from what he himself would have been had he remained in Austria or Germany or Poland. Had he remained in the areas of dense Jewish settlement, he would have been in large part a medieval man, in outer status at least.

Here he was no outsider, certainly not in his own estimation, and that estimate of his sense of "belonging" was accepted by the majority of the people about him. Ever since his earliest days in the colonies he had conceived of himself as a natural and necessary part of the larger general community. Here, in those cities where he built his Jewish communities, he was certain that he had found his niche in society, that he was making a place for himself, and that he was receiving some recognition, modest though it was. He, the immigrant of only a few years, was exhibiting a rather unusual capacity to fit into the new scenes about him and to adapt himself to the time and to the place. This integration was not only economic, but also spiritual.

The American Jew of the second half of the eighteenth century was fast becoming a distinct type. He was changing. Back home, across the seas, if he himself would study no Talmud in a leisure hour, he would have doffed his hat, mentally, to the man who did. Back home he faced the past; his hope for the future was a Messianic redemption in the Promised Land. But here, on these shores, even as he said his prayers for Restoration, he knew that this was his Promised Land. The Jew of this country was secure in his belief that his present and his future lay here.

This American was in the process of "becoming." Moving steadily out of his colonial status as a second-class citizen, he was becoming the political, economic, and cultural peer of his fellowmen. In many communities he had long been accepted as a social equal. There was an alchemy at work effecting the change, and we know of some of the elements that made for it. One was the distance from Europe with its bad traditions; another was America itself with its few traditions; a third was the fact of economic opportunity and the need for willing hands. There was a magic chemistry at work that took Haym Salomon, a

Pole, Jonas Phillips, a German, Aaron Lopez, a Portuguese, Judah Hays, a Dutchman, and Mordecai M. Mordecai, a Lithuanian, threw all of them into the colonial melting pot, and brought forth something new. They might not have recognized it, but they had changed. They had become Americans.

When, in 1790, President George Washington sat down to read the letters addressed to him by the "Hebrew Congregations," what, at that time, was an American Hebrew, an American Jew? One thing is certain: he was not a British Jew even though both spoke English. English Jews were ritually Ashkenazic or Sephardic. Ethnic, cultural, and social divisions and institutions were sharply maintained in London. The two groups lived in two disparate worlds. In 1772 the *mahamad* of the Sephardic Bevis Marks synagogue refused to allow Asser del Banco to marry a *Tudesca*, a German Jewess. It was almost as bad as marriage to a Gentile! (Be assured that some of the English Sephardim of that day thought it worse!)

The American Jew had no such ethnic prejudice against his fellow-Jews. Naturally, he cherished and enjoyed his social prejudice against newcomers, but that, of course, disappeared when they started to get ahead.

In matters of ritual, all Jews in this land followed what had become the American rite. Actually, it was the standard Sephardic Spanish-Portuguese liturgy accepted by all Jews on this continent even though most of them were Germanic by birth and training. Religiously the American Jew was completely oriented to Europe with its century-old traditions. Was he then, this new Jew, a European with American manners and mannerisms? No, he was much more than that; he was a man who had established a balance between his European religio-cultural folkways and the emancipatory spirit of America. In his case adjustment was not self-effacement; adaptation through assimilation was to prove itself a successful technique for survival as a Jew.

But let us note other details about him. Though an immigrant, or the son of an immigrant hailing from Central or Eastern Europe, he employed English as his vernacular. He sported no earlocks, wore no Jewish garb; he was no ghetto man. His dress and appearance were typically English, his house and its appointments, like those of others. There were no mass settlements; there was, frequently, a Jewish neighborhood, dictated by the need of ready access to a kosher butcher shop, a ritual bathhouse, a school, and the synagogue.

What sort of *Jew* was this American? On the whole, he was a "good" Jew; that is, he was observant. Survival, religiously, meant everything to him. Let there be no doubt whatever on that score. And if anyone had told him that the Jew could not survive in this land of freedom, he would have pointed to the minister of Shearith Israel, Gershom M. Seixas, who was a third-generation American on his mother's side. It was essential to the well-being of the American Jew that he surround himself with religious institutions; they were for him indispensable necessities, and he was willing to be taxed for their maintenance. Being a Jew required no sacrifice on his part. There was no objection by the mass of Christians about him to the communal organization which he had set up. To many church groups, his services may have seemed exotic but were not deemed objectionable. To the enlightened political leaders of that day the synagogue was just another house of worship. If the Jew did not belong to the Christian world, he was at least within the ambit of a very familiar tradition.

Here in America, on the rim of European civilization, one should not peer too critically at the Jewishness of that generation. The typical Jew was not interested in Jewish learning. There were no rabbinical jobs here, no ecclesiastical courts; America was no place for a rabbinic school and its cloistered devotees.

This typical urban businessman of whom we speak had no particular desire for more general education. On an occasion he was willing to buy and to read a good book in English, on a general or a Jewish topic, particularly a reference book of some sort. But he was busy; he had his business and other chores; and he could not take time out. He had no passion for learning. He would make no sacrifices to educate his children, not because he did not love them dearly, but because education had little utility in eighteenth-century America. What could you do with book-learning? You could not feed a family on it. Learning for learning's sake? Some Jews here would have understood that. But only a few; the typical Jew would have smiled deprecatingly. That type of learning was a luxury.

* * *

On December 13, 1790, a Jew, Manuel Josephson, called on Washington and personally presented him with a memorial address from four of the American synagogues. It would have been an interesting coincidence if, at the moment when the visitor was announced, the President had been reading Crèvecoeur's *Letters from an American Farmer*. Might not Washington then, with Crèvecoeur, have asked himself this question: "What then is the American (Jew), this new man?"

If the man who stood respectfully in the presence of Washington had been typical of his fellows—as it happened, he was more than a cut above his Jewish neighbor— he would have been a city dweller, a member of the middle class, literate, but not literary. He would have been a merchant, skilled, enterprising, venturesome in commerce and shipping, a man of courage. Good common sense and a willingness to work hard were among his chief traits. He was an individualist, more vigorous in asserting himself than the typical Jew in a well-regulated, urban, European Jewish community. There could be no question of his loyalty to his faith, but, like his Christian neighbors, he was not submissive to religious authority, such as it was.

This man looked just like his neighbors; his features were not particularly "Jewish"; he had the suspicion of a foreign brogue, but he was obviously a person who had sloughed off the externals of Europe. His culture was English. Conversation with him would disclose that he was politically an equalitarian, a republican.

As one who had lived for years among Gentiles, this Jew numbered among them intimate friends whom he admired and trusted. He was willing, when he could, to join them in common philanthropy. Like Rivera and Lopez, who had been close to President Stiles of Yale, he was happy to do anything that would be "honorable" to the Jewish "nation." Good relations with a neighbor, with the wider community, were important. Sign a petition to re-open the theatre? Of course! Politics? An office? Why not? If he needed anything to help him make up his mind, he had only to look about him to see everyday men whom he knew occupying the highest offices, sitting in the cabinet with the President himself. I'm just as good as the next man, was his unspoken thought. This fellow believed in himself; he had complete confidence in his future in this land.

After the departure of Josephson, Washington might well have picked up his book and continued reading. The very next passage began: "Here individuals of all nations are melted into a new race of men. . . . The American is a new man, who acts upon new principles."

Notes

1. MS., Rosenbach Collection, American Jewish Historical Society Library, New York City.
2. MS., true copy, Etting Collection, Historical Society of Pennsylvania Library, Philadelphia, Pa. Published, with minor changes, in W. V. Byars, *B. and M. Gratz, Merchants in Philadelphia, 1754–1798*, Jefferson City, Mo., 1916, pp. 36-37.
3. MS., Etting Collection, Historical Society of Pennsylvania Library. Translation, except for minor changes, taken from Joshua N. Neumann, "Some Eighteenth Century American Jewish Letters," *Publications of the American Jewish Historical Society* [= *PAJHS*], XXXIV (1937), 79-80.
4. MS., Historical Society of Pennsylvania Library. Printed in Kenneth P. Bailey, *The Ohio Company Papers, 1753–1817*, Arcata, California, 1947, pp. 211-13.
5. MS., Etting Collection, Historical Society of Pennsylvania Library. Published in Byars, *B. and M. Gratz*, pp. 101-102.
6. MS., Gratz letter book, Historical Society of Pennsylvania Library. Published in Byars, *B. and M. Gratz*, pp. 100-101.
7. MS., C.O.5:1352 (Virginia Papers), 151ff., Public Record Office, London. Copy in Division of Manuscripts, Library of Congress.
8. MS., The Library Company of Philadelphia.
9. MS., Mayer Sulzberger Collection, American Jewish Historical Society Library. Translation, with minor changes, taken from Joshua N. Neumann, "Some Eighteenth Century American Jewish Letters," *PAJHS*, XXXIV (1937), 100-102.
10. MS., Gratz letter book, Historical Society of Pennsylvania Library.
11. MS., C.O.5:40, p. 241, Public Record Office. Copy in Division of Manuscripts, Library of Congress. Translation, with minor changes, taken from *PAJHS*, XXV (1917), 129-31.
12. MS.. Rosenbach Collection, American Jewish Historical Society Library. Published in *PAJHS*, XXXIV (1937), 271.
13. MS., Historical Society of Pennsylvania Library. Published in *PAJHS*, XXIII (1915), 177.
14. MS., Historical Society of Pennsylvania Library. Published in *PAJHS*, XXIII (1915), 178.

15. MS., United States applications for office under Washington, Division of Manuscripts, Library of Congress.

16. MS., original, if not destroyed, was to be found in Tit. LVIII, Vol. II, No. 7, pp. 182-83, General Controlle, Königl. Geheimes Ministerial Archiv, Preussisches Geheimes Staatsarchiv, Berlin. Copy in Division of Manuscripts, Library of Congress. A copy of the German petition was published in *PAJHS*, XVI (1907), 85-88.

17. MS., Emmet Collection, New York Public Library.

18. *The Pennsylvania Magazine of History and Biography*, XVI (1892), 216-18.

19. MS., Mendes Cohen Collection, American Jewish Historical Society Library. Facsimile in Joshua Trachtenberg, *Consider the Years, etc.*, Easton, 1944, opposite p. 64. Printed in *PAJHS*, III (1895), 151.

20. MS., McAllister Collection, Ridgway Branch Library, The Library Company of Philadelphia. Printed in Byars, *B. and M. Gratz*, pp. 169-70.

21. MS., William L. Clements Library, Ann Arbor, Michigan.

22. MS., Historical Society of Pennsylvania Library.

23. MS., Etting Collection, Historical Society of Pennsylvania Library. Printed in Byars, *B. and M. Gratz*, p. 182.

24. MS., Lopez Papers, Newport Historical Society Library, Newport, R. I.

25. MS., archives of Mikveh Israel Congregation, Philadelphia. Photostatic copy in the American Jewish Archives, Cincinnati.

26. *Pennsylvania Archives* (First Series), Philadelphia, 1854, X, 731.

27. MS., Papers of the Continental Congress, No. 41, Vol. IX, pp. 58-59. Division of Manuscripts, Library of Congress. Printed in *PAJHS*, I (1905), 87-88.

28. MS., Rosenbach-Oppenheim Collection, letter book of Haym Salomon, American Jewish Historical Society Library.

29. *Ibid.*

30. *Ibid.* Printed, in part, in Charles Edward Russell, *Haym Salomon and the Revolution*, New York, 1930, pp. 230-31.

31. *Ibid.* Printed, in part, in Russell, *Haym Salomon*, p. 231.

32. Letter book of Haym Salomon.

33. *Ibid.* Printed in Russell, *Haym Salomon*, p. 234.

34. *Ibid.* Printed, in part, in Russell, *Haym Salomon*, p. 232.

35. *The Freeman's Journal*, Philadelphia, January 21, 1784. Printed in Russell, *Haym Salomon*, pp. 301-303.

36. MS., Lopez Papers, Newport Historical Society Library.

37. MS., Miscellaneous Petitions, Michael Gratz, Req. C/4780, The State Library of Virginia, Richmond, Va. Printed in Byars, *B. and M. Gratz*, p. 215.

38. MS., archives of Mikveh Israel Congregation. Photostatic copy in the American Jewish Archives.

39. MS., Samuel and Moses Myers letter book, 1785–87. American Jewish Archives.

40. *Ibid*.

41. *Ibid*.

42. *Ibid*.

43. *Ibid*.

44. Typescript copy in the possession of Emily Solis-Cohen, Philadelphia.

45. MS., Lopez Papers, Newport Historical Society Library.

46. *The South-Carolina Gazette*, July 28, 1759. Reprinted in Barnett A. Elzas, *The Jews of South Carolina, etc.*, Philadelphia, 1905, pp. 50-51.

47. MS., Brown University Library, Providence, R. I. Printed, in part, in *Hebrew Union College Monthly*, March, 1941, pp. 10ff.

48. *Commerce of Rhode Island*, I, 358-59, *Massachusetts Historical Society Collections*, Vol. LXIX, Boston, 1914.

49. *Ibid.*, I, 394.

50. MS., Lopez Papers, Newport Historical Society Library. Printed in *Commerce of Rhode Island*, I, 425-26.

51. MS., Lopez Papers, Newport Historical Society Library.

52. John Drayton, *Memoirs of the American Revolution, etc.*, Charleston, 1821, II, 363-65, supplemented by the version of this letter in R. W. Gibbes, *Documentary History of the American Revolution . . . 1776–1782*, New York, 1857, pp. 24-26.

53. R. W. Gibbes, *Documentary History of the American Revolution . . . 1781 and 1782*, Columbia, S. C., 1853, pp. 182-83.

54. MS., Colonel John Walker Papers, 1736–1909, State Department of Archives and History, Raleigh, N. C.

55. MS., archives of the Society for the Propagation of the Gospel in Foreign Parts. Copy in Division of Manuscripts, Library of Congress.

56. *Ibid*.

57. *Ibid*.

58. *Commerce of Rhode Island*, I, 242, *Massachusetts Historical Society Collections*, Vol. LXIX.

59. *Ibid.*, pp. 374-75.

Notes

60. *The South-Carolina and American General Gazette*, December 3, 1778. Reprinted in Elzas, *The Jews of South Carolina*, pp. 88-89.

61. MS., New York Public Library. Printed in *PAJHS*, XX (1911), 159-60.

62. MS., Sheftall Papers, Rosenbach Collection, American Jewish Historical Society Library.

63. American and West India Papers, Public Record Office, London. Printed in Allen D. Candler, *The Colonial Records of the State of Georgia*, Atlanta, Ga., XII (1907), 454-56.

64. MS., Sheftall Papers, B. H. Levy Collection, Savannah, Ga.

65. MS., Papers of the Continental Congress, No. 78, Vol. XX, folio 629, Division of Manuscripts, Library of Congress.

66. *PAJHS*, XVII (1909), 182.

67. MS., Sheftall Papers, Rosenbach Collection, American Jewish Historical Society Library.

68. MS., Sheftall Papers, B. H. Levy Collection.

Index to Volumes I and II

Elizabeth Whitlock), II: 185, 190-191

MORDECAI, MOSES (infant son of Jacob and Judith Myers Mordecai), II: 202

MORRIS, ROBERT, I: 100, 191; II: 65-66, 69-70, 94, 114, 134, 140-142, 152, 162-164, 196, 367-368, 418, 525, 542

MOSES (as a family name), II: 393

MOSES (family), I: 91

MOSES, HANNAH, II: 13-14, 401

MOSES, ISAAC, I: 99-103; II: 60, 125, 128-130, 185-186, 192, 196, 198-203, 367, 393, 408-409, 426

MOSES, ISAAC, AND COMPANY (business firm); see Isaac Moses, Samuel Myers, and Moses Myers (business firm)

MOSES, LION, II: 141

MOSES, MYERS, MRS., II: 362

MOSES, PHILIP (cousin of Haym Salomon), II: 326

MOSES, PHILIP (merchant of Savannah, Georgia), II: 326-328, 421

MOSES, RACHEL, II: 362

MOSES, SAMUEL, I: 126-128

MOTTA (family), II: 371

Music, II: 8-9, 497

Music Club (of Philadelphia), II: 8

Muskingum Valley, II: 54

MUSQUETO, JACOB, II: 50

MYERS (family), I: 174, 280

MYERS, MASTER, II: 46

MYERS, MR., II: 56-57

MYERS SISTERS (wives of Mathias Bush and Barnard Gratz), II: 70

MYERS, ASHER, I: 166, 172; II: 157, 397

MYERS, BENJAMIN, II: 327

MYERS, HYAM, I: 211-212, 219-224, 236-238, 277, 280; II: 193, 204; see also Mears, Hyam

MYERS, ISRAEL, II: 148-149

MYERS, JACOB, I: 222

MYERS, JUDITH, II: 192-193; see also Mordecai, Jacob, Mrs.

MYERS, MANUEL, I: 280; II: 444

MYERS, MORDECAI (merchant of Georgetown, South Carolina), II: 267-269, 422

MYERS, MORDECAI (American army major), II: 327

MYERS, MOSES, II: 192-193, 195-215, 408, 416, 495, 511

MYERS, MYER, I: 99-101, 121, 166, 172, 280; II: 193, 397

MYERS, NAPTHALY HART, I: 72; II: 49

MYERS, SAMUEL, I: 59; II: 147-148, 192-193, 195-210, 212, 214, 408

MYERS, SAMUEL AND MOSES (business firm), II: 147, 192-193, 195-197, 204, 208, 212-215

MYERS, SOLLY, II: 202

Nantucket, I: 132-133, 143, 149

NAPTHALY, ISAAC, I: 52-54

NATHAN (family), II: 175

NATHAN LEVY AND FRANKS (business firm); see Levy (Nathan) and Franks (business firm)

NATHAN, SIMON, II: 125, 128-129, 157, 175, 186

National American Jewish synagogal community, the question of the creation of a, II: 491-493

"National church," Jewish, the question of a, II: 491-493

Naturalization, I: 38-39, 41-42, 88, 103-104, 117, 119, 128-129, 219; II: 9-10, 70, 155, 166-168, 178, 229, 259, 281, 321, 337, 515-516, 520, 545

Navigation Acts, I: 16, 38, 41, 118-119, 160; II: 20

Navy purveyors, I: 200-201; II: 91, 406

NEHEMIAH, MOSES, II: 165

NESBITT, DRUMMOND, AND FRANKS (business firm), II: 94, 108-109

New Amsterdam, I: ix, 15, 22, 24-34, 45, 115, 117; II: 3, 155, 165, 380-382, 384-386, 400, 429, 436, 516-517, 525, 538

New England, I: 35-36, 89, 102-197, 200, 277; II: 194-195, 205, 235, 238, 245, 252, 284, 325, 386, 389, 404-405, 421, 430-431, 466, 468, 497, 519-520

New Hampshire, II: 195, 388, 519-520, 537

New Haven, I: 171

New Jersey, II: 51, 65, 95, 105, 110, 369, 389, 466, 520

New London (Connecticut), I: 119, 160-161, 167; II: 469

New Mexico, Marranos in, I: 3, 19

New Orleans, I: 75; II: 19, 138, 174-175

Newport, I: 81-82, 92-93, 105, 116-120, 123, 126, 128-130, 137, 142, 153-154, 159, 167, 179, 181-185, 188-190, 193-194, 196-198, 222, 236-237,

239; II: 3, 20, 60, 122, 124, 159, 170, 217-218, 227, 234, 236-238, 241, 250-251, 254, 281, 290, 317, 321, 323-328, 330, 336-337, 355, 386, 388-389, 392, 399, 403, 405, 413, 415, 424, 436-437, 441-442, 447, 449, 458, 462-463, 473, 475, 486-487, 493, 497, 499-500, 512, 519-520, 536, 539

"New Synagogue" (of Beth Elohim Congregation, Charlestown, South Carolina), II: 276, 340

New York (City), I: 33-101, 115, 121-123, 128, 152-153, 158-160, 162-163, 166, 174, 178, 189, 198, 204, 206-209, 211, 213, 216, 219, 221-225, 231, 246, 272, 276-283; II: 3, 6, 11-12, 43, 45, 50, 55-60, 65, 70, 74, 78-79, 95, 103, 108, 110-111, 113-115, 117, 121, 124, 129, 133, 135-139, 143, 146-149, 159, 161-162, 164, 182, 191-193, 196-202, 204-207, 209-210, 212, 214, 216, 218, 227, 229, 231-232, 238, 246, 253, 272, 279, 290, 292-296, 321-322, 328, 340, 348, 386, 388-389, 392, 394, 398, 400, 403, 405-407, 409, 414-416, 419, 424-427, 436-437, 442-444, 446, 448-449, 452, 461-463, 466, 471-473, 477, 481-482, 486-489, 491-493, 495, 499-500, 505, 517-518, 531, 540, 542; *see also* Shearith Israel Synagogue (of New York)

New York (State), I: 231, 247, 259; II: 24, 158, 195, 290, 444, 514, 516, 521, 529-530

NIETO, ISAAC, II: 237, 471

Religious tests for office; *see*
Christian oath; Oath of office
Religious tolerance; *see* Tolerance, toleration
Retail trade, retailers; *see* Commerce and trade; Merchants;
Shopkeepers; Traders
REVERE, PAUL, I: 190; II: 326
Revolutionary War, Jews in the,
I: 175, 254; II: 73-78, 150, 159,
184, 186, 218, 226, 256, 261-
265, 277, 292, 330, 332, 335-
336, 346-348, 350-355, 360-
361, 363-366, 408, 486, 529,
531, 539, 544-545; *see also* Soldiers, Jewish
REZNIKOFF, CHARLES, II: viii
Rhode Island, I: 4, 42, 64, 116-
118, 126, 128, 141-157, 236; II:
155, 169, 240, 246, 254, 281,
317, 319, 321, 323, 325, 328,
386, 394, 431, 449, 515, 517-
519, 521, 524, 536-537
Rhode Island College (Brown
University), II: 246-248, 340,
500
RIBIERO, NUNEZ (as a name), II:
321
RICE (Anglicized name of
Jews), II: 249
RICE, PATRICK, II: 95, 108-110
Rice trade, II: 196, 209-210, 235-
236, 241, 243, 251, 253, 325,
329, 403
Richmond (Virginia), II: 123,
145, 150, 172, 177, 181-182,
184, 187-188, 190-191, 204,
208-209, 213-220, 223-225, 397,
402, 413, 421, 437-438, 445,
469, 475, 478, 488, 493
Rights, civil, I: ix, 14, 16, 32, 35,
96, 106, 117, 119, 141-142, 156-

157, 160, 199, 201, 250, 273;
II: 10, 12, 68, 82, 94, 130, 155,
157-158, 167, 177, 182, 227-228,
231, 241, 259-260, 287, 335-
336, 378, 382, 384, 386, 487,
523, 526-530, 533, 544; *see also*
Disabilities; Rights, political
Rights, economic, II: 10, 12, 169,
217, 232, 337, 378, 382, 384,
387, 494, 515, 526-527, 548; *see
also* Disabilities
Rights, political, I: ix, 13-14, 32,
39, 41, 117, 119, 128, 201, 251,
274; II: 10, 12, 26, 32, 68, 82,
129, 154, 158-160, 164, 166, 169,
177-178, 180-181, 217, 227-228,
230-232, 241, 259-260, 265, 269,
271-272, 318, 330-333, 335-
337, 373, 378, 382-384, 386,
422, 486, 490, 494, 501, 512,
514-537, 544, 546-548; *see also*
Church and State; Disabilities;
Emancipation; Equality, political; Rights, civil
Rights, religious; *see* Freedom
of religion
RITTENHOUSE, DAVID, II: 480, 501
Ritual (of the synagogue), II:
438-439
Ritual, American, II: 438, 485,
549
Ritual, Ashkenazic, I: xii; II: 54,
56, 72, 390, 438, 549
Ritual, German; *see* Ritual, Ashkenazic
Ritual law, ritual observance;
see Observance, religious
Ritual murder accusations, II:
524
Ritual, Polish, II: 56, 72
Ritual, Prague, II: 56
Ritual, Sephardic, I: xiii, 82; II: